From Concept to Cult

Printed in Finland by WS Bookwell, OY

Published by Sanctuary Publishing Limited, Sanctuary House, 45-53 Sinclair Road, London W14 0NS, United Kingdom

www.sanctuarypublishing.com

Text excerpts from the musical used with permission from Rocky Horror Company Ltd ©.

Jim Sharman interview derives from his Rex Cramphorn Memorial Lecture 'In the Realm of the Imagination: An Individual View of Theatre', revised by Suzanne Kierman and published in the Sydney Review 79 (September 1995): 10-12

Photographs courtesy of John Jay (via MPTV), Perry Bedden, J Dewe Mathews, Hugh Cecil, Sadie Corre, Kimi Wong O'Brien, Michael Amendolia and Scott Michaels

ISBN: 1-86074-383-8

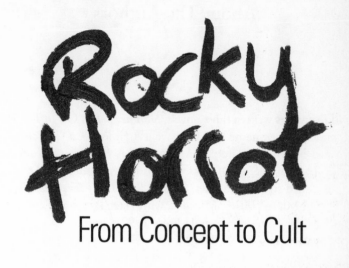

From Concept to Cult

Scott Michaels & David Evans

Sanctuary

About The Authors

David Evans has written three novels, *Summer Set*, *A Cat In The Tulips* and, under the pen-name Ned Cresswell, *A Hollywood Conscience*, all published by Millivres Books. A sequel to *A Hollywood Conscience* entitled *The Other Side Of Sunset* has just been completed. David has also published five biographies: *This Is Real Life – Freddie Mercury*, with David Minns; *Mister Mercury*, with Peter Freestone, about their friend Freddie Mercury (Tusitala Press 1999, Omnibus Books 2000), *The Boy Who Looked At The Moon – The Life And Times Of Cat Stevens* (Britannia Press 1995), *Scissors And Paste – Dusty Springfield* (Britannia Press 1995) and *Glamour Blondes – From Mae To Madonna* (Britannia Press 1995).

David Evans' short stories are embraced in Mammoth, Prowler and Zipper collections. A volume of short stories, *The Bad Boys' Book Of Bedtime Stories*, was published by Prowler in September 2001. 'I remember how I felt, coming out into Sloane Square on that first night in June 1973, empowered and validated by what I had seen. I felt such surging joy, such euphoric elation... I know I must have been grinning from ear to ear for hours. I realised that at least one other person on this planet recognised the fundamental importance of fantasy in our everyday lives...'

Scott Michaels grew up in Detroit City and spent most of his adult life in Chicago and Los Angeles. In 1997, he moved to London, England, where he currently resides. He was formerly 'director of undertakings' for the popular Grave Line Tours in LA, which escorted devotees to notorious Hollywood locations associated with the demise of the rich and famous. This lead to his creating the internationally praised website www.findadeath.com. His extensive knowledge of the motion picture and television industry has landed him many research roles in the development of books, contributions to magazines such as *Bizarre* and *Guitar World*, as well as internet and television programs, most recently for Rapido and Sky TV. 'I decided to go on a Trannie hunt. I always thought of them as the Munchkins of Transylvania. They were the freaks I adored. Once I found my first one, Sadie Corre, all the pieces started to fit into place. Phone numbers were becoming available...'

Acknowledgements

The authors would like to thank the following people for their contributions to this book: Graham Norton, David Quantick, Jane Bussmann, John Mckay, Lauren Iannuzzi, Larry Viezel, Ruth Fink Winter, Steve Cox, Sadie Corre, Perry Bedden, Imogen Claire, Michelle Martin, Peter Straker, David Johnson, Kimi Wong O'Brien, Chemene Sinson, Karen Krizanovich, Rick Michaels and Christine Fritsch Paul of Ken Paul Antiquities.

This book is dedicated to David Toguri, Charles Gray, Rufus Collins, Ramon Gow, Anthony Then, Frank Lester, Peggy Ledger, Fran Fullenwider, Colin MacNeil, Jon Berkinshaw, Kim Milford, Graham Freeborn, Ernie Gasser, Bruce Silke, Lili St Cyr, Ben Fencham, Ishaq Bux and Marie (a costumier).

Contents

The Story

In London in 1973, a new rock musical was performed for the first time at the tiny Theatre Upstairs at the Royal Court Theatre in Chelsea's Kings Road. Nothing remarkable in that. Dozens of new rock musicals opened every month all over London. And closed. With a budget of only £2,000, out-of-work actor Richard O'Brien's first attempt at writing a musical show was an explosive success, as hot a ticket as the controversial *Hair* and *Jesus Christ, Superstar* had been before it.

The controversy continued when the show's producer, Michael White, gained control over the property from UK records boss Jonathan King and sold the American rights not to a Broadway producer but to Californian record producer Lou Adler, who put the show on in Los Angeles at the Roxy, a club he co-owned with record label Asylum's David Geffen.

Despite the show's huge 'alternative' success with the Hollywood *cognoscenti*, the movie of the show had a slow and vulnerable birth and was far from a traditional multi-million-dollar Hollywood musical. The weekend before the first day's shooting in late 1974, Twentieth Century Fox threatened to pull the plug.

They didn't, though, and the movie was made, starring the unknown Susan Sarandon and Barry Bostwick, Meat Loaf and the show's star, Tim Curry, playing Doctor Frank N Furter, the 'Sweet Transvestite from Transylvania'. It was the greatest drag performance of all time and the movie was the making of all their careers. Except it nearly wasn't…

In March 1975, the Broadway Production was savagely panned by

East Coast critics resentful of this 'transfer' from California, which had always been thought of as the cultural desert. The show closed at the Belasco Theater after only 45 performances. The word-of-mouth climate on *Rocky Horror* amongst the American chattering classes did not augur well. The movie opened in August 1975 to terrible reviews. Fox executives wanted to bury it in videoland as quickly as possible. And so what? It had only cost $1 million.

In 1976, a resourceful Fox executive introduced the movie as late-night schlock-horror filler into a couple of late-night Manhattan movie houses frequented by gays, students and punks. They loved its irreverent zaniness.

The word of mouth on the streets soon spread, and by 1977 *Rocky Horror* was playing every weekend on student campuses and on over 100 art-house, alternative screens countrywide. The legend was born. The cult of *Rocky Horror* emerged, like Rocky himself, from an accident...

Preface
'The Masculine Feminine Me'

In November 1998, Peter Straker held his customary birthday party. For a certain section of London's *theatrati*, Straker's party is a much-anticipated annual event. (At this juncture, it is not necessary to flesh out the fame and form of Peter Straker. He looms larger in this story than merely as host of a birthday party.)

The usual suspects were in attendance: an appearance by London's most famous former landlady and sometime crossover-to-rock hopeful, Anita Dobson; occasional Equity-registered 'Transylvanians' on loan to a theatre on Earth from Alien Productions headquarters on Planet 9; good old gals like Gaye Brown and Annabel Leventon, two-thirds of Rock Bottom (also once crossover-to-rock hopefuls). These Transylvanians have a more significantly traceable pedigree than even they would care to admit. Transylvanian blood is thicker than anything.

And, of course, there was The Master himself, Richard O'Brien – Ritz – and his wife, the second Mrs O'Brien. Richard, it must be said, was also high on the crossover-to-rock hopeful list. He had made several forays into da music biz, schmoozik biz...

Surprising though it might be to his many fans, and even to those merely casually interested, earlier in the day Richard had called Straker – yet another crossover-to-rock hopeful – to enquire whether it would be all right for him to come to the party wearing a dress.

Was it all right? No question. It was more than all right!

And so, indeed, there he was in the dress. And earrings. What shoes he wore were obscured, as the dress – cut on the bias from a very clinging material – was shin-length and flared at the hem. So the ultimate symbol of any self-respecting cross-dresser's drag – the bats – were hidden. Was he wearing stilettos? Was there a hint of fishnet?

'Bats' is theatrical-speak for shoes, like 'drag' is theatrical-speak for dressing up in women's clothes. It comes from the camp *parlare* of the 1940s and 1950s. And the 1920s and 1930s. And the 1960s and 1970s, and 1980s and 1990s.

But make no mistake. We are not – repeat *not* – talking drag here.

The language and lore of the theatre is simultaneously vibrant, mysterious, magical, glamorous and arcane. It is the theatre that is the touchstone in the saga of *The Rocky Horror Show*. Whether onstage or on screen, the piece was and is and will always be a theatrical event. It was never, is never and never will be merely a musical. Neither was it just a play or a play with music. It was never even mildly mainstream music business. Its very pedigree, conception and gestation ensured that it was never a serious candidate for crossover-to-rock. But examination of all these grand assertions can wait. They might even prove worthy of being ignored and forgotten altogether.

Now, merely be content to behold...

Behold the real star! In full regalia once again. Not Rocky Horror, the wet-dream-made-dry, not the popinjay Frank N Furter but the real Master. Once mere 'riff-raff' in Frank's sparkling diamante scheme, the butler is now revealed as the ultimate power. Behold the career alien:

'I made you! And I can break you just as easily!'

Ladies and gentlemen, we give you Mister...Richard...*O'Brien*!

Some 25 years after the birth of his incubus, in private, in the company of friends, acolytes and the far too polite to stare, we witness once again Frank N Furter's new commander, suitably cross-fertilised, 'dressed', meeting his public and still taking prisoners. To what Mrs O'Brien was wearing, no one gave a thought nor cast a glance. The Mistress doesn't even get a look-in here. The mortal women in the room are instantly eclipsed by the alien presence.

All attention is riveted by The Creator... Yes, heresy though it be to say in these oh so politically correct times, God is only man in this tale of Rocky Horror.

It gets a man thinking…ummm…then and now.

Introduction
Punk, Porno And Pantomime

If we may, we'd like to start at the beginning.

The King's Road in Chelsea, London, is so named for one of the Stuart monarchs who used it to gain access to his mistress who lived somewhere opposite where the Chelsea Fire Station now stands. Mistresses. Infidelity. Sex. Night-time frolics, discreet comings and goings in closed carriages. The King's Road has always been associated with the unmentionable, the clandestine, the bohemian, the eccentric and the naughty. It was the haunt of artists, writers and musicians for three centuries and ultimately, in this tale at least, the stomping ground of Quentin Crisp. (He was the elderly man in the purple hair who turned heads in shock horror for years before he was discovered by the intellectual cool hunters.)

What would the cool hunters of today have made of the King's Road 'scene' of 1973? Those men and women who are paid by clothes manufacturers and shoesmiths to patrol the beaches and boulevards frequented by the groovy and the trend setters and report back to HQ? Would they have spotted the proclivity for bondage trousers sold in so many gross by Vivienne Westwood and Malcolm McLaren? Would they have seen *The Rocky Horror Show* and whispered to their bosses that all men would be wearing corsets and stilettos next season? Viv did very well out of corsets and aberrantly tall-heeled shoes. Who exactly was it who invented punk? Who first married the word with the movement? Who first coined it, and where? Or is there no natural mother to the trend that redefined youth culture in such a tribal way? Simon Barker, one of the first punks identifiable as such on the King's

Road, believes that honour goes to an American journalist called Lester Bangs. But don't write in...

If one is to believe the chronology in Jane Mulvagh's 1998 biography of designer and style guru Vivienne Westwood, punk as a genre can't even be properly identified before 1974, for it was in that year that Vivienne Westwood and Malcolm McLaren opened their shops Sex and, later, Too Fast To Live Too Young To Die (the biker-gear business) in the shop at 430 King's Road. Later, in 1977, their shop Seditionaries began to sell the clothes that are generally identified as 'punk'.

Vivienne Westwood and Malcolm McLaren were their own cool-hunters. Identifiable punk clothing and accessories had, as do all fashion and style developments, a mixed pedigree.

Punk is, after all, an American word whose connotations have nothing at all to do with flamboyantly mohicanned young people in torn, dirt-stained jeans and slogan-emblazoned T-shirts held together with safety pins. A 'punk', from the 1930s onwards, was a worthless, ne'er-do-well, probably with criminal and certainly violent antisocial tendencies. But surely that's how many people in the 1970s would have themselves described Simon Barker and his fellow band of Bromley boyz 'n' gurlz, who would at weekends wander down the King's Road, Chelsea, in what was then outrageous and shocking attire, and with a confrontational, threatening attitude. And that, too, is a pretty accurate character definition of Eddie. Eddie from *Rocky*. All of them punks. No-good kids. One weekend party, the Bromley Bunch organised in some unsuspecting absent parents' tidy, nice, cosy little suburban home and rejoiced in the title of the Easter Nuremberg Porno Olympics. Get the picture?

The accoutrements of that movement, subsequently legitimised under the 'punk' umbrella, had been seen on Manhattan streets as well as in bands such as The New York Dolls and Television. Similar on-street manifestations had been noticeable in the King's Road for a couple of years. Nell Campbell herself, nominated with Vivienne for a newspaper story on the phenomenon, was more punk than prankster, and was seen every weekend tap-dancing on the King's Road pavements.

It seems that with posters advertising *The Rocky Horror Show*, first at the Sloane Square end and then halfway down at the old (now demolished) Chelsea Classic Cinema, and finally at the Essoldo Cinema at the World's End, the King's Road and its denizens would have been pretty familiar with Sue Blane's costumes. Coupled with the sexual fetishism, which was only later picked up by the sexually unadventurous Vivienne and Malcolm as a sales point, it would seem that *The Rocky Horror Show* was a more than significant ancestor in the family tree of punk. Contrary to what could be believed, the mum and dad of punk, Viv and Malc, were terribly squeamish and easily shockable.

Simon Barker knew Viv and Malc and punk and the King's Road very well. He is now an acknowledged authority on the punk movement as it was observed in its London incarnation. He contributed hugely and generously to Jane Mulvagh's biography of Vivienne Westwood and is set to collaborate with Ms Mulvagh on a HarperCollins graphic volume covering the era of which he was such an important part.

It was Simon and a group of his school friends and peers from the London suburb of Bromley who became the first identifiable punks in London (although he maintains that it was all an accident! Pure coincidence!). Bromley was fecund territory. It had already given the world David Bowie, significantly in the guise of the painted and dyed-red-haired Ziggy Stardust. Indeed, Bowie was a fellow alumnus of Simon's, although Bowie had left the school a few years earlier.

Simon, Siouxsie (of The Banshees) and (later) Jordan from Seaford – as well as a large boy with raggedy long brown hair, who was later to metamorphose into the phenomenon known as Billy Idol – with several other core members, formed this particular band of teenagers who began in their mid-teens to experiment with a non-conformist visual look just as hundreds and thousands of disaffected youngsters all over the country were beginning to push back the boundaries of style in dress, music and thought.

The punk thing wasn't merely a London phenomenon. Punks surfaced in several British inner cities with fertile suburbs.

Entirely unconnected with sexuality or fetishism, the Bromley 'look' evolved depending on the use of clothes, accessories and surreally juxtaposed haberdashery, together with an exaggerated use of make-up. It was a look of glamour, glamour based not on the glossy, perfect world of Hollywood but on the ancient root of the word, *gramarye*, having to do with magic, mystery and necromancy. The look was born from a chosen lifestyle and itself evolved into a lifestyle of its own.

Thus glamorised, the now-magic Bromley Brigade would venture forth from their suburban boudoirs, first into the streets of Bromley, then neighbouring suburbs and finally to the very acme of the London 'scene', which was in those faraway days of the 1970s the King's Road, Chelsea...

They would take the train from Bromley to Victoria, then the Circle Line on the Underground to Sloane Square, and spend shopper-crowded Saturday afternoons walking the length of the King's Road, calling at several points along the way, including the Markham Arms pub, the second hand market called Antiquarius, where there were a couple of important clothes outlets, and on, westward ho! They became celebrities both unto themselves and to the unacknowledged wider world. Incidentally, according to Simon, equal celebrity in this King's Road pantheon had already been accorded to the as-yet-unsung Richard O'Brien and Nell Campbell. They were already head-turners. Their hair colour alone had already become a thing of reputation. Much of it was acquired via Anny Humphries, then at Vidal Sassoon, before she came to the King's Road. The contingent would go in and muse over colour – 'Yeah, maybe blue today' – and, hey presto, blue hair it was.

Joe Public's head, naturally, was powerless to resist being turned in this unusual wake. To the Bromley Brigade, their look was everything and the group all-encompassing. However, there was frequently a sour side to this sweet coin: today, *Rocky Horror Picture Show* fans who make the pilgrimage to the silver screen by public transport are fully accepted and thought rather amusing. In 1973, however, the King's Road phalanx of punks and fetishists were frequently grievously abused for their anarchic and anti-establishment 'look'. Then, the pre-punks were like aliens visiting a backward planet. Members of the Bromley Brigade were aware of the reaction they provoked, but they didn't care. Contradictorily, though, they did care about their look, because they cared what the group thought, what their peers thought. As to what others thought, however, they gave not a damn.

As Simon Barker says, 'We didn't care about the consequences of what we did. Money didn't matter. If we ran out of bus or train fare, we'd just walk back to Bromley. Or hitch-hike... We'd just spend money and...well, if it ran out, fuck it! We'd just hitch-hike back...'

It seems a bizarre stretch of the imagination, but it is an entirely credible and legitimate stance. It accounts for so many instances of American tourists being told to 'Fuck off!' when they took that one picture too many. It was 'the look' that was the liberating factor, both for those who wore it as well as those who saw it. Derek Dunbar remembers his father being confronted by the zippered, rubbered and fetishised Jordan, and being obviously reduced to jelly by the implied opportunity to play the submissive. As someone might have sung, 'Something in the way she looked...made him want to be her love slave...'

And this was a woman who was daily seen on the train from Seaford, every evening witnessed walking the length of the King's Road pavement in search of her supper. Jordan was not merely giving a performance like the strutting Frank N Furter, she was for real. Frank – he of the spotlight, the footlight and limelight – was only make-believe, the ultimate great pretender.

So what else motivated the Bromley Brigade on the King's Road, a length of strut and fret that has been described in all seriousness as the 'longest catwalk in the world'?

Music? According to Simon, most of his group weren't into retro anything, least of all the undressed-up pastiche songs of *The Rocky Horror Show*. Unlike the safety-pinned street trash look of Manhattan icons like Richard Hell and Tom Verlaine from the band Television, and the others of the much later New York anticulture, King's Road culture in 1973 was all about Bryan Ferry and Roxy Music, David Bowie and (to a lesser extent because of his defection to glam rock) Marc Bolan.

There was also an inherent theatrical/performance quality to which Simon and his friends were attracted. Theirs was also, essentially, an exhibition of actors on the stage. Simon remembers specifically a band that never made it, whose lead singer dressed in a sort of vampire-cum-academic gown, which billowed out over a body that had been liberally powdered with flour and talc before the performance. Even over a short distance, the image created onstage by a gyrating black cloak swathed in white dust was patently mesmerising. Pity about the music...

Movies figured, too, in suburbia, where televisions had only recently escaped from the family sitting room into the children's bedrooms. Movies that probably had never been seen by the under-18 generation: sci-fi late-night television movies, B-movies in general, the whole James Dean 'live fast' genre.

In 1973 Simon and his friends were more than aware of Andy Warhol and his Manhattan Factory, where much of the transatlantic punk recipe was being concocted. Drag queens and porn stars in electric celluloid juxtaposition made meat for hungry young imaginations. Divine, Holly Woodlawn, Candy Darling, Jackie Curtis and Cherry Vanilla teamed with beaut-boyz like Joe d'Allessandro. More than the stuff of dreams and fantasy. These were fantasies made flesh in movies and shows like *Flesh* and *Pork* respectively. Achievable images. Famous for 15 minutes. Porno, like the gestating Eddie and the embryonic Rocky Horror, was in labour and was soon to be delivered.

A Clockwork Orange and *Cabaret* were also two huge favourites of the punk pundits. The latter, having immortalised the image of corsets and tawdry laddered stockings, is strangely reminiscent of another King's Road cast dressed in stockings and suspenders. Despite the moralistic caveat epitomised by Sally Bowles' unwanted pregnancy, *Cabaret*'s promise of careless sexual abandon and illicit wanton fulfilment appealed far more deeply and widely to the core of the human psyche than its creators could have imagined.

Sexually, the punks and the King's Road have been, from their inception, pretty much tolerant. Simon explains how Siouxsie was the one amongst them to have discovered a club called Louise's in Poland Street in London's West End that was patronised mainly by lesbians.

Siouxsie had gay connections from an early age. The punks developed realising instinctively that they were rarely hassled by gay people, and that fashion and style were as important to their gay peers as to themselves. After all, many if not all, major fashion trends – even male liberation itself – had begun in the gay arena.

Siouxsie and Lindy St Clair, followed by the rest of the Bromley Brigade and attendant hangers-on, began to patronise Madame Louise's premises. Although the resident dykes of Poland Street kicked up a fuss at the unwanted attention foisted upon their meeting place by the platoon of punks, Madame Louise, who presided, was not averse to the extra revenue and interest they generated.

As to punk body-part piercing, which probably upset more people than any other manifestation of the phenomenon, there was little evidence of this in 1973. Simon particularly remembers being almost expelled from school at the age of 14 when he had his ear pierced – a commonplace act now, but almost revolutionary in those days. Not really a lot to get upset about, but his school was duly outraged. Surely having had Bowie as a pupil, it could see its way to putting up with the odd earring at morning assembly? Tattoos like Tim Curry's false ones ('D'you have any?') were also introduced as part of 'the look' and became *de rigueur* in the panoply of the biker/punk *faux* macho statement.

And so, one night in 1973, the Bromloids were confronted by the Androids at the Chelsea Classic cinema-turned-theatre. Simon doubts that, had the show been playing anywhere else, he and his friends would ever have gone to see it. Anything in the West End was establishment and old hat, and the punks' basic tenet was discovering and adopting things for themselves.

To discover *The Rocky Horror Show* on their own turf must have been hugely validating. Not that they would have cared that their philosophy was being taken seriously, mind you.

Fashion and style; sexuality and fetishism; music; celebrity and stardom. Although these four facets are the main elements of *The Rocky Horror Show*, the context of the theatre in which they come together was no accident.

The thesis of Richard O'Brien's show employed the very basics of the psychology of 'theatre'. It plugged into the very essence of why audiences find such magic and glamour in 'the theatre', why people fall in love with 'the theatre'. The theatre, and the lifestyles and world it creates and sustains, are so different from the *milieux* of ordinary people. The actors and the audience are separated not merely by a row of footlights or an orchestra pit, just as the punks and the public were separated by more than mere costume and make-up; the theatre breeds a sense of being different, apart, not ordinary... *That Despicable Race*, as runs the title of Bryan Forbes' history of his own profession.

Freedom is only a perception. Being 'free' is what the Bromley Brigade and the Androids onstage nightly at the Chelsea Classic were perceived to be. The theatre provides an alternative life, an escape, if only for a night of dressing-up and interacting with a stage or a screen. For some it holds out an eternal promise, the opportunity to lead a life of real freedom.

Coupled with a life of exhibitionism is the spectre of celebrity – stardom. People who aren't famous are fascinated by those who are. The fascination is almost spooky, as though fame and being well known somehow endow the celebrity with a magic, magnetic attraction.

The search for fame, the trying to look like you're famous, the desire to know famous people, the basking in the reflected glory of famous friends – all this is in *The Rocky Horror Show*, too, and is endemic to the human race. Even the famous and the celebrated rarely ignore the famous and the celebrated.

Simon, who later went on to be Malcolm McLaren's assistant and who travelled widely with The Sex Pistols, remembers the lyrics of *The Rocky Horror Show* songs more than the music, which would not to have been to his gang's Roxy tastes. Simon loved the lyrics, found references such as the mention of Steve Reeves fascinating, and was inspired to find out more about what to him were obscure to the point of being unknown, the point being that he *could* find out. Simon liked the 'story' nature of the songs, the way they furthered the action and filled in the characters' natures and backgrounds, dreams and fears. He is surprised at the ongoing success of the show, but understands completely why the music and songs have never had a life outside the visual context in which they are heard. 'Without the visual,' as Simon puns on Richard O'Brien's rhyme, 'it was all too abysmal.'

After seeing the show, Simon was inspired to reify some ideas of his own. Having acquired a cine camera, he wrote his own script and, although it was never made into a full movie, the camera allowed him to film the titles of all the other movies he would write. Nothing else – just the titles. Creating, making and then filming the titles was tantamount to having made the films. If Marshall McLuhan a decade earlier had made the medium the message, to Simon and the Bromley punks, the fantasy was the fulfilment.

And so the Bromloids and the Androids found themselves allied forces. Not that there was a great issue, but no longer was the street frightened of the middle-class, establishment phenomenon of the successful play.

The fusion of commercial theatre and super-street chic whetted commercial appetites. The world watched and people like Duggie Fields, Derek Jarman and Andrew Logan assessed the possibilities. As Simon says, cults cannot be created, they can only evolve. Jarman's *Jubilee* was, therefore, far from being made. To the punks, the likes of Jarman were merely spectators, casual acquaintances of punk, unmotivated except by 'voyeuristic intentions'.

However, the music that made the crossover from beyond the pale to within it was not Rocky's but the more designed and tailored version bred by people like Malcolm McLaren and The Sex Pistols, The Clash, The Stranglers and Bromley-girl-made-good Siouxsie with her Banshees.

The music business ignored the dangerously theatrical parent and instead adopted the malleable musical child. Early Sex Pistols audiences were not unlike the people who now dress up to go and see *The Rocky Horror Show*. In the upbringing of the infant bands of the 1970s, the role of theatre in the punk movement was marginalised until the advent of the musical *Rent* in the mid 1990s.

Meanwhile, Tim Curry, Nell Campbell and Richard O'Brien all became customers at Sex, at 430 King's Road, where McLaren's much-publicised 'rubberwear for the office' was in plentiful daily supply. The phenomenon, for Simon, assumed a new dimension when one day he was astounded to find that the occupant of the apartment above his turned out to be no less an alien than Magenta herself, from the planet Transsexual in the galaxy of Transylvania – the lovely Patricia Quinn.

‹‹‹‹irememberdoingthetimewarpirem
emberdoingthetimewarpi›››

1 'Let's Go See The Man That Began It'
Richard O'Brien

The world revolves around creations. They are as fascinating to us morbid creatures as ends. Of the two, creations are rather more difficult to pin down and appreciate accurately because, as Doctor Frank N Furter was to find out, creations are usually unpredictable and notoriously accidental, and trying to recreate creations precipitates a succession of casualties, the first and most mortal of which is often the truth itself.

That sounds like one of the Narrator's lines.

I, David Evans, have a passion for *The Rocky Horror Show*. Not only have several of those most intimately involved with it been dear to my heart, the show itself ranks alongside the Royal Shakespeare Company's *Nicholas Nickleby* as the best piece of theatre I've ever experienced in this 53-year-long life. I remember how I felt, coming out into Sloane Square on that first night in June 1973. I felt such surging joy, such euphoric elation... I know I must have been grinning from ear to ear for hours. I felt empowered, validated and no longer alone.

I realised that, apart from me, at least one other person on this planet recognised the fundamental importance of fantasy in our everyday lives. Fantasy breeds the ability to generate glamour, whether externally, in the form of feather boas, seven-inch-high strappy stiletto sandals or 16-foot-long trains of white fox fur, or internally, in the dreams we need to refresh the drab everyday nature of our individual existences. Listen, I loved Dusty Springfield, but she was no more real than sliced bread. Did I care? Had I believed that Cliff Richard was as wholesome as brown bread? Get a life.

The Royal Court Theatre had been the first proper, professional theatre I had ever visited. Our history teacher took a school party up to London from Malvern in Worcestershire in 1963 to see a Brecht play. The Court was the flagship of 'new' British theatre and it was guided for many years by George Devine, best remembered for his policy of 'Here, we give you the right to fail'.

Subsequently, the Royal Court Theatre had figured largely in my early 20s, too. I worked for a theatrical agent called Barry Krost, a man who is to figure somewhat in this story. Mine was a job where failure was not only unconscionable, it was a dismissable offence. Barry Krost represented, amongst many others, writers like John Osborne, to whom the Royal Court was second home; directors like Robert Kidd, then an up-and-coming young man of Sloane Square; and actresses like Jill Bennett, Osborne's wife, who more than often trod a shining path across the boards of the tiny stage of the main house.

But those pieces of theatre never moved me. I found them irrelevant to my life, hung on characters who were dreary, uninspiring and often incomprehensible. Our theatrical agency was fast changing into a music-management company. We were in the swim, in the thick of the groove of the time, our fingers firmly on the pulse of the future. Our top client was Cat Stevens and it was in the direction of rock 'n' roll that my principal, Barry Krost, was moving as he opened an office in Los Angeles. There was an incredible amount of money to be made if you hit it right. Robert Stigwood had found that out with The Bee Gees and John Reid was discovering the same thing with Elton John. London was on a wealth-alert standby and there was a long queue of the hopeful waiting to sip from the same cup.

Trouble is, the content of the cup is as unpredictable as the efficacy of the Midas brew itself. Some plotted and planned and thought they had drunk the magic draft...but it was not always to be.

What *Hair* had spawned in the way of wealth and fame *Jesus Christ, Superstar* continued. *Godspell* jumped on the surfboard, too, and the theatre had started to breed what it hadn't bred for years: music stars and music that the non-theatregoing public also bought. Not since Noël Coward and Ivor Novello had there been such a killing to be made for performers, writers and musicians alike, although the reality was that the new music industry and the theatre were as immiscible as oil and water. There had grown up a mutual suspicion, which had resulted in 'serious' rock 'n' roll being as divorced from 'serious' theatre as Richard Burton from Elizabeth Taylor. Flirtations were permitted, brief marriages tolerated, but serious inter-breeding, never. There was a hard edge to the rock business, whereas the theatre, although bitchy, more camp and equally poisonous, was ultimately vulnerable.

The money for rock 'n' roll came from small investment, hunger and greed being the visceral motivators. The theatre, even with burgeoning Arts Council public funding, ran on the enthusiasm of 'angels', wealthy people who were prepared to gamble on a whim on the advice of a 'gentleman' producer. It was acknowledged that rock 'n' roll started and finished in the gutter. The theatre, though known to be lewd and loose and frequently lascivious, was still respectable enough for the establishment to dally with. In those days, a third of a century ago, despite glam rock and Danny La Rue, scandals were still scandals; men in suede shoes and pink socks were obviously sodomite spies and real men would rather die than admit to having nibbled on a quiche. It was why, when it finally appeared, *Rocky* found such a ready pool of supporters.

But I contend that *The Rocky Horror Show* could never have been created and developed by anyone from the British theatrical tradition. *Rocky* would have been too visceral, too raw and confrontational to have been entertained by any of the London managements of whatever colour. Those most intimately involved with the nascent *Rocky*, with the exception of Richard Hartley, were all children of the colonies.

This chapter is devoted to Richard O'Brien. That other assorted antipodeans and ex-colonial connections like Kimi Wong O'Brien, Jim Sharman and Brian Thomson, Nell Campbell, Peter Straker, David Toguri and Freddie Mercury join the party later is a further treat in store.

<<<<<irememberdoingthetimewarpirememberdoingthetimewarpi>>>>

Richard O'Brien

19 September 1999

DAVID EVANS: Straker's right – Rocky is not a musical, or even a play or anything to do with the mainstream music biz; it is a rock 'n' roll show.

Richard arrived with Peter Straker about 7:30pm.

There were so many questions I needed to ask him, but I had been warned that to dive in too quickly and to be too earnest could put him off. I decided we'd let the evening just roam and find its own way. My friend, the journalist Andrew Marshall, had told me that Richard had a low boredom threshold. I spent all evening trying to detect one. Only once did a faint glaze come over the face of the wonderfully loquacious and enthusiastically garrulous Mister O'Brien, and by that time it was way past 1:30am. Could the glaze have been sheer exhaustion?

We started gently, did the Joan Crawford in *Trog* thing, and then went through all the Hollywood stories and talked about the television programme that had then recently been broadcast about the manager Don Arden and his music-management family. Then we swapped a few Freddie Mercury stories, as Richard had been privy to several of 'the family's' get-togethers and admitted that they had all wanted to be in the music biz, in the mainstream. Him, Tim, Nell...they had all been fascinated by Freddie Mercury, who was part of our society at the time. Freddie, from Zanzibar via Bombay and Poona, was also a devotee of B' and 1950s movies of early rock 'n' roll.

Richard is patently very passionate on the subject of his children. They and his perceived obligations to them, as well as the joys they bring, are very important to him. His eldest son from his first marriage is Linus and he has two younger, a boy and a girl, from his current relationship. He is also much concerned about his wider family. They still mean a great deal. I gathered that his relationship with his mother left something to be desired, although he was effusively complimentary about his sister, calling her 'one of the most lovely human beings on the planet, with a heart the size of Texas; she lost two of her little boys'. Of his brother he is equally fond: 'Bit of a chauvinistic old bastard...has morals and ethics that are very strong, and very honest. But he's the one constant...'

I found these fluidly expressed visceral passions surprising. His basic, raw humanity is palpable. The family man, the non-celebrity, would have appeared at odds with his other, crafted persona. We talked of his old country, New Zealand, which I had visited for the first time late in 1998, and especially of the North Island, where he has just bought a piece of land. I rather thought North Island, New Zealand, was not un-akin to a vast golf course, so close had the nibbling sheep eaten up to the grassline, but on Richard my silly ribaldry was rather lost because he waxed almost rhapsodic about his own recently acquired piece of somewhere to go home to. Made me think about Frank's song at the end of the show: 'Going Home'.

As a fellow writer, I wanted to draw him on writing. Perhaps I put too many words in people's mouths, although on this occasion I don't think so. Although I said it first, he agreed entirely that he now finds it very difficult to write originally and on spec. ('Spec', for those thankfully spared from and therefore ignorant of the torture, is the process of having an idea, writing it all down and then presenting it to 'the powers that be' for their due consideration. The process – which can often take upwards of six months, depending on whether a novel, play, musical or album – is agony. For the 50s, it is pure unadulterated hell and only sanely undertaken by the irredeemably masochistic.)

I fear that unrequited, unrecognised feeling goes down the line from scriptwriters, to playwrights, to lyricists. Makes me think of all the effacement Bernie Taupin has had inflicted on him. Without him, there would never have been an Elton John or a Rocket Records, and I have no qualms about asserting that without Richard O'Brien there would never have been a *Rocky Horror Show* for people to have become so greedy about.

I'm sure that even God had to have a great deal of help, and I'm sure if He or She or It is as fair-minded as they say, then He, She or It would be the first to acknowledge that storm, fire, flood, collision, disaster and accident have had as much to do with the current state of the universe as that first big bang. And I am equally sure that, if Richard O'Brien ever had seven minutes' air time and didn't need to plug the product he was currently involved in, he would be first to acknowledge that directors, writers, choreographers, make-up artists, costume designers, musical arrangers, lighting designers, publicists, producers, musicians and actors have all played their part in the finished aural and visual aspect of 'his show'. Indeed, in the case of a flop, all of the above would be the first to clamour to their agents to have their names disassociated from the corpse of their endeavours. Everyone, it seems, likes to be credited with success but few wish to have such intimacy with failure. I have to say, however, that in the way that showbusiness is currently comported, these people are employed to come and participate in and contribute to, in a creative and interpretative manner and to the best of their ability, the development of the basic idea on which they are all being *paid* to work. I have never come across any successful play or show or album in which every creative input is acknowledged in the source copyright. If that was the case, there would only be lawyers. There would be no artists left.

Please write in and correct me if I'm wrong.

I asked Richard about current work. Work in hand. He said he thought that he would be OK being commissioned to do something with a specific brief, but...but...

Believe me, these are big buts and difficult times.

As far as his 'other career' is concerned, the all-singing, all-dancing version, he recently released a self-financed album, *Absolute O'Brien*. Straker thinks it's his first album in 25 years, and thus he *still* hasn't cracked the music biz. He has a deal with a small label in the States. He confirmed that he still enjoys writing songs, however – even on spec. It was truly joyous to hear him expanding rapturously about finding a chord the other day and it inspiring him – because of its shape and colour and mood – to write accompanying lyrics.

Richard noticed the Burne Jones stained-glass panel in the room where we talked, and admitted to liking arts and crafts and gothic as well. We chatted on about styles and things, and he said he was not fond of the garish bright Clarice Cliff-type stuff. He told us about how he had worked in a shop called China and Charm in Hamilton during his teenage school holidays and before returning to England, and now sees stuff he was selling as new turning up as collectibles in bric-à-brac shops.

We started talking about writing and I wondered whether, like Richard Hartley, he was surrounded by new musical technology. He isn't. He freely admits to being a technophobe. Doesn't like technology and only has the standard four terrestrial television channels.

DE: Can I press you now, regarding Tim...?

RICHARD O'BRIEN: I freely admit that I did resent the attention going all Tim's way. It did seem to be a one-way street. Not that he didn't deserve it, but...

I remember when the show hit LA, seeing the posters, which read, 'Lou Adler presents Michael White's Production – starring Tim Curry in *The Rocky Horror Show*.' I wasn't anywhere on the poster and had no biography in the programme. It wasn't Tim's doing but three people knew the value of billing and someone had decided to keep me away from it. The same poster appeared in Times Square, still no mention of me. So, since then, I've insisted on my name being above the title. 'Include me' is my mantra.

DE: But why would you have been so sidelined?

RO'B: I could see the showbiz side of Tim with his looks and talent. I just couldn't understand why they were rubbishing the talent aligned with that: *moi*.

When *Rocky* closed in New York, we got moved out of New York on a Sunday night, the two of us. Be ready to hit the road right after the show comes down, they said. They were putting us on a flight to Los Angeles to plan the show's future. I came offstage, out of the dressing room, into the limo, onto the plane, first class to LA.

Tim's [staying] with Barry [Krost], and I'm at the Sunset Marquee;

we go to the meeting the next morning, and I'm not even spoken to. Since that day, I've turned around to Lou Adler and said, 'I think you backed the wrong horse, and I never understood why you did that.' There is a difference between creative artists and interpretative artists. If you've got the creative artist on your team, surely you're better off than having an interpretative artist, because everybody is waiting for the good songs. A bucket is very useful, but not if the well's dry.

DE: *How do you feel about John Goldstone?*

RO'B: He's very nice. Truthfully. When we were doing that movie, I assumed he was at least in his 40s. Always assumed he was ten years older than I was.

DE: *I always found him charming. Totally self-effacing.*

RO'B: I've always had a huge problem meeting people that suddenly turn on that sort of 'star' kind of vehicle, this diva turn. Where's it fucking coming from? That kid Damien who recorded 'The Time Warp'; I met him up at Ilkley. We're going to go on and do a few sets, and he's doing *my* song, but it's like all of a sudden he's the star of the evening and I'm the hired help.

DE: *A little thank you goes a long way, doesn't it?*

RO'B: If you really want to make our creative work sing, try to be ego-free. It's really important, otherwise it over-embellishes and takes away from the pureness of the heart of your approach to everything. I've met a few divas and I just think... I don't understand it. Why do you really, honestly believe you are such a big effing star? Why are you doing this diva kind of gig? I think to myself, 'Just *stop it*! Who are you? Where do you come from? What have you done? How have you changed our lives? What have you given the world? Why do you think you're better than me? Why do you think you are better than anyone is?' How does that kind of complete bullshit confidence come about? Some people have an incredible amount of belief in themselves.

I stood onstage in the King's Road, our very last night, and Peter was very kindly doing a party that evening. I'm leaving the show to do the screenplay for the movie and Tim's leaving to do the show in Los Angeles. I step forward and gesture to Tim...

DE: You mean to take a 'company bow'-type thing?

RO'B: Well, I thought we might share a moment, but he never turned to me, he never made eye contact, never acknowledged me in any sense of the word. He went forward and took bows, and it was as if nobody else on that stage existed or mattered. Just a smile, that would be nice. A wave, a hand... [sighs]. We have a contract with life: the more intelligent you are, the more responsible you are. The more intelligence that's given to you as a gift, the more you have to give back to society, the more your responsibility to make change, to improve things, is incumbent upon you. That's the deal. When people play your intellectual superior – and there is no doubt that indeed Tim is... I was in adolescent-ness for too many years, that's my nature. I can't be any cleverer than I am... But to be dismissed like that is sad. Surely the job is just that. It's so easy just to say, 'And thank you for the songs...'

PETER STRAKER: All of us came through Peace and Love and *Hair*, and all that shit, whether you believe it or not. At the end of a show that's done you very well in London, you can't *not* turn round and acknowledge the hand [he is referring to the composer]. You might... I don't know, you might hate them, but at least you do the bow.

When we worked together doing *The News*, for instance, we spent most of the night going like that to each other [he means 'acknowledging'] and genuinely meant it. It's no big deal.

RO'B: You have to do a movie that has got two or three Americans in it, and I'm not referring to just *Rocky* here. You turn up on a wet morning and the fourth assistant director says, 'Oh, Richard, you're over there' [he points somewhere vaguely, way off in the distance].

Would they have done that to the three Americans, earning all that? How do you expect a performance out of me today, because now I'm angry. I was *going* to contribute to the art form here, and now you've turned me into a c∗∗t. A real fuckin' angry c∗∗t! I can turn from Mother Theresa into Freddy Kruger real quick!

PS: I had no idea that was going on. I was Tim's friend at the time, and he never said anything horrible about Richard.

RO'B: I have to say, hearing all these names again…I'm transported back to 1975, to Los Angeles, to Barry Krost's apartment in some street a bit in the hills above Tower Records. I know I'm going to this awful rock 'n' roll hotel and Tim's being looked after because Barry met him at the airport. And I'm thinking, 'Why am I the country cousin here? Why am I being treated like, "Oh, we had to bring the ugly one"?' I did feel awfully like that, especially when I discovered I wasn't needed, that they had little interest in my being in LA. I was left stranded at the Sunset Marquee, had to pay my own bill and was taken back to the airport in the A&M mail van!

Rocky was such a wonderful calling-card for so many people. It was, after all, *Rocky* that took Tim to Los Angeles… *Rocky* gave him his moment in time. In the sun. *Rocky* gave Jim Sharman a movie to direct that he wouldn't have been able to direct otherwise, gave Brian Thomson a film to design. To whom do we say thank you for these gifts, gentlemen? To each other.

When we were in New York, I was upstairs at the beautiful, bloody Belasco with Meat Loaf. Downstairs, Tim has a huge dressing room, with another huge dressing room next to it, for the people who might want to sit before they go into his dressing room. Then, of course, the show went down the fucking tubes. Day one. Terrible fucking reviews. Anyway, Kimi comes in, and the stage door person says to her, 'No, you can't go upstairs!'

I say, 'Hang on just a second. Who says she can't come upstairs?'
He says, 'Lou says.' It was a general rule, but…

I say back, 'I know Lou is the producer of the show, and I realise
he's employing you, but who do you think wrote this fuckin' show?
That's me. If Britt Ekland wanted to come upstairs, would you stop
her? I don't think so. Give me a fuckin' break here.'

After about two weeks at the Belasco, Tim comes to me: 'Why are
you upstairs?'

Now, mind you, we're in a flop and he doesn't have the people
turning up at the end of the show, because it's going down the fucking
tubes. 'You should have the dressing room next to me!' It was a little
late in the day.

'I'm staying with Meat Loaf,' I reply, 'and Meat Loaf kisses so
nicely.' [Laughs] He did. Really did. He had a sweet kiss, Meat Loaf.
Really soft kiss. Delightful. He only did it the once, though. He was
and is a honey.

PS: When we went to NY to see Tim that night [at the Belasco], we
went after the show with Tim to some apartment opposite the park,
overlooking the park. John Reid was there. It was me that took the
papers to him.

RO'B: We went to Sardi's, and Tim had decided to bring along a
model, Gay somebody [Gay Beresford, later remodelled as Zoe
Cadillac]. I think that apartment you mentioned was in the Sherry
Netherlands, wasn't it?

The show at the Belasco needed a better entrance for Tim. It was
wrong. They wanted to put in more seats. That's all I'm saying. It was
my biggest disappointment through the whole fucking show. No
matter who plays it, the entrance has to be wonderful.

DE: *When you first arrived back in England from New Zealand, did
you not have a second agendum? Even a first agendum?*

RO'B: Absolutely. I used to walk into recording companies. I went to

Decca one morning and the girl at the desk asked if she could help me. I said, 'I've come to sing some songs.'

She asked if I had an appointment.

'No,' I said, 'I haven't, but you're a recording company, aren't you? You make records, don't you?'

'Yes.'

'And people write the songs, don't they? And people sing on these records, don't they?'

'Yes.'

'Well, I'm a singer/songwriter, and I've come to sing some songs to whoever.'

'Oh,' she replied.

I'm not embarrassed, she's embarrassed. I'm from New Zealand with a guitar in my hand. So she says, 'Just a minute,' and Dick Roe came through. Of course, I wasn't aware of the history he had with The Beatles and he was terrified to make another mistake, so he saw me. Because I was there. He went, 'Young man, we don't regularly do this. It doesn't work this way, but you're here.' This was 1965. It was 1965 that I came to London.

DE: How old are you?

RO'B: Now? 57. Then, 23. But in those days, I played anything I could.

DE: Did you feel marginalised by that initial period of rejection?

RO'B: I never used to take it as rejection. I came along and played you my songs. If you don't want them, then all right. I didn't beat my head against the door. I always wrote songs. I wrote my first song when I was 15. A three-chord derivative rock 'n' roll song, no change there. But I actually wanted to be a comedy actor. I wanted to do what [Peter] Sellers was doing. I wanted to play comedy character roles.

DE: Did you sell any songs before Rocky?

RO'B: No. But I remember I rode horses in a show called *Carry On Cowboy* and I remember thinking, 'I know what I'll do, I'll write the title song for them.' So, I went home and wrote this song about Marshall P Knutt.

DE: *That was* your *song?*

RO'B: No, it wasn't. But I went along to the studio in Dean Street, and recorded it onto acetate. I took it out and took it up to Peter Rogers' room. He wasn't even there. You could get into people's rooms in those days. I left it on his desk. The next time I saw him, I said, 'Mr Rogers, I left an acetate on your desk of a song you might consider using for a theme for your movie.' He said, 'Oh, we've already got the writer for that.' But I still think my song was the better song. But then, I would say that, wouldn't I?

DE: *Do we conclude that those Rocky songs were really you? The deep and down and dirty you?*

RO'B: A lot of people said I was being very brave and up front and out there. Even at the time, I didn't get it…

DE: *At least you were never banned, although I've always wondered why some of the stage songs weren't in the film. Do you think there was some censorship there, from Fox? I mean, 'and deep inside, the beast was feeding'? Satanism? In middle America?*

RO'B: I've never thought about that. They're just songs to me. You know, I met up with this guy Arthur Kelley in 1967. He went to school with George Harrison. He was going to be a Beatle, but he turned it down. So Arthur and I spent some time writing songs together. We used to get the shilling for the song from a publishing company called Planetary something. We didn't have any success whatsoever, but I had plenty of songs in the drawer by the time I wrote *Rocky*. I was able to form some of those, which made life a lot easier.

I remember finding myself down at the Baghdad House in 1967. Donovan [Leitch] was there, and I remember playing him one of my songs. He won't remember this night because he was Donovan and I was nobody. I can't even remember the song I sang. Those things used to happen.

DE: How did you – do you – write? I mean, on what?

RO'B: I always worked with a guitar, and three chords really do go a long way.

There was an innocence and simple joy driving me along then. I think what happens is that when you do things when you first start out, you aren't intimidated by history or peer-group pressure. You're living in your own adolescent world. The writing just comes pouring out. Then, of course, you reap some success and people make some kind of critical evaluation, compare you to someone else. Suddenly you start to look at your work in a different way. You become intimidated by the need to succeed. Those other variables weren't in your mind before. Success can undermine innocence.

DE: Did you think your life was going to be easier as a songwriter after the success of Rocky?

RO'B: That changes on an hourly basis. Now I wish I could stop giving myself jobs to do. That's where I think I fuck up. I give myself a job, and am therefore kind of half-hearted about it. So then I go and find ways to hone my avoidance skills so I don't have to face up to what I've set myself to do. I could give a master class in avoidance. I come up with all sorts of reasons for not doing what I should be doing. I face up to my responsibilities, but I'm very good at doing a runner. Let's be honest, I'm a sheep in wolf's clothing.

DE: But you made it through to tell the tale. What if…shuffff! All gone?

RO'B: I know that, if everything was taken away from me tonight, I would survive. I know that my possessions mean nothing to me. Some may have sentimental value, but it's all expendable. Personally I couldn't give a fuck. The only thing I feel any responsibility for is being a parent. Though my missus and I haven't lived together for the last five or six years, I still feel very strongly about being a parent – emotional, moral and financial stuff. I'm relieved that I can take care of most of those. Linus is 27. I have another boy of 16 and a girl of 10. Good kids, very good kids.

DE: I thought that Helen Montague was in some way a sort of unifying force at the Court.

RO'B: She was one of those people you wanted to have lunch with. But no more than Gillian Diamond or Nicky Wright or Harriet Cruickshank. [Harriet Cruickshank is now a theatrical agent, while Nicholas Wright later directed Richard's *TZ And The Lost World* at the Royal Court Theatre.]

DE: Was Robert Fox involved with being supportive?

RO'B: He was an ASM [assistant stage manager] at the Royal Court and then he went to work for Michael White. Michael says that I went and sang the songs to him, which is not my memory. I never sang the songs to Michael, ever. I sang them to Jim and Richard Hartley.

Yeah…the Court. Robert was there. He was a 20-year-old, rather good-looking boy. It was kind of like we were groovy, and he was groovy, too. I think he was working for Michael when the movie was made. By that time he was together with Celestia. [Celestia Fox's maiden name was Sporburg, casting director on the movie. Her later marriage to Robert Fox was the only *Rocky* romance that came to anything.] Michael knew how to pick good people to work for him.

DE: It's a talent most successful managers have, too. Barry Krost, John Reid… Did you have much to do with the production of the movie of Rocky? *I notice you aren't credited.*

RO'B: [Laughs] I remember sitting with Michael White in Los Angeles around a pool, outside Lou Adler's offices, with a chap that we were trying to talk into becoming the director of yet another kind of *Rocky Horror* project, which Joe Roth, the then head of Fox, had commissioned. Michael turned around and said to this person, 'I'm not very good at business. I'm not a businessman at all.' I wanted to say, 'Could you tell me exactly what your fucking function therefore *is* around this table?' Business is surely the one thing that producers should excel at. But I bit my tongue, because Michael is a sweetie.

DE: *I'm amazed that so many projects that have turned into huge successes ever got started.*

RO'B: Michael's initial investment in *Rocky* was two grand, I think. Or his was a grand and the Royal Court matched it. Something like that. Our wardrobe budget was £200 out of that. I think Brian had £600 for set, seating and lights. And we had one microphone. We could only afford four musicians, so we had to get a bass player who doubled on sax.

PS: Fortunately, Upstairs at the Court was such a tiny room, and they all had good voices, so you didn't need the mics.

DE: *Sound is always such a touchy subject with musicians and performers.*

RO'B: When we went to LA in 1974, there was a guy called Abe Jacobs who did the sound at the Roxy and it was…delicious! The music that Jacobs was providing for that show was concert music. Suddenly, we were looking at the show so very differently. He was one of the greatest sound people in the world.

At the beginning, at the Theatre Upstairs, the single microphone came through a series of pulleys. Because it wouldn't drop down, we had to put a three-pound weight of iron on it to drop it down to the floor. Only then could you pick up the mic to sing. You'd watch this mic swinging around over people's heads when they were done with it.

After LA, we'd come back to the King's Road and listen to the show. This is a piece of shit. I'm sitting in the back and the sound is crap. It is so second rate. I just got back from LA. The audience liked it because they didn't know. Thank God for modern sound production and good engineers.

DE: Any thoughts about Phil Sayer?

RO'B: Philip Sayer. Ummm. I remember at his memorial, at the Aldwych Theatre, some woman came on to me and started going on about him in a lyrical manner: 'He was a colossus standing on a mountaintop.' I thought, 'Is this the man I remember?'

Then, Martin Sherman came forward and said, 'We all knew Philip, and we all knew he could be a little difficult from time to time.' I thought, 'Thank God. Now we're dealing with the human being we all knew, understood...and loved. For what he really was. Warts and all.'

DE: Did you know Michael White isn't keen on Rocky *being out on video?*

RO'B: I don't know his deal with Lou. The video idea was awful and because there was no original video provision, the thing as far as I was concerned was... [shrugs] well... They released it after 15 years at the movies for a two- or three-week lock-off period. They sold 400,000 copies for $99.99. They gave me £12,000, which I thought was rather cheap. I wrote to Michael and Lou and said that it makes no sense whatsoever. We're looking at 18 million in profit, really. They said, 'Well, actually, our cut has been pretty abysmal as well.' I finally got £34,000 for that period of sales.

DE: Are you and Rocky *on an everyday basis now?*

RO'B: I have nothing to do with anything except the stage shows. I think they've squeezed the lemon pretty good, as far as *Rocky* is concerned. Remember, you're talking about a film that shouldn't have got an audience in the first place. But money always seems to be a *major* problem... I did a television biography for New Zealand and they couldn't even afford the clips. Success has many fathers, a flop is born an orphan. That's Hollywood. It's the general rule.

DE: *That's a line I shall remember 'til I die. I can't let it go. Elaborate – in more than ten words... More wine?*

RO'B: I remember when *Rocky* went on. I was mostly divorced from it, and watching the thing happening I never thought, 'Oh, I've got a hit.' It wasn't part of my nature to be so out there, so visible. Nothing like that went through my brain.

But things happen. Earlier, before it opened, I'd sung some songs to a guy I knew. The show had been running for about three weeks, and he was ringing up the Royal Court saying, 'I've got a share in this. Richard came and sang a few of the songs over at my house.' People see success happening and want to be part of it. And it's not something I ever looked for. I once had a woman write to me from America. She wrote me, 'Dear Richard O'Brien, how clever of you to take my story that I wrote for the *Village Voice* (or whatever) and turn it into a musical. I wish I had that idea.' I didn't know where she was coming from. Then, strangely, a copy of this story came my way. I read it. It was *Dracula In The Chelsea Hotel*.

Anyway, I was in New York, and someone said that there was a telephone call for me. I knew it. I absolutely knew the minute someone said it that it was this woman. I have no idea how I knew it. She said, 'Mr O'Brien, I wrote you this letter.' I said, 'I *knew* it was you. You think I ripped off your fucking story, and you're fucking wrong. Both of us should be down on our knees, you to Bram Stoker and me to Mary Shelley, as it happens. Both of us have ripped our stories off from someone else. Nothing is created in a vacuum. No one that thinks they are original has any sense of history. I'm sorry.'

She says, 'Do you think we can go out to dinner?'

[Shouting] 'I DON'T THINK SO! I may be stupid, but I don't want you in my life.'

I can recognise a flake at 3,000 paces.

[As an aside, ordinary writers without the luxury of representation cannot get their work read unsolicited by, for example, Steven Spielberg's Amblin Entertainment. Try sending in an outline, a treatment or even a script. Three weeks later your work is returned unread. There's even a letter stating in very legal terms that it is unread.]

The only time I flip is when people try to take it away from me. Not in monetary terms, but in intellectual terms. I have to go back to Brian. Brian says, 'I don't understand why Richard thinks he's the only person responsible for the show.'

However, when I go on daytime television and they announce that they have the creator of *The Rocky Horror Show* – and I didn't feed them the lines – what am I supposed to do? Me being 'the creator' is a way they've found for explaining my being there. They decided to come up with it as a generic term. I'm not going to turn around and, say, spend all seven minutes I have to sell whatever I'm there for to explain the whole of the ins and outs and the whys and wherefores of *Rocky*. Fuck it. No one is interested in that.

DE: Quite right. Smacks of whingeing and boring old sour grapes and 'Where's the remote? Let's surf to Richard And Judy *instead.'*

RO'B: I wrote the book, music and lyrics. I realise I didn't actually *write* the music down in notation, but the thing was mine. Is mine.

DE: And that, as far as both legal and moral copyright goes, is what a creator does and is. The way the copyright system works, there has to be a source. A single, unique source.

RO'B: Quite.

DE: And so, in a nutshell?

RO'B: *Rocky* started as a way for me to spend winter evenings when I was an out-of-work actor. It was the very first thing I'd ever written. I didn't even see it as writing, really. To me, it was just like doing the crossword or making a collage. I just wrote some songs that I liked. I wrote some gags that I liked. I put in some B-movie dialogue and situations. I was just having a ball. It's all an exhibitionist kind of need, the work of an arrested development. There's nothing wrong with it. I think we all need to make believe.

DE: And as a last word?

RO'B: When Rocky was born, somebody asked Tim my age. He replied that I was 31 going on 13. He was right on the money. I was and, until recently, remained locked into pubescent adolescence. *Rocky Horror* is a thumbprint of my psychological pathology. *All* the midwives at the birth were just what the mother and child required. Excellently so. The doctor was a perceptive man who drew songs out of the patient with deceptive élan. We are all marked by the experience and our differences may never be resolved. I think it's unlikely that Brian T and I will ever be friends again, as he veers towards emotional bully while I am most assuredly an emotional coward. I don't think Jim ever said, 'OK, boys and girls, let's make magic,' but he could have done, and we did, in spades.

‹‹‹‹irememberdoingthetimewarpirememberdoingthetimewarpi››››

2 'I Can Show You My Favourite Obsession'
Behind The Scenes

Kimi Wong O'Brien

There is an old adage, well worn, scuffed and commonly derided but often true: behind every successful man there is a woman. Richard O'Brien's catholic sexuality needs no more trumpeting, but suffice it to say that his proclivities either had to be entirely embraced by the women in his life or there would have been no women in his life. In 1972, there was only one woman in his life, his wife Kimi, whose own family background of 1950s rock 'n' roll (her father having an abiding passion for movies) made her a soulmate.

Despite the women's lib movement and the charred ashes of a zillion bras, Kimi was the wife who followed where her husband led. His dreams were her dreams, and she was prepared to support him. It was what Mary Austin did for Freddie Mercury, what Cynthia Lennon did for John, what the wives and lovers of thousands of artists throughout the ages have done to enable and empower their husband-children.

But that's just my opinion. I have a proposition, though. I think there should be a *Rocky Horror* ombudsman, who could help maintain that same joyous enthusiasm that flourished in *Rocky*'s own Garden of Eden when the apple was still safely on the tree.

Born in South Africa, Kimi's late and much-loved father was Chinese. Her mother is from Mauritius, a small island off the coast of Africa, although she now lives in Canada. Kimi has five brothers and a sister. The family left South Africa when Kimi was four, when Apartheid kicked in. Her father was classified as 'yellow' and her mother 'black'. Her father loved movies and opened a drive-in movie site, as well as restaurants and a fish 'n' chip business, while her elder brother loved 1950s music. Her father sold all these business interests. Kimi thinks the family would have been split apart otherwise. The Wong family came first to England but didn't settle easily and so moved on to Monastery Park, Dublin, Ireland, where Kimi was brought up and where her father realised his 1950s dream and founded Wong's Drive-In Restaurant.

Kimi, whose own mother had started her family at the age of 12, met Richard when she was 16. Was she Richard's Yoko Ono? She sang beautifully, had a great eye, took excellent photographs.

She keeps the past very safe, wrapped in a very tight pink ribbon. Her memory, despite her years of drug addiction, during which she abused it, is still accurate, although remembering seems to surprise her. She allowed Scott unlimited access to her most private papers. They're like her treasures. She's like a little girl with her treasures garnered in a time capsule. They validate her. They are her importance. She appears not to have realised how much she was loved. She is now 48. When Scott approached her, asking for an interview, she remarked, 'Fate plays a strange card when you least expect it.'

It sounds like a line from the show itself.

SCOTT MICHAELS: *So you have nothing to do with the business any more?*

KIMI WONG O'BRIEN: I've got a friend with a guitar, and we're looking for a venue. I want to get back into singing. I work as a phlebotomist at the Whittington Hospital at Archway and I've just got these ten days off. I bike to work. I would like to get back into the business. I'm insane, you know. Sane but insane. But whatever I tell you about *Rocky* will be absolutely true. I've got all the diaries, from when Ritzy [Richard O'Brien] and I were together. I tend to go off the rails a bit, but I have it all. I've got the original handwritten script with all the scribbles. He rewrote it tidily and threw it out. I saved it. It is going to be part of history. And I was the only one on the first day of filming to have a camera and I took so many shots. I've got pics of Lou [Adler] and the cast in LA and New York. I also even have eight-millimetre film of the rehearsals.

SM: I appreciate your honesty. Everyone that I've spoken to has volunteered to be so. However, you have memorabilia and photographs that I could use. I would buy the use of them from you.

KW: Now I have to get an agent. I told my lawyer friend that I'm going to do it. He told me, 'Look, Kimi, if you want to do a book, you have to be careful.' I have that sort of personality. If I'm asked something, I'll do that. I haven't even said 'Let's discuss it first.' I feel, if I say yes and do it, within myself I won't be truthful. Within myself. My brain has gone weird, but it hasn't forgotten things. I showed your letter to Linus [her son with Richard O'Brien] and he said, 'If you feel safe, then go ahead with it.'

With you, I'll be truthful. I'm not a bread-head – however, I need money. The main thing is to keep my head above water, [so] I pay my bills and the things that matter. I don't want to go through that again. The advice I've been given is to talk to you and tell you how I feel. I could deceive you, but I don't want to play those games. You are either open or not. I have got more information (I'm not bragging), more knowledge and papers and photographs than anyone has. More memories in my diaries and in my head, from before *Rocky* was even conceived. My information deserves it. The fans have been very loyal. That's the way I work.

SM: I detect an aura of…well, I don't think it's been a bed of roses for you. Am I right?

KW: One thing I resent: I started to make this wonderful scrapbook with everything Richard did, before *Rocky*. Richard asked me what I was doing. I said, 'One day you are going to be big. I just know it. Don't ask me how, I just do.' When we split up, he took it, unbeknownst to me, and I know he still has it. How can one argue, 'That's mine?' But it is mine. I made it and kept it for us. However, I'm not going to quibble about it. I got the main thing, which I was offered a lot of money for: the original script. I just said no – that is a legacy for my son. Now, I would be prepared to give you photographs. This meeting is basically you and I getting to know each other. You can pick my brain and write things. There are certain things I am not going to say until we get to know each other better. Then we make a deal or whatever. Then you can be the first one in there, for a *Rocky Horror* book. I don't even know what you want from me.

SM [having explained what I'm after]: Why don't you just start by talking...

KW: Well, we were at the Royal Court and it was the last night. Everyone was putting their make-up on and I was working on lights. I ran up and said, 'My God, have you seen who's down there? Elliot Gould and Mick Jagger.' Everyone was excited. The next thing I knew everyone slowed down. I asked what was going on. I heard Ritzy shout, 'OH MY GOD!' from behind a curtain. He came out and pulled me aside and said, 'You won't believe it. Raynor has got glitter up his cock.'

'So?' I said and Ritzy said, 'So. The doctor told him not to do it. Just go and have a look.' I expected nothing, really, and opened the curtain and gasped. I ran out and said, 'Oh, shit!' His legs were spread wide and his balls were like tennis balls. We had to carry him out, with his legs like that. The show was cancelled. Tim was so very angry.

Raynor was excellent for the part because he loved himself. I'm not saying that in a nasty way. He had that style of how to do it, and he looked good. Nell started going on about considering playing other parts. I said, 'You can't do that. You just have to come to terms with the fact that you ain't going to do the show tonight.' Ritzy said, 'You're right.' Tim was slowly putting on his make-up, and when I said that, I remember his hand going down and he thought, 'Right,' and he got out make-up removing cream and he started taking his make-up off. Then it was announced and everyone – Lou and Britt were there – couldn't believe it. I think it was Brian who gave them their money back.

SM: *That must have been quite a night.*

KW: There's more. As we were leaving the theatre, it was Ritzy, Brian, Pierre [Perry Bedden] and myself. We were walking towards our cars. We heard a voice calling, 'Richard! Richard!' and it was Jonathan King, offering to produce the first recording. And it was done, in one night, just before the Chelsea Classic. Jonathan was already in the music business. I remember him being quite respected in the business. It couldn't have been the last night because Raynor was there. We worked from about eight o'clock right through 'til seven or eight the next morning. Everything was put down. Julie Covington was not on the original album. By that time, they auditioned Belinda Sinclair. Richard and I had known Belinda from *Hair*. Belinda went down to Sarm Studios that night. Sarm stood for 'sound and recording mobile studios'. It was owned by a dear friend of ours called John Sinclair. When Richard brought the idea up, John and another guy called Andy were also there.

SM: *So, like the song says, was it great when it all began?*

KW: We were living in our little flat in Maida Vale in Oakington Road, W9. I remember Richard suggesting a horror story based on rock 'n' roll, and I remember thinking it was a great idea. But John Sinclair didn't seem that eager because he was getting his own thing together with the studio. Richard had quit the tour of *Hair*. A guy that played Herod in *Jesus Christ, Superstar*, Paul Jabara, was playing it and he could only do three months. Richard had quit and he became very downhearted. Then he met up with Jim. He heard about *Superstar* and thought he wanted a change, so he auditioned for it. He had two rehearsals, and he told Jim that he didn't want to do it like Jabara did it, which was very camp: tap-dancing with a top hat. Richard wanted to do it like a rock 'n' roll style. Paul Nicholas was playing the lead role and a girl named Dana Gillespie played Mary Magdalene. So Jim agreed to that.

I'm at home with our son. It was a Friday afternoon and I get a call from Ritzy saying, 'Oh my God, I'm on tonight. I'm on this afternoon [matinée] because Robert Stigwood wants to see what I'm like.' I wished I could come and see it, but I couldn't and wished him well and said, 'Just do the best you can, which you can do.' He did it. Remember, he only had two rehearsals. From that Friday to the following Friday, we waited to hear if he'd got the part. The phone rang and it was Robert Stigwood's underdog, Bob Swash. Robert and Bob were producing *Hair* at the time. He basically said that Robert wasn't satisfied with the performance.

Richard was devastated and so was I. I thought, 'How the fuck could they do this to him?' They broke his heart. They spent about two grand on his outfit. Rufus [Collins] was the choreographer [and future Transylvanian] and he was taking Richard for rehearsals. Richard had some strength left, so he got on to Equity. The man in charge of Equity was Peter Plouviez, or something like that. He told him the events that occurred and Peter told Richard he could sue for breach of contract, because Richard had signed one. We went through all this shit and all they came to was £300, [although that] was a lot of money at the time. Now Richard lives in luxury and I live the opposite. Not a dump, just not as suave.

We had a very good relationship, you know.

SM: Money was pretty tight, then?

KW: I'd done my O-level examinations and, after seeing an ad in the *New Musical Express*, I came over from Ireland to audition for *Hair* with my dad's blessing and 20 quid. David Toguri auditioned me. I was asked to sing 'If I Had A Hammer', then told to freak out all over the stage. They were amazed that I had flown from Dublin to audition. Then I had to come back for a second audition. James Werner even quoted me those immortal words: 'Don't call us, we'll call you.' But I got to sing the Frank Mills song, totally alone onstage. I was really upset and I went home only to go down with gastroenteritis for two months. Then I got a call from Frank McKigh [to say] that I'd got a role in the first national tour.

I met Richard in the first line-up. He was the coolest of them all in his skin-tight Mister Freedom pants, a wide-brimmed hat. I thought I'd found my own John Lennon. I went weak. He used to tease me a lot. Called me Bridget, 'cos I came from Ireland. He took me under his wing. We were just friends. He had his girlfriend and I always remembered that he wasn't free. And I was still a virgin and very scared of that side of, well, relationships. I had no idea. We became closer, of course. We were about six months into the tour, in Nottingham, before I lost my virginity.

Then suddenly Richard announced he was going to leave the tour. My heart just fell apart.

By the time we got to Aberdeen, there was this guy called Glen Conway who was had a real crush on me and at one point even asked me to marry him. He never gave up. Always there for me. I'd love to meet him again. Glen used to go down to London at weekends and stay with Richard and his girlfriend, Kate Garrett, at a house they lived in then in Chesilton Road, off Fulham Road. It was owned by Jane Stonehouse, the daughter of the infamous vanishing Member of Parliament John Stonehouse. Kate had finally got into the London show and was having an affair with an American, which really upset Richard. So, via Glen, I always knew what was going on.

When I came back to London from Aberdeen, they'd asked me to take the role of Chrissie in *Hair* at the Shaftesbury Theatre. I stayed in Peter Straker's flat in Holland Park. My girlfriend Jeanie MacDonald and I stayed there. Jeanie was a good friend of Yasmin Pettigrew, who'd been living with Straker off and on in the Holland Park flat. Straker was away somewhere – Norway, I think, or Germany. One night at the end of the show, when the audience come up to dance, there was Richard standing in the prompt corner and he smiled and waved. I really didn't want to get involved in that all over again. I'd only just lost him, after all.

I saw him again later in the pub but I didn't pursue anything. But he called me later and asked me to meet him in Kensington Market. Said he'd meet me outside. He told me he wasn't with Kate any more. We spent the night together at Straker's. Then we started seeing each other again. We got married on 4 December 1971, when I was pregnant. In fact, I worked 'til I was eight and a half months pregnant.

SM: So when you got pregnant, did you plan that?

KW: No. It wasn't planned. I was only 19. I had Linus on 1 May, when I was 20. I was given 30 April as his birth date, 1972. Richard wasn't working and so he took care of our son. I had to go back to work, too. I used to get £45 a week, which was a lot of money. You got paid by the line. If you said so many lines onstage, you got £1 for every line you said. I knew the show inside and out. I was playing a bloody man at one point, a policeman. That was the only time I didn't do the nude scene. That's how I made the money.

I do feel, and felt, a great deal of resentment – all that shite I read about afterwards, about how Richard looked after the child, and I've never been mentioned. If Richard took care of the baby, who brought the money in? Do you know what I'm saying? I'm not begrudging him. I hold no animosity towards Richard. I would love to meet my ex- and only husband and first love, meet him and talk to him. I feel that I've grown up tremendously. I just turned 48 this week and Richard is 58 and our son is 28. That really hurt me. There was this enormous spread in *The Guardian* about how well he's been doing, and of course it came to talk about *Rocky*. A person that I met in treatment sent me the cut-out. It stated, 'Of course, Richard stayed at home with the baby and changed nappies,' and there was never a mention of me! I feel I contributed so much to that. My parents, too. My dad bought us a Mini, a little black Mini, so we could get around. I gave so much support to my husband that just a little bit of recognition would have been nice. A bit of self-esteem. Not because it's just in black and white for people to read. I don't care about that. What I care about is the recognition.

With hindsight, that is Richard's way of dealing with things that might go wrong: blot it out completely. I don't blame him for that. Some people don't want to deal with certain issues, and yet some people need and have to deal with issues. Like I have to deal with a load of shite, a load of crap, because I went into a state of drug addiction. I felt like I was a little girl thrown out when we broke up. Thrown out, not knowing what to do, where to go. I wasn't physically thrown out, of course. I came home from shopping one day with

Linus, on a sunny day like today – and you are the only one I've told this to – and Richard is walking out of our front door with a suitcase. What am I supposed to think? I'd just come out of the bloody Priory [the rehab centre] and at the same time my father died.

Being the spouse of a famous person is very difficult. I found out who my friends were, and no one was my friend. They were our friends, but when Richard left, nobody wanted to know. Nobody. There I was, living in a relatively large house with our son 'til things were sorted out. Of course, there were exceptions. Brian Thomson was always really kind to me and to Linus. Brian was very close to all three of us (ie including Richard) at the beginning.

[She expresses sweet surprise when Scott tells her that Richard told us of the incident at the Belasco when the security wouldn't let Kimi into the theatre.]

Even then I was quite naïve. I look back and think, 'Don't knock yourself, because you did bloody well. Of course, you went down a road that people frown upon. They don't really look at the real motives.' It was drug addiction, 'cos I've never drunk in my life. I've never been recognised at all, not in any way, other than to be used, but I never allowed myself to be used. I had to learn to walk again on my own. I didn't know what way to go. Aside from the chemicals that were in my head and in my body, I was just so very naïve. If I'd known then what I know now…I would have gone that way he wanted me to when he talked about being 'friends'. Then I just thought, 'I don't want to be your friend, mate! I'm your wife!'

SM: *So what happened to your family, to Linus, after Richard left?*

KW: Linus was with me for a certain amount of time and at boarding school. You have to be separated for two years, and if either party files for divorce the other party either agrees or disagrees. Then the person who wants the divorce has to wait for three years, so it's five years total. So I thought to myself, as fucked up as I was, 'He wants to go with this other woman [Jane Moss].' He was on his own for a while, before Jane. He left me in 1979. I moved to my house in 1982. We both agreed not to inflict anything upon our son. Then I received the decree. I am always on my own when I have to face those things. It's heartbreaking. People don't realise how hurt I really felt. I wasn't ready for it to be over.

SM: I get the feeling you felt there was nothing you could do?

KW: The decree came and my attorney said, 'Kimi, you make the decision. If you don't agree and Richard really wants the divorce, he could take you to court, and it could get ugly.' At that time, I was petrified and thought, 'Well, what's the point in hanging on for another three years, and one party doesn't want it?' I agreed. I gave complete care and control of Linus to Richard, yet we had joint custody. That was a fucking hard thing to do. I wasn't thinking of myself. It was the worst thing that has ever happened to me. I still cannot get over what I did.

But for some reason, as fucked up as I was, I had the greatest sense to know that our son mattered. I could not give him what Richard could: the education, the stability, the security. I was incapable of even taking care of myself. That's one of the major things in my life that seems to recur. There was a time when I would express my anger about Richard and Jane to my son. Linus would tell me to stop. Gradually, as happens in life, one learns how to deal with certain things. I would love closure with Richard. Is he here today? No. Will he be back? No. My dearest old friend Sally, Linus's nanny, once said to me, 'Kimi, it's time to take Richard off the pedestal.' When she said that, those words stuck in my head. Even now in my eyes, I tend to protect Richard if someone says anything derogatory.

Now, when I do see him on television or in a magazine, I say to myself, 'You were there when he wasn't known. You were there from the beginning, when nobody knew anything. You were there for the hard times, which were probably the good times.' When it comes down to it, money talks. That and celebrity. They're what talks today.

SM: Certainly seems that way a lot of the time.

KW: Pat Quinn and I always got on very well. She is a very open woman, very much like myself. At one point, the two of us were going to get a book together. I'd already written a transcript, but it's not polished. It needs somebody to work on it, someone to get to know me. If that means spending 72 hours a day with somebody, then you do that. Then you get the deep down truth of that person. I took a brave step last night when I called you. I thought I mustn't ignore you. The voice in my head said, 'Ring him and help him.'

SM: *That's kind but, no, I don't think so. I don't think I'm capable. I can offer you financial help with pictures, etc. I'll include you as best I can, and help in any way I can.*

KW: As much as I need money, I am not a materialistic person. Just look at this room. I just want to survive. I want to move on from the hospital and things like that. I'd like to get back into the theatre. The reason I left entertainment was because I thought to myself, 'You've broken up with Richard. His fame is at its peak. No matter what I do, I'll always be known as his first wife. His ex-wife.' I probably still will, but I'm much stronger with my mental health, and more of an individual. I've begun to realise that. I'm still wanting to grow and I feel I still have things to offer.

SM: *I just noticed from this original script you have from the rehearsals at the Theatre Upstairs that the character of Brad was originally called Ricky. Was that Richard?*

KW: Never thought about that, but I can tell you that Magenta was based on me. I came home from doing two Saturday shows of *Hair* and my voice was really screwed up. I remember coming home to Oakington Road. In the basement was a girl called Kim. On the ground floor were two gay guys and we had the upstairs, and that was it. We just had a front room, bedroom. The guy that lived there before us was the friend of a very good friend of Richard's, who became my friend. Her name is Chrissie and in those days she was married to Scott

Messenger. Chrissie was the sister of Jean Shrimpton, the model who went out with Mick Jagger, and Chrissie was a really well-known model too. Anyway, I came home and Jim Sharman, Ritzy and Richard Hartley were there.

Jim said to me, 'There's our Magenta!'

'Get off!' I said, 'No way.'

Richard said, 'Come on, sing "Science Fiction".' I was very shy, and though they kept insisting I sing the song, I just wouldn't.

SM: Do you regret that now?

KW: I don't know. I regret it in one aspect and I don't in a major aspect. If I had done that, I wouldn't have learned as much as I did. But I was there again, in the background. I was working with the workers, on lights and that. When we did matinées at the Chelsea Classic, I used to run out and get coffees. I did get to play Magenta at the King's Road, as understudy. I loved it. I really enjoyed it. Jim Sharman is a fantastic director if you're right for the part. If you are, then all he does is tell you where to stand and where to go, and he knows he will get the goods. That's how Jim knew it would be with Susan Sarandon and Barry Bostwick. He knew they would be great, and they were.

I mean, Chris Malcolm had been offered the role of Ralph Hapschatt in the movie. I know from Jim that Chris had hung up the phone and he's never spoken to Jim ever again. He could have had the role. Turning it down was on his own head. And Brian Thomson, he had an amazing input into the way the whole thing looked and felt. Some wonderful, like, satirical moments that he contributed to. He and Jim and Richard were a fantastic team. But it started with Richard. If it wasn't for Richard, neither Jim nor Brian would have had anything to be part of. The resentment that you talk about…well, when it comes down to it, it's Brian's problem, isn't it?

SM: If you had played Magenta, you could have owned a bit more of the history.

KW: Yes. I know what you mean. I would be at the forefront of it. People only remember the faces. If I'm being honest, there was a point... But the sort of person I am, I think, 'OK, but at least I was in the movie, and no one can take that away from me. No one can take away my memories.'

SM: *Talking about 'Science Fiction', just when was it written? In fact, how many songs were written before* Rocky?

KW: Richard wrote the 'I'm Going Home' song for me ages before *Rocky*. He wrote loads of songs for me. Ian, a weird friend of the actor Gary Hamilton, was always outside the stage door. He kept tarantulas. Horrible hairy things. We used to call Ian 'Spider Face', Diane Langton and I. Anyway, he wanted Richard to do a song or something for a show he was putting together for Christmas at Elstree Studios. I told Richard when I got home that I'd committed him to it. He said he couldn't do it.

Then he started thinking. I saw him... I knew we wouldn't be getting to bed that night until I'd talked him round. We got the movie books out and I said, 'Go on, what movies do you like?' He said, 'You know what movies I like.'

Anyway, we sat and picked them out, all the weird ones, the horror stuff. And that's when he wrote 'Science Fiction'.

Writing that started to bring him out of that flat period. I didn't go and see the Christmas gig, 'cause of Linus. John Sinclair went with him and Andy, too. Nice Jewish people. Jill was lovely too, John's sister. She's married to Trevor Horne now.

'Over At The Frankenstein Place' wasn't written for the movie but he used that for *Rocky*. 'Touch Me' was written for Julie. They all said that she had to have a song.

He wrote 'The Time Warp' for the show. It was Ritzy and I at Oakington Road who put the Time Warp dance together. I said it had to be simple but it needs a bit of this, a bit of that. Then he came up with the lyrics. He did 'Eddie's Teddie' overnight, too, 'cause it was needed for that gap in the show. I did a single of that, just called

'Eddie'. It was the B-side for a song Ritzy and I did together called 'Merry Christmas, Baby'. They all said I sounded just like Ronnie Spector. You remember The Ronettes? It came out on Epic and sold about 12,000 copies and it got on the BBC playlist. Got a great review from John Peel, too, a very big DJ then. His opinions really counted. We sold it at the King's Road Theatre. We gave them to all the crew members at the end of filming, just a little token to say thank you.

When we were in New York we went to see someone, some record company guy at Epic. Then, when everything went crazy, the records weren't so…

SM: What happened with Epic, then? Why didn't they want you to go on and do more?

KW: I think Richard rather lost his confidence after the Lou Adler thing, when Lou only wanted to know about Tim. Richard was dumped, you know. Being the wife, I realised that he wasn't into going on with the records, and so I just never said anything, never did anything else. I always depended on him saying what he wanted to do. And something happened to Ritzy after his great success. I think he changed. Not only towards me, but changed.

SM: I'm guessing, but surely it must be very difficult to have such a huge hit on your first time out and then know that whatever you follow it with will always be compared.

KW: It brings such pressure. We were all under pressure. I guess I dealt with it in my way, he dealt with it in his way.

SM: As you know, I'm heavy on the Transylvanians. What was it like actually being one?

KW: We rehearsed in Oakley Court, having to traipse through fields of mud from Bray. The place was all decaying. We were all banned from going any further than the second floor. Ritzy and I went further, though, and we even nicked a piece of the place for a souvenir. I have it still.

SM: Pam [Obermeyer] said she remembers you coming to the film set with Linus in his pram.

KW: Can't understand that. Linus was always with Sally [his nanny] at home. Pam didn't have much to do with us on the set. She wasn't very social. The only time I brought Linus was at the end, for the 'I'm Going Home' song. I think they had to do at least two takes 'cause Linus called out for his daddy!

SM: Sorry. It was Superstar *Pam said she remembered you coming to. Was Transylvania as cliquey as it's been rumoured?*

KW: Well, Gaye was always very outgoing. Quite overpowering, really. So was Biggins, though in a gentler way, yet he was really keen to get on. Very keen to talk to me. Annabel not so much, not so 'pushing'. But you know the scene in the film with the motorbikes in the rain? That's Annabel, Gaye and me. Jim just said at the end of that day, did we want some more filming. So we did. I was the last one coming through. Annabel was on the first one, then Gaye, then me.

There was another guy, Tony Cowen, who was Henry Woolf's replacement for two days. We all would sit with each other, but he kept to himself. It always seemed he thought, like, 'What the hell am I doing here, amongst these nutheads?' That's the impression we got. We tried to bring him in with us, because we were a separate entity compared to Tim, Nell, Pat and Susan etc. We were, like, apart, you know?

But it was fun. I remember being with Perry [Bedden] on the set. (Don't forget, I call him Pierre. Can get confusing!) Pierre and I would drive up and one day we were smoking this joint and we passed our exit and ended up in Oxford. We were the last two to arrive, and Jim just glared at us. He did give us a bollocking, really shouted at us. We used to drive around in this little car, this little runabout that Brian had bought him, and one day the floor almost fell out. I could see the tarmac on the road as we were driving along Kensington High Street!

I remember David Toguri taking me aside and going with him to another room. He was so nervous about showing people how to do the Time Warp. I said, 'Come on, you. They don't know how to do it, so what're you nervous for?' So I went back and I did it with him to show the others. I was so chuffed. This was the guy who gave me my break.

But it was Ritzy and I who originally worked out the first version of the Time Warp. Then Jim Sharman sort of took it over and asked David, 'Can you help me out here?'

I remember Peggy Ledger and Fran Fullenwider from those times. Peggy was wonderful. I remember they put little frail Peggy up by one of the statues as the stunt rider was driving the motorbike up the ramp and she had to snap off the head of that statue. Perry and I had to just leap over the railings. Jim told us to leave jumping out of the way 'til the very last moment. Jeez... The stunt guy was well qualified, but the bike was still sliding all over the place. Terrible wig, they gave him. Some of the other Trannies thought they couldn't talk to me 'cause I was Richard's wife, but as we got into filming I was just one of them.

SM: How about the others?

KW: I know Stephen [Calcutt] felt a freak. He looked so ordinary usually, but as a Transylvanian, well... He was so thin but that hair made him look even taller and thinner.

There was no one I didn't really get on with. Lindsay Ingram was always a bit quiet. Henry Woolf was wonderful, too. The bit with Perry Bedden as the photographer – great. Tony Milner was very quiet, too. I've seen him do stuff lately, so he's still around.

On that first day of filming, it was the wedding scene. My Transylvanians carried me into Henry Woolf's van. I was freezing, but there was such a happy atmosphere as we got into our wedding-guests costumes.

SM: *What about Tim?*

KW: He found the *Rocky* thing too much to handle. He was getting scripts on the basis of being Frank and he wanted to be this great actor.

SM: *And a rock star...*

KW: Really? He made it his role, though. No one could take that away from him. He was very good to me, though. Gave me some lovely presents.

SM: *Sorry, I interrupted you about the Trannies.*

KW: Richard and Jim were arguing about the dialogue, and then there was that almost fatal moment when the elevator drops just as Barry Bostwick had got out of it on one of the takes as Frank is taking Brad and Janet up to the lab. I remember it. There was this whoosh, this release of air, and down went the lift. Was there a yelling!

Jonathan Adams was such a divine man. What you saw was what you got with Jonathan.

However, I have to say there was a lot of 'us and them' on the set. The Transylvanians were not allowed to come and eat in the proper place where the 'actaws' were eating. So, we'd go into the canteen where the crew and all the gaffers or whatever went. We did feel a bit like, 'Fuck off!', you know?

SM: *I can't believe you were treated like that.*

KW: I'm not trying to portray that I feel hard done by, although I have to tell you the facts. I've learned a lot from going through therapy and all the shit I went through. Way back then, Richard got me to go to a psychotherapist for evaluation. I went along and answered all their questions. I went along with it because I wanted to save our marriage. Binkie [her pet-name for her son Linus] was sweet... He asked all the usual questions: 'Will I see you? Will I see Daddy? Will you see Daddy?' Richard wanted to come around but I didn't think it would be good. We had to take things to a different space. It was very difficult for me to say no.

He did come a couple of times but we only sat and talked about trivia. I heard through Tim that he was seeing Jane [Moss]. She'd been the costume designer's assistant on *Disaster*. She'd been going out with Brett Forest, who'd been in *Hair* with Richard and I. I'd met her before at Brett's house.

SM: Could I just ask you something that will clear up one of my little mysteries. Just what did Pierre La Roche do?

KW: Pierre La Roche? He did the David Bowie sleeve cover of him and Twiggy, the ones with the masks drawn on their faces. Pierre was brought into the show and the artists, like Tim, didn't like the original make-up. They thought it was far too heavy. They wanted it toned down. The artists did their own designs for make-up at the Court. Sue Blane drew the costumes and the images, but they all did their make-up. Both Jim and Richard had a vision of what the characters should look like, but it was the actors who brought the final influence to bear. Pierre was brought into the movie to synthesise all the ideas.

SM: You worked properly with Richard in another show, didn't you?

KW: I was in *TZ* [Tarzan] *And The Lost World* at the main house in the Royal Court. It wasn't directed by Jim and it didn't get great notices, but it lasted the five weeks. Warren Clarke was in it, too. Nicholas Wright directed it and he wasn't right for it. In fact, he wasn't strictly a director. The Edgar Rice Burroughs estate wouldn't allow Richard to use [the word] Tarzan. Brian's set was incredible. Without that, it would have been shit. The set was a circus ring. Jim Sweeney played the Angel that comes down and talks to the Tarzan character. Sue Blane did the costumes, of course. Richard Hartley was musical director. Di Langton was in it, too. She played Princess La. It was all based on Armageddon in Los Angeles. Richard played a geeky sort of scientist and Belinda Sinclair played his love interest, Alison.

After that closed, I went on to do something with Ken Campbell, but I was never comfortable. I think he wanted more from me than just a performance onstage. That didn't last.

SM: I can't thank you enough, Kimi. I just hope that one day you can find someone who can take care of Kimi the way Kimi wants to be taken care of.

KW: I thank you, Scott. You've given me back my voice. I've got a voice again. Looking through all this stuff, which I knew I had but which had been put away for years, I just think to myself how lucky I am. How lucky. I feel I have a very compassionate nature, which at times has been taken advantage of. I have to live in the moment, though. I have to do what I need to do for myself.

I need to include myself again. I'm a human being. I've got feelings. I need people to know I was there.

<<<<irememberdoingthetimewarpirememberdoingthetimewarpi>>>>

Perry Bedden

Why does the dream always work out and reality never does? 'Don't Dream It, Be It' is all very well but it's not as easy when the house lights come up at the end of the show and the magic dust is put away again 'til tomorrow. And, when all's said and done, most people don't want to be free. Freedom is a very frail flower and needs as much daily TLC as any lover or friend.

Speaking of friends, Jim Sharman and Brian Thomson were friends from Australia and they became fast friends of Richard and Kimi, and they were the first to join Richard on the road to *Rocky*, when *Rocky* was called *They Came From Denton High* and Brad only existed as Ricky.

As we were initially unable to contact Brian Thomson or Jim

Sharman, and were indeed given to believe by people who *did* know how to contact them that neither would have any interest in contributing to this book, we are extremely grateful to Perry Bedden for giving up his time to fill in a few factual details about the wheres, hows and whens of Jim Sharman and Brian Thomson becoming involved with *Rocky*.

Perry is uniquely qualified to shed light not only on the making of the movie – he famously played one of the Transylvanians – but he was also involved in a close friendship with Brian Thomson, the designer of both the play and the film, and therefore knew Jim Sharman, the director.

Although we were able ultimately to talk to Brian Thomson, we failed to enlist direct contributions from Jim Sharman, although Perry very kindly allowed himself to be quizzed on all aspects of the *Rocky Horror* phenomenon.

DAVID EVANS: *So where did the friendship between Jim and Brian start? Because this is pretty pivotal to the whole story, isn't it?*

PERRY BEDDEN: I think they met in a coffee shop. It was a Sydney association. The theatrical thing with them started in *Hair* in Sydney. Harry Miller was the producer. The first thing Brian ever designed was the foyer for *Hair* in about 1969. From there it followed on to him doing the production design of *Hair*, which must have been in Melbourne or somewhere in Australia, for Harry Miller. Then Harry got them both to do *Jesus Christ, Superstar*. Then there was a movie involved, which I never saw, called *Shirley Thompson Versus The Aliens*, which they both did. Then they went on from *Superstar* in Sydney to *Superstar* in London.

On the *Superstar* thing – which I was in, by the way – the producers were going to get the Paris production over into London. Robert Stigwood, who ultimately produced it, just said, 'No, we're not going to have it.' I think there were frantic phone calls during the night, and they got in touch with Jim. I think they got something like a week's notice to get from Sydney to London to start rehearsals. Something tells me that they both knew Stigwood; he must have been out there [in Australia] for the opening night, and he had lots of Australian connections. The Bee Gees were originally from there, weren't they? Anyway, the Sydney production came to London, and it was from there that they went on to do *Rocky*.

DE: *But there was a tour of* Hair *or something, in between?*

PB: In that period, it seemed as though Jim and Brian always worked together, and they did loads of things in Australia after *Superstar*, too. After *Rocky*, they went back to do *The Threepenny Opera*. Brian did *Joseph And The Amazing Technicolour Dreamcoat* without Jim, I think, in about 1975. Rufus Collins was directing it. Brian was living here by then. He'd come over in 1972 and stayed until 1981, but Jim kept going back and forth. They both came back to do the second *Rocky* transfer, to the Essoldo.

DE: *That's when Brian put the ramp down the middle of the theatre.*

PB: That's right. Later on in the day it moved over to the left, because Michael White wanted more seats. It used to be in the centre, then it went to stage right. I say Michael, but it was whoever wanted the money. I remember in 1976, when I played Riff Raff, the catwalk was down the centre. I remember having to go right around to the back of the auditorium as a spaceman.

DE: *Talking of Michael White, did Lindall Hobbs [White's then girlfriend] know Jim and Brian from Australia?*

PB: I think so.

DE: *Do you think she recommended them to Michael?*

PB: I think certainly Brian knew her before, I would have thought. She was a reporter on Thames Television news. Helen Montague's name did pop up quite a few times, too.

DE: Were Jim and Brian aware of the significance of the Royal Court as a venue? How impressed were they by it?

PB: I think the main theatre was pretty prestigious, but to be Upstairs, that was just an experimental piece of space. It was exactly that. When *Evita* came up, I know Jim was up for it, but he turned it down.

DE: Had Jim fallen out of love with musicals?

PB: No, I don't think so at all. I just think he wanted artistic control that he wouldn't have got with *Evita* and didn't get with *Superstar*, to be allowed to direct properly. I think that, within limits, in Australia they were able to do their own production of *Superstar*. But after the Paris nightmare, they got to London and they weren't able to take control as they thought they should have done. Paris was done for real. Victor Spinetti directed it. You know how religious the French are, and it was a very religious piece that they put on. It was very dark and big wooden crosses. Real costumes. And it did about two nights, then it didn't go well. I was there for the opening-night party. God, the atmosphere... People walked out.

Of course, Jim didn't want anything to do with that production. We were opening in August, and this was already summer. That's when they got Jim and booked Brian.

DE: And was everything plain sailing from there?

PB: We had disasters here, too. Jim cast this girl to play Mary Magdalene. We were about to go to previews and he sacked her. He didn't like the way she played it or the way she sang. Then we had problems with the costumes. The designer didn't actually look at the set. When you put the costumes on, you couldn't work onstage or get through those tunnels, because the costumes were so wide and made of stiff, heavy furniture fabric. They were incredibly heavy and hot. I remember Jim had us walking onstage in costume and he went down the line: 'Take the sleeves off that one, get that one off the stage...'

We did our very first preview and we were told that we could wear anything we wanted. I thought, 'This show is going to die.' All the girls came in drop diamonds. I felt so embarrassed. I just don't know what the audience thought. The next day, the wardrobe mistress was told to dye all the jeans brown and all the T-shirts brown. You know that Jesus came on in a white dress? Only bits of the costumes were saved, tiny bits.

DE: So what can you remember about the genesis of Rocky?

PB: Their projects, Brian and Jim's, mainly came through Jim. Jim would say what they were going to be doing. I don't think they still work together now. *Rocky* took up a lot of their lives. More Brian than Jim. They worked together on *Rocky* in London, Australia, LA and New York. Jim didn't do Japan, but Brian did. Jim really stopped having anything to do with it in New York. I remember asking Jim if he was going to see a revival of *Hair* or *West Side Story*. He said, 'I never see revivals. You never get that same experience that you get when you see that first production,' which is very true.

Brian did work in opera. He did *The Macropolis Affair* at the Adelaide Festival and *Death In Venice*. He didn't have any great plans that I'm aware of.

Jim was very quiet and very observant. Very Warholish. He was always watching. He's amazing at casting. He really has an eye for talent.

DE: Did they know Nell Campbell from Australia? I understand that there wasn't a Columbia character, originally.

PB: I don't think either Brian or Jim knew her from there. Jim may have done. She was tap-dancing outside the theatre where *Superstar* was playing. She was a busker outside the Palace Theatre at the end of Shaftesbury Avenue. Even when she came to Jim's attention, there wasn't a song for her. Nell had to get her Equity card, and I think that's why Jim thought he couldn't use her.

DE: She was a show-off, not a show person, although she became one.

PB: She was sort of like Annette Funicello. That's what she wanted...

<<<<irememberdoingthetimewarpirememberdoingthetimewarpi>>>>

Brian Thomson

Friday 5 May 2000, Soho, London

We met Brian Thomson two days after the opening night of his production of *The King And I* at the Palladium. The show had been slated, except for his sumptuous sets, partly the result of his having spent time in the parts of Asia in which the story of Anna and the King is set.

Neither of us had never met Brian before, nor laid eyes on him. The very first thing that struck us was his simmering creativity. He told us that he had first wanted to be a painter, fell to being a designer, tried his hand at directing and is now primarily a designer again. But what the world knows a man for is not necessarily what the man is. He bubbles with ideas, slants, interpretations, additions – both graphic and literary.

Brian Thomson is the essential creative man, the eye of synthesis, through which all experience is extruded into an identifiable, communicable medium. Who else would think of putting in the skeleton clock, where the face of eternity stares out of a handless and motionless timepiece? Why do we remember that clock from the *Rocky* set so vividly? It is an intimation of mortality more incisive than the Reaper's scythe itself.

A native Australian, the son of a banker, Brian Thomson grew up in Perth and studied architecture at Perth Technical College and then the University of New South Wales. He went on to design sets for many opera, theatre and musical productions, including *Hair, Jesus Christ, Superstar* (Sydney and London), *The Rocky Horror Show* (in London and in the United States and on Australian tours), Barry Humphries' *Housewife Superstar* (in London and New York) and *Grease – The Arena Spectacular* (in Australia). Brian has won many accolades for his work, including a Tony for *The King And I*.

Nowadays, Brian designs for opera, film, theatre, television and dance. 'That range keeps me focused and keeps me on my toes. There's always a challenge.' He has worked on *Aïda* and *Summer Of The 17th Doll* for the Victoria State Opera and *Medea* for the Sydney Theatre Company. He was commissioned to design the medal podiums and closing ceremony for the Sydney 2000 Olympics and the 2001 Australian Federation Centennial Ceremony.

Since talking to Richard O'Brien, Yasmin Pettigrew and others, we had been only too aware of the phenomenon of bad blood that has existed between Richard and Brian Thomson. As angry as Richard O'Brien is, Brian is equally so. There is no need to repeat the words each uses about the other; they're probably deeply litigious.

Brian agreed that his emotive feelings have, as much as Richard's, polarised acutely. It's as though both men are imprisoned in a whirling vortex, their feelings and emotions hurled by centrifugal force to the opposite sides of the spinning chamber which, as long as *Rocky* is popular, will contain them both.

The polarisation is at the moment beyond repair. It has a way to run. There are other cooks stirring what seems an irredeemably spoiled broth. In as much as it takes a whole village to bring up a child, the total long-term breakdown of a once strong, ongoing relationship between two people is infrequently the sole responsibility of either. Furthermore, it should be borne in mind that the generation of great wealth in turn generates great jealousy and great envy and great greed. Both Scott and I were quite surprised by the widely held belief that such success should be shared amongst all the participants as though by natural right. We never heard the complementary view expressed that, should such a project have gone wrong and lost money, the participants would join together in contributing to the losses.

From the advantage of an independent overview, the problems of the initial artistic team originated because, in the beginning, they shared professional representation. In short, in 1972 they all had the same agent. Although how these problems get solved is another matter.

With the benefit of hindsight, Michael Linnit, who was to drop out of plans to restage the show in the West End in the late 1980s, should never have represented Richard O'Brien, Brian Thomson, Richard Hartley and Jim Sharman in the same endeavour. Down the years, the echoes of the gnashing and grinding of the teeth in a huge potential conflict of interest are deafening and palpably obvious.

Maybe, in those pioneering days, Michael Linnit hadn't yet grasped the significance of rock 'n' roll shows in the spectrum of theatrical possibility. Maybe, way back then, the need to formalise arrangements regarding a tiny show on a tiny budget in a tiny space seemed less pressing. Maybe the finding of other agents to 'temporarily' represent the interests of the four individuals for what could only have been seen as a one-off event was too difficult and risky. Maybe, but it was an accident waiting to happen, even without Richard O'Brien. Jim Sharman and Brian Thomson worked as a team, and sooner or later another Richard O'Brien would have come along with another show to which the pair would have applied their Midas touch.

Such a confusion would never have happened in the music business, even then, and in fairness to Mr Linnit, what could have been interpreted as carelessness had everything to do with the genesis of the show itself. To be able to separate the creative strands in order to identify each and negotiate accordingly for those responsible would have been an unenviable task. To create a copyright covering the whole and yet protecting the individual contributors would have been beyond the pale of showbusiness law as it then existed, certainly beyond the pale of experience of a workaday theatrical agent. Not that it would have been impossible, merely a situation that, even then, never arose to be thus dealt with.

Some 28 years later, the resulting confusion and the real pain all the participants feel was the thrust of Brian's agreement to meet with us. He admitted that he had insisted that Richard O'Brien was not to be allowed into the Palladium for the first night of *The King And I*. Brian's anger is visceral when he refers to the posters papering London's walls at the time of our meeting, advertising the current incarnation of *Rocky*.

BRIAN THOMSON: I mean, 'Richard O'Brien's *Rocky Horror Show*!' Give me a break! I really have to have this thing explained once and for all. I have to tell my side of it... It's all to do with how the show came about.

DAVID EVANS: *Fire away!*

BT: It started with the London production of *Jesus Christ, Superstar*. Jim was directing and I was designing. There were a lot of politics involved in that. Paul Jabara was playing Herod. A really campy performance. The understudy was Ziggy Byfield, but he'd broken his leg and so Richard was called in to audition as the understudy. He was playing it much butcher than Paul, like a real rock star version. Like a teddy boy. But Stigwood and Lloyd Webber just hated Richard's interpretation and so he left the show.

DE: *Left, or was he pushed?*

BT: Let's just say he left. Time passes and Jim and I are doing *The Unseen Hand* Upstairs at the Royal Court. There's this part of Willie the Space Freak and Jim asks me what I think about bringing Richard O'Brien in for it. Now, this is important. To me. I could have said no. I didn't. I knew Jim was feeling quietly guilty about Richard's chance at playing Herod being thwarted. Whatever.

Anyway, I said, 'Fine. Bring him in.'

I remember we put a tattooed hand over his head. Can't think it could have done the health of his hair much good, but that was then...

DE: *I'm sure he doesn't blame you for that. He looks great now. Better with no hair.*

BT: Richard Hartley would sit at the piano and play doo-wop songs and Richard O'Brien would play his songs too. Whatever I think now, Richard [O'Brien] is one of the best lyricists around. I've always thought so. Jim heard these songs, all disparate, separate songs, and put them all together. They put them on a tape and Richard wrote a very simple script which involved some kid watching TV and bringing in this narrator character, who told a story of the alien thing and ended with the kid back watching TV again.

And that was all there was. From there on in we all put our own spin on our various responsibilities and contributions. Mine was definitely seeing *Cabaret* – the movie. Richard O'Brien saw the whole much more like a *Star Trek* kind of science-fiction thing, but when I went to see *Cabaret* in that movie house, there were trailers playing. Or those short movies that got shown before the main feature? Then, the curtains would close between everything. Remember? Well, the ice-cream girl came on in those breaks in the screening. This one looked totally bored and completely uninterested and it got to me. I suggested this as an alternative opening to the show. In fact, it was Jim who was responsible for the final title. *They Came From Denton High* doesn't have quite the same ring, does it?

DE: *And was it true about them wanting Marianne Faithfull for Magenta?*

BT: Sure. Why not? This was the Royal Court, remember? We also had Ralph Richardson down to play the Narrator. I have the script back home with all these names pencilled in.

DE: *Did you have anything to do with the original graphics or the advertising? In fact, who was it who did the original woman's face?*

BT: That was definitely Michael English. It's changed a bit over the years. Lou Adler altered it a lot for New York.

DE: *I have this theory that, without you guys – including Nell, of course – having come from the old colonies, Rocky would never have been bred by native Brits. The Royal Court would never have even considered it.*

BT: I think you're right. You know what Jim's background is. We all shared this real love of trashy films, B-movies and rock 'n' roll. Look at me and my Annette Funicello obsession.

SM: You have a whole collection, right? So do I.

BT: Boxed sets. Everything. *Hawaiannete*, the lot. And in Sydney, we have a very strong tradition of drag. It's like nowhere else in the world. It's very masculine. Jim was very into that and he also had all that experience from when he was a kid with his family of conning people to come into a tent to see a show. We all come from that sort of culture. It was Jim who wanted 'The Time Warp'. He said, 'I want to invent a new dance craze.'

DE: That was the time for it. I remember seeing all those massed ranks of homos madisoning their way up and down Studio One in LA the very next year.

BT: You see? Anything was possible. And talking of 'The Time Warp', Nell was very much on our wavelength, too.

SM: Did you and Jim know her before, from Australia?

BT: Jim didn't. I knew Nell from about 1969. She was very involved in the birth of the show. Everyone was involved, even down to parts of the script, like, 'Doctor Von Scott...' That's my line. Tim Curry, too, was very contributory. Frank N Furter never just jumped off the page. He wasn't there until Tim invented him. Timmy never played it as a drag part, nor did he ever have to resort to cheap jokes. He always played it very, very straight. He also brought that Sloane Ranger/Knightsbridge accent to it. That's what turned it for him, finding a voice for that character.

I had no budget to speak of and so I had to invent like crazy, too. The lab was just a Coca-Cola ice box we borrowed. I borrowed the tarpaulins from a company called Cox. Paul Cox, I think. The cinema seats came from the Glasgow Citizens Theatre. It was being refurbished.

DE: When did the Acme logo appear on the tarps?

BT: At the Classic. The Acme Demolition Company. Yes.

SM: Were you all being paid the same, then?

BT: It was all fine, then. I forget what our weekly wage was, but money wasn't such a thing then. Like the flat I stayed in – it was a protected tenancy. You just took over from who was there before, started paying rent and if the landlords accepted your rent cheque, you could stay, secured, for as long as you wanted. What I do remember is that there was a production of the show in Holland where all that the Dutch had done was completely, faithfully reproduce what Jim and I had created in London. That was when Michael Linnit wanted to protect us all beneath the show's copyright and when Richard started paying Jim and I a royalty because he said we had to be protected. As it happened, nothing was done about the copyright of the show and the royalty went on until Richard arbitrarily stopped it in 1989.

I mean, people ask me why I'm not so all fired up about not getting anything from, say, *Jesus Christ, Superstar*, which was as much Jim's and my staging as anything. It was our version of the show that Andrew Lloyd Webber had seen at the Capitol in Sydney and that he wanted in London, as he couldn't stand what had been done in New York. The point is that, there, we didn't help create the show; with *Rocky*, we did.

SM: A lot of people have said that you all knew it was going to be a smash from the very first.

BT: Well, I didn't. I knew we'd all done incredibly well and that it had gone down well, but more than that...? How could you even begin to conceive it? I did know it was unashamedly erotic. But it was erotic in a way that had never been done before. Also, it did pick up with what was happening in music at the time – The New York Dolls, Lou Reed, David Bowie. *Rocky* had a real edge to it.

I remember the first night, when Coral Browne and Vincent Price came. She was playing in Edward Bond's play *The Sea* in the main house downstairs and they came up afterwards to see our show, which of course started after the main play. I even brought them up that other staircase there. 'I'll be your personal usher,' I said as I took them through the other ghouls. I remember a load of the seats fell over where we hadn't screwed them to the floor. Anyway, they loved the show, really loved it, and so I asked them to tell the cast that. I took them back to this tiny room where everyone was crammed in, all in their knickers and underwear. In they went and Vincent said his bit, in that great voice. The cast loved it.

DE: *Enter the King of Schlock Horror!*

BT: Absolutely.

DE: *And then you and Jim went back to Australia to do* The Threepenny Opera. *That was before the Classic, yes?*

BT: No, after. That was for the Sydney Opera House. We came back to do the transfer into the Essoldo, which became the King's Road Theatre.

DE: *Would you have come back from Australia if there'd been no transfer?*

BT: Oh, yes. Jim's plan was yet to happen.

SM: *Jim's plan?*

BT: Sure. There was this great scheme that Jim had that he was going to take over the National Theatre. As that wasn't immediately possible, he thought he'd start with the Royal Court. We were the only team to have shows running simultaneously both up and downstairs at the Court.

DE: *Where did you two meet, by the way? You and Jim?*

BT: In a hamburger bar.

DE: *Just like that? Right. So who found the Classic for the transfer?*

BT: It must have been Michael White. The only thing Jim and I contributed to that was our refusal to have the thing go into the West End, to an ordinary theatre, especially one where there was a balcony, a circle. We resisted all that like crazy. I think Jim's lost his way now, but then he had great plans and he was so talented. He was way in front of Trevor Nunn, doing serious theatre work and then slotting in the odd really commercial musical here and there to fund the rest of the plan.

DE: *Is it like the Philip Prowse thing? So brilliant and so obviously brilliant at early age and now not much heard of?*

BT: Yes.

DE: *And also like with music people. Three or four albums and then, burn out? Gary Numan stuff?*

BT: Yes. In those days, Jim could have done anything – *Evita, Phantom Of The Opera* – but not all the time. Like me – I need to have those challenges, new things and not just new, commercial straight stuff...and in 1973 I had a job to go and work with Tony Richardson at what was to be the Globe, working with Vanessa Redgrave on *Antony And Cleopatra*.

DE: *That was where Julie Covington went, isn't it?*

BT: Julie was keen to work closely with Vanessa Redgrave, but it wasn't mutual. Jim'd been Tony Richardson's assistant on *Ned Kelly*, by the way.

SM: *Is that where the Mick Jagger idea for the film came from? And is it true that Jagger was one of the options to play Frank?*

BT: When the film happened, Jim had two choices: either a really big-budget thing with stars like Jagger playing Frank or a very small budget with unknowns like Tim.

SM: *Is that why the film sticks pretty much to the stage show?*

BT: For the movie, both Jim and Richard wanted a much more sci-fi look and feel, and I said, if it was going to be that, I didn't really want to do it. Not that I had any initial vision whatsoever of what I thought it should look like, but when we went down to Bray Studios and we were asked if we'd like to see the old Hammer House...well, it all became clear.

SM: *Your models for the sets are exquisite. I've only seen two, Rocky's black bedroom and the church, which I reglued for Kimi the other day.*

BT: I've always made models, since I was 19. It began with making models of houses I designed. I've never been formally trained and so I'm not held back by any formal ideas of what should and shouldn't be, what material should or shouldn't be used. I just pick things from other worlds and put them all together onstage.
DE: *So the stage or the screen is a frame for all these eclectic choices?*

BT: A canvas, yes. The movie script of *Rocky* was meant to start with just the velvet curtains opening and then pages being turned, I think. The lips idea came from the Man Ray poster on my wall, and of course the whole thing was planned to be in black and white until Frank comes down in the lift and we just see his lips in colour.

SM: I see. Is that why the Trannies were all dressed in black and white?

BT: Yes. It was all planned for. I did so much experimenting with what it should look like, mainly watching TV and turning the colour knob down. Jim and I made this low-low-budget movie in 1972 called *Shirley Thomson Versus The Aliens*. That was the pedigree for *The Rocky Horror Picture Show*. It has a sort of cult following, too. Anyway, I was then asked if I wanted to see the Hammer warehouse, and of course I immediately said yes, thinking there'd be a fantastic hoard of stuff to raid, like they'd filmed every piece of mad scientist laboratory equipment known to man. But this great warehouse turned out to be nothing more than a shed behind the buildings at Bray, and I have to acknowledge Ian Whittaker here – he was the set dresser with a lot of experience. This was my first movie job in Britain, and although I'm pretty inventive, Ian took me to places I never dreamed existed.

SM: The clock?

BT: Yes, we got that. And all those dead animals. Writing Magenta's shopping list on the wall of the laboratory. Weird went into overdrive to make the set look something. I remember the day those Fox executives arrived. They couldn't believe it. And I've never had a call from Hollywood since!

SM: And Fox did refuse you the logo, right?
BT: Yes. I had great ideas for that, the spotlight picking up Nell as it shifted around and then Tim being there in the middle on a podium.

DE: But you – you and Jim, that is – obviously had a different financial arrangement for your work on the movie?

BT: I still get money from the movie, yes.

DE: *And the video?*

BT: I suppose. I think it's all in together. I know I noticed I got a whole lot more when the video was issued first.

SM: *Moving to New York and the Belasco, what did you feel about that?*

BT: There was a kind of a bad omen from the start. Some down-and-out guy outside the theatre told me that 'nothing succeeds on this side of the street', and the theatre was really run-down. Should have been fine, as *Rocky*'s always open to possibilities, but the whole place was badly neglected. Upstairs, David Belasco's flat had holes in the roof and pigeon shit all over the place. The whole place was gutted. Lou ripped out so much. I was blamed for the side boxes being ripped out. I still haven't been forgiven for that, but the truth is that it wasn't me. I could have used those boxes.

SM: *Wasn't Richard [O'Brien] a last-minute thing in New York?*

BT: The guy cast to play Riff Raff had an accident playing in a Tom O'Horgan show and couldn't do it. So that's when Richard was called in.

DE: *He must have felt pretty marginalised, not being cast in the first place.*

BT: He was very uptight. I remember taking him outside the theatre to show him the billboard advertising the show: 'TIM CURRY in...' There was no mention of Richard. Maybe they hadn't yet filled in his name as the writer, but he went crazy. But everyone seemed to be at odds in New York. Jim was pretty much tired of the show by then, too.

DE: *And then the music-business ambitions took over. Richard was really disheartened by all that fuss over Tim Curry. You wrote lyrics too, didn't you?*

BT: When we were doing the music for the movie, I wrote some things for Meat Loaf. He'd met Jim Steinman, of course, but nothing was happening. I remember we did a reggae version of *Stand By Me* with him. Tim's material, when he got around to choosing it, wasn't good. I remember that gig he did at the Roxy. He really hadn't got it together as to who it was he was supposed to be doing. They'd fitted up some kind of ending to please the fans, with him singing 'I'm Going Home', but it was never right. But he was beautiful as Frank. Beautiful to everyone. Men and women both.

DE: *Did you ever think of moving to the States?*

BT: I enjoy the range of opportunities in Australia. In New York, I would've been put in the 'exotic musicals' category. After I did *Superstar* in London, I got offered all the religious musicals. After *Rocky*, I got offered all the transvestite musicals. When *Rocky* got so panned in New York, I knew what it was like to do a disaster like I knew what it was like to do a hit. And I think that was probably a very good grounding, to have done the flop...

DE: *You went on working with Richard didn't you?*

BT: We did Sam Shepard's *Tooth Of Crime*. Jim and I gave him the idea for *TZ*, which was originally written for Meat Loaf. That was all written in couplets. And I contributed a lot to *Disaster*, too. I know it didn't work, but it was a great idea. By the time we got to do *Shock Treatment*, you notice I got my designing credit and also one that said, 'Additional ideas by Brian Thomson.' We scouted for locations for Denton in the USA. Wichita, Kansas, came nearest. I remember being at a Holiday Inn in Wichita and there was a Shriners' convention going on there, everyone wearing fezzes.

SM: *Sounds Transylvanian to me.*

BT: Right. And then John Goldstone said we should go on to Dallas, and so off we went.

DE: *And after* Shock Treatment *you did lots of different things, right, including directing?*

BT: Being a director is the worst position to be in. Yes, I did direct. Just before the *Mad Max* movie, I directed Mel Gibson, both in a play and then in a movie. It was a detective story, with Terence Donovan, Jason's father. And you know about *The Stripper*, don't you?

DE: *We've been told there was a big blow-up between you and Richard.*

BT: Richard O'Brien had written this script. He'd read a lot of Carter Brown detective stories and he'd come up with a script that was far too long. It really needed condensing. I was directing it with Richard Wherrett as associate. The rehearsals were not going well and all the actors were having trouble with the lines. The dialogue was very repetitive, and so I started working on it. Richard O'Brien wasn't having any of it. He refused to have his script touched and got really pissed off. In the end, I refused to have him in the theatre.

DE: *Ouch. And then Richard stopped giving you the royalty?*

BT: When he started working with Chris Malcolm, yes. I wasn't asked to be a part of the revival, either, at the Piccadilly.

SM: If you could redo anything on Rocky *now, what would it be?*

BT: I think now, so far on, it'd be the alien thing I'd concentrate on more: the approach rather than the details.

DE: Have you ever taught? I mean lectured, in a college or a university?

BT: At home we have the National Institute of Performing Arts and I get all my assistants from there. We need that youthful input.

DE: And what's next for you?

BT: I'm working on productions of *The White Devil* and *Suddenly Last Summer*. Paul Dainty has the rights for *Rocky* now in Australia and he's wanting Richard Wherrett to do a new production and me to design it.

SM: You know your Rocky *scrapbook is out again, don't you?*

BT: I didn't, but I'd love to see it. I have so much stuff at home. I spent hours photocopying and putting those pages together as montages. I'd love to have a copy.

‹‹‹‹irememberdoingthetimewarpirememberdoingthetimewarpi››››

Jim Sharman

Some *Rocky* authorities seem to think that, in the London of 1972 there was 'open sexuality', and this opinion is based on the phenomenon of David Bowie. Like all phenomena, Bowie is best understood in hindsight. If there *was* open sexuality in London in 1972, it was the same that Quentin Crisp wrote about autobiographically in *The Naked Civil Servant*, and it was an open sexuality that had always been there. To most, the love that dare not speak his or her name was not a subject to be entertained publicly, except in the most cerebral of senses, and any openness was confined to theatrical circles. In the cut and thrust of rock 'n' roll, a queer was still a shirt-lifter was still a poofter was an un-man, to men and women alike.

Once again, Scott and I did not have the benefit of an interview with Jim Sharman. What follows is our précis of other comments and quotes from interviews and lectures given by Jim over the years. Other than these precious few lines, there are many references the actors themselves make to Jim, both personally and professionally, which we hope you will find illuminating in the respective actors' segments of this tale.

Jim's association with *Rocky* covered the London years in the King's Road, a production in Australia in 1974 (in which Reg Livermore starred as Frank), the Los Angeles production and the movie, terminating with the Belasco fiasco.

'...Richard said he'd written a musical. I said, "I hope it's not religious." He turned out to have written the one musical that got its own cult.'

'...There may well have been other actors that I considered initially for the role of Frank. I can't remember them. I just remember Tim Curry walked through the door of the Royal Court Theatre saying, "Rip it up!" And he got the role.'

'...I seem to remember an initial discussion whereby one was offered a reasonable budget provided we stocked the film with currently fashionable rock stars. The alternative was to use people like Tim Curry, who had been in the original production, on a very modest budget and a very tight shooting schedule. I went for that option.'

'...It's a home movie for extraordinary people.'

And from the Rex Cramphorn Memorial Lecture, which he gave to an audience in Sydney on 23 July 1995 at the Belvoir Street Theatre, Jim's remarks about himself and *Rocky* ran like this:

'...Storytelling would also have been part of traditional culture. In the legends and tales crucial to any society is a direct connection between past and present. It's a small step from the tribe clustered in a cave around a storyteller silhouetted by a camp fire's reflected flames to our modern tribes gathered in a theatre, or in that labyrinth of caves known as a cinema complex. A movie audience sits in the dark, hypnotised by coloured light reflected onto a sheet, collectively agreed that this play of shadow and light represents real people in real situations, telling of universal legends.'

'...Politics aside, our modern tribal gathering is engaged in what has been termed "public dreaming", an extraordinary act of imagination by the audience.'

'...For me, theatre is at its purest and most alive when it appeals directly to the imagination, when it offers the least literal and most poetic use of words and images, when it acknowledges the presence of the audience and requires its active participation in what amounts to a spiritual communion. This is the alchemy of artists and audiences creating, out of the air, something that is not actually present; it hovers in the air, in the realm of the imagination.

'My own introduction to this kind of theatre was at the circus. I grew up in a world of travelling side-shows, carnivals, circuses, boxing troupes, Chinese acrobats and tent-show vaudeville.'

'...Before being shuffled off to school, I filled in time around show grounds, side-shows and, especially, the circus. I came to admire those artists who performed on the trapeze and the highwire – the aerialists. Artists who worked without a net seemed to my young eyes the true aristocrats of this vagabond world and the real icons of the circus. It was only for the aerialists that the crowd would hold its collective breath. My strongest memory is of a masked face, fear painted white, with a slash of red lips and a blotch of blue mascara, nailed to the sky-blue canvas by a cruel spotlight – or was it, in my child's imagination, an apparition from the heavens?'

'...Another aspect of the carnival world was its racial mix, which we would now call "cultural diversity". The carnival world spoke many languages.'

'...From as early as the production of *Hair*, I have attempted to accustom audiences to the world we are going to live in, rather than to the middle-class, Anglicised ghetto that so often prevails.'

'...At this time – 1976 – I had been directing for a decade. My first production had been a revue – *Onstage Oz*. I had continued with a volley of mostly experimental work until I earned my professional wings and took off to create a series of populist musicals that spanned the globe. They culminated in *The Rocky Horror Show*, the one musical I was involved in creating from its first tentative steps, through a series of stage productions in London, America and Australia, to the now well-known film. After this, it was to Sydney and *Sarsparilla* that I returned. My interest now was in Australia and its writing.'

'...Gloria Dawn, the soubrette in Sorlie's *Varieties*, went on to play Mother Courage in an MTC production staged by a Berliner Ensemble director and also played Mrs Peachum in my staging of *The Threepenny Opera*. This production – in the opening season of the Drama Theatre of the Opera House – made a direct connection to the vaudeville tradition, though I have generally avoided specific reference to my colourful past, choosing to let its influence be felt in more subtle ways. The exception was *The Rocky Horror Show*. Here, Brian Thomson's blue-canvassed cinema-under-demolition set turned virtually every theatre or old cinema we played in into a tent. The transvestite hero of that musical might have owed something to German gothic cinema, but was also derived from childhood memories of Bobby Le Brun, Sorlie's famous panto dame, who looked like a stevedore in drag. Tim Curry, who created Frank in my original production at the Royal Court, kept asking, "How far should I go?", and I always replied, "Just stop before you throw Fantales to the kiddies." The audience thought they were seeing a hip, streetwise character in a rock 'n' roll show; we knew it was a panto dame in mufti.'

'...All the theatres of that era went: the Empire, the Palladium, the old Royal, Phillip Street (the home of revue) and the Palace, where as a teenager I first saw Patrick White's *The Ham Funeral*. Later, I was pleased to help encourage Harry M Miller to revive the old Minerva at Kings Cross as the Metro for the long run of *Hair*, the Capitol for *Superstar* and the Paris Theatre – designed by Walter Burley Griffin – for a brave if short-lived experimental theatre company created with Rex Cramphorn.'

'...After 30 years spent creating theatre, film, musicals and opera, I must confess to now having little sense of anything but the present moment. It is almost as if someone else created that body of work, and I am sure that many of my colleagues privately share this curious feeling of having participated in the art of creating forgettable illusions. For theatre exists only as a shared moment between artists and audience. Once that moment has passed, it resides solely in the realm of individual memory, there to be re-invented in some other way, at some other time, with the assistance of scripts, production photos, old programmes, archives of contemporary reportage and the regenerative power of the human imagination.

'Perhaps there is value in the fact that our theatrical illusions are swept away along with the other achievements and with the detritus of our lives and times. Perhaps it's better that only the song survives, and only the one with a strong and memorable melody at that. Maybe art in general – and theatre in particular – is a perfect reflection of our lives. Passionate and central to our experience in the present, quick to evaporate, lingering in spirit as a record of our inner life, which is lived in dreams, in the imagination, in memories that form part of our link with other lives and other illusions in some infinite, if elusive, universal continuum.'

'...Artists are both the creators and curators of the illusions that speak of our lives and times in beautiful lies that, at their best, reflect universal truths about the terror and wonder of our lives.'

‹‹‹‹irememberdoingthetimewarpirememberdoingthetimewarpi›››

3 'I Really Love That Rock 'n' Roll'
The Music

DAVID EVANS: About three years ago, in an extremely dusty and battered cardboard box I found a reel-to-reel tape I hadn't seen since the early 1970s. It was a tape of Cat Stevens singing the demo songs, just voice and guitar, for a musical he had conceived called *Revolussia* all about the last days of the Romanovs. Though I toyed with the finders-keepers theory of ownership and alloyed it with the old 'possession is nine points of the law' misperception, I returned the tape.

But what happened to the tape Richard O'Brien produced in cahoots with Richard Hartley? Now that'd be worth a fair bit at a Rocky convention, wouldn't it?

Richard O'Brien wrote and composed on guitar. By hybridising his songs using Richard Hartley's keyboard-based discipline, the songs in *Rocky* achieved a new and controllable dynamic.

So, let's give it up for the *maestro*...

Richard Hartley

14 December 1999
'I need a friendly hand and I need action'

It was a freezing-cold day in Shepherd's Bush. Scott and I were early for our 12:30 appointment and I had taken Scott to show him Freddie Mercury's old front door at 100 Holland Road, which he photographed.

We met Richard at his house. He introduced us to his cats young (the Bengalis, Frank and Brad) and old (a black and white job who had to be protected from the virtually feral Bengalis). Scott thought

Richard himself rather catlike. He has an expression that breaks into a wreath of contentment from a face that, in repose, is almost inscrutable. It's as though he is waiting to be amused. His memories of *The Rocky Horror Show* obviously amused him as they unfolded during the two hours we spent in a Thai restaurant in the Uxbridge Road a few hundred yards away from his front door and where we were the only customers. When we met in December 1999, he had recently won an Emmy for his work on *Alice In Wonderland* and his *Don Quixote* for Hallmark USA was due to be screened in the States the following March.

After he had been thrown out of school (he never even got a Music O-level), Richard had come to London from Yorkshire. He had then lived in France, in Paris, for a while where he had played in an R&B band called The Witchdoctors with a bunch of other Brits, gigging all over France to some success. France can be very kind to Brits – remember the revitalised careers of Petula Clark and Murray Head? Being British in France in the mid 1960s was to be very special, as indeed was being in King's Road when Richard returned to London.

He settled first in 1967–8 in Sloane Street, just around the corner from Sloane Square and the Royal Court, before moving first to Fulham, where Richard O'Brien also lived, and then to Shepherd's Bush, where he has been for some 16 years.

He studied later for many music exams after his earlier academic failure and, on the strength of this academic work, began a career in music. He met the film producer Jeremy Thomas, son of Gerald Thomas of Carry On movie fame, and subsequently worked for him on several projects, including *The Last Emperor*.

He professes not to have had the rock 'n' roll bug in the same performance measure as Richard O'Brien and Tim Curry but was nonetheless, like Richard O'Brien, an ardent fan of basic, everyday, non-elitist rock 'n' roll. We started by telling Richard who else Scott and I had and hadn't talked to.

RICHARD HARTLEY: I saw Nicky Wright recently – he'd be very good to talk to. Nicky and Harriet [Cruickshank] ran the Theatre Upstairs. But

Nicky was the one. We were doing this Sam Shepard play, *The Unseen Hand*, which Jim was directing. Jim was an experienced director, and he had great grasp of theatre, and he came from a family of entertainers. His father used to do boxing troupes in Australia. Jim was a great showman.

I was writing the music for the play and it had need of a lot of rock 'n' roll songs. Richard [O'Brien, who was acting in the play] told us he had an idea for this musical and so Jim and I went around to his flat one night.

It was late – after rehearsals of *Unseen Hand* – and it must have been after midnight. And basically, that's how it started.

Jim then persuaded Nicky – because they had these little slots for three weeks when they didn't have anything else – to put *Rocky* on. We needed some more money, and that's how Michael White got involved. Producers were very aware of how much money could be made in music too. The play before us at the Theatre Upstairs was directed by Pam Gems and that was a cabaret-type show. It had a stage, and so we rehearsed on the stage.

DAVID EVANS: So where did Michael White come in?

RH: Michael White and a few more producers was on the board of the Royal Court Theatre, and you know how that is. If any play at the Royal Court looked like a transfer, then they used to get there first... The Royal Court was *the* theatre – the writers' theatre. Jim really enjoyed working there.

I think Michael put £500 or something like that into *Rocky*. But it was Nicky who was the one who gave us the slot.

Jim had just done *Jesus Christ, Superstar* with Brian; we all were working on *Unseen Hand*, and Richard was in it with Chris Malcolm. It wasn't a musical. Sam Shepard, the playwright, loved it. From doing that, I did the music for another of Sam's plays, *Tooth Of Crime*. Malcolm McLaren was always at that production. It was all about rock 'n' roll – the new replacing the old, the wannabe versus the has-been. Malcolm had the Sex shop then. He had that kind of anarchic thing. *Tooth* was the first play about the changing rock 'n' roll phenomenon – how things have to die so that others can live and everything has its turn. Just like in *Rocky*.

DE: *I remember it very well. With Mike Pratt and Di Langton. What happened to it?*

RH: Sadly it didn't do well. It could never be mainstream, because it was very intense.

DE: *I also think that people didn't and have never appreciated the finer workings of the rock business, the politics and the drama.*

RH: *Tooth* was initially going to launch Sam from the fringe. I think after that he went back to America. We used to go greyhound racing together. I've still got the demos from us putting the songs together. He wasn't a big fan of *Rocky* – it was a bit too lightweight, too much into light entertainment for his taste. It was, really, although it was intimidating to some people. He was into country-rock, that kind of stuff. More Kris Kristofferson-meets-Lou Reedish kind of country.

DE: *What was your musical aspiration?*

RH: I wanted to be a composer. I was in a band called The Witchdoctors in France in the 1960s. We were all English. We were quite successful and we played big places. Then we went to Beirut at the end of 1966. After that, when we left – at the end of the war – I didn't want to play much any more. Ironically, I did audition for Procol Harum, but I didn't get the job. When we did *The Rocky Horror Picture Show*, half of Procol Harum were the band, the guitar player and the drummer, who is dead now.

DE: *Any reason for using them, other than old times?*

RH: We wanted the film and the music to be more gothic than the play.

Big and Phil Spectorish. Atmospheric. In fact, before they were Procol Harum, they were an R&B band – The Paramounts, I think. I reminded BJ Wilson once. I said, 'You don't remember me, do you?'

DE: *Did he?*

RH: [Laughs] Anyway, I then starting doing arrangements. I wrote string quartets, etc. I used to do arrangements for TV shows and variety shows. When Chappell's [which became Warner Chappell publishers and is now part of the Time Warner group] was an acting and theatre kind of publisher, they had a string of people that would work for them.

DE: *Almost in-house?*

RH: Yes. And I used to do things for Island Records too. They used to bring over reggae songs from Jamaica and other Caribbean places, and I would put strings on them to make them sound white. And all out of a Nissen hut in Neasden. I've got some amazing original recordings somewhere!

Harry J is a name I remember. It was Chris Blackwell's partner that I used to work for, David Betteridge, who was in charge of Trojan. They would bring the lacquer up, we'd put them on a multi-track, then add the strings. They became very popular. I worked with Dandy Livingston, who was a producer. They did Bacharach songs. You know how complicated Bacharach songs are? And they managed in the reggae version to get them into four chords. 'Don't Make Me Over' is a classic.

DE: *I'm amazed you stayed with the theatre.*

RH: It all combines. Through Chappell's I met Anthony Bowles. He's dead now. He was a musical director and used to teach at Lambeth. Very high voice. And he gave me my first real break. He was doing a musical with Ron Moody, being put on in Coventry. Anthony was in charge and I did the orchestrations. It was at that time that people were doing classic stories, updated. Modernish musicals based on classics.

DE: There seemed to be a new one every week in those days.

RH: Shortly afterwards, when they did *Superstar*, Bowles was the musical director. He called me up one day and said, 'We're auditioning all these people to sing. They need to have popular-music voices and I don't know anything about that. Would you do the auditions?' So I went along, and that's how I met Jim Sharman and Brian. They worked together a lot. I didn't work on the show, just the auditions. Rufus Collins was the choreographer. He was relentless. He can tell if someone has a little bit of a spark when they are singing. Rufus would put them through these tortuous routines.

DE: And the musicians?

RH: That's how I met Jimmy and we got on very well. I didn't play with Rock Bottom. Ian Blair did, though. After that I did a musical with Straker, Keith Washington and Suzanne Bertish in Harrogate, then a Rob Walker musical called *Dionysus '73*, first performed at Watford.

Actually, before that we did a musical called *Mother Earth* at the Roundhouse in Chalk Farm in the summer of 1972. After *Mother Earth*, Jim called me up and said, 'We're doing this Sam Shepard play. Do you want to write some music for it?' I said yes.

DE: There was a very tight group of people who seemed to be at the core of a lot of theatre at that time.

RH: After *Mother Earth*, I used to play with Straker in his band. We did an album together, *Private Parts*. I met Ken Howard and Alan Blaikly, who wrote the songs for *Private Parts* through Count. Ken and I were friends, and it was he who said that Straker needed some help with arrangements. Straker had a manager friend named Sydney Terry. Sydney was much egged on by his wife, Joyce, and daughter, Lorraine. Anyway, he had got an option on the rights to *V*, which was an ecological musical written by Toni Tennille. They wanted to put on a one-night version of it to raise money for investors. Straker, Tim Curry,

Angharad Rees and Helen Chappelle – that fantastic voice. All we had were a few demos. I arranged all the songs, and we put it on for one night. It was a revue, songs and sketches between the songs. That's how I met Straker. And so *Mother Earth* did go on at the Roundhouse. It was multi-media, with film and projections. Helen Chappelle wasn't available for the full production and neither was Tim. He was only around for the one-nighter. Probably a good thing. He and Straker were very competitive, even then. A lot of the people from *Hair* were in *Mother Earth*. We rehearsed at the YMCA in Tottenham Court Road. It was so hot, that summer.

DE: That must have been 1972. Which brings us up to Rocky.

RH: Jim called me up and said, 'Nicky Wright is looking to put that musical of Richard's on.' Richard and I did some demos for the songs with a tape recorder on a table. We went around to Jim's flat. I think it required a bit of money to make it possible. Jimmy went around to Michael White with the tape.

DE: And it was just this tape?

RH: There were three or four pages of script. All of the Narrator's stuff was in it, I remember. But it was a first draft, with dialogue. I remember vividly that night we did the demo. Kimi was there, and Linus about three months old. They were sat in the corner, and Richard was there with a guitar, singing songs. It started off with 'Science Fiction' and it reminded me of Françoise Hardy because it was very slow when Richard did it. He took five minutes to sing it. I thought it was fantastic. I'd never heard anything like it. There was no 'Time Warp' then. A bit after that, we did this demo of about five or six songs. Then we did a bit of work on them. 'Whatever Happened To Saturday Nite' was there. There were two guitars on the demo and we put in a few vocal backing ideas to give it more of a show sound – some oohs and ahs.

DE: What is it they say about tiny acorns and great oaks?

RH: At the Royal Court, we got £15 a week. Everyone made the same. I didn't make any more than the rest. I had to improvise wildly when we needed the thunder and lightning effects. They just grew and grew as the rehearsals went on.

DE: *So you couldn't have possibly written a score until the last moment?*

RH: Its best possible form was probably on the afternoon of the first performance. We knew we had a hit on our hands as soon as that first performance ended.

DE: *Do you think there is a difference between guitar and piano songs?*

RH: Generally, guitar-composed songs are simpler. In Richard's case, he has a somewhat limited musical vocabulary, but it suits what he wants to do. The songs took on a form that was part of the show after I started on them. When we did it in the theatre, it was very fast, furious and basic. That was because we had just two and a half weeks' rehearsal. We rehearsed the band in Victoria one Sunday and we had to do everything. Everyone had to learn everything in a day. We couldn't afford a sax, and since there were only four people in the band, the bass player doubled on sax and the guitar player played bass when the sax was on.

DE: *Necessity being the mother of invention?*

RH: It was very complicated and there was no room for a piano, so I had a little electric organ. That was it. We had to make all the sound-effects, like lightning – I had a little sound-effect spring reverb and I would crash it. Eventually it broke. All the sound-effects were either done by the cast or the drummer or the reverb, improvised. There was nothing on tape. We decided we would invent it all. Tapes were being used then, but we didn't want that. It was all invented, which is what made it. The initial show music was played fast and furious and made the one-hour initial length of the production seem even shorter. The band itself was sort of like its own theatre company.

DE: *And you had some great voices to work with.*

RH: We had Julie, Tim and Richard, who could sing. The rest had interesting voices. I was there for all the auditions. I had seen hints of Tim's performance in *Mother Earth*. A very seductive quality. The casting was done by Gillian Diamond. She called the people in. The person who was going to play Frank was Jonathan Kramer, who played the transvestite in *Midnight Cowboy*. He's dead now. He was auditioned, and after the first load of auditions it was almost decided that he would be Frank. Then, at the last minute, Jim changed his mind.

DE: *On such moments, careers are made and lost.*

RH: I think Jim thought that Jonathan was going to be too outrageous, in drag terms. Jim knew that that kind of showmanship had to be avoided. The Royal Court had previously been the demesne of a drag artist known as Mrs Shufflewick and any association with drag would not have been appropriate. Jim thought it would be better to have a slightly more sinister overtone. In hindsight, he was absolutely right. My recollection of the rehearsals was that the part of Frank was straighter. Tim Curry, even without high heels from the outset, showed that he had the necessary acting funds to furnish the right blend of nastiness, viciousness, temper-tantrum and oily charm required of the part. In the heels, he was a lounge lizard run rampant, and yet he mustered that vulnerable, self-mocking quality that saved the character and gave Frank the required sympathy to make him immortal. If the reprehensible Frank hadn't been immediately likeable and, most importantly, accessible to and embraceable by women, we wouldn't have stood an earthly.

DE: *This show did so much for so many careers.*

RH: Julie Covington disliked having to be partly undressed. In the simulated sex scenes behind the screen, I was sitting there playing the piano, and the guitarist had to crouch down, otherwise he'd be seen.

She used to loathe doing that. It's not smutty, and it has a morality about it. She was perfect for it.

DE: So many people have told us about the additional songs that you found were needed.

RH: 'Eddie's Teddie' was written for the Classic move. All the others were in by then. 'The Time Warp' and 'Touch Me' were written in rehearsals. Jim would say, 'We need a song here.' Richard O'Brien would go home and come back the next day with almost a full song. Then we – Richard and I and whoever was singing it – would go back to my flat and fiddle with it; I'd find a key and would teach it to the person and put it in the show. 'Touch Me' was actually put in very late, just before the first preview at the Theatre Upstairs.

DE: Sort of necessary for the plot, too.

RH: Jim wanted a song for Julie's character because after the first song, which was completely different, you can see the change she had gone through. That's what that song is all about. In the show, it's a dodgy part of it. That song saves it. After that, she's regretful. 'The Time Warp' was put in partly for Nell. Jim thought that the three people in the house needed a song. Nell's character, Columbia, wasn't originally in the show.

Jim did know her, kind of, from Australia. It was Brian Thomson and I that persuaded him to have her in. I love Nell. Every time I saw her, she'd be dancing on somebody's table. The part of Magenta was always there, and Columbia was written in. Jim did quite a bit of work with Richard. 'The Time Warp' was put in so Nell could have a tap routine. I used to rehearse the routine with her.

Richard wrote that very quickly. I remember he got so far, to this particular chord. He wanted to get back to another chord – that's the four chords in the middle, joining it together. If you use that chord, then you get led back to the first chord, then you get back into the verse again.

DE: *There should be a soundtrack to this part of the book!*

RH: Because, in fact, it's one of the strangest intervals – it's called a tritone. It's a very unnatural interval in popular music. It's very difficult to get back to – it was written in A originally, and ended the verses in B – and the chorus starts in F. From F to B are three tones, thus it's a tritone. It's a very strange interval. It does give it quite a shock. It jars. And all more by accident than design.

DE: *Isn't that how the best things happen?*

RH: 'The Time Warp' began as a song and it afforded the opportunity for Nell to have a tap routine, so it killed at least two birds with one stone. It was an ensemble piece for the three people in the house, and it's a plot song. And it showed off the relationship between Riff Raff and Magenta, too.

DE: *You didn't stay with the show as a musician?*

RH: Immediately after it transferred, Jim, Brian and I went to Australia to do *The Threepenny Opera* for the Sydney Opera House. Then we got a call saying that *Rocky* really was doing well. The only reason it went to the Classic in the first place was that the building was being demolished and had closed as a cinema.

At first, Jim and Brian didn't want to do it in a cinema again. I remember we looked at the Mayfair Theatre as a possible alternative, but we all knew it wouldn't work in a conventional theatre with a proscenium arch. We came back and moved it to the Essoldo, at the other end of the King's Road, and that's where we first started to slow it down a bit.

DE: *Why?*

RH: I think partly because the band were in a different place. In the Theatre Upstairs, the band were behind the stage; at the Classic, they were very close on the side above the stage. We had a power failure on the first night. We had to do the floorshow with no microphones and one follow spot. Fortunately, we had a real piano, otherwise we wouldn't have been able to do it. All the electric stuff was played on acoustic guitar. It was scary.

DE: And from then on...

RH: It went all over. I didn't go to America with it. I gather it was more Las Vegas than Transylvania on tour. The play did London, Los Angeles, Australia, then we did the film, then the Belasco in New York. I was doing another film by then and when I got a call about going to New York to play in the band again. I said, 'Forget it.' I didn't go to America or Australia. Not that time around.

DE: But you were obviously involved in the recordings. What was the story with the first cast album?

RH: As I said, the gothic thing with the film score came about in the studio. That first cast record was done in a day and a half, when the cast had the time off between transfers. It was recorded at Sarm East, in Osborne Street off Aldgate roundabout. It was used because Richard and Jill Sinclair's brother, John, were very good friends. The album came out on Jonathan King's label. I don't think the recording would have happened without him. He was the first. Jonathan paid for it. He was a fan of the show, and he said, 'I want it to be like the show.' We just went in and did it. Same band, same people. A couple of the sax solos were done by someone else – by Phil Kenny, in fact. When we went to the Chelsea Classic, we became a five-piece band, so nobody had to double. Phil Kenny went on to play with people like Rod Stewart. The musical technology was still abysmal at the Classic. There were still no stage monitors.

At the Classic, the ramp was down the side, but we got permission to put it down the centre at the Essoldo. That made Frank N Furter's entrance spectacular. As I said, we slowed it down and, at first, this didn't work. I still feel that 'I'm Going Home' was ultimately much, much too slow. I know it's a torch song, but sung too slowly it was often lost in that low area of Tim's.

The first preview was terrible. It was depressing beyond belief. It was such a big theatre compared to anywhere else. The Classic was intimate and oblong, so the audience was closer to the stage. The Essoldo was the other way, and the band were further away and had monitors. It all started to become kind of proper. It was very disappointing. It was to do with the fact that no one got used to the catwalk. We didn't have any real time to prepare. It got a bit more sophisticated, and it didn't really work, so we sped it up to the way it had been.

By then, Tim had moulded that part – it was more of a big one-man performance. I think we had more lights, more bits. The performances were not rising to the size of the room. When we sped things up, it got much better and the performances got bigger – they had to be – and when it did change, then we slowed it down again. By then we had the audience eating out of our hands so that, when Tim came on, that was it. 'I'm Going Home' got very slow, because he used to milk it.

DE: I presume you didn't share Tim's hunger for the music biz? Or Richard's ambitions?

RH: Richard did have rock ambitions, but they were kind of for himself. *Rocky* attracted people like that, people that didn't want to do conventional theatre. *Rocky* was so successful for such a long time that a lot of people passed through it, people who not necessarily became rock singers, but alternative comedians and people that do a bit of everything. It would be interesting to get a list of all the casts, to see who has been in it. The girl from *Not The Nine O'Clock News* was in it. Yasmin Pettigrew would know her name [Pamela Stephenson]. You see, I was only there for three months. I would go in every now and again to fix problems. I couldn't stand playing it after three months.

DE: None of the songs had a real life outside the show, did they?

RH: I don't think they are commercial songs outside the context of the show. I think that's both a strength and a weakness, the way they are done as you might do a record. The only one that has been a huge hit was 'The Time Warp'. The single is one of the best-selling singles in Australia, from the film, but the others, they don't lend themselves. You can't hear Barry Manilow... Oh, I don't know, though. 'I'm Going Home', I suppose, is a torch song, but very old-fashioned in terms of pop songs. The other thing, of course, is that Timmy's versions of those songs are pretty definitive. Not that that's exclusive.

DE: So what about Tim's music career?

RH: Tim's career. I think he just made bad choices of people to work with. The songs he should have been singing were... I remember talking to him one time and, well, I didn't think his material was good enough. He should have evolved and taken an old classic and redone it his way.

Tim is a great interpretative performer but he's not the greatest voice. Timmy's range is actually quite small. I don't think it's strong enough, although his Frank is an incredible performance. I think Timmy should only do the songs he could perform. Some of those songs were very dark. Of course, he wanted to completely disassociate himself from the monster he made. I remember we were in New York in 1977, when the film was really finally taking off. I said, 'You should really do an album. You should start off by doing somebody else's songs and it would be a bridge between what you do and a bigger audience.'

But he didn't. He didn't have the motivation. Tim didn't grab things. He didn't want to be seen doing the wrong thing. During *Rocky*, he was as cool as he could get.

DE: And Richard, in this context of career?

RH: Richard, I feel, left it too late. He could have been really big and he does have the voice.

DE: *And you?*

RH: I'll never deny the fact that *Rocky* helped me have a career, although it's not the only thing I've ever done. I was never dependent on it. It was a fantastic period in my life. Fortunately, I wasn't in the spotlight onstage. It was a hit very quickly and it carried on being like that for such a long time. I don't know why, really. It's a rock 'n' roll pantomime.

DE: *It was life-changing for some people, for performers as well as the audience.*

RH: Partly because they found something they could perform in that didn't expose them. They could give a million per cent; it's that kind of show. You don't have to be the greatest singer/actor/dancer, just as long as you can do a bit of everything and you are prepared to throw yourself in and make something of a fool of yourself onstage, you can get by. It's slightly deceptive, in a sense. However, a lot of people did that and had a great time.

DE: *Same for the audiences.*

RH: Absolutely. When we went to the first convention – Richard and Pat, and Meat Loaf, Susan and Barry – it was somewhere in Long Island. I'd never seen anything like it, 2,500 people. They ran the film and some of the audience's comeback lines were absolutely astounding. Total commitment to sitting down and coming up with this alternative. I said to Richard, 'These lines are better than the ones in the show!'

I know there is a theory about the reasons for the audience participation. It's because the film is so slow. It's so boring that people had to make up lines to make it entertaining.

DE: *It restored the theatricality.*

RH: You are absolutely right. There is a little world there. You go into that dark room with the screen, you're brought into a world with these people. Yes, you're right about the audience bringing the film to life. I've seen it with a straight audience and it was pretty dull. All of us went in the beginning. Michael White was appalled. It just didn't have that spark that the show had. But then the show, even without the audience, is funnier than the film.

DE: Do you realise that the play is completely gone now? You could never do it again.

RH: When we revived it at the Piccadilly, at the first preview you couldn't hear a word. I think Tim McInerney lost his voice. It's now a completely new experience. It was so important to a lot of people: 'Don't Dream It, Be It'. It was at the time, in the early 1970s, that the sexual liberation permeated, apart from a couple of blocks of central London. The glam rock thing, that just happened, too, at that time. All those elements – it was pre-punk in the style sense. Just the right collection of people in the right place at the right time. Sue Blane was noted for her style and is still consistent, in a different way. Jim with his showmanship. Brian Thomson, too. The idea of putting it in front of a screen was fantastic. He was one of the first minimalists.

DE [having left the Thai restaurant, on the way back to the car]: The play could never be done again, could it? It's been left behind, like a host that the parasite has drained. The original is an empty conceit now. It's been voided of relevance.

RH: Yes. Agreed.

<<<<irememberdoingthetimewarpirememberdoingthetimewarpi>>>>

The audience participation is now so deep-rooted in popular perception that the play has been buried deep beneath the charade. Richard O'Brien's simple little idea has become a charnel house of unexhumable remains.

Sadly, the original significance has also been lost under a mask of 'fun', 'dressing-up' and a populist, vulgar, unsophisticated lack of any real intellectual appreciation of the original meaning. As Susan Sarandon recently quipped to the British TV presenter Johnny Vaughan in an interview when he protested how shallow he really was, she said, 'But you have such a deep surface.'

So, for those who contend there is and never was any meaning other than a 'fun' hour and a half's 'entertainment', go strut your empty mortal illusions and miss out on the chance of running your own mental mind-fuck…

DE: I originally thought that line was spectacularly overblown with no real meaning. I have changed my mind.

A couple of days after we talked, Richard e-mailed Scott with the following lyrical variation on 'The Time Warp', which had been composed by someone called 'B and B'. It had been inserted into the call sheets distributed to cast and crew on the movie, which Sadie Corre had given Scott. It amused us.

'Let's do the time sheets again…
It's just a NLB to the left
With a NSB to the right
With your hand on your wallet
You bring your hours in tight
But it's extended days
Which really drive you insa-a-a-a-ane
Let's do the time sheets again…'

And in another e-mail, Richard provided us with the definitive list of the backing singers on the film soundtrack album: Liza Strike, Helen Chappelle, Clair Torrey, Brian Engel and Barry St John and, on certain tracks, Meat Loaf.

<<<<irememberdoingthetimewarpiremembardoingthetimewarpi>>>>

Sue Blane

2 March 1999
'Put these on. It'll make you feel less...vulnerable'

The last member of the creative team to be brought on board for that first production was Sue Blane. She is not hugely well known outside of the British theatre, but where she is known, those who know her make the most complimentary claims...

SCOTT MICHAELS: *So what's your take on the Rocky and punk and 'which came first' thing?*

SUE BLANE: I wouldn't dream of taking the credit for inventing punk! Frankly, Malcolm McLaren should take the same attitude. It grew, and *The Rocky Horror Show* was definitely a big part of that build-up. It was happening at a time when the King's Road was boiling up to something. I think certain elements of punk – for instance, ripped fishnet tights and glitter, and the funny-coloured hair – a lot of those aspects of it were directly attributed to *Rocky*. At the same time, there was another thing going on, which was indeed all about Vivienne Westwood and Malcolm McLaren and all the things they were doing. In my opinion, the whole emergence of the punk thing was a genuine build-up that quite quickly turned into what was afterwards called punk. Virtually simultaneously with *Rocky* becoming popular, you were seeing kids on the street with stilettos and pointy shoes, wild hair, safety pins and fishnets. It all kind of generated into punk. I think it would be quite wrong to say that *Rocky* itself was the reason for punk.

SM: *The shops came after you'd opened, though.*

SB: We bought Magenta's shoes and the space boots from Sex. They were the stiletto pixie boots in black patent, with gold lining. We used them in the film, as well, but we had to remake them to be stronger for dancing. A big chunk of my budget went on those shoes for Pat Quinn. Yasmin probably still has them. I would love to have bought everything at Sex, but we were on such a tight budget. We didn't have the money.

SM: People say some of the clothes ideas came from other productions you'd worked on.

SB: Lindsay Kemp, the mime performer and director, takes credit as well because we did a production called *The Maids*, based on the thing by Jean Genet, with Tim Curry at the Citizens Theatre in Glasgow. The minute I knew what I was doing with *Rocky*, I rang the Citizens and asked them to send the corset down that I found for Tim for *The Maids*. Lindsay directed *The Maids* and he has an extremely keen visual sense, but nevertheless I was the designer on it and I feel quite at one with that. In fact, it was me that found the old corset and decided to turn it upside-down and turn it into this weird thing, and paint it to look like leather. Lindsay might have a problem with what I've just said, but I feel quite comfortable with that. What Tim looked like in that production was out of my development.

SM: To an extent, everyone's plugged into the same style influences, aren't they?

SB: My approach kicked off, not only because of Lindsay's influence but because of the artist Allan Jones. He was a massive influence. He was the painter/sculptor who came to everyone's attention because of his wonderful coffee tables made from kneeling bondage girls. He was fantastic. Still is. I thought he did the original poster for *Rocky* but it was Michael English. Allan was most famous for those mannequin coffee tables, the big bondage S&M thing. It was all the kitsch surrounding the B-movies – pointy breasts, etc – way before JP Gaultier and Madonna. The biggest influence for me, because I was from the Citizens, where Philip Prowse had invented a way of doing the classics, a radically new way of approaching and presenting classic plays. He pioneered this way of doing exotic classics. All of that influence was there, too.

SM: From what I gather, the original piece needed as much bringing to it as possible.

SB: I really think you should not underestimate Jim Sharman's contribution to it. In every sense, he had a very good vision of how to deal with the piece. It's the same with Brian Thomson. I wasn't privy to their initial meetings or which one of them specifically came up with the idea of setting it in an old B-movie cinema. Brian's original concept, with screen and old cinema seats, was fantastic. The fact that *Rocky* was able to transfer to that Chelsea Classic Cinema was just fantastic.

SM: At least no one else can take any credit for the costumes.

SB: I think the other thing I did with *Rocky* that wasn't happening in fashion – and I feel very strongly about this – was that all the costumes were distressed to a great extent. From day one, they looked like they came out of a ragbag. Particularly Riff Raff. The entire dramatic silhouette with him was achieved because it was broken. The appellate hanging off, the tails being really thin and mean, all his laces hanging down – it was a gothic spectacle. Same with Tim. The crazy lacing like he was stoned when he did it. It was all very deliberate, from my point of view. I made it a very sexy gothic look. It seemed to suit the piece, in a very theatrical sense. I think that did get taken through to punk. You were allowed to rip things and paint them.

SM: And you turned a green hospital smock into a couture *creation.*

SB: That surgeon's gown worked well as a cocktail outfit, didn't it? We had little money, but I could afford to go to a hospital and buy some old gowns. The pink triangle thing was weird, because it was already on the gown from the beginning. I didn't put it there. We continued to use it, but it was by accident. It was completely genuine for surgery. It was red, but over the years it washed out and became pink. It certainly wasn't intentional, as if it was some kind of sick joke. Had I known the significance of that symbol, I would never have used it. I thought it was weird. Because we didn't know what it was, we kept it. But I love Tim in that green gown. I think it's so sexy with the pearls and the way it splits up the back when he walks.

SM: *They broke the mould when that one left.*

SB: Recently we did it again with Jason Donovan. I designed the very newest one. I redid the designs for 1990. Not hugely successfully, I have to say. It was the first one Chris Malcolm produced. We changed it a bit, but it didn't need it at all, the new one. I tried to put back into it as much of the classic one that I could.

SM: *And by that time you had the audience in on the act, too.*

SB: The incorporation of the audience is weird. Funnily enough, the dress rehearsal was the only time you could have seen it in its original form, ie before the audience comes in and heckles it. The only way you can deal with the audience now is to build it in. It is very funny, but on the other hand it doesn't allow you to see what a damn good piece of theatre it is. The script is really tight, very funny. The music is sensationally good. You will never witness the original again because of the audience participation. But then, that's also why it's a success. I don't think anyone feels bad about that. In fact, we celebrate it.

SM: *You see, I can't imagine what it must have been like without the audience. I only ever saw the movie.*

SB: I was justifiably scared to do the film, when they asked. I had never done a film before. It interfered slightly with my other work and I knew we didn't have major resources. I can't pretend I enjoyed it very much. It was such hard work for me, and since I was the only non-union member I had to do most of the work myself. But I am enjoying the results of it very much. I get money from it still. It was a nice enough company. I was the only person who could stay late at night in order to stick sequins on. I had a nice team of people, and they pulled their weight wonderfully.

In fact, originally, I didn't even want to do the play. I think the budget was £400 for everything. I honestly don't really remember. My fee was £50, which I shared with Colin MacNeil, who sadly is no longer with us.

SM: How was working with Tim Curry?

SB: I think Tim must have known that *Rocky* was the performance of a lifetime. He created that role and went a good long way to creating the success of *Rocky*, full stop. It was very hard for him to handle. He didn't want to play Frank for the rest of his life. He knew he could sing well and act, and he was desperately keen to have a career in his own right, too.

I think he was very keen to rid himself of it, because it was such a famous role. He never quite succeeded. I wouldn't say it was the performance of his life, but you would never get another part that fitted you quite so perfectly. It really was a niche he was in, and perfectly created. Once the movie was made, that was it for Tim.

The shoes normally do it for people. It was like that for Tim. Shoes are so important for every role, in every theatre piece. They change your attitude to everything. The shoes for *Rocky* came from two sources. In the stage show, Tim had a pair of gold shoes for the floorshow. I knew they were up in Glasgow. They were early 1950s and quite tatty. The main shoes were bought in a shop. I don't think they lasted beyond the Royal Court.

A theatre shoemaker built the ones in the film and I stuck all those rhinestones on them myself. I still have a bag of them at home.

I think Tim was a size eight, English, so with a shoe that was open-toed he could just about slip into the largest ladies' size. We were able to just buy them. The fact that they were too small for him was part of the look. Technically his feet came just over the edge, but that all helped the look. He wasn't meant to be in those shoes. If they were made to fit, they would not look like ladies' shoes, just shoes that a drag queen might wear.

SM: Did you like the movie?

SB: I think I've seen the film maybe ten times. It's quite an extravagant, ambitious film. For the movie, I was there every day, sometimes all night, on my own, in a hut. It was terribly spooky. I was definitely on my own the night before we shot Meat Loaf. I was painting the back of his jacket, and the security man came to lock up. I told him I hadn't finished, so he just locked me in overnight. Since I was non-union, I was the only one that could stay. I did get a wage.

I mercifully didn't have to maintain the costumes. There was a team of people that washed the knickers and tights. It's quite a tricky job, because you had to do the continuity as well. Richard Pointing, who was the costume supervisor on the film, he worked so hard. It was a very difficult show to produce. You couldn't just wing it. You couldn't go out like nowadays and pick up a bit of lycra. A long time ago these things were not available, and you had to go into sex shops.

The stilettos for the floorshow were from Cover Girl in Islington, a shop that caters to cross-dressers and drag artists. They are still in business. I still have one of Barry's and one of Nell's stilettos. I saved Barry's because it was the biggest, so I just popped it in my bag. They were in such agony. The heels were something like seven inches. They were absolutely unworkable. And working in them wet as well...

SM: Did you keep much yourself?

SB: I gave Frank's corset to Dori Hartley, who was a big fan. I thought she deserved it. I must have taken it over for the tenth anniversary. I loved it when the fans started to dress in such a witty way. They have a great imagination. They are so resourceful. They are so important to the success of the production.

SM: And since those days?

SB: I did *Shock Treatment*, of course. Imogen Claire's costume was very special to me as the costumier.

SM: It seems to me there should be a Rocky *referee. So many people seem to have so many axes to grind.*

SB: Brian [Thomson] is quite tough. I've been told both sides of it so many times, I just don't listen. It's very sad to me because they are all people I respect. I haven't been implicated personally. I see Brian fairly regularly. He's a terribly clever man. The fact that the production is still going on without Brian is a bit sad, but I've managed to put that guilt away long enough to accept my royalty cheque. To be brutally honest, I was lucky because I managed to get a royalty on the film. It was courtesy of Jim Sharman, who gave me a quarter of his percentage. It's not very much, but my God, it's kept the skin on my back for many years, in one way or another.

‹‹‹‹irememberdoingthetimewarpirememberdoingthetimewarpi›››››

Michael White

4:30pm, 14 September 1999 at 48 Dean Street, London W1
'And now all they needed was the money...'

David Evans: I had telephoned Michael White, who had picked up the telephone himself. Rather unlike days of yore, when he could be very difficult to contact. One of the clients of the company I had worked for in the 1970s was the writer Charles Laurence. *Snap!* One of Charles's plays, which starred Maggie Smith and Barry Denham, had been produced by Michael White. I knew Michael rather well. He had completely forgotten me. And why not? I rather felt at the time that writers weren't Michael's favourite human sub-species. After our conversation, I was convinced of it. 'Yes,' he said when reminded of Charles Laurence and his play, 'and wasn't he lucky to have had Maggie agree to do it?'

Scott and I, never late, were buzzed in and walked up to the first-floor suite. The walls of his rather smaller and humbler office – compared to that of the glory days – were completely covered with posters of his past successes, of which the *Rocky Horror* complement is by far the largest. His assistant was charming, very welcoming. Michael was not so, handing us his 'own' book, *Empty Seats*, and telling us to read it before we talked to save him answering some 'unnecessary' questions.

After doing our relevant homework and paying appropriate homage, we were called into the inner sanctum.

DAVID EVANS: Was the Royal Court the initial commissioner of Rocky Horror?

MICHAEL WHITE: The Royal Court wanted to do it based on an outline of what the story would be, particularly because of Jim Sharman. They needed £2,000 to get it going and Richard O'Brien rang me and asked me to come and listen to some of the music. Eventually I did. I went to Richard Hartley's flat, and they told me the story outline. Very simple, very immediate. But when I heard the songs, I thought they sounded great.

DE: So it was hearing the songs that coaxed you? The music clinched it?

MW: No, and the story.

DE: So there was no script at that time?

MW: No.

DE: Was Helen Montague involved in any way?

MW: No. I had already done a number of things Upstairs, at the Royal Court. *Tooth Of Crime*...

DE: Had you ever worked with Jim Sharman?

MW: No. I followed him with *Jesus Christ, Superstar*, which he did here, which was the best.

DE: So was he one of the up-and-coming directors at the Court?

MW: No. He wasn't a Royal Court director. He was Australian. He came here with *Jesus Christ, Superstar* and hadn't worked at the Royal Court before, to my knowledge.

DE: So Jim was a crucial factor in it?

MW [beginning to get tetchy]: I heard five songs and heard the story outline. I met Jim Sharman and thought he was very talented. His production of *Jesus Christ, Superstar* was the best of any around.

DE: Did they produce a script at all?

MW: No. Eventually they did. It was very much on an *ad hoc* basis. I think that Jim Sharman's contribution was enormous, on the development of the storyline and the script.

DE: Was there a deal within the Royal Court, with Jim, to do Rocky?

MW: I don't think that's true. Apart from Richard O'Brien, there were two crucial people in this. One was Richard Hartley, the other Jim Sharman. And, to a lesser extent, me. I never interfered, except for the very end, because I totally trusted Jim Sharman. Nobody else had any effect whatsoever on anything.

DE: Were you consulted with casting decisions?

MW: I knew a few of the people, but I didn't interfere. Jim said, 'I want Tim Curry.' I didn't say boo. I didn't want to, either. I knew Tim Curry, but nobody knew him the way he became. The ratio of importance, without Tim's performance initially, which is one of the ten best performances I've ever seen, that made a huge difference. The show was impeccable on the first performance and remained that way. It wasn't like, 'Oh my God, we need to cut 40 minutes.

That song doesn't work. That actress doesn't work.' There was nothing to say.

DE: *After it got to be so successful, was there any other film company interested?*

MW: No, quite the reverse. The only way the film was made was because of Lou Adler's influence in Los Angeles and his record as a very successful person in the LA music community. Nobody wanted the film. Fox didn't want the film. They tried to stop it three days before we started the filming. Jim and I were summoned by the head of Fox to come to Los Angeles on the Friday before we were going to start filming on the Monday. We were told that, if we didn't come, the film was going to be stopped. Jim refused, so I went with Peter Beale, who was the head of Fox in the UK. We got to Los Angeles on Friday night, and on the Saturday morning (or Sunday) we went up to the house of Bill Immerman [this may not be the correct spelling of his name], I think, who was the head of financing. We managed to convince them not to pull the plug.

The budget was $1 million, which even in those days was quite a small budget. Very small for a musical.

DE: *What do you think would have happened if they had pulled the plug on the film?*

MW [now rather cross]: Let's get this clear. Crystal clear. The show was very, very successful onstage in London. It was very successful at the Roxy in Los Angeles. It flopped in New York within ten days. It did not get done anywhere else, as far as I know, before the film was started. I very much doubt if we would have found the money elsewhere to do the film. We might have. The fact is that Fox went into it very reluctantly. After we were filming for two weeks, the whole operation of Fox had been replaced. Alan Ladd Jr became the head of Fox. He came to London on a fact-finding tour and came to the studio. He looked around and looked quite bewildered, like he didn't know what was going on. It was a very grey ugly day in November. He hung around for about 20 minutes and left. That was the end of it. When they saw the film, they didn't like it, as indeed none of the English critics did, apart from the *Sunday Telegraph*. It got very bad reviews and did no business here, and the same thing happened in America. The famous story is that, coming back from San Francisco from some pre-screening, one executive said to the other in the front of the car, 'How soon do you think we can dump this on TV?'

So anybody that says that *they knew* or *it was certain* is talking absolute rubbish. The film was a disaster. I shouldn't think that more than 3,000 or 4,000 people saw it during its London run at either the Rialto or what is now the ABC Haymarket. You can come back and I'll show you the press clippings.

DE: Did Fox ask to see the film before Jim's final cut?

MW: No. Peter Beale saw stuff, but he was on our side, I think. The truth is, the film takes some getting used to. It's just one of these quirks of fate that it went on to be successful. It was mainly due to a man who liked it, who owned a theatre in Austin, Texas. (I think Austin is the biggest university town in the United States.) He kept playing it at midnight on Saturdays and eventually, after a slow start of about a year and a half after the film had been released, gradually this thing grew. Then it started in New York, and then it really took off. After the Eighth Street Playhouse, it spread like a rash all across the United States. There was no video at the time, and TV only bought films like *The Sound Of Music* – more successful films. Now you can switch on and see every quirky film ever made. That didn't exist then. In fact, in our contract with Fox, there is no video clause, because video didn't exist.

DE: People have told me the video is unobtainable at the moment.

MW: I think it was a mistake to bring *The Rocky Horror Picture Show* to video and allow it to go to television. I think the film should be seen in the cinema, not at home. I tried to fight it, but I have no power to fight it. It was nothing to do with me. The power always does reside with the film company.

The only thing I knew, going way back, was the first night at the Royal Court, which goes down with maybe half a dozen shows I've done, where at the end of the show I knew we had a mega, mega hit. I'm not talking about the film but the show. It was absolutely clear to me that it didn't matter what the critics said. We had a big, big hit. Then I was very correct and worked against my own interest in the sense that I insisted on keeping it in a small space. I was offered the Shaftesbury, the Cambridge…big theatres. I wouldn't let it go. I didn't even discuss it with them. That's why I'm very annoyed now, when Richard and Chris Malcolm put it in a 1,600-seat theatre. I thought it was really greedy. Stupid. The show doesn't work in a big theatre. It never has and it never will. I thought it was very naughty, short-sighted and hurtful [to the show].

DE: *Can you remember if it was the film coming out that knocked out the overseas productions?*

MW: I think there were some in the pipeline. The film didn't nudge anything, but it was a negative influence, because it was badly received. We did no business and we got no good reviews.

DE: *Did you participate in the making of the albums?*

MW: I went along, but I didn't say anything.

DE: *Are you friendly with Lou Adler?*

MW: Of course. Why not?

DE: *Much is made of Curry's distancing himself from the role. Do you find it surprising?*

MW: No. Tim does not want to be Frank N Furter. Tim is Tim Curry, who played a part and played it completely brilliantly. When he came to the 20th anniversary of the movie at Fox, and all the kids came from all over America dressed like you wouldn't believe, Tim came in a suit and a tie. I don't understand why people don't get that. Like Billy Wilder said, people meet him and expect him to make witty remarks all the time. It was such a definitive performance that hadn't been done before, the greatest transvestite performance of all time. I can't think of a better one, can you? Maybe in *Some Like It Hot*, but they were kind of timid performances. Great. Tim as Frank, it's like, 'I don't give a stuff, honey.' Of course, completely different from the way he is in real life. So that's a performance. It's not like he's like that, like Harvey Fierstein.

You walk down the street with any star and people come up and gush about any performance. Jack Nicholson gets the 'Here's Johnny!' thing. People act as if they know you. The public thinks that they have the right, because someone is a performer, that they know them and own them. Maybe his denial is a quirk or a failing in his character. Particularly when you meet him, he is so different. If you talk about Harvey, they are more like the way they are onstage than offstage. Tim isn't, and that's why it's such a great performance.

DE: Do you remember if Richard really wanted to play Frank?

MW: I never heard that, but knowing Richard, that is quite possible. I don't think so, really. That's why I say the people that really know are Hartley, Jim and myself. I take a lot of pinches of salt with everyone else. Including O'Brien.

DE: When the first production was done and the film was made, did you actively look for anything else, product-wise, from that team?

MW: Yes, I did several things with them, but none of them worked. I did *TZ*, that Richard wrote . I did a play that I wish I hadn't done called *Top People*. We did another film called *Shock Treatment*, which would be fantastic if there were no dialogue and no story. If you just took the songs, which were great... I did it the other day, after 15 years. I ran the film without anything but the songs.

DE: *There was nothing else you could coax out of them?*

MW: He's done nothing since remotely comparable. I did three shows of his after that. Not the kind of subject to dwell on. It's not true of actors. They can go on to other things. Sometimes writers just have one great thing in their head. There are very few things in my career that I regret, but *Top People* was a nightmare. I never ever sat through a more awkward first night.

DE: *Were you surprised that Tim's career as a rock star failed?*

MW: No. I'm not surprised by anything like that. You are talking to a very old man. It's either there or it ain't there. If it is there, it melts pretty bloody quickly as well. It's a different genre. Some start when young, *à la* McCartney and Sting, develop in a different way and go on. Most people just come to a grinding halt. They have their two or three years and that's it. It doesn't go on because the generations change every three years and they don't want to know. They want to know about Britney Spears and Jennifer Lopez. Next will be someone else.

DE: *There is a great irony in the show. Did you get any of it? 'Don't Dream It, Be It'? And then, in the end, you get nothing?*

MW: Yes. Judy Garland.

DE: *It's about stardom?*

MW: Yes.

DE: *When you said after the first night, 'I knew we had a mega hit,' what specifically made that feeling?*

MW: It was incredibly enjoyable, simple as that. There wasn't one minute in the whole show where you looked at your watch or wanted a drink. I've sat through probably more shows than most people in the world. You know. When your bum starts to ache, you know there's a problem. *Rocky Horror* just went *wham!* from beginning to end. Every minute of it was enjoyable. The critics loved it. Did you see it?

DE: *Yes. On the first night, like you.*

MW: There were no dull moments or performances. Critics liked it because it was so unexpected and so different than anything else that was on. It was such fun. People that read all this symbolism into it are just talking through their hats. It's just the enjoyability.

DE: *Those people who didn't see it when the film came out but saw the show, what's the difference?*

MW: I don't think the film is less enjoyable. I think it's less good. There's something magic about seeing a live performance. When the theatre works, there is nothing better. No matter how great a film is, it cannot convey the magic of that moment for you, in front of you, live.

DE: *Do you think that was the problem initially with the film? Don't you think it conveyed that?*

MW: Well, obviously it didn't. The difference is the *live*-ness of the presentation.

DE: *How did Lou Adler get involved?*

MW: My friend Hercules Belleville, the producer, either told Britt Ekland, who was going out with Lou, or took her to see the show. She rang Lou and said she saw this great show in London that would be great for the Roxy. Lou saw it and went back to LA. Jim Sharman and my then girlfriend, Lindall Hobbs – who also had quite a lot of influence because she was Australian – we arrived in LA and called Lou. I'd had other offers in NYC to take the show there. I felt it was a good idea, rightly or wrongly, to go with someone in rock 'n' roll rather than a theatre producer.

Lou kept us waiting, and after four days we still hadn't seen him. Jim said, 'Let's split. He's treating us rudely. Let's do the deal with someone else.'

Finally, after the fifth day, we saw Lou. He was very enthusiastic. But we very nearly left. I don't regret taking it to LA. If it went to New York first, it would have failed and we would not have gotten the film. The run in Los Angeles helped to get the film. America is quite difficult to crack. The Roxy was the perfect venue. Lou at that time was very well connected. He brought a lot to the party. And, he is very smart.

DE: I have to emphasise that Michael's business was to raise money to finance theatrical production. His 'angels' were therefore of primary importance. Without their willingness to invest in him, there would have been no plays. It's a notion that should be borne in mind through any examination of an artistic phenomenon. Michelangelo couldn't have done what he did without the patronage of the Pope, and without the Pope Michelangelo's Sistine centrepiece would never have been reproduced on the bottom of Frank N Furter's pool, which would also never have happened without Michael White's angels' initial investment, which launched the show.

Theatrical production is essentially a chain of trust. Angels trusted Michael with their money, Michael trusted Jim Sharman with his, Jim trusts his own judgement and the whole thing teeters on whether the bones of Richard O'Brien's and, later, Richard Hartley's ideas can have the flesh of the designer's art and the cast's potential performances grafted onto it.

Scary or what?

<<<<irememberdoingthetimewarpirememberdoingthetimewarpi>>>>

Jonathan King

Friday 14 July 2000
Magenta: 'I ask for nothing, Master'
Frank: 'And you shall receive it, in abundance'

I met Jonathan in the first-floor bar at the Royal Lancaster Hotel at midday. 'My office is in a frightful state. It's being done up.' He is well known at the Royal Lancaster and I was directed by the concierge exactly to our rendezvous, together with two young women, recording hopefuls, who were before me in the audience line-up. Jonathan arrived, phone in ear, and set about his appointments.

As I sketched out my questions at a table across the bar, I overheard his conversation. One is hard pressed not to overhear Jonathan's conversations. On his own admission, he talks loudly, and tells the story of Sir Edward Lewis, chairman of Decca Records, with whom Jonathan worked very closely both as artist and business executive. Sir Edward once asked that Jonathan kindly lower his voice. Jonathan politely but firmly pointed out that Sir Edward and Decca had made a great deal of money out of his having a very loud voice and it being heard, not hidden. Sir Edward, apparently, stood down.

His meeting with the girls involved him telling them about the progress of their demo tracks, which he had been trumpeting inside the industry. As well as this progress report, his career advice to them was concerned, deeply avuncular and peppered throughout with caveats about the fickleness of fame and the minefield that can be the aftermath of success.

I listened, my heart gladdened that I was about to meet a man whose concern for the artist and the material and the project outweighed the usual greed and conniving endemic to a lot of the music business. I was therefore amazed to hear his pronouncement to me that 'I hate all artists. They're difficult, unreasonable, egotistical. They have the morals of a viper and have no responsibility.' When I checked that I could indeed quote this opinion, he was adamant that I could. Why is it that I choose not to believe him? Because he is half artist himself, his first hit having been 'Everyone's Gone To The

Moon', which he racked up when a recent graduate from Trinity College, Cambridge, in 1965. I think he protects himself from the possibility that, as he also said, 'All artists are c**ts!' When I enquired if these beliefs stemmed from his own celebrity as a performing artist, he replied, 'Possibly.'

Jonathan King is a fascinating enigma. He is a man for all seasons and all people. He has been the progenitor of more music-business projects than could probably ever be listed. Indeed, the music business honoured him in 1997 as its Man Of The Year. He believes that the heads of record companies, film studios and publishing houses should not be artists themselves or anyone with a bias to any one aspect of the industry. 'People who head those organisations have to be people people,' he explains, 'people who can put teams together and look at the whole picture, not specialists.'

Whether this dictum applied to him, I hesitated to ask, but suffice to say that, in 1973, well after 'Everyone's Gone To The Moon', he headed his own record company, UK Records, which in Britain was distributed via Decca and which existed in its own right in the USA.

DAVID EVANS: *And you were quite happy with this business* milieu *in which you found yourself?*

JONATHAN KING: Absolutely. I'd found out, thankfully early on, that to go around singing my current hit song or, worse, my hit song of five years ago, every night, eight shows a week was something that had no appeal at all. I remember asking Elton once how he could possibly face singing 'Goodbye Yellow Brick Road' every night on his endless touring schedules and he told me that he just lived for it. I don't share that feeling at all.

DE: *But I would nonetheless call you an extremely creative man.*

JK: I have a creative imagination. I can see things. I can spot a hit before anyone else, and usually when most people say it won't be. And I love starting things, helping things along, nudging people or projects to fruition. If I earn money out of it, so much the better. If not, well, there's always something else. I really can't take myself that seriously, to be that obsessive. I think karma has a lot to do with what happens to us and I just go with that.

DE: *Which brings us to the* Rocky *karma. Was this business or pleasure?*

JK: It started out as both...

DE: *Implying what? That it ended up as neither?*

JK: Richard's show has always been a pleasure. Always. I notice you're starting your chapters with little lines from the show. I use the lines all the time, quote them constantly, and I play the album all the time, too. I never get tired of it.

DE: *So let's start at the beginning. How did you first get to see the show?*

JK: My great friend Jack Tinker – who's no longer with us – used to write for the *Daily Mail* and he reviewed *Rocky* on the first night at the Theatre Upstairs. In his review, he didn't even mention that it was a musical but just said that it was the most brilliant piece he'd seen in a long time. The next day, I rang up and got tickets. Quite easily. I had planned an evening out with my friend – and he's also no longer with us – Donald Torr, who was a dancer in The Young Generation – and asked him if he minded going to see it. Well, it was wonderful. Afterwards, I went backstage and met Richard O'Brien and told him that I wanted to sign it up and record it, produce a cast album.

DE: *Did you know that the show had legs, then? When you first saw it?*

JK: From the very first. I knew the show would have a life. I have to say that the songs themselves I didn't like too much, as songs. I've told

Richard this, so it's no great revelation. I just thought the whole show was tremendous.

DE: So then you met…who? Michael Linnit or Michael White?

JK: White. He was already the *de facto* producer. Along with the Royal Court, of course. Linnit was only Richard's agent. Richard had already signed away his executive powers with his initial contract with Michael White. I got on very well with Richard immediately. I really liked him and I could tell he was keen and was keen for me to be involved. So, the next day I found myself in a meeting with Michael White, who also knew he had a hit on his hands and wanted it to transfer. He told me it would cost £100,000 to transfer it, so I proposed a deal that I would invest £20,000 and have 20 per cent of whatever would come from *Rocky* in perpetuity. For that, I also got the rights to make the cast album.

DE: Sounds like a good deal.

JK: It was a very good deal, for all of us. It was concluded quickly and Michael had my cheque immediately.

DE: Presumably the publishing wasn't on offer?

JK: I wasn't particularly interested in the publishing at the time. Cast albums didn't usually sell a bundle, although if the show was successful – which I knew this one was gong to be – they sold steadily. I didn't see any future outside the show for any of the songs as possible covers for other artists – except maybe 'The Time Warp' – and so the publishing was taken up by John Sinclair. I was left to get on with the making of the record.

DE: Did Sarm approach you or vice versa? It was John Sinclair's studio, after all.

JK: I can't remember which way round it was. Probably I was prompted to go to Sarm, but I do remember that they offered me a very good deal, which in the event warranted going there, as I was very specific about how I wanted to make this record.

DE: Which was?

JK: I had to preserve that raw, rough and ready, totally fresh and exciting feeling that had come over in the Theatre Upstairs. And that ethos of amateurishness, that thrown-together quality, as though the singers had only ever sung the songs through twice and the band were not slick and rehearsed. So I thought that, if I could do the whole thing – recording to mixing – in 24 hours, it might work out. The cast were not allowed to leave the studio – some of them even slept in corners on the floor – and the band were completely exhausted.

DE: So you were pleased?

JK: Delighted, and still am. I loved the links that were put in, too, between the songs. That was my idea.

DE: And the rest is history?

JK: The rest is a nightmare, as far as I was concerned. The theatre and the music business have never understood each other. Always mistrust, wariness, suspicion. Don't know when all that started but it's still true today, even with the television industry and the music business, and I should know as I'm deeply involved in both. When it opened at the Classic, I used to go and see the show a lot and took all those people to see it, like Robin Nash at *Top Of The Pops*, and got all the media involved who could talk the thing up as a sort of culty thing for young people to be involved with, as opposed to the usual people who composed 'theatah' audiences. I was the super-angel, after all, and it was in my interest to be pro-active like that. As far as I was concerned, I knew I'd found my 10cc of 1973!

But, as it turned out, there wasn't going to be a future. Not for me, at least. Michael White's costs and charges were horrendous and there was very little in the way of a return for ages. There was always an unexpected charge for new scaffolding or some such exaggerated thing, and in retrospect the cost of the transfer from the Court to the Classic was astronomical and quite unfounded. But life moves on and I had other projects brewing, although Michael and I would keep in close contact. When the idea was mooted for an American production, I was vehement that the show should not follow the time-honoured path and go to a big theatre on Broadway. In fact, I thought it shouldn't even go to New York and should open in some little club – like the Roxy, in fact, where it ended up.

DE: So who came up with Lou Adler?

JK: I can't say who told him or how Lou was made aware of the show in the first place, but I was in contact with Lou from an early stage. Michael White knew nothing about the music business, so it was natural that I should push the project in that direction once the big theatre/Broadway idea had been knocked on the head. And I had equally strong feelings about a New York production. Not the big Broadway theatre but an off-off kind of thing, which would let people discover it for themselves and its own sake as a show. Not as a hyped-up phenomenon.

DE: So you were pleased it ended up at the Roxy?

JK: Delighted it ended up at the Roxy, but not delighted that, just before that, I noticed that my royalty cheques had dried up.

DE: Say again?

JK: When my lawyers got onto the case, they discovered that Michael White had bankrupted the original company with which I had contracted and had transferred the rights to *Rocky* – ie the company's stock – to another company with whom I had no contract. Ergo, he had no reason to pay me anything.

DE: *And this is legal?*

JK: Watertight. It's a loophole that is being used all the time. Moves are constantly afoot to change the legislation, but nothing yet.

DE: *And so the sale of the American rights excluded you by consequence?*

JK: Excluded to the point that I was refused grand rights to allow UK Records in America to issue and promote the cast album. In the end, I was so incensed that I caused to have imported 20,000-odd records produced in England and sold in the USA as just that, imports. I took the billboard on Sunset Strip across the road from the Roxy and advertised to that effect. The *original* recording!

DE: *But we're talking millions of dollars as residual and earnings from your initial investment here.*

JK: Tell me about it! I've done all right from the cast album over the years. I was at least left in control of that and I suppose that, after the return of my initial 20 grand, I earned about 50 more on top of that but it's peanuts when you consider what 20 per cent of *The Rocky Horror Show* in all its guises could have meant.

DE: *All the cast members are still very grateful for you never having abandoned them. They treasure your cheques!*

JK: Well, that's nice.

DE: *And you might not be blamed for never having had anything further to do with it.*

JK: I was there in New York for the first night at the Belasco. Awful. Just what I didn't want to happen, where it should never have been played.

DE: So I presume you were not involved with anything about the movie?

JK: That's right, although I had already expressed strong feelings about how the film should look. Whereas it ended up looking a bit too much like a low-budget Busby Berkeley concoction, I thought it should look like a gritty black-and-white schlocky British horror-genre sort of thing, with only occasional flashes of colour.

DE: That's how it was originally written. It was all going to be black and white until Frank arrives in the elevator.

JK: How interesting. So, that's the history... I never abandoned the album soundtrack, either. I kept pushing it even after the movie flopped. No one could have known about the audience participation thing. Karma, karma...

DE: Sad that there seems to be so much bad feeling between so many of the instigators.

JK: If there is, it is sad. It was such a collaborative effort. Jim Sharman was – is – a very under-estimated talent. Thomson, too, is wonderful, as is Richard Hartley, of course. I watched them working together as the show transferred and it was wonderful to see.

DE: And Richard O'Brien. Are you surprised that he hasn't repeated his success in quite the same way? Commercially, I mean.

JK: Yes. I would have thought Richard would have come up with something else, although it is often who you collaborate with.

DE: Do you still write? Songs?

JK: Only very occasionally. I'm a much better lyricist than I am at the music. I'm very critical of myself. There's been lots of attempts at collaboration. Well, a few, because I really don't like collaborating. I have worked with Roger Greenaway and Elton, and I always talk about it, but I have so much else to concentrate creative energy on.

DE: Did you make any separate offers to Tim Curry at the time or any others in the cast vis-à-vis recording?

JK: No. I love Tim, and I always thought he was a wonderful actor and performer, and I am surprised in one way that he didn't go on to get success in the music business, although from knowing him in New York, when he went there to play in *Amadeus*, I can sort of understand. He is an actor, really. I'm also surprised that he hasn't become a bigger star as an actor. I saw him the other day in some Stephen King thing. He was playing something hugely evil in deep dark sewers and playing it as a clown.

DE: And what of Jonathan King now?

JK: My big pride and joy is my publication of *The Tip Sheet*, which brings new tracks, songs and acts to the attention of the office-bound music-business execs. It's been going seven years now and is a huge success. It's distributed throughout the music business and I'm pleased to say people pay a lot of attention to it. Its greatest claim to success is the Chumbawamba phenomenon and 'Tubthumping'. It was an unsigned track and went on to sell four and a half millions albums in the USA alone.

DE: I presume you've never been an 'angel' to anything theatrical since Rocky?

JK: Indeed no. The last thing where I really felt that the same magic had been generated was seeing *The Lion King* on Broadway with my god-daughters and their mother. The children were entirely enraptured, caught by that special magic.

DE: And any stand-out memories of the piece?

JK: Oh, yes. Sitting in the Theatre Upstairs when it was raining. The place had some sort of tin roof. It was so loud at times, you could hardly hear the dialogue.

DE: *On such stormy nights, accidents were more than likely to happen...*

JK: I see you shiver with anticipation...

    ‹‹‹‹irememberdoingthetimewarpiremememberdoingthetimewarpi››››

4 'When Worlds Collide'
The Actors

Gillian Diamond, together with Harriet Cruickshank, was responsible for the casting process at the Royal Court Theatre. Once the basic show of *Rocky* had been scheduled, having received the OK from Nicky Wright and had its funding guaranteed by the Michael White production investment, the wheels were set in motion. The casting director, in consultation with the play's director, sent out the calls to the theatrical agents according to the preliminary lists of alternatives in order of preference the director had drawn up.

We've heard how Tim Curry wasn't first choice for Frank and we've heard that Kimi could have been Magenta. This chapter deals with the thesps, the actors, those who were once described as 'that despicable race'. Those who themselves brought magic and glamour from those dark, forbidden, taboo areas that actors were long thought to inhabit. Those who also contributed hugely to the human form assumed by Richard O'Brien's paper aliens.

<<<<irememberdoingthetimewarpirememberdoingthetimewarpi>>>>

Patricia Quinn

'There's a guiding star'

Pat Quinn's extensive theatre credits – other than in *AC/DC* at the Royal Court, which won the Best Play Of The Year award, and as Sarah Bernhardt in *Sarah B Divine* – include appearances in *The Threepenny Opera* at the Prince of Wales Theatre, *Murderer* at the

Garrick, *Strip Well* at the Royal Court, *Macbeth* for the Bristol Old Vic, *Bedroom Farce* at the Prince of Wales, *Can't Pay, Won't Pay* at the Criterion, *A Bright Room Called Day* at the Bush, *Light Up The Sky* at the Old Vic, *Another Love Story* at Leicester Haymarket and *The Real Inspector Hound* at the Palace Theatre, Watford.

Patricia is also Lady Stephens, widow of the noted Shakespearean actor Robert Stephens, who was with the National Theatre Company alongside Laurence Olivier, John Gielgud, Ralph Richardson and Anthony Hopkins. Robert was knighted just before he died, in 1995.

After *The Rocky Horror Picture Show*, Patricia was in *Hawk The Slayer*, the Fox feature film *Monty Python's Meaning Of Life*, *The Outsider* for Paramount and Richard O'Brien's *Shock Treatment*.

On television she has appeared in *A Christmas Carol*, *Fortunes Of War*, *Bergerac*, *Lost Empires*, *The Professionals*, *Tales Of The Unexpected*, *Hammer House Of Horror*, *Minder* and *The Countess Alice*. She also played Christabel Pankhurst in *Shoulder To Shoulder*, was in the BBC's *I Claudius*, in *Beauty And The Beast* with George C Scott and has featured in *Doctor Who*, yet another cult success with worldwide appeal.

However, she will always be remembered for not only for her role as Magenta in *The Rocky Horror Picture Show* but for the iconic status of her lips, which were recruited when the producers found they needed an original way to present the opening song, 'Science Fiction'.

Onstage in the original production, Patricia Quinn sang this song in the role she created of the Usherette. For the screen, it was decided that she would film the opening sequence in blackface and glistening blood-red lipstick. Forget Dali's classic red-lips sofa – surely Patricia Quinn's lips are now the most famous in the world?

Recently, Lady Stephens attended Michael Bourne's Broadway-bound *Cinderella*. When the cast heard that the original Magenta was in attendance, they begged her to show them how to do the Time Warp afterwards. She hadn't forgotten!

SCOTT MICHAELS: *Back to basics. Where were you born and raised, as we say?*

PAT QUINN: I grew up in Belfast and studied acting in London. I remember having an interview at the Playboy Club when it first opened – to be a bunny girl. I had to wear a swimsuit and high heels and make-up. I then went into a cloakroom, changed into a little dress, took off all of my make-up and went to the drama centre to do my audition.

I got my audition at the drama school; I met Don Hawkins, my first husband, in drama school. He was an actor. He was with The Moody Blues in the beginning. Too bad he left them! He then went on to Hamburg and Paris. He really fancied himself as the new James Dean, walking like him, talking like him. He introduced me to all of the James Dean movies. Don was a big movie buff. He used to go to the movies five times a week.

Don appeared in the film *The Virgin Soldiers* with John Dexter, who directed my future husband, Robert Stephens, in *Royal Hunt Of The Sun*. He was one of the best theatre directors in England. Don went to Singapore. Wayne Sleep was in it, too. There were two gay characters in it, walking through the swamp, and the leeches were getting to them. Wayne was screaming. The film was delightful.

Dexter always had a whipping boy on his films and Don was his at the Old Vic. Dexter was gay. Zeffirelli was the same with Bruce Robinson on *Romeo And Juliet* and Robert [Stephens] was in that, too. He played the Prince. Robert said to Franco, 'If you don't leave that boy [Bruce] alone, I am walking off the film.' [Bruce later went on to write *The Killing Fields* and *Withnail And I*.] Ned Sherrin told Don to either put up with it or take the first plane home, because it's not going to change. I don't understand the pleasure of that.

SM: *Back to you for a bit. Tell me about how you started with* Rocky.

PQ: Simple. I auditioned. For Richard O'Brien and Jim Sharman. They really wanted Marianne Faithfull fpr the role but she was unavailable. I remember Richard was wearing a teddy-boy coat. I thought they were very with-it blokes. Richard played 'Science Fiction' for me on the guitar. Then I sang along with him. Afterwards I waltzed down the

King's Road, thinking, 'That's one of the best songs I've ever heard.' Half an hour later they called and said they wanted me.

My agent said, 'You haven't read the script. There could only be four lines.' I went to the Royal Court and picked up the script. My agent was right. It really was four lines.

SM: So you hadn't known them before auditioning?

PQ: No. I found out pretty soon that Richard had always been a fan of old sci-fi B-movies, and he had penned a few songs and a bit of dialogue, which was eventually going to become this amazing musical. He had been Herod's understudy in *Jesus Christ, Superstar*. I think this was around 1972, and Brian Thomson and Jim Sharman were working on it. A few months later they were doing a Sam Shepard play at the Royal Court, and got Richard in for it. During rehearsals, Richard was toying around with some of the songs and Brian and Jim were approached by Richard about the possibility of his musical coming to the stage. He sang them 'Science Fiction' four times! Jim and Richard made a tape for Michael White and he gave them £1,000, and the Theatre Upstairs at the Royal Court matched it. That was the original budget.

So we did our rehearsals, and because we had no money for a set, Brian Thomson, who is an absolute genius, thought they would make it look like a decaying cinema house, so the stage was a blank cinema screen and the band was behind the screen. The set was the theatre, and the walls were covered with scaffolding at all different levels, so you could climb it. There was a ramp down the middle so you could get around the whole theatre and still be onstage, and that gave Tim Curry probably the best entrance of his life. In the film, he had the elevator, but in the play...

The great thing about the whole *Rocky* thing is, because of the lack of money in the production, wonderful imagination was used. There was no choreography at all. We did everything ourselves and Jim directed it. Jim wanted the style to be very serious. Even though you are doing something that much fun, you play it to the hilt in the sense that everything matters. It was good over evil and all that.

Jim Sharman used to have only two expressions to let us know if were following his directions. One was sort of down in the mouth, looking at you miserably, and the other was a big smile. You knew what both of those meant and you acted accordingly.

If he smiled, I would think, 'You liked that? I'll do it better!' That is my favourite kind of direction. I don't particularly like to be told what to do. I know what I'm to do. Better than the director sometimes!

In the old days, you never had such things as directors. Nowadays, it's become the director's show. 'Nunn's production of...' 'Spielberg's film so-and-so...' Lots of egomaniacs and power maniacs. They never shut up about the text and the play so you can carry on acting.

Jim was not that kind of director, thank God. One day, Jim Sharman said at rehearsal that we were going to improvise a car. I hate improvising, even though I went to Drama Centre and improvised for three years – in great pain, mind you. I never liked making things up, Stanislavsky and people like that. I've always liked a text.

So for Jim, we had to really use our imaginations. We had no props. Brad and Janet were supposed to be in a car, walking around the ramps like they were travelling, pretending with a steering wheel, and since it was supposed to be raining, Janet had to move her hands like windscreen wipers. They were just walking around and singing, but you believed they were driving.

There were no Transylvanian dancers in the play. It was just all of us. Richard, Nell, Tim and I were the only guys from Transylvania.

When we started at the Theatre Upstairs, we didn't wear wigs, because there was no money for them, so I came on as me, Pat. Then I left and put on Magenta's frock and came on again, the same as the Usherette.

The house opened with all of these ghouls dressed as ushers and usherettes, seating people. They wore masks and talked to the punters. The people loved it, because nothing like this had ever happened to them before. They were terrified, yet they really enjoyed it.

I was standing centre stage dressed as the Usherette and Jim Sharman had me covered in a transparent sheet and lit from underneath. His vision of her was that she was almost a ghost, in this dilapidated cinema. She's very naïve, and singing about her most favourite films. I don't mean in a Shirley Temple way, but just charming and delightful. I think this was brilliant of Jim, for me not tearing the house down with 'Science Fiction'.

The entrance to the theatre was off to the side, so when the audience entered the first thing they saw was me. They had to pass me to get to their seats and they'd just stare at me and touch to see if I was real. We called the Usherette character Miss Strawberry Time, because of the sign on her tray, but she never really had a name; she was just the Usherette. In America, instead of calling her Miss Strawberry Time, they gave her a name: Trixie.

So then all of the ghouls came along and said things to the audience like, 'Glad you could come tonight,' and then took the sheet off me. Then I began singing 'Science Fiction' and handing out sweets and lollipops. That was a fantastic beginning and the people loved it! After the song, I walked off the stage to change into the Magenta costume.

Magenta and Columbia were meant to get along well, and Nell and I really did in real life.

SM: It sounds as though Jim gave you all pretty much free rein.

PQ: Absolutely. We each had to find our characters. Tim was really struggling to get his character together and Sharman was quite hard on him. He found the voice, which was a send-up Kensington voice of the Queen: *hyse* not *house*, *slayab* not *slab*, and instead of *down* it was *dine*. That was his key to Frank. For Magenta, I found her partly in her voice too, which I made sort of German/Dietrich. That really threw people off, when they met me after the show! Jonathan Adams was cast as the narrator and Doctor Scott. Nell found her own squeak, but that wasn't new. She was always squeaking. Riff Raff found his voice and his hump, so we were set to go.

SM: And so it began...

PQ: Yes. We weren't all strangers. I met Tim from around the Royal

Court, and I was pregnant with my son and I was asked to do a play with Tim called *The Sport Of My Mad Mother*. Tim was sort of in awe of me because I was quite successful and he was just beginning. He hadn't quite cracked it yet; *Rocky* did that for him. He was still doing small roles here and there. I remember going into a pub around the corner from the Royal Court and we met. He is really quiet and quite introverted in real life. Quite serious. It seemed that he was really thrilled to meet me. A bit fannish, if you know what I mean. I don't mean to say it as such, but that's the truth.

We all got together and started rehearsals and had a great time. Richard [O'Brien] talks about the times we sat on the steps in front of the Royal Court to have our lunch and we would be playing music, Julie Covington, who could really sing, and Tim and Richard [Hartley]. I was the only one that was married, with a three-year-old, all the rest of them were single and free. I also had a nanny, whom I paid £18 a week, Equity minimum wage, which was exactly what I made doing *Rocky*, so I would just hand her my £18 once a week; but in those days, somehow the money didn't matter. So I was a lot at home bathing the baby and I couldn't do the hanging around with the rest. Years later I was on the Gloria Hunniford show with Richard, and he said, 'Rubbish. Don [Hawkins, her first husband] was bathing the baby! You *were* on the steps with us.'

SM: *So, opening night...*

PQ: For our first dress rehearsal, we went to the White House Hotel, in Earl's Court. They had a big rehearsal room that we used. Sharman set up chairs like the theatre so we had our aisles to make our entrances. That was the first night I got my costume, complete with ice-cream tray and high heels. Tim got his shoes on for the first time and he finally 'found' his Frank character. The shoes absolutely transformed him, and off he went, like a duck to water. It was amazing, because he wasn't quite sure of himself until that moment.

Just before opening, we realised the show was too short, and Richard Hartley and Richard O'Brien went home that night and came back the next day with 'Eddie's Teddie'. I hated that song. It's one of my least favourite songs.

Jonathan Adams was brilliant, because he is very straight, and his comedic timing is great. There has never been a Narrator since who is more amusing than Jonathan. When he became Doctor Scott, with the stockings, the place went wild!

In the film, they wouldn't let Jonathan be both Narrator and Doctor Scott. They wouldn't let me be both the Usherette and Magenta. They couldn't figure out how to use the Usherette on the screen, so they had to come up with a different idea and that's how they decided on my lips. Jonathan chose Doctor Scott and Charles Gray was cast as the Narrator.

Since the film, so many people have gone into this thing in massive depth. There have been psychology books and articles. At the time, all I knew about the show was that it was sex, drugs and rock 'n' roll. At least, that was what was going on when we were there. Everyone wanted to know what Richard meant – the whole sexuality, 'Don't Dream It, Be It', cross-dressing thing.

SM: But that's what must have pole-axed most audiences.

PQ: When Tim Curry made his entrance, he did it from the back of the theatre, not the stage, so the audience didn't know what had hit them! He began with his 'How'd'ya do? I see you've met my...' and the audience whipped their heads around and thought, 'What the fuck is *that*?!', because the impact of it was stunning! Down comes this transvestite, and he frightened the life out of everyone! Tim's energy was amazing, it was like Mick Jagger, Bowie, just everything rolled into one. His performance was fantastic. At first, Tim had had great difficulty with the part. It took a long time for him to create Frank. It wasn't the best writing in the world.

SM: And, of course, all this was without the benefit of hindsight. You were all just mucking in together, then.

PQ: We all had to change in the same room at the Theatre Upstairs, an office. There was no other option. One night, Rudolph Nureyev came late to the show, and the policy was not to admit latecomers, but they made an exception for him. He couldn't go through the door into the theatre, so he had to go through the office and around the back. So Nureyev says, 'I'm terribly sorry, do you mind me disturbing you? I'm late and I have to go through.'

I was thrilled and could only respond with, 'Oh, I'm so delighted! That's lovely!'

To think of all the people that came to that show, it was fantastic and it was all word of mouth on the street. Soon we had David Bowie, Lou Reed... We had no idea that it would become what it became. Just another job to begin with. Nell and Brian Thomson, both Australian, never stopped taking pictures, all the way through the film. I never even owned a camera. I was never into taking photos. That's why Brian had so many photos for the scrapbook. I do have some snaps of Richard, Jonathan and myself in the play *Disaster* and a few of a party at Tomb View, Jonathan Adams' house.

SM: *What about the cast album?*

PQ: The record producer Jonathan King came to see the show one night (post-Julie Covington), just for pleasure, but ended up thrilled with it and proposing a 20 per cent investment in the show, to record a cast album, for 20 per cent of the profit. We recorded the album in 24 hours at Sarm Studios. It really captured the innocence of the production, although I was less than pleased with 'Science Fiction'. I thought it sounded very amateur, but that was exactly what he was trying to convey. Recreate.

We were supposed to be upstairs at the Royal Court for three weeks, but they extended it to five. I didn't really want another two weeks at 18 quid a week. On the last night, Pam Gems was supposed to be coming, the playwright I did *Sarah B Divine* with. There were two entrances to the building: one in the front, up the stairs.

On this last night, I was coming in and at the top of the stairs were standing Elliot Gould and Mick and Bianca Jagger. I remember Bianca had on a white suit and carried a cane; that was her trademark at the time. I very coolly walked past them and went upstairs and then just gushed, 'MY GOD! Mick Jagger is downstairs!'

I was dumfounded because everyone was looking miserable as fuck. I didn't know why. I always went downstairs to the loo to get changed, because I didn't like getting undressed in front of everyone; I guess I was a bit shy. So I went into the loo, and I heard this agonising moan coming from the shower. I said, 'Who's in there?' and it was Raynor, who played Rocky. I said, 'Raynor, Mick Jagger is in! What's the matter?' He said, 'I got glitter in my dick and it's swollen up out of all proportion and I can't move, so I'm showering it.'

So everyone now knew Mick was in to see the show and Tim Curry could have just killed Raynor. Raynor suggested he do the part without moving, but Sharman said, 'That's it. Let's close the show.'

So that was the last night, and we were going to a party for the close of the show. Mick, Bianca and Elliot had to go home.

We were wearing glitter every night, and glitter in those days was made of glass. You could feel it prickling your skin. My bed was covered in it! It was everywhere and the glitter just got in the wrong places!

Of course, Tim was out-Jaggering Jagger in that show, anyway. But no one forgave Raynor for that night, although since I was a working mum, I was quite happy to have the night off and the party was the most miserable party in the world.

People don't realise that, even though *Rocky* was only an hour and 20 minutes, you really had to get out there and work. It's like going to a party every night. You can't do it half-arsed. It's not like a Noël Coward comedy, sitting with teacups in a drawing room. It was physically quite gruelling. So that's how the show closed at the Royal Court.

SM: *And you were persuaded to stay?*

PQ: Michael White found a new home in a beautiful little cinema next to the Pheasantry Club in the King's Road called the Chelsea Classic, which was about to be demolished, so we could do as we pleased. We ended up succeeding in turning a cinema into a theatre. It's usually the other way around! And since the set is supposed to be a crumbling cinema, it fitted our needs perfectly. We put up our scaffolding set again, and the critics thought that they were really there to abolish the cinema, so it was art imitates life imitates art.

Everyone from Princess Margaret to David Bowie came to see *Rocky*. During this time, we were *it*. We got invited to all the parties and were the talk of the town.

Robert Stephens, my future husband, came to see this original production. On the advice of a friend he took it in – the friend dating a French girl from the *Day Of The Jackal* – and took her along, too. There was a lot of buzz amongst the cast that the great Robert Stephens was in the house, so the three of them came to the show, and afterwards they came backstage and went straight to Tim Curry to tell him how terrific he was. He really went straight to Tim, bypassing me. An odd, fleeting moment with my future husband.

Julie Covington left the show to do *Antony And Cleopatra* with Vanessa Redgrave, directed by Tony Richardson, oddly enough, in a tent where the Globe Theatre has now been built, on the south bank of the Thames. The night I went to see it, the tent blew down. Julie's *forte* was singing. She was fantastic. She was in *Godspell* and then *Rocky*. She left after the five weeks at the Royal Court to be a 'serious actress' – that is, to play Charmian the maid to Vanessa Redgrave. Bad mistake. Tents blowing down. She really wanted to be a great actress, not a singer, where her great talent is. She turned down *Evita*. She made the record and turned down the show. The record was made first and sold all over the world. She went on to Sadlers Wells to do *Seven Deadly Sins*, which is an opera.

Julie was replaced by Belinda Sinclair and at first I found it difficult to work with a new Janet. You see, there is a possessive feeling, when you invent something or a character that has never been done before. You get very attached and protective towards it. Belinda was a lovely girl and excellent, but she wasn't Julie Covington.

They couldn't put the ramp down the middle of the Chelsea Classic due to fire precautions, so it had to be from the side. But as a theatre idea, it was fantastic. I mean, today everything is sophisticated – people are always running down from the back – but in those days people just didn't. It was very, very imaginative.

At the Chelsea Classic, there were no entrances or exits because it was a cinema. So when Richard and I got into our space suits at the end, we had to go out into the street to make our entrance. Walking up the street in our pixie high-heel boots and space suits, just chatting away like normal. We would have to go outside at the front of the cinema and, therefore, come in at the rear of the auditorium for 'Frank N Furter It's All Over'.

SM: You didn't stay forever, though. Like Magenta, you were off.

PQ: I have to emphasise that I am an actress and I really wanted to act, not hang around, so I got very bored in *Rocky Horror* because I had nothing to do. I did it for three months at the Chelsea Classic, then I was offered an eight-month contract by the BBC to play Christabel Pankhurst, Emmeline Pankhurst's daughter, the suffragette who helped win the right for women to vote. It was a massive project and a great opportunity for me as a new actress, playing Christabel, one of the greatest politicians in the land.

Michael White released me from my contract, if we even had one, now that I think about it. He very kindly said that I could leave. I had to be in Halifax the next morning to be on a soap box outside a mill, making a passionate political speech about socialism and rights for women. Michael said that I had to do the two shows and take an overnight train to Halifax. Between the two shows, the cast threw a party for me and Richard wrote me a song called 'The Day Magenta Went Away'. My understudy took over the part. I remember Kimi was at the party and they bought me an ornament of a cowboy boot.

SM: You were very King's Road. You know about the punk thing.

PQ: You know, Vivienne Westwood is given a lot of credit for starting punk. In fact, I would wear her clothes. But I think Sue Blane and *Rocky Horror* started punk – the ripped stockings, the leather jackets with all the badges. There were Vivienne and Malcolm in their 'shoppe' down the road. I started buying their T-shirts. They would have rips and lesbian and bondage connotations.

<<<<irememberdoingthetimewarpirememberdoingthetimewarpi>>>>

There couldn't have been a better person who Jim Sharman could have cast to have played the original Rocky Horror than Raynor Bourton. There were many other actors who could have filled the trunks, but the creation of such a delicately balanced character required other talents than the skills of acting craft. To be loved equally by men and women and to be able to convey the knowledge that love – both emotional and sexual – is requited is a tall order. Raynor Bourton has no side to him. He is not one of those people who professes to be tolerant and pays only lip-service to sexual equality. It is a quality that Rocky had to have in his demeanour and behaviour, to appeal equally to the woman in women and yet not disaffect the man in men.

There is much more to Rocky Horror than meets the eye…

Raynor Bourton

19 October 1999
'I've been making a man with blonde hair and a tan'

During our lunchtime interview, it quickly transpired that there is a lot of jealousy and envy connected with the initial cast members and the creative team of the first production of *Rocky*. However, Raynor freely acknowledged that, at the time of our meeting, 27 years after it all started, if anyone should be credited with the show, it should be Richard O'Brien, despite all the misgivings and the unforgiving.

Changing and honing is, after all, what directors and actors are paid to do, contributing their own personalities and observations. It should all make for a perfect society, everyone using everyone else for their own purposes, but Raynor would have liked to have been acknowledged for his input. His Rocky was indeed a much more substantial character than Peter Hinwood's interpretation. For a start,

Raynor's Rocky had lines.

What has happened with the *Rocky* creative core is what happens in most rock bands/pop groups, from The Beatles to Take That, Queen to Oasis. The creative pressure makes for an over-deep bonding. When the individual pressures can no longer be sublimated into the collective core, the collective pressure explodes in a big bang, which accelerates the individuals faster and faster away from each other and the initial core. It's basic 'band' psychology. Add to that the huge amount of money being seen to be made and perceived to be disproportionately shared and the bang is often terminal. It was 18 years before Raynor and Richard O'Brien buried their hatchet. Raynor stresses the part that Jerry Jenks had in the initial lighting of the first production. Jenks was from the Citizens Theatre in Glasgow, as was Tim Curry and his replacement, Philip Sayer.

Raynor told us a wonderful showbiz coincidence story about just having been for his *Rocky* audition and going into a café with actor Mike Gwilym and meeting up not only with Tim Curry but also with Lindsay Kemp. Raynor had a base in London in Mike Pratt's flat (this was Mike of *Randall And Hopkirk Deceased* fame, who later went on to star with Richard O'Brien in *Tooth Of Crime*).

Raynor remembers sitting with Tim Curry and Jim Sharman at the first screening of *The Rocky Horror Picture Show* and neither of them liking the movie. He acknowledged that the creation of David Meyer's character in Lindsay Kemp's *Flowers* was not a million miles from Richard O'Brien's creation of Rocky in *The Rocky Horror Show* and he confirmed the likelihood that a straight director on *Rocky* would have made just another sleazy vehicle for the dirty-old-men-with-newspapers-on-their-laps brigade. Sharman was very honest with Raynor about the movie and told him directly that he would not be right for the part.

For the initial production, Raynor was sent by his agent, Jeremy Conway, for the part of Frank. Jim saw him and immediately said, 'That's Rocky.' That Jim Sharman fancied him, Raynor had no doubt, although later overtures Raynor parried with no acrimony whatsoever.

He was at pains to emphasise the great bonding felt by the first company. There was a great love at work, although he considers his relationship with Pat Quinn the best, the most enduring, of all the people he worked with.

Raynor had a music career in Japan when he went there for two tours of *Rocky*, directed by David Toguri, and did lots of gigs. He appeared as himself, singing Rolling Stones songs with a Japanese band called Geddo, when he would descend from the skies on a wire like the arrival of an alien from outer space.

The characters in the play of *Rocky*, which were created by whatever means in whatever workshop situation, touched basic chords in all human beings about the struggle to be human and the struggle to be divine. The white-god-good/black-god-bad is only what we have been told. It's not necessarily true – black god also good for a lot of people; dark side, wild side, very good to walk, on as Lou Reed told us. Where Frank could never sustain his 'Don't Dream It, Be It' philosophy, Rocky is the noble savage, the feeling beast. The beast within everyone. Rocky is the character whom we all either want to be or take care of or advise or have as our best friend. Something untameable. But for both, living the truth renders one very vulnerable, as there is nowhere else to hide.

DAVID EVANS: *So, from a theatrical tradition where boys dress as girls to be boys and where men dress as women to be comedy dames, we get* The Rocky Horror Show?

RAYNOR BOURTON: Yes.

DE: *And from sexual repression and the emergence of the androgyne – like Lindsay Kemp, Bowie, glam rock, Bryan Ferry and Roxy Music,* The New York Dolls, Lou Reed *– we get Frank N Furter?*

RB: Yes.

DE: *In a play that's all to do with stardom and ambition and envy?*
RB: Yes.

DE: So, come on, set the scene for us. Little background required…

RB: Well, it was, of course, the most extraordinary thing. It was basically a fringe thing, at the Royal Court Theatre Upstairs. The Royal Court was a very prestigious theatre. I didn't want to do it at first, but because it was the Royal Court it had kudos to it, which was good for your CV. It was a three-week rehearsal, three-week play, £18 a week, which was very good for fringe. You didn't get anything like that in normal fringe. It was the Equity minimum at the time. I was on retainer with the Glasgow Citizens for £12 a week, so I was getting like 30 quid a week, which was brilliant for that time.

DE: And what happened was quite a surprise?

RB: At that time, all the attention and focus was put upon Tim Curry and the character of Rocky Horror: me. The very first poster for the Theatre Upstairs was a drawing of Rocky. Rocky was the push – he was very prime, in terms of focus. Then the publicity people did come up with this wonderful face, which everyone said was Little Nell.

DE: And was it?

RB: It probably was. Like I said, Tim and I were getting all the attention, all the photographs and press. I went back to Glasgow and Tim turned down two television roles. Television roles were very important in the early 1970s and incredibly well paid, compared to the theatre. Brave of Tim at the time. He turned two down to stay with this 18-quid-a-week show. When I look back on it, I know now that I had never seen anybody so ready to perform and to do that role. It was as if someone was sitting on his shoulder and said, 'You know, if you stay with this for a couple of years, Tim, you are going to be a big star.'

He just sort of knew it. He was so ready and wanting. Straker said that, when Tim did the tour of *Me And My Girl*, Tim called it 'the Get

Thin, Get Rich tour'.

DE: Do you think he had any idea about how and why he was going to be this big star?

RB: Through the show, he created this fantastic character; he created another David Bowie character, almost. What was onstage was not Tim Curry, it was stardust. I remember Tim coming to rehearsal one day at the Theatre Upstairs and saying, 'I've just been sitting behind these two women on a bus, coming in to Sloane Square. I couldn't believe it. One of these women said to the other, "Tell me something, Deirdre, do you have a *hice* in *tine*?"' And of course he used that. He incorporated that into the performance.

DE: I have an idea he had other role models too. That voice and delivery was a bit Peter Straker as well. He used to wheel around like some sort of demented black duchess. His diction was like cut crystal.

RB: Sure. But unlike a duchess, I never remember Straker having any money at all, but living in these beautiful places and being welcomed everywhere he went. And he played it to the hilt. I was a fan of Straker's before I even met him. I met him through *Rocky*. I was in awe of him. Every time we saw Peter, we'd always end up going out to dinner, which would take all night…

DE: Sexuality was starting to be more evenly spread in those days.

RB: Exactly.

DE: I think both Richards drew on the fact that they knew a person like Frank. Straker was a Frank.

RB: And Paul Jabara, too. Jabara was in *Superstar*. Richard told me that he got the line 'Tell me, Brad, do you have any tattoos?' from Paul Jabara when they were invited to St Paul's or something. It was a publicity thing. It doesn't seem that bad now, but in 1973 it was outrageous.

DE: Jabara's dead now, isn't he?

RB: Yeah. One of the many. I know that Riff Raff is now a major character, and I am very saddened that Rocky's character is now portrayed like he is. And it was the film that did this. In the play, Rocky was actually a very powerful character. And I know I created it. Jim Sharman helped bring him out, of course. [Pause] Yes, Rocky was a big-time character. Now he seems very minor. He was Pinocchio, a very nice sort of good character, and that was brought out very strongly in the original production. Riff Raff wasn't the second star that he is now. He was just a servant. Paddy always seemed the odd man out to me. When we originally did Rocky, Paddy O'Hagan was cast because he could play the sax. Paddy never wanted to be an actor. Last I heard, he left *Rocky* to do publishing. Funny that Eddie and Paddy were both the odd ones out. We never hear of Paddy O'Hagan.

DE: So what about you, your life?

RB: My story is that I was born in Birmingham and was brought up with an aunt. I am entirely untrained as an actor. I was, in fact, a milkman in 1969. Since we finished at midday, I got a backstage job at the old Birmingham Rep[ertory] Theatre, in the flies, literally pulling the ropes. Since I finished my milk job early, I could go to the theatre and watch the rehearsals. Before the performance that I was pulling the ropes on, I would go up to the ASM and ask if I could sweep the stage too. 'Of course,' he said. This was in the days before Equity minimum, and before all those restrictions came in, so they could really work people. I was 19. One day, between the matinée, the director came up to me and said, 'Understand you want to be a fucking actor?'
    'Yes,' said I.
    'I've got four lines for you in *Hamlet*.' And that was it. The four lines in *Hamlet* was in Richard Chamberlain's *Hamlet*. It changed his career. I wanted to be a classical actor. When I got to the Glasgow Citizens I

thought that was the most fantastic place I'd ever been. It was extraordinary. To give you an idea, when Philip Prowse did *Antony And Cleopatra*, they felt the whole thing was about the beauty. He thought that Cleo should be very beautiful, so he chose the most beautiful member of the cast, which happened to be a man. Nobody questioned it, because the beauty was there. That was the sort of thing they did. They would use live chickens and horses, and it was extraordinary.

DE: *It was at a time that male beauty was allowed. As long as you were confident in your sexuality, whatever it was, nobody gave a damn.*

RB: I used to wear make-up – foundation, nail varnish. It was never considered odd; it was just something that was done. I liked doing it, and I felt better for it.

DE: *The ultimate incarnation of this is Richard himself. Richard was ripe for this.*

RB: I would agree.

DE: *He stepped into it as if it were a relief that he didn't have to pretend any more. That was his first flowering, really.*

RB: Again, I would agree. As I said, I wanted to be a classical actor, and here I was in Glasgow – and the old guy that was the founder of the Edinburgh Fringe, Andrew Cruickshank, had three daughters. One was an actress, one a director and Harriet, the third, was the administrator in Glasgow. She left that summer to become the administrator of the Royal Court. She put my name forward as Frank N Furter, for the casting, so I went to see Gillian Diamond for the role of Frank. The first thing she asked me was if I knew any musclemen. I recommended a couple of guys. Then I went to audition for the part of Frank N Furter, having never sung, other than panto in Chesterfield, where I sang 'Long-Haired Lover From Liverpool'. It was one of those awful rooms where the people waiting can see the people auditioning.

I was full of confidence, I was young, I was in the company of the Glasgow Citizens and that's where I wanted to be. There was no desperation for me whatsoever. I was sitting there and Jim Sharman told me later that he turned to Gillian and asked why I was there. 'Frank,' was her reply. 'No, that's Rocky,' was his reply. I had not even spoken to Jim; this is the story he told me. I went up to do my piece and I sang 'Long-Haired Lover From Liverpool'.

Richard and Jim showed me 'Sword Of Damocles' and asked me to sing it. I sang it. I thought it was very ponderous and dull and slow when Richard played it on guitar [compared] to the way it finally turned out when played by Richard Hartley, who was a keyboard man. They asked me if I could camp it up a bit. The only thing that came to mind was that I went into this natural falsetto. I understand that Richard was still not sure because I wasn't muscled, though I was fit. Apparently, Jim was convinced and Jim got his way, and that's how I was cast.

DE: Had Jim Sharman been straight, do you think he would have cast you?

RB [laughing]: Ha! Probably not.

DE: I have a theory: Rocky *came along at a time when male porno stars were creeping out of the closet, and female ones, too. But, as a gay man, Jim would have appreciated that.*

RB: Let me back you up on that. A little-known film came out in 1973 called *Tarzan*. I'd never seen it. There was a very beautiful young man in it who had a very similar hairstyle to me. I cut out this picture of him from a newspaper, took it in and stuck it on the fridge at the Royal Court as a joke. When Jim saw it, I told him it was me, and we laughed. Then he said, 'Leave it.'

People probably don't remember this, but that newspaper stayed up there for what turned into the whole five-week run at the theatre. When we moved from the Royal Court to the Chelsea Classic, we had to rehearse, and we all knew what we were doing, except for Julie Covington. There was a slight tendency to mess about, because we were confident. This new song they gave us, called 'Eddie's Teddie', we put that in for the transfer. From my point of view, I didn't have a lot to do in that song. There's a part of it where Jonathan said, 'And a motorbike,' and I remember going up to Jonathan and picking up the mic and going, 'VRROOOOOOM VRRRRROOOOOOOOM!' and putting the mic back.

Everyone looked at me, and I told them I was just a bit bored from doing it over and over again. Jim Sharman said, 'Keep it in.' It's the same as the newspaper cutting: 'Keep it in. Leave it.' There was an excitement of contributing. I didn't realise how sexy my 'vroom vroom' could become. My Rocky had an incredible amount of truth, and an immense amount of naïveté. Rocky wasn't Raynor. Rocky was a much more intelligent being than he is now portrayed.

DE: I think Jim was obviously the one to be able to pull together Richard's ideas. There must have been great trust between them.

RB: I make no bones about that. Without Jim, Brian and Susie Blane to a certain extent – and I'd even credit Jerry the lighting designer with some of this – and Richard Hartley in particular. O'Brien wrote the show, but it wouldn't have been the show without that team. I was very pleased, when I spoke to Richard O'Brien recently, that he actually managed to encompass the original cast on this occasion, the 25th anniversary of the play with Jason Donovan. He said, 'It was all of us. I had the idea, but it was everybody else…'

I asked Jim once about when Richard came to Jim with the story, when Richard left the cast of *Superstar* and Jim cast him in *Unseen Hand* at the Royal Court Upstairs. It was there that Richard showed Jim what was to be *The Rocky Horror Show*. Jim told me that, 'When Richard passed it over to me, I just yawned. Out of politeness, I actually read it.'

If you read that first script, it was nonsense, really. I only saw the script once I'd been cast. My agent must have seen it, because he didn't want me to do it because he didn't think it was any good.

But, because it was the Royal Court Upstairs, we went along with it. Jim said, 'I love rock 'n' roll, I love camp humour, and those two ingredients are there.' Within weeks of starting the show, it just took off. Jim said then, 'It constantly amazes me. I never thought it would have turned out like this.'

Brian's cinema setting was brilliant and the ghouls who showed the audience to their seats came about because there was a performance going on in the downstairs theatre. It was called *The Sea*, by Edward Bond. Because we were rock 'n' roll and noisy, we couldn't perform at the regular time, because it would interfere with the play downstairs. We would go on late, at 10:30pm, after their performance. That simple little thing meant that the theatre then could not afford to pay the usherettes at the Royal Court Upstairs. We could therefore not have usherettes. I couldn't be one, because I had to crawl under seats to get into position, and my fake tan and everything. Obviously Tim couldn't be one. Nell, Paddy and Richard were therefore the original ghouls. When we moved to the Chelsea Classic, where we actually had understudies, we had back-up singers and more ghouls.

DE: Now let's have the truth about the glitter!

RB: The glitter. Probably the most famous glitter story in the world! It's quite simple. I believe the only glitter you could get then was made of glass dust. Unlike the film, where Peter Hinwood was quite muscular, I was quite slim and [laughs], of course, attractive. We used this false tan with baby oil. Instead of doing the shadow on the pecs, which we originally did to try to accentuate the muscle line, it didn't actually work, so we came up with the glitter.

Now, the only costume change Rocky had was to change from the gold lamé shorts to the black ones for the floorshow. Of course, being a very cheap production, we had no bathing facilities, so it was a quick change, whip down this pair of shorts, whip up the other pair, and after a while a little bit of glitter would come off. Eventually, with the oil as well, it would start to stay within the briefs. I'd put the briefs on and arrange myself, and a piece of glitter... Oh, and I did wear a cocksock in the end, which is another story, but at that time I didn't. What happened with the glitter was I got some (I am circumcised) and I got it under (there's not much foreskin), just with the oil, and it just sort of stayed there *[SM: Can we draw this out any more?]* and I just cut myself.

Didn't realise it at the time. It was a Friday, because we had to cancel Saturday, the last performance at the Theatre Upstairs. I woke up in the morning and my cock was throbbing. It had come up, swelled up, but of course, not having trained or anything, I simply thought, 'The show must go on.'

I crawled into the theatre. My cock was huge and I just could not go on, and we had to cancel the show. It really is as simple as that – except, of course, Mick Jagger turned up that night, thinking it was the time we normally start, at 10:30, but on Saturdays we started at 11:30, 'cause of the matinée. So there was Jagger sitting in the auditorium from 10 o'clock, waiting there all by himself, and the show wasn't going to go on until 11:30 anyway, and then it got to about midnight, and they decided to cancel the show.

The funny part about it was when they told him that the show was cancelled. He asked, 'Why is that?' 'Because Rocky's got something the matter with his cock.' Apparently, Mick turned and said, 'Well, haven't we all, love? Haven't we all?' It made medical history and a paper was written on it because of the pus, and I had to have it lanced. I won't show you, but I still have some scars.

Jim was very angry with me. He said, 'If you'd told us three hours sooner, we could have put Nell on as Rocky and adapted it.' As I think about it, Nell may have made a better Rocky than I did at the time.

DE: *Who'd have played Nell?*

RB: They'd have just cut Nell. Easily cut Nell. Don't forget, she was only ever an appendage anyway. I don't mean that the way it sounds. I also believe that, very quickly after that, they did invent a new glitter, which is now paper glitter and won't do that kind of damage. At that time, glitter wasn't being used for the reasons we were using it.

DE: So after the initial rush at the Royal Court?

RB: Yes, indeed. Two weeks after the incident, until they opened at the Chelsea Classic. I couldn't move for a week. I got antibiotics and a beautiful drug I had an out-of-body experience with. It was the best drug I had ever taken.

You know, I had never seen a drug taken in *Rocky Horror*. By us, I mean [coughs]...

But anyway, after the five weeks at the Theatre Upstairs, which we all agreed to do, including Julie Covington, they found the Chelsea Classic and we all transferred there. Julie said no, because she was going into the tent, which is now the Globe, and so she was replaced by Belinda Sinclair. They asked me to do it and I said no, because I was going back to Glasgow at the end of September, or something like that, so I couldn't do it. They came back with a six-month offer. I said, 'Nothing has changed. I am still going back to Glasgow.'

Then they offered me a three-month contract. I said, 'No.' Finally I remember them saying, 'Well, how long will you do?' I said seven weeks, which would take me to Glasgow, so I agreed to do that. Pat Quinn left before me, so I was the third person to leave the cast, but it always looks as if I was the very first.

DE: But what was the story about the Chelsea Classic?

RB: They found it because it was going to be pulled down. We didn't know if we were going to open at one point, because of the fire regulations. We did open. Tim always tells this funny story: we had to share lavatories with the audience, and no showers. There were two boxrooms, one slightly bigger than the other. The men were in the one room and the women and Tim were the other. They needed more. I always remember Tim coming back from the loo and saying, 'You're not going to believe this, Rayn, but I've just had a piss with Tennessee Williams!' So I rush straight to the loo, unfortunately just to see

Tennessee disappear back into the auditorium. As I said, we even had to share the loos with the audience!

And we had a lot of IRA bomb scares in those days. One night we had one, and I hadn't gone on the stage yet. We had to stop the show. There was nowhere else to go, so all the cast and the audience were mingling outside together, all just chatting away. About an hour and a half later, we got back onstage and I think Jonathan Adams started it by saying, 'Sorry for the interruption...'

DE: Did the transfer go all right?

RB: Yes, but Jim Sharman was not in attendance so much after the transfer. Jim was going to do something at the new Sydney Opera House, which had just opened. He took Susie Blane and Brian Thomson as well. Once there, they struck a deal for *Rocky* to go. So *Rocky* went to Australia quite quickly. I seem to remember that it went to Australia before Los Angeles. Jim used to come to the Theatre Upstairs because he was also doing a show downstairs. I remember him coming up one night and giving us a right bollocking. I went out for a drink with him afterwards. He said, 'You really upset me.' Now, I didn't really feel like it was a bad show, not enough to warrant this outburst. 'I come here to enjoy myself,' he went on. 'It always lifts me up. I had a bad day in rehearsal and I thought I'd get a lift by seeing *Rocky*, and you were all crap.'

I said, 'Jim, you probably had a bad day, actually.'

But before he went off to Australia, Jim rehearsed in the songs for the transfer. I left before they moved on to the Essoldo.

DE: Do you remember people from Michael White's office being in attendance?

RB: Yes, Michael and Robert Fox.

DE: According the Michael, Robert worked for the Royal Court.
RB: That's right.

DE: *I remember Celestia, whom Robert married soon after, was Michael's secretary.*

RB: Michael was going out with Lindall Hobbs at the time. I met so many people, then. You know, all I had ever done was one television play and been at Chichester, and the rest was rep. To suddenly walk into this West End scene – *the* scene – half the time I didn't know what I was doing, and the other half I was really enjoying what I was doing. To have Huntington Hartford, the American zillionaire, single you out and say, 'Will you join me and my entourage?'

This is Huntington Hartford!

I was gobsmacked. Michael White was very generous. I remember he took us out a lot. He would always pay, which I thought was very generous.

DE: *Michael said that everything was on trust. He maintains that there was hardly a script.*

RB: Not what I would have called a script. What I can tell you for sure is that Richard O'Brien and Jim said that *The Rocky Horror Show* did not come together until they were doing *The Unseen Hand* at the Theatre Upstairs. Jim had another play to do Upstairs. His contract was two up and one down, and he chose *Rocky* when he was in rehearsal for *Unseen*, and that's from the horse's mouth. The rest of it, I don't know.

DE: *Who changed it?*

RB: Jim. That first day we read it through and Richard O played it on guitar and we said our lines. It was nothing of nothing. It was when it hit the floor that it really began.

DE: *Would you call it a workshop situation?*
RB: No, I would call it a Jim Sharman brilliant brilliant situation. Jim

said to me once, 'If you cast it right, you are 80 to 90 per cent there.' There was a great bonding. Even though we didn't know what was going to happen, we were aware that it was a peculiar piece. Nothing like this had probably been onstage before. There was a very quick bonding, a great amount of love, more than anything I've come across.

Jim took us all out one night. 'You are all coming out with me tonight, to the Notting Hill Gate Cinema. You are all going to see your characters in a film, *Beyond The Valley Of The Dolls*.' We all got on the tube after rehearsal and went to watch it. Afterwards, we went to the Pizza Express next door and he asked us, 'Did you see all your characters?' We did.

DE: Good company spirit?

RB: I fell in love with Pat Quinn. She is the one I've stayed in touch with, as a friend. I do say friend, as opposed to those I just see occasionally. They wrote another song called 'Toucha Touch Me' for Julie. I used to spin Julie around. At the Theatre Upstairs there was a massive concrete pillar in the centre of the screen. The position of where you were was absolutely critical as to how I would spin her. I remember bringing her around one time and smacking her head into this pillar, and I heard it above the music. I looked at her and her face – and she was *still* singing. We finished the song, and I had to literally drag her off the stage. I kept apologising. It wasn't my fault – well, it was in that there were inches involved. It could have happened to anybody. The next day I brought her in flowers, and she had this face covered in black and grey. We carried on and did the show. She was probably the best known of all of us. It was lovely, just a lot of concern. I hate to say it because it sounds very '60s and '70s, but there was a lot of love in that show, a lot of special feeling. And this was before the explosion.

Nell was an extraordinary character, would nip off at lunchtime to go busking, come back with 20 quid in her pocket. Jim found her busking in front of the Palace Theatre. He got Richard to create a part for her.

I did work with Jim again in *Shock Treatment*. Jim had the idea that the audience should be made up of anyone having to do with

Rocky Horror over the years. I played a singing GI. I'm the middle one. Annabel and Gaye were right behind me. After that, Jim didn't do very much over here. When I saw Jim on *Shock Treatment*, Jim did fancy me. If he didn't, I probably wouldn't have got the part.

DE: Rocky could not have been directed by anyone other than a gay man.

RB: I get what you mean. I think Jim made it very clear. At the same time, I was also very fortunate, knowing Jim. Forget the fancying thing – at that time, for me to kiss a man, or lie in a man's arms, even though I'm straight, it was a very natural and comfortable thing. Probably not for everyone in the world.

DE: It gave the world, the audience, the freedom to say, 'It's all right.'

RB: By the time we rehearsed the orgy scene in 'Don't Dream It', there weren't any hang-ups at all. I do remember Belinda Sinclair when she started her rehearsals, and when we got to that scene, she ever so slightly... I could tell she wasn't comfortable. Mind you, we'd been doing it for five weeks, and Belinda was just coming into it. Regarding Pat again, I remember I introduced her to Robert Stephens. I liked him. He came backstage looking for Magenta and I brought him back to introduce them, and I am telling you that is the truth. They did hook up near that time, certainly by the time *Shock Treatment* came around. I was always trying to pull Pat Quinn...

I went back to Glasgow to do *Happy End*, playing Doctor Nakamora. I had just had three months of high glamour. I'd gone from having just a nice ordinary sort of girlfriend to having a supermodel.

Everything I wanted was available to me. We were hits. We were stars of the town. I certainly never viewed myself as a star of the town, but I enjoyed the benefits of it. Going into any club, going to the front of the queue. I thought it was me, but it wasn't me. It was the show.

DE: But you decided to leave?

RB: I shouldn't have gone back to Glasgow. I should have stayed. In hindsight, I should have stayed with *Rocky*, though I don't regret it now. There's very little I regret, other than not learning to smoke at an early age and not learning the piano. But at the time, it was a mistake not to stick with the character. With Rocky. And, of course, I fell in love with the glamour.

It was Jeremy, my agent, who really wanted me to go back to Glasgow. I never really had a plan for acting; I fell into it. Not going to drama school means you miss out on a lot of things, other than training, such as how important agents are and what's your career plan. I was just happy to be offered a job. I got with Jeremy on a fluke. I wrote to a lot of people to be my agent, and another stage manager (I've been very lucky with stage managers) knew Jeremy. My career took a nice little turn from the time I was with Jeremy. I was never out of work. I never realised how important he was. Then I was poached from him, and now I'm on the other end of the scale, and I realise how important Jeremy was.

After the season ended in Glasgow, I got very unhappy and left and came back to London. I had a taste of 'it', that's what happened, and I wanted to do that again. It seemed, in my silly way, that London was the place to be. Then I was cast as Nugget in the National Theatre's production of *Equus* with John Dexter directing. However, we clashed on several levels and it was always going to be a difficult production for me, but I was surprised when they took the role from me, stating I was not good enough.

Gillian Diamond called Dexter and said, 'I'm not going to let you do that to Raynor.' She said, 'Go and see Peter Hall.' Peter made me laugh. I don't have all the time in the world for him, either. He said, 'Despite what you may have heard, Raynor, I run the National Theatre, not John Dexter. I guarantee that you will be back here within a year.'

Well, 23 years later I did go back to the National, but nothing to do with Peter Hall. I will qualify that now, because after that John used to write to me and I used to write to him asking him questions, because

I did think he was a brilliant director. He told me that I was the new star of the National Theatre and all the good parts were going to be mine. What he didn't tell me was that I had to shag him. I never thought of actually prostituting myself to get a job.

DE: *But you all radiated sexuality in that first production. Some may have mistaken that quality for 'coming on'.*

RB: I saw Tim Curry turn men and women on, like couples, people who were together. Something amused me a few years later. I decided I would create this character and take him everywhere with me. I decided he was going to be a policeman type – fairly straight. This is Raynor the actor, trying to create an image to get cast in. I remember going out with a friend of mine to a wine bar in Covent Garden and these girls were talking to us and I was giving it a try. It must have been working because one of them turned to me and said, 'God, Raynor, you're so straight. You should go and see *The Rocky Horror Show*.' Admittedly, I was working on them. I jacked the policeman character, because he didn't get the results!

DE: *Where did your life take you subsequently?*

RB: I founded and edited the magazine *Applause*. I got incredibly bored with acting. I was chasing fewer jobs, with fewer lines. We're talking between 1992 and 1994. I found myself not wanting to face acting. So I had a lover at the time who worked for the ticket agency called Applause. They had bought out this brochure called *The Arts And Music Club*. It offered cheap tickets and package tours. It did maybe two reviews. They took over Theatre Express. You would get these businessmen getting tickets from Glasgow to see a show and it would cost them a third. I'd seen it, and the editor was about to leave. My friend Maggie asked me to write an article for it, because they were desperate. They actually paid me £100. I wrote another one and they paid me £75. I went in and did a lot of work to see how it would become a proper magazine and I took it to Paul Burnett, who was the chief executive, who bought the idea. It turned into Britain's foremost theatre magazine.

SM: Have you ever done the Rocky *conventions?*

RB: I met Sal Piro on the set of *Shock Treatment*. Pat does the guest thing quite a bit. She and Chris Malcolm both were going on about it and I thought, 'Why am I never invited to be in one of those?' But it's all to do with the film, isn't it? I must say that there were times that I was very embarrassed when I would go to see *The Rocky Horror Show Picture* and see Rocky. I used to just feel sorry for the actor. I felt it was a much better part. Poor Peter Hinwood. That silly walk! What was that all about? That was nothing. OK, it made him vulnerable. I just hated it, though. There was a time I wanted to grab people and say, 'No, you don't understand. Rocky wasn't like that. He wasn't like that. It wasn't like that!'

DE: It was like a sequel to Hair, *really.*

RB: The *Hair* thing was very much a thing of our time. I always say that *Rocky* is a family show. Even after all these years, if anybody finds out if I was the original Rocky, you can see a physical transformation. It doesn't matter who they are. What *Rocky* did, it went beyond that. It grabbed your mum and dad and your niece into it. Some people say *Rocky* started punk, but it all happened at the same time. It was a jolly little show. There was nothing offensive in the original *Rocky Horror Show*. Jim took out a line. It was something like, 'Your star sign is something, your rising is in Uranus.' He said, 'That's offensive.' That was at the time. Even the tasteful ways we did the fuck scenes.

DE: Did you ever go back to Rocky?

RB: I directed the show in New Zealand, with Gary Glitter as Frank, and I played Rocky. I had written a show called *Let The Good Stones Roll* for the West End. Stewart MacPherson asked me if it were at all possible for me to approach Tim Curry to play Frank in New Zealand. 'No,' I said, 'but I can find you a good Frank, if you want one.'

'What about you?' he asked. I said, 'No, I'm Rocky!' It was Straker I was thinking of.

MacPherson says, 'Well, I've got Gary Glitter.'

I said, 'If you've got Gary Glitter, take him. He would make a great Frank.' This was 1978. 'And if you want a Rocky, I'll do it.' They came back, 'We want you to play Rocky. And will you direct it as well?'

I was absolutely thrilled. I knew what I was doing, because all I did was copy what Jim did. Why change it? We got a great cast and yet Richard still came and asked what it was all about. [At this point Raynor asked us to turn off the tape recorder.]

<<<<<irememberdoingthetimewarpirememberdoingthetimewarpi>>>>>

Jonathan Adams

9 July 1998
'I was feeling done in'

Laconic, dour, dry and academic – just a few of the adjectives to describe the character of both the Narrator and Doctor Scott. Another adjective is 'essential'. It's interesting to note that the Narrator was the only fully formed character and dialogue in the original script because, without his explanations of both plot and character, the plot-driven play would be all but incomprehensible, based as it is so entirely in fiction and imagination. The science of this piece of fiction is that, like the strongest steel cable, it is wrapped around a tungsten core. However over the top the individual performances became, the actors always had to return to the plot. Jonathan Adams was the creator of both roles onstage.

SCOTT MICHAELS: I went to Jonathan's house in East Finchley, an area of north London bordering on the St Pancras and Islington Cemetery. I went armed with a bottle of malt whisky. Once settled, Jonathan drank his coffee from a Rocky Horror Anniversary coffee mug. He now concentrates on making collages and does voice-over work.

SM: So, how has life treated you since Rocky? *I see from the coffee mug that you don't deny your association. Some do, you know.*

JONATHAN ADAMS: But I don't do much acting now. I don't even own a copy of the film. I have the soundtrack on cassette. The original one with Jonathan King is still available. I get about £100 a year from that. I don't get anything from the film. Has it made a lot of money? I don't know. We don't get paid anything from the movie. We got paid at the time and that's that. I remember being in a studio in Barnes – Olympic Studios. Don't remember where we recorded the play. I did do a recording of something called *Metropolis* and we did it in Abbey Road, The Beatles' studio.

SM: How did you get the part?

JA: At the Royal Court, I just auditioned for the job. I had no connections. My agent put my name forward: 'There's a weird thing being cast at the Theatre Upstairs, some show with transvestite people. You should audition.' I have to say, it was odd wearing the fishnet stockings. It's not the kind of thing I usually do, but I took it with aplomb. I had rather good legs at the time. People used to remark on them. We did a month or so at the Royal Court in the beginning. It worked out that, eventually, I did it for a year. The energy and excitement was amazing. Frankly, I thought it was going to be a fringe show that would die pretty quickly.

SM: Do you mean you thought it lacked substance?

JA: The original show was so simple, just a cinema coming to life in front of the screen. It should be played seriously, not like in a pantomime. Richard O'Brien keeps referring to the 'dark side' of it, and that's absolutely right. It's not all 'ha ha!'. There's a threat of darkness. There's an edge to it. A comic edge. Richard O'Brien drew the original poster himself, you know, for the Theatre Upstairs.

SM: Really? Perry Bedden thought it was done by someone called Michael English, a friend of Michael White, and Sue Blane said it was a man called Allan Jones.

JA: Well, that's my memory, that it was Richard.

SM: You must have been cast because of your ability to come over so straight. No one can expect your character to go astray. That's what makes the ending so hilarious.

JA: Originally, when I was the Narrator, I said my lines normally. People listened and laughed. Then, when I came back to it years later, it's all completely changed. All this shouting from the audience. It's a bit of a shock to begin with, but once I got settled in, I quite enjoyed playing with the audience. It's another dimension to drama, isn't it? Sometimes it would go on for two or three minutes before I could say my lines. Lots of people have played the Narrator since. Nicholas Parsons claims he came up with the idea that the Narrator wears tights.

[A phone call interrupts the conversation. Jonathan announces that it was for a job on the radio. More voice-over work.]

I suppose you've heard the story about Raynor's glitter problem? The show was cancelled. I think it was Mick Jagger in that night. Coral Browne and Vincent Price were there.

SM: But your own bit of immortality came with the film, right?

JA: They asked me to be Doctor Scott, instead of the Narrator. It was more money. Being the Narrator on the film would have been very boring. That part was only a day's filming. All those bits and pieces. I had three months' work and was paid each week. I got much more money for that role. We filmed at Bray and Oakley Court, of course, and I remember it being a happy set. I found it quite relaxing. Of course, I spent most of the filming in a wheelchair.

SM: *Any particular memories?*

JA: When I broke through the wall, it was plastic or something. I remember coming down in the wheelchair. It looked dangerous. The set was slightly amateur, but I don't remember feeling vulnerable to death or destruction.

SM: *Even in the dinner scene?*

JA: The dinner scene? You mean with the body under the glass table top? Nothing is a surprise when filming. I don't see how it could have been a surprise to anyone.

SM: *Did you partake in any sex and drugs with your daily rock 'n' roll?*

JA: Drugs? They don't bother me. Was there a lot of drugs? I don't know that. Maybe in the dressing rooms. Alcohol is all I do.

SM: *Terry Ackland Snow, the art director, was telling us about spray-concreting your wheelchair. [We will come to our meeting with Terry in Chapter 6.]*

JA: And the making of the plaster casts. We had to lie down, and they put straws up our noses so we could breathe. They also put muslin on our bodies to keep it sticking to our flesh. They then poured the plaster on us. It was very hot. I wouldn't mind having my statue now, actually. It's probably been broken up by now. People would pay for that today.

SM: *You were obviously comfortable with the cast from the play. What about the Americans?*

JA: Barry Bostwick struck me as being the least good, in a way. No sense of comedy in *Rocky Horror*. You don't laugh at him. He's not comedic enough. Susan Sarandon is.

SM: What did you think of the finished movie?

JA: I saw one of the previews of the film. It started off with a lot of raving and then everything went flat. People just stopped. I did go to the premiere. That was loud and exciting. The crowds were fantastic. Maybe the Piccadilly. Somewhere like that. Now, of course, the film is a real phenomenon. I've seen it about ten times. I don't know anything quite like it in this world. People re-enacting it in front of the screen, it's almost like a religious phenomenon. They try to get it as accurate as possible.

SM: You go to the conventions now. Do you enjoy them?

JA: I've been to New York three times for fanclub conventions. They're good-natured. I just wonder about their sanity levels. You know Sal Piro, I suppose. He stayed here once or twice in years gone by. Friendly chap. Obsessed a bit. It's like a holy church, and the script is the holy text. They're obsessed with themselves. No, with the movie.

I went to the 25-year thing in Richmond. I met Richard and Pat there. Even I shouted at the narrator a couple of times, 'You got no fucking neck!' But I don't understand the ethos of the film, I don't know why it's become such a success. It's a pantomime for adults, I suppose. But I don't understand this obsession.

SM: So at least you have fans, then?

JA: I've never been a 'fan' type of character. Everyone else seems to have hundreds of groupies; I have one.

SM: What happened in life after Rocky?

JA: I was basically an actor, not a singer or dancer. I went to a convention in New York and, while there, I did some cabaret. I do write some music. *Rock 'n' Roll Vicar*, that was at the Duplex, a tiny theatre. I don't write songs now. I've been to three or so conventions.

They wanted me to go to Los Angeles for the Roxy cast, but Equity wouldn't let me.

Richard O'Brien has gotten mixed reviews in the things he's done since. I was in another play called *Disaster* by him. Terrible name to call a play. I enjoyed that. You should judge a person by his best works. We all go up and down with our creativity. I was an art student, an artist, so now I do collages. I've done these all my life, as well as act. Now I concentrate on these. It takes me two or three days to put one together, sometimes a few hours. I do sell them. Make me an offer now and I'll give you a good price. I say that to embarrass people.

SM: Do you live alone?

JA: I have been married. No kids. I'm infertile. [Laughs] That usually kills the conversation. [Smiling] Pat Quinn's a lady now. You'll never interview Tim Curry, will you?

‹‹‹‹irememberdoingthetimewarpiremember doingthetimewarpi›››

5 'I Just Love Successes'
Tim Curry

The major casting coup came, of course, with Jim's decision to settle on Tim Curry to play Doctor Frank N Furter. And yes, Jonathan Adams, you're right – we never got to interview Tim Curry.

Usually, we could let it go at that and merely allow the observations of others to explain the phenomenon of both Tim's persona and his performance, but in Tim's case we can't because, as one of his closer friends for several years until he too was dropped from Tim's mate-list, David has a privileged insight into him. Thus, rightly or wrongly, he feels he has the knowledge that allows him to try to fill in some of the questions about Tim and his subsequent renunciation of a time of his life that he used as a springboard to achieve his current lifestyle, status and career.

Although, as the years bring dotage to us all and it becomes more and more difficult to remember, it is far, far more difficult to forget.

What follows is taken from David's memoir *Inside Out* and, the later material, from his journals.

It was 1973...

Rocky Horror transferred no sooner than it had opened, first to the old Classic cinema (now demolished) halfway down the King's Road and later to the old Essoldo, renamed the King's Road Theatre in the show's honour. The building is now back to being a movie house. Apt.

Rocky's star, Tim Curry, had given a hugely bravura performance; cross between a megalomaniac boarding-school matron and a deranged circus ringmaster. The flagrantly ambivalent sexuality of the show's hero, Frank N Furter, made us howl. I just loved it.

But it was not until a year later that I was really to get to know the depth of Tim's bravura, which was, ultimately and rather disappointingly, the antithesis of the androgyny which he paraded every night onstage and which had become fashionable. David Bowie was braver about things like that then, Peter Straker had fearlessly made it his trademark and someone called Mark Feld wished but didn't dare and became Marc Bolan instead. Glam rock as a genre lessened the highbrow profile of the threatening queer aspect of androgyny and brought the pantomime aspects of men in make-up to *Top Of The Pops* every week on Thursday nights. Sweet, Mud, Slade… Aaah! That smell of sweat and Chanel.

Straight men in layers of Max Factor had never had it so good, and not a drop of blood had been shed. The gay boys had already done all the fighting for their straight brothers to come out in a bloodless coup.

And in 1974…

It was my first trip to America. I'd first gone to New York and I had then flown to the capital of Dreamland, Los Angeles.

In the four years I had worked for him, I'd lied for Barry (Krost, my boss), cheated for him, censured him, sulked and made up, and even helped him to 'befriend' lovers and clients. Why I still loved him (in the purely male sense), I have absolutely no idea. I even understood why he wanted his new home in Los Angeles. It wasn't my idea of home, but it was his. Someone once opined – I was told it was David Hockney but that's probably apocryphal – on being asked what Los Angeles was like, 'It's like the Holloway Road but with perpetual sunshine…'

It's not. I live near the Holloway Road and I know that, even from its furthest end and even on foot, it would take me no longer than an hour to reach home.

Home, as they sort of say, is where the art is, and Los Angeles had a lot of artists. Tim Curry had been enjoying huge success at Lou Adler's Roxy Theater on Sunset Strip in *The Rocky Horror Show*. Tim was the first person I met in Los Angeles. He was swimming in Barry's pool when I arrived at the house on King's Road. Tim was one of those people I ought to have met years before, but our paths had only touched, never crossed.

I introduced myself as a friend of Peter Straker's and we were friends from that moment on until...

When I met Tim, although Barry Krost had been trying desperately to acquire him as a client, Tim hadn't signed. In this context, signing is not a form of communication for the aurally challenged but a rite of passage in which artists and performers seeking fame and fortune are blooded by giving away 20 per cent of their lives to people who say they can make fame and fortune happen. It's the greedy leading the greedy, of course. But who am I to judge?

For Tim, his future's prospect then was more than merely pink – it was cerisely rosy! As there was a *Rocky* cast album in the offing, Tim had also been promised a great record deal with Ode Records via A&M via Lou Adler, Carole King's producer, and he knew he would be opening at some point in New York with *Rocky Horror*.

Tim was living in the Chateau Marmont Hotel at the time before he moved to an apartment in the gloriously Art Deco Sunset Tower on Sunset Strip, in which he was amassing Deco and Post-Modern artefacts, which he loved. Barry made bloody sure that Tim and I got on together even more famously than we would have done if left to our own devices. I'm afraid at this point I have to admit that I wasn't being particularly loyal to Barry. I told Tim not to sign.

But, hey ho, a lot of art was involved and both Tim and Barry, after all, still call LA home.

I was also, of course, sent out yet again to woo my friend, writer/director Colin Higgins, the creator of *Harold And Maude* and later *Foul Play*, *Nine To Five* and *The Best Little Whorehouse In Texas*. I was pleased to be able to introduce Tim to Colin to ensure the wisdom didn't dry and flake off when I went home. Colin was also getting seriously famous. His script of the remake of *Silver Streak* had just been shot and studio heads were nodding with great approval. The cash-register bells associated with Colin's talent were also beginning to ring.

Although Barry asked me to move to LA, to relocate and live and work for him, re-establishing the artists' management company we had had in London, I declined. I didn't really think too long about refusing, and I'm so pleased I refused because if I had gone I would have been amongst the first to be culled by AIDS – like Barry's LA assistant, the gentle Bruce Silke, in 1983.

And again in 1974...

The second time I went to Los Angeles, Barry Krost didn't have to pay for anything. Chrysalis Records paid because, by then, with Barry safely 6,000 miles away, my client list had grown somewhat to include the then-popular Brian Protheroe. No longer was I just representing Twinkle. My other client, and still my close friend 25 years later, was Peter Straker. Straker deserves a chapter on his own. No, Straker deserves a whole book. His immediate CV runs: *Gang Show* at the Palladium as a child, *Hair* in London from 1968, *Hair* in Norway in 1970; groundbreaking, spuriously autobiographical album *Private Parts* in 1971 for RCA, produced and written by Ken Howard and Alan Blaikly; starred in Ned Sherrin's movie *Boy Stroke Girl* with Clive Francis, Michael Hordern, Patricia Routledge and Joan Greenwood in 1971; couple of out-of-town jobs in 1972...

That Peter was not a major star in 1974 when I first saw him perform at the King's Road Theatre on one of those Sunday nights, *Rocky Horror*'s day-off gigs, was inconceivable. Backed by people like *Rocky*'s Richard Hartley and Ian Blair, and with composer Don Fraser in the band onstage, Peter appeared on Frank N Furter's catwalk at the back of the theatre in a voluminous John Bates haute-couture black silk gown looking like the spawn of Diana Ross, Marlene Dietrich and the long-dead pharaoh Akhnaten. It was like the divine Frank N Furter had been granted his wish: TeeVee immortality in Movie Stellar Heaven.

Peter sang Ken Howard and Alan Blaikly's allegorical, sexually dynamited *Cock Robin* on his raked way to the stage and brought the house down. Goosebumps still rise all over me as I write this 25 years later. All the women in the audience loved him and most of the men wanted to be him. He vamped his way through the rest of the evening, backed with superbly apt work by Rock Bottom. The creation of Don Fraser and Annabel Leventon, Rock Bottom also comprised Gaye Brown and Diane Langton and were collectively Howard Schuman's model for the acclaimed 1970s telly series *Rock Follies*, which made stars instead out of Julie Covington, Rula Lenska and Charlotte Cornwell, and in which Tim Curry played the part of Stevie Streeter, a character who Howard modelled on Straker. Small, small, cruel world. And I say this wisely, for I truly believe, that if Frank N Furter had a temporal original, that inspiration was surely Peter Straker. He didn't have to dream it to be it. Straker already was it.

Beautiful, mysterious and hedonistic, this accident of occident and orient, this world person, this androgynous spawn of *Hair* was extravagant in almost everything he said and did, being as infamous offstage as he had ever been famous on it. Straker cared little for money and always assumed he had it. His manner was that of a crazed duchess, a sort of thin, black Bubbles Rothermere. Even his manner of speaking and delivery could sometimes be pure Princess Margaret. And yet, in the next sentence, he could dive into the broadest Jamaican patois in the most incisively suggestive way... Remember the line 'Do you have any tattoos?' It made for a fascinating juxtaposition. Tim Curry's version was pretty good, too...

Straker was also known for teetering on every known sexual brink and had, better still, been known to launch himself into the abysses, soaring and flying over the vertiginous taboos and – *and* – returning safely. Into his bed strayed the intrigued and entrapped of all sexes, magnetised by his riveting, paralysing charm. He was like a giant spider, hurrying and scurrying busy-busy-busy all over his web. He gave the most wonderful parties and exotic Sunday lunches; it seemed he only ever drank champagne and, when the French stuff ran out, assumed with vigorous and unarguable bravado that the German sort had bubbles and was therefore just as exciting. And he knew everybody in that certain raffish circle of London thespianism. He knew Richard O'Brien; he knew Tim Curry, with whom he too was close friends; he knew Howard Schuman and his friend the director Bob Chetwyn.

And you know, just like in the show, just like poor old Frank, used and abused and eventually tossed aside when the mission was done, everyone took from Straker, basked in Straker, learned from Straker, let Straker lead, but in the end declined to follow and gave very little back. And most of them were much too scared to follow. As, strangely, was he. Where innuendo and hints would suffice, Straker was quite content never to dot his Is or cross his Ts. Peter would tease but never, ultimately, dare... What you saw was what you got. Unlike Bowie, there was nothing left to re-invent. Nowhere he could go.

Beneath the outrageousness, and the make-up and the frock, there was a career that was deeply compromised both by its conception and its infancy and, oddly, what others thought. Peter is Jamaican...but he's not your standard-issue BMW, go-fasta Rasta. Educated, more English than the English, Peter is like Semtex. In the wrong hands, *whoomph*. In his own hands, take cover!

And, of course, [he was] a nightmare to cast. Positive discrimination in casting is seldom successful. To heap difficulties onto problems, Peter also only sang; he didn't dance, he didn't write and didn't play an instrument... Hard to pin a music business label on that. Hard to get that one in a standard agent's closet and make the drawer stay shut. When he gaily insisted that I be his manager, I kind of knew it was an impossible task and, rightly, started off by saying no.

He asked me again.

And again I said no.

And again and again, and then...

He wore me down and so we ended up having a go. I did him no great service, professionally, although our friendship was forged in alternate links of red wine and tears and debts, and our lives have since been rendered indivisible. He had, and still has, a unique voice that no one has used either as orchestral instrument or solo performance. He still waits for the stardom I contend should have been his years ago. He says it's better to still be waiting for it than to have had it and to have lost it.

There are, of course, many artists who have been blessed with no greater talents than Straker's but who have been bankrolled to the tune of hundreds of thousands and further funded with that expertise of those who are paid to know what it is that makes a particular career take off at a programmable time.

Of course, we know all about the material having to be sound, the artist–producer relationship being fecund. We know about the need to have the record company solidly in support, we realise the importance of strong management reflecting the essential interest of the artist. We understand the cumulative acceleration of interest that successful reviews of low-key showcases and enthusiastic initial radio airplay can generate. We know about good publicity, angles being just right and spread evenly across the industry so as not to cause any competitive, resentful backlash amongst the journalists. We know about good photographs. We know all about that.

What we still don't know about is stuff like the 'X factor', that factor which defines the indefinable, the moment when thousands upon thousands of individual punters decide to take up the product the industry has presented them and make that product successful. We know it's about fashion, we know it can be contrived, but we also know that a great deal of the matter is about one uncontrollable phenomenon.

Luck.

I'm going to quote Rupert Everett: 'You get what you want in the form you deserve.' I've used this epigrammatic observation so many times. I'm convinced that if it's not gospel then it's a pretty invariable rule of thumb. Everyone who strives and heaves and pushes and forges ahead because they nurse a sore ambition will ultimately get somewhere along the road they wish to travel. Where they haven't got is where they haven't been allowed because…their membership dues haven't been paid or they've forgotten an essential ingredient or they're not as good as had been thought; unforeseen competition, acts of God contemporaneous with the push…

Dammit, but I don't believe that any of the above apply to Straker. I'll be there rooting for him 'til they come with the long box.

And this *milieu* and these friends and colleagues were Tim Curry's schoolroom, this was where Tim learned the arcane arts and the canon of crafts of being a star. Straker had been once very celebrated, fêted and betted on. Tim was now in the same situation as his close friend and determined not to follow in the same footsteps.

And so I make my damning and damnable assertion. If my contentious contribution to this book of Scott's and mine has any teeth at all, the teeth snarl that it was the reality of Peter Straker who gave birth to the creation of Frank N Furter. Tim had seen it all before. And Tim too was to get what he wanted … in the form that he deserved.

But by 1975…

Tim opened and closed in *The Rocky Horror Show* at the legendary Belasco Theater on Broadway. Big blow. It opened on 10 March, ran 45 performances and closed Sunday 6 April.

Many of us had made the journey from London for that first night, including Straker and me. Where Barry was, I don't know, but although we stamped and hooted and hollered our way through that first night, the reviews were resoundingly pooh-pooh. The show had not come as virgin to New York, and I am convinced that the theatre critics and the New York theatrical establishment could not forgive this flouting of convention, this reversal of tradition. The producers had, after all, had the audacity to open *Rocky Horror* on the West Coast! Culture in America moved from east to west, not nice versa. *Quel rocky horreur* indeed!

After the show, we ended up at someone's apartment on the Westside, near the Dakota building, and waited. I think it was perhaps John Reid's place. Peter Straker and me and Tim. Little gang of Englishmen abroad contemplating a cruel sea of ink.

At last. The reviews came in.

Tim read them and then went and stood in front of an open window, several storeys up, and looked out over the firefly lights of the New York night. His silence was oceans deep and I felt so, so sorry for him. He had wanted so much to conquer New York. Straker and I both went and put arms around him, but there is so little comfort in way of gesture or word that can reach to the bottom of such a bleak void at moments like that.

Sure, no one had died, but that's what it felt like.

Exit stout party.

However, Tim was to get his wish, sort of, in a way, not like he wanted, but when *The Rocky Horror Picture Show* came out, it ran – and I believe still runs – for decades at a New York movie theatre. Like the movie of Colin Higgins' *Harold And Maude*, in Paris.

And, of course, Tim Curry got to know Clodagh Wallace. Clodagh was Peter Straker's agent for his theatrical work.

In summer 1975, I was about to leave Barry Krost and go and work for John Reid. In those days, Reid's acquisition of the coming band Queen had made his the largest and most significant management company in the rock 'n' roll arena. No wonder Tim was watching me, too. Tim wanted to learn from just about anyone he could. Basically, Tim was desperate at the time to become a rock 'n' roll star as well as a star actor. And guess who was now an intimate member of our magic circle? The divine Miss M. No, not *her*, silly! Miss Mercury. Melina, as Elton John famously dubbed the most famous Bohemian in the world. Freddie Bulsara that was, then Freddie Mercury, about to become Peter Straker's best mate and boozin' buddy.

I still had a ways to run before my friendship with Tim really blossomed. Because he was playing in *The Rocky Horror Show* in America for the time I was with Reid, I saw little of him. Despite Reid's interest in the person of Tim Curry, whom he had got to know closely in Los Angeles, Reid never expressed an interest to me in wanting to participate in the management of the career of what the music business could easily have viewed as a drag queen. But Reid liked challenges. If managing Tim had a future, it would have been an easy enough development for Reid to have made.

However, Tim – sporting himself as Frank N Furter – despite the attentions of Lou Adler and the quizzical, avuncular appraisal by Jerry Moss at A&M (and therefore Ode) Records, was a whoops-perhaps-not phenomenon on the cough, spit, snort and curse American music-biz scene.

I think, in those days, even Liberace's psycho-psyche was left unassailed, safe on the outer limits of the off-limits closet.

Showbusiness, whilst founded on careers of rock-solid negotiability, has to have its gold rushes, the perceived motherlodes whose claims people grab for, fight over and then abandon. As far as Tim being another Iggy Pop or Billy Idol, the future was entirely Meat Loaf's

So, like I said, Tim's and my real time as friends was yet to come, for he was there and I was…hey ho. But Straker's and my time had come to an end, and the professional parting was amicable enough. Freddie wanted to turn his new best friend Peter Straker into a rock star by giving him a record contract and producing the albums. Tim must have been green with envy for he must have heard of every step of the way from Clodagh Wallace, who also became Straker's manager. In hindsight, looking back, Straker's foray into Mercury's orbit could almost have been observed by Tim as another dry run. I say 'another' advisedly. Way back in the late 1960s, whilst both Tim and Straker were in *Hair*, Peter was established with a manager by the name of David de Yong. Tim wanted to be represented by David, too, and tried very hard, only to be rejected.

In the fullness of time, I left John Reid's office and retired at the grand old age of 30 from the music business. I went to live in Scotland, in Edinburgh, with an antique dealer, Ed Murray. Tim visited us several times in Scotland and we saw him often in London. I have no diary for these years and my memory is not good for this time of change and withdrawal. Had Tim harboured any thoughts of being managed by me, I was no longer in a position to be able to fulfil any such ambition, but I was a still a good listener and a good facilitator, and by any other name might still be thought of as management. But free advice never comes cheap…

However, in November 1977, I did start to keep a journal, of which the following are extracts. Ed and I moved down from Edinburgh to a large country house in six acres of park and gardens near Bath. Tim had gradually become closer. To us both.

MONDAY 31 OCTOBER 1977
It was moving-in day. We arrived at Homewood on the dot of 8:30 in the morning… Tim arrived at midday. What a friend! By evening we had a lot of furniture in place… It is home. I love it. A feeling of cosy wisdom seems to lurk in every corner.

Tuesday 1 November
Tim decided to stay all week and the family seems complete... Early to bed, early to rise. As Tim says, Kate Hepburn hours.

Saturday 12 November
Tim and Minns [Freddie Mercury's lover] came down. Lovely to have Tim back... Tim very tired. Too many late nights, I think. He has bought a car. Why? He can't drive... Minns misses Freddie [Mercury] a lot. Three thousand miles is a long way, although apparently the first concert went very well [Queen's 1977 US tour] and Freddie is enjoying the shows. Ha! Wait until the seventh week!

Sunday 13 November
Took Tim back to the station in the evening... Returned and had long chats with Minns – mostly about Freddie and the mysterious Clodagh Wallace... What does she want to do? I know she wants as much to do with Tim as possible, but as agent? As manager?

Monday 14 November
Ed and I drove up to London with Minns... Had drinks with Clodagh and Jason [Wallace] and collected Tim's little Honda car, which we have agreed to park/garage for him. Clodagh had arranged for it to be serviced and then insured for me to drive. Hope that Tim will start to learn to drive when he comes back from JP Donleavy's in Ireland. I wonder if he will do the play or not? It seems that any piece based on The Beastlies can hardly be Beefy's play... Clodagh told us that Tim might be going to America in December. We shall see... Minns is flying out to see Freddie on 1 December. He and Tim will be in New York at the same time...

Thursday 17 November
Tim rang to say that he might have to go to Los Angeles on Monday. His meeting with Jerry Moss had gone very well and Moss wanted him to start as quickly as possible on recording with producer Bob Ezrin. Tim said he will try and come down on Sunday for the day. We will

miss him if he goes. He'd be away at least two months if he does begin recording immediately. [Tim was in the throes of buying a new apartment in a mansion block overlooking the River Thames at Putney Bridge. It was rather a dark, gloomy old place which he intended to thoroughly redecorate. His mood was Presbyterian and pine and pastel taupe at the time. Stripped Presbyterian and stripped pine. And definitely nothing in pink.]

FRIDAY 25 NOVEMBER
Tim flew off to New York today. He sounded much better on the phone, although there is some huge new hassle to do with his flat...

FRIDAY 2 DECEMBER
Had a lovely telephone call from Tim, who is now in Los Angeles. He says he'll be back in London by the 8th.

MONDAY 12 DECEMBER
Clodagh called. Tim had asked her to ring to say he wouldn't be back in London until at least the end of this week but that Minns would be returning from his trip to see Freddie in America on Wednesday... Must start reading all those gardening books of Tim's. I have a feeling I shall be needing them! I have a feeling Tim ain't gonna be here much to help!

FRIDAY 16 DECEMBER
Tim came back today but no call as yet. I have to admit, after calling in at Clodagh's yesterday, all my old music-biz feelings came flooding back. Tim's apparently almost definitely going to have to tour in America. If he does, I don't mind confessing I wouldn't mind having a hand in it somewhere. I miss it...

MONDAY 19 DECEMBER
Tim called to say he'd be down on Boxing Day evening on the train. His flat completion is apparently on Tuesday. What has he lumbered himself with? He says that he is to return to New York about 20 January to work with [Bob] Ezrin on material for the album for six

weeks. Plan is to then record in Toronto with the album coming out in May/June and live shows in June/July. No manager, no organisation, and on top of that he says he will have to rent out his flat for three or four months as it is costing him over 80 quid a week. Is he mad or does he so want to exorcise the rock 'n' roll ghosts that he doesn't care about diving headfirst into a bucket of blood?

Monday 26 December
Drove up to London and collected Tim from Clodagh's. He had apparently hitch-hiked down the A1 from Lincolnshire! That's what I like in a star – style!

Tuesday 27 December
Tim seems very nervous and restless… I got Ed to talk a little. He agrees in the end that there is 'an atmosphere' that isn't quite right. But, as long as we are aware of it, we shall overcome… The Ardens, the whole family – Don, Mrs, David and Sharon – who were supposed to be coming down today, never arrived. Papa's Roller blew up on the motorway. Horrors!

Wednesday 28 December
Bit of a row between Ed and me in the morning as I was determined to get OUT and spend the day poking around Bath with Tim. We did go and had a lovely day. TC found his old chiropractor and had a bit of a pummel. That old back strain from *Rocky* still takes its toll. Afterwards we took his theatre prints in to be framed.

Saturday 31 December 1977
Dug up all the dahlias. Planted a couple of rows of iris tubers. Replanted some pinks… We decided to hole up and go nowhere… Tim called to say Happy New Year. Freddie had called earlier, too… We seem a long way away from the other real world…

Monday 9 January 1978
7:15 departure for London… Went on to see Tim. The flat, I must

admit, looks lovely; he has really worked very hard... I still feel, however, that his commitment to A&M will have to be encouraged by everyone, and we shall wait to see if his yen for the theatre and film will either balance or outweigh his desire to be a rock star. And whether, he out of all of them, will be allowed the luxury of the crossover!

Friday 13 January
Tim called to say that there is a possibility of his not going to the US, as A&M have not yet concluded a producer's deal with Bob Ezrin. He is obviously reluctant to go away so soon after having done so much hard work in his new flat...

Monday 23 January
We delivered Tim's wretched pine plate warmer cupboard, his blind and the framed theatrical prints. He confided, too, that he was all but completely broke and that, even after doing the A&M album in the States, he is still going to be broke at the end of it. Jeez. He really has to start earning some money to keep this huge edifice he's started going. Sad to have to admit, but it was not an uplifting visit. I was really worried for him...

Saturday 4 February
...and so drove up to London to Tim's, where we all changed to go to the birthday party that Freddie had arranged for Minns.

Richard O'Brien was there – as crazy as ever but, as genius he undoubtedly is, then crazy he'll probably remain. Chris Malcolm was also there – the original Brad in *Rocky Horror* – and he comes down to Somerset, apparently, with his girlfriend, whose parents live there and so said he'll give us a call when they're next coming down. Party was at Shezam – food, normally so good there, was meagre and lifeless under banqueting conditions. But always good service. Sat next to Sarah Harrison and had good gossip with her and then Clodagh, on my right, also poured out her sad soul about Peter Straker. She wants to sack him as a client. (And replace him with Tim?) So, 'the family' gathered for yet another birthday. One day it will gather for its first funeral. I wonder whose it will be? There's bound to be a party afterwards. It's in the way of families...

Tim off to New York on Monday.

Wednesday 1 March
Lovely joint phone call from Tim and Minns in New York. (Who paid, I wonder?) Both seem well... Tim said he was going to LA for a couple of weeks and probably won't be back in London until they have done a month in the studio for basic tracks and vocals.

Monday 27 March
Tim called from LA to say that he would be back in England either tomorrow or Thursday for a while as Bob Ezrin has gall bladder trouble and the Toronto recording schedule has been postponed from 10 April to 10 May...

Sunday 2 April
Drove all the way into Temple Meads in Bristol to collect Tim's friends, Brooke Adams and her 'lover', John. Strange way to be introduced, I fancied. He's a morose Californian. A real pain. I felt that Brooke, a very natural girl for an actress, would have been better without him. We went for a 'run' in the car, although the occupants were so smashed that I doubt if they will remember anything we showed them... After taking the Americans into Bath to catch the train back to London, we went to the pub in Hinton and then the Garrick's Head in Bath singing songs from the musicals in the car. Great night!

Had a long chat with Tim in the course of the evening about him touring. He listened and says he doesn't want to but I intuit that A&M will MAKE him tour. He still doesn't understand the record business. He doesn't WANT to enough. Want to WANT to. I hear echoes of the Brian Protheroe/Chrysalis saga... He wants to be an actor AND a recording artist. The record company don't trust this. They WANT him, nay INSIST that he commits. It never happened for Brian Protheroe, either...

Now Tim tells us that he is joining the National Theatre next year.

Like I said, we shall see which side wins out, the footlights or the bright lights.

TUESDAY 18 APRIL
Tim called from Toronto very happy with the progress on the album. Clodagh is due to fly out there tomorrow for his birthday as well as Jerry Moss and Jim Beach (who had just taken over management of Freddie and Queen).

SATURDAY 29 APRIL
Bob and Francesca Ezrin came with Curry and were MUCH more fun! Tim looked very tired. Cooked a big dinner in the evening and we all went out to the George at Norton St Phillip for a drink. Had a good chat with Ezrin and Francesca, who seem nice people and not totally steeped in 'the business'. Tim seemed bored and very quiet. 'You get a bit fed up hearing about trumpets,' he confessed to Ed. And his line 'I get the feeling we're making a hit record' is more one from a corny Presley movie or a scene from *Happy Days*.

FRIDAY 5 MAY
Ed gave me so much stick today over the Tim Curry entourage arriving last weekend. So now what to do? Minns has just called and asked if he could bring Margaret Trudeau down for the weekend [the then recently ex-First Lady of Canada].

SUNDAY 21 MAY
After the family [my mother and father] had gone, I drove up to London to John Reid's party... Really surprised to see Tim there, just back from Toronto, although I should have known that he would have come back for Tom Stoppard's *fête-champêtre*, to which Peter Wood and entourage were also going. Tim asked me to go outside with him and he played me three of his tracks in Clodagh's car. I liked the third one, entitled 'Birds Of A Feather Flock Together, Yes They Do'. Yes! They do! I opined that I thought it needed lots of backing vocals, some jangling rock 'n' roll piano and t'could be a hit. He was

desperately insisting I turn my attention to the words. I think they must have been his. I have to admit I felt privileged that he wanted me to hear the songs before anyone else...or was I the only person available to hear them?

THURSDAY 1 JUNE
At the Cannes Film Festival, Curry's film *The Shout* had a special prize and he is mentioned in all the reviews, even though his part was small...

TUESDAY 13 JUNE
Tim as Will Shakespeare was our treat of the evening at nine o'clock... It's all *Portrait Of The Artist As A Young Man* stuff but the casting is all good, which gets it over the tittiness of John Mortimer's script. I don't know what it will do for Tim but I suppose it can't do him any harm. 'Aspiring Rock Icon Takes Quality Time Out For Shakespeare' isn't quite how *Billboard* might interpret our hero's career...but I liked it.

SATURDAY 8 JULY
I must remember to send a card to Timmy, who has his first concert on the 16th...

TUESDAY 18 JULY
Freddie called from Montreux in the evening and reminded us about Tim's last appearance as Shakespeare...

FRIDAY 28 JULY
...then went into Bath at 5:40 to collect Minns and Tim from the train. Tim looks well, slimmer and obviously over the moon about his successful shows in California. The record is also very good. Tim's vocal performances are all very good and Bob Ezrin has really excelled himself. He must be a minor genius...

SATURDAY 29 JULY
Our new friend Robert Thomas, the antique dealer, came over along

with his friend Christopher (a shop assistant from Cardiff – oh, it's all too Dylan Thomas to be true!)

After walking around the park, we had dinner. Tim must think he's in some kind of glass cage. He is suddenly SO conscious of his semi-stardom, so covetous of it and yet so fearful of being recognised and pinned down because of it. If only some macho-being would pin HIM down and beat out of him who he REALLY is.

First with Ed and later with me, we heard paranoid ravings about 'being recognised'. And yet he was the one on the phone on Thursday who wanted to go out and 'behave badly in Bristol'. It really is unbearable – the protection one has to give people like Tim Curry (or Freddie or any publicly known friend) takes away from the enjoyment of being with them anywhere other than in the privacy of a non-oriented restaurant or in one's own home.

SUNDAY 6 AUGUST
Watched Tim in *City Sugar* – a very good play and a great performance, I must admit...

MONDAY 28 AUGUST
Bank holiday and a good lot of sunshine, too... Robert, Chris and a friend of theirs, Kevin, a florist from Bloxwich in Birmingham, came over. We took the horses and rode through Friary Wood. At least, the Welsh rode. The assorted friendly foreigners walked behind. Surprisingly lovely day...and we went on to the Oasis [a gay dancing club in Bristol]. Tim and I had a long talk about his career, of course, but there's nothing more I can say to him in my role as...as what? Surrogate manager? Friend? He needs to make up his mind what shape he wants the structure surrounding him to take. No wonder he feels insecure and unsure. To do what he is doing and wants to do, he has to have an organisation around him. At the moment, he's shouldering everything himself. I think he knows the theory all right – he should do; he's been watching and studying long enough. He knows he NEEDS proper integrated management! His problem is committing to what he has all but in name chosen. I think his is a problem of ultimately trusting...

Oh, to bed… Please, dear God, to bed!

WEDNESDAY 30 AUGUST
I stayed in bed whilst Ed very kindly took Tim back into the station for the 8:12 back to London and, for him, reality. Laden with a bundle of old weeds from the country meadows.

THURSDAY 31 AUGUST
The swallows darted about the house for an hour this evening, waiting for the final rallying call that would take them southwards to Africa. They left and the summer was suddenly gone. I went out and called aloud to them: 'Come back… Come back!' I felt like crying for a minute but I didn't. So much seems to be flying away at the moment…

THURSDAY 28 DECEMBER 1978
Minns and I went off to Beaulieu to spend the day with Clodagh at her cottage. Ed decided to stay at home, which I think was a wise decision as Tim Curry was still there having spent Christmas with the Wallace family. Although he gave me a very nice blue and white soup plate, I have to say that I too have lost much of my close feeling for him… Drove Tim up to a pub in Beaulieu for cigarettes. He told me that he was going back to the States to make another album and do a tour in late summer. Oh, well. That's showbiz…

THURSDAY 25 JANUARY 1979
Spoke to Clodagh, who sent love from Tim…

FRIDAY 2 MARCH
After months of argument and acrimony, I finally left my partner, Ed Murray, and the beautiful house at Homewood Park forever. I really needed people then, friends to help me over what was going to be a bleak and difficult time.

Although I telephoned Tim several times, I never got through. Nor did he ever once call me. It was as though I had been excommunicated. I understand that Tim remained in touch with Ed for some time and even visited Homewood again. I only saw Tim once more, in the street in Covent Garden, when he was being the Pirate King in *The Pirates Of Penzance*. When I asked if he still had the same telephone number, he replied, 'Sure. Do use it.' After such a warm invitation, I decided there wouldn't be a lot of point, for either of us...

I understand that Tim has decided to distance himself as far as possible from the *Rocky Horror* phenomenon. It has been widely remarked that he rarely refers to his role as Frank, and when someone else does he appears to find it irritating, infuriating or embarrassing, depending on the company he is in and how far he feels he can express his displeasure.

I have a photo of him as Frank N Furter taken by Johnny Dewe-Matthews in the first few days of the show's opening at the Royal Court. In one of the spotlight beams, he has written 'To David' with the addition of an X. A kiss. In the other, he has written 'Recognition at Last, love Tim XXX.'

AFTERTHOUGHTS
29 OCTOBER 1999, RESEARCHING THIS BOOK
I've been thinking about him more and more and why he didn't make it as a rock 'n' roller in the mid to late 1970s, when he had all the big guns firing on his side. His voice...something about his voice.

I always remember Freddie Mercury explaining that to be a rock singer you had to sing in a very stretched register, to push your performance to the edges of your vocal range. He also explained that a natural-register voice – like the one he used on a song on *Barcelona*, where Montserrat Caballé insisted he try singing in his natural register – isn't necessarily exciting when recorded; he demonstrated that singing 'strained' makes the recorded sound more vibrant, arresting, and consequently creates an entirely different performance concomitant to the effect required of the medium. The vocal performance has to sound equally great on all sorts of speakers – home stereo, disco, concert mega-volume and via radio airplay.

Tim's natural voice, which he used as Frank, was not exciting *per se*. His performance and his magnetic presence were exciting, but not the voice, not in a 'recorded' sense. He never changed his register, never shrieked, never strained for a note. Result, coupled with all the other negative aspects of his personality, attitude, and commercial and organisational situation, Tim's was not a rock 'n' roll persona that people who hadn't seen the show could take to their hearts.

And then there was his material:

'Darkness has conquered'

Tossing and turning the other night, pondering on this *Rocky* book, I think I finally understood something about Tim. Freddie always said that the rock star in him was a different person, a character he played. Mister Mercury, he called him. I think Tim used his other person to play Frank and therefore couldn't use him to play Tim Curry, Rock Star! If that is true, if I were Tim, I suppose I would hate Frank, too, because it could be seen that Frank screwed things for Tim. Frank was fixed in eternity, immutable, undevelopable. The audiences who came to see Tim live in concert would also want a blast of Frank and the undeclared Tim couldn't find another character able to deal with Frank. Who could?

As a codicil, should you require amusement on some long, dull evening, try playing the Casting Game. Just who else could play Frank N Furter now in any remake of *The Rocky Horror Picture Show*? Some names mentioned have been Robert Downey Jr, Alan Rickman, Alfred Molina, Gary Oldman, Guy Pearce, Johnny Depp, Kevin Spacey, Joseph Fiennes. But, after much discussion, the only name that emerged as unassailable was that of...*Robbie Williams!*

<<<<irememberdoingthetimewarpiremememberdoingthetimewarpi>>>>

6 'In Another Dimension, With Voyeuristic Intention'
A Celluloid Jam

The scheduling of the movie focused the Midas perspectives of participants and producers alike. It expanded the parameters of the concept of the original show and, by bringing on board more alien castaways from Transylvania, rebranded the *Rocky* phenomenon as *The Rocky Horror Picture Show*. The making of the film occupied an eight-week schedule from 21 October 1974 until Friday 13 December 1974 – hardly an auspicious date. The finished product premiered in London at the Rialto cinema on 14 August 1975 after a series of disastrous pre-screenings in the United States.

To make the unreal real and yet maintain the unreality – there was the rub. It was some brief. Film involves the work of professionals whose expertise essentially bears the hallmark of anonymity. Onstage, it doesn't matter whether the actors' make-up can be seen from the third row; it doesn't suspend the suspension of disbelief if a wooden scenery flat flaps in the wake of a stout party's exit; in a movie, the audience must never, ever see the joins, unless the joins are meant to be seen.

So, it's good to be able to pay tribute to some of that team of seamless technocrats whose contribution brought *Rocky* to the mortal earthlings in the cheaper seats.

‹‹‹‹‹irememberdoingthetimewarpirememberdoingthetimewarpi›››››

Terry Ackland Snow

16 September 1999
'Brad, what kind of a place is this?'

DAVID EVANS: *What was the background to you doing* Rocky?

TERRY ACKLAND SNOW: I worked on the film of *Tommy* as assistant art director. John Comfort was the production manager and John Clark was the art director. I got on with them very well. When it finished, John Comfort and John Clark were going on to do *The Rocky Horror Picture Show*. John Clark was involved in a lot of architectural work and, in the end, Clark decided not to do *Rocky*, to pursue his other interests so he very kindly recommended me to John Comfort to be the art director. So, *Rocky* was my first film as art director in my own right and I was 29 years old. That's exactly how it happened. I went in, got the job and had a budget of £75,000. I went to the film finance people for them at Twentieth Century Fox, which was headed by Peter Beale in England.

DE: *Did you know what you were getting into? Had you seen the show onstage?*

TAS: I'd seen the show once, before I started to work on it. By the end of my stint on it, I'd seen it a total of nine times, I think, to get a real feel of it. Of course, they let me have free tickets! I think the technicians were encouraged to see the play. I certainly thought it was important for people to understand what we were doing. I would take the crew, people like Ben Fencham, the painter. He's dead now.

DE: *And the working atmosphere? What were the producers like?*

TAS: The producers worked out of Bray Studios. I dealt a lot with John Comfort. It was very consultative, though. I remember Jim Sharman asking if I could put a ceiling across this certain scene. 'Yes I can' was my reply.

Can, but couldn't. Money.

I went to Michael White and told him that there wasn't enough money to do it. Michael asked if I had told Jim that and I said that it wasn't my job to tell him that. He asked me if Jim's scheme was possible. It was. I could do the work and get the people to do the work, but I can't do it without paying them. Fair do's to Michael. He said, 'If you need the ceiling, you've got to have the ceiling.'

DE: Did you know the film almost never happened? That on the weekend prior to shooting, Fox almost pulled the plug?

TAS: That is something I never knew about. But then, it shows you what a good producer is, because if that did happen, if we had known about it, we all would have had a big problem with it. We would not have had our hearts in it.

DE: It was Brian Thomson's first film, too, wasn't it? Something of a quantum leap for a stage designer to be designing a film.

TAS: Brian Thomson certainly gave me the designs and ideas; I just took them on board and got it all organised. I worked quite well and quite closely with Brian. I know that Brian went to New York to do the show there and left the film. Everyone's ideas were always in our minds. After all, we had all the pictures and the records. But there were no storyboards for *Rocky*. None at all. Brian did his ideas and it was up to me to carry them out. I knew everything about film-making. What you could get away with, which lenses would suit, etc. I got on well with Jim Sharman as well. I don't mean to be detrimental at all to Brian, but I always felt that, if I hadn't done a first-class good job, Brian would never have gone to New York. I elaborated on his designs. Of course. That's what I was there for, to achieve what I felt was the best possible. We had a great team, too. Ben Fencham I've said about. Dick Frift. Ian Whittaker. Bob Spencer. Colin Chilvers on the special effects and, of course, Wally Veevers. He was the brains.

I worked with Helen Lennox the other day. She was one of the make-up team.

DE: *Was there a lot of decision-making 'on the hoof'?*

TAS: The church, in the opening scene. It was my idea to put it where it was. At that particular time, there were trees and bushes and a field beyond it. We had the famous drawing of it ['American Gothic' by Grant Wood] and we reproduced it. The interior was inside a small stage in Bray Studios. If you notice, they shot the exteriors from the side, to give it that 'dead man's area'.

DE: *What is this 'dead man's area'?*

TAS: It's a term I use. To get through continuity problems with the design of the set. When characters enter and exit, basically. They exit from one set and, in another set-up, they enter from what the audience has to think is the same place. So, you have them exiting by turning a corner or going through a door, or you have some architectural detail visible in both set-ups. In this particular case of *Rocky*, there was a little bit of the house architecture showing on the ballroom side of the enter–exit interface.

I went to Oakley Court, which was there anyway, and it was the right type of follyish building, right next to Bray Studios. I think I went over there on my own to look at it. What was apparent at that time was that the first and second floors were very dangerous. There was dry rot to the point where you could see through other rooms. Where you see Riff Raff at the window, we had to put boards up there so he could walk up to it. It was a dilapidated house, and inside we wanted to put the lift, which we used, in the laboratory. We went up through the centre of Oakley Court and through the gallery and continued up to the geodesic dome, which was supposed to be the top of the laboratory. The idea was that it would all be black and white and then, when you went up into the lab, it all changed colour.

DE: So a lot changed along the way?

TAS: Jim was very interested and involved. I think it was a learning experience for Jim and Brian. I've worked with many first-time directors, and I believe in the film industry. I believe that you've got to give as much help as you can to everybody, use your own expertise to improve other people's. Originally, Brian Thomson and Jim Sharman wanted a Wall of Death in the laboratory for Meat Loaf to ride his motorbike around. That was almost impossible, especially for shooting. I don't quite remember how, but I came up for the idea of the ramp. When we did the tiles, the construction manager said to me that he'd done these eight-feet-by-four-feet sheets of six-inch tiles, in pink. I said, 'No.'

He didn't understand because, doing it his way, we'd be saving so much money. I wanted the tiles to be different colours. Sometimes you can see, on real walls, they are different colours. It's absolutely subtle, but it's there. Also, I wanted them all put on individually. It was a big set! I know it was quick to put the sheets up, but it was not what I wanted to do. So we had two machines cutting out six-inch pieces of hardboard, bevelling them off. The painters were told to paint some of them in one colour of pink, the others in another shade. Then I wanted them all mixed up, and then to have them put up one at a time. I have a great belief in getting things as real as possible.

DE: Any hairy moments?

TAS: We put a lamp too close to that tank that Rocky was born in and cracked the glass when it was full of water. We had to drain it and replace it. And the lift caused us problems. It was pneumatic, run on compressed air, because it was cheaper. The air compressor was outside the building and hoses were run in.

SM: Isn't this a flaw in the film? While they are going up in the lift, some hosing can clearly be seen on the floor in front of the lift.

TAS: Well, the lift actually broke down in the laboratory, with the cast in it. The cast were very good about it. It stopped halfway. It was rectified. And, of course, it had safety shoes on it.

DE: *The proximity of Oakley Court must have been a great bonus, especially to you guys in the art department.*

TAS: I copied the entire look of Oakley Court for the sets. I used the detail of the arches, of the windows, and all that sort of architectural style, but we made them four times bigger.

SM: *Can I ask you about little details?*

TAS: Sure.

SM: *The clock?*

TAS: The clock was in the house. And the dome? We did actually build a dome. In those days, we never had CGI or computer graphics. What you see onscreen was a fibreglass geodesic dome. We had to crane it up to the roof. The diameter was about 25 feet. We constructed it. Then, when we needed to reproduce it in the interior of the laboratory, we just used painted stars overhead. I was in Egypt and saw the stars on the ceiling of some of the tombs, so I used that idea.

SM: *And what about locations?*

TAS: A great belief of mine is to go to the local shops when you've chosen a vague area and pick up postcards. Those have got to be one of the best shots of the locality. If you are on top of it, you won't see it. You have to get down into the places. Know about the potential. I used to take my kids to a picnic area called Marlow Woods on Marlow Common. What was stunning about it were these tall, tall trees, with no undergrowth. That's what you saw in the film when Brad and Janet were driving through in the woods, when the motorcycles come past them. I used the same location in *Batman* as well. It's fairly near Bray.

SM: *The swimming pool must have been a big headache?*

TAS: The colours of the Michelangelo on the pool bottom all had to be different from the original, because it was to be seen through water. Bob Spencer painted it. The colours were more vibrant and we had to take into consideration the green of the water. We painted the perimeter step gold to make it look like a frame. They really wanted that RKO tower, but we had to get permission from Lucille Ball. It was a tightrope situation. At one time we were going to use the BBC logo as a back-up, the Alexandra Palace thing. When we finally got permission and were able to build the tower, stuntmen were involved and everything like that. There was no water in the tank at the time we were rehearsing with it. The stuntman said, 'No problem at all.' He went up, down it went and he just landed on some sacks.

DE: *Any other trade secrets?*

TAS: Meat Loaf and the motorcycle were covered in hot candle wax that we sprayed on to look like snow – the ice from the cold room. I used spray snow for touch-ups. And we put together those plaster casts for the statue scene. The biggest thing was the wheelchair; we sprayed it with liquid cement. It was the only thing that took shape. Those statues of David had to be sculpted, and it wasn't that easy. They were mirrors of each other, one left and one right. Same as Janet. We moulded Susan Sarandon's face but didn't necessarily use her body.

You know, I watched the film yesterday and I cringed when I saw the glass bricks we used in the laboratory. In the 1930s it was quite fashionable, but now everyone has them. I did think, 'That's a bloody good film. It gets better all the time.'

DE: *There are some who say the film wasn't a success because there was no reality about it.*

TAS: But the entire concept of the original show is unreal. I mean, take the laboratory. How often do you go into a house that has a laboratory like that? I knew that I tried to make it look as real as it could. Had to.

I was absolutely pleased that this was my first film as art director. I was overwhelmed by it. I'm a bit of a sentimentalist, really. When I finally see the finished product, because we usually only see the rushes at the time, it's like seeing something come to life, and it's better than you think. I went away from that set thinking, 'I'm really happy with that.' If I were able to change anything now, due to technical advancements, it would definitely be the television monitors on which you see the various approaching characters. It was a very complicated system to achieve that effect on the monitors, and now it's much easier. I have a feeling that we had to do live television when Doctor Scott was coming up the stairs. That was *live*, two sets of action going on at the same time. These days also, computer-generated imaging could make things like the house blowing up at the end different. But we must not forget how old the film is and we had to work with what was around at the time. Budget-wise, I don't think I would have done much different if it was now. Maybe I would have done more of the night rain sequence. We wet the trees, you know, and that picked up the lights, gave it that effect.

DE: *And what did you think would happen to it when it was released?*

TAS: I absolutely did not think it would be a hit. Not like it is now. I think it's unique. Nothing I've seen is like it. It's a very brave thing to have done. I am so happy that it is successful.

I would love the pleasure of saying that I designed *The Rocky Horror Picture Show* but I didn't. But it was the biggest break I ever had. It takes a chance for a person like John Comfort to give me a break like *Rocky*. And then there's the people you work with. I remember asking Dick Frift – who at the time was one of the top set construction managers in the world – if he knew anyone that was a construction manager that could help me with this picture.

He said, 'I do know someone.'

Rocky's script

THE
ROCKY HORROR
PICTURE SHOW

PETER HINWOOD

A SCREENPLAY BY JIM SHARMAN AND RICHARD O'BRIEN

Adapted from "The Rocky Horror Show" a musical
with Book, Music & Lyrics by Richard O'Brien

18th July, 1974.

Richard O'Brien, the man who started it all, *circa* 1969

Richard O'Brien, aged about 18, New Zealand

Richard O'Brien, unknown and Pat Quinn on steps

Director Jim Sharman, 1973

11 Oakington Road, where *The Rocky Horror Show* was created and Kimi and Richard lived

The Royal Court Theatre on Sloane Square, London. The theatre upstairs is where *The Rocky Horror Show* premiered in June 1973

Richard Hartley at Brian Thomson and Perry Bedden's typical Sunday-lunch gathering, 1973. Note the T-shirt's Olympic Studios legend, where the film's soundtrack was recorded

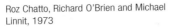

Roz Chatto, Richard O'Brien and Michael Linnit, 1973

Tim at Sunday lunch, 1974

Tim as Frank – inscribed 'Recognition at last – Love Tim xx'

Tim and Jane Cameron at Tim's PA in
New York, 1974

Sarm Studios, where the original London cast
recorded the music with Jonathan King

John Sinclair from Sarm studios, 1973

Michael White and Lindall Hobbs, 1974

Richard O'Brien and Jim Sharman outside the Hard Rock Café in London, 1974

Nell strikes a pose in Charing Cross Road, London, 1974

Tim and Perry at Nell's flat in Charing Cross Road, London. The mouse ears are Nell's. Brian thought that Columbia should wear them, too

Richard O'Brien having fun with Dr Scott's wig, 1974

Michael White, Lou Adler and Richard O'Brien in the Green Room, New York City, March 1975

Richard O'Brien and Lou Adler (on the phone) at Lou's Malibu home

Brian Thomson, Perry Bedden and Linus O'Brien in New York, March 1975

Kim Milford and Tim on stage in New York City, 1974

Richard O'Brien, John Sinclair and Andy Leighton on the UCLA campus, March 1974

Happier days – Richard O'Brien and Brian Thomson in Los Angeles, March 1974

Kimi and Ritz at Broderick Crawford's star on the Hollywood Walk Of Fame

Tim posing for the Sunset Boulevard Billboard and film picture disc, March 1974

Tim Curry outside the Roxy on LA's Sunset Strip, preparing for the opening, March 1974

Tim and Richard Hartley

A rising star –
Tim, the Christmas
angel, 1974

Pat Quinn reading the NYC playbill, 1975

Meat Loaf at the Roxy in Los Angeles, 1974

Peter
Hinwood,
coverman,
March
1967

THE LEADING BRITISH BODYBUILDING MAGAZINE

MAN'S WORLD

and REG PARK JOURNAL

1967
MARCH
2/6

Brian Thomson's original model of Frank and Rocky's wedding bed, 1974

Brian Thomson's original model of the Denton church interior, 1974

Susan and Barry enjoying the party,
October 1974

Barry Bostwick at Perry Bedden's surprise
birthday party, October 1974

Meat Loaf at
Perry's surprise
party

Sue Blane and Jim Sharman

A toast! Richard O'Brien at Perry's party

MICHAEL WHITE PRODUCTIONS LIMITED

C A L L   S H E E T   NO: 28

PRODUCTION: *THE ROCKY HORROR PICTURE SHOW   DATE: Tuesday 26 November
                                                            1 9 7 4
DIRECTOR: JIM SHARMAN   UNIT CALL: 9.00 am Stage 1

SET: INT. BALLROOM   SCENE NOS: 41,43,45,46,47complete
                                                                48,50,52,53

ARTISTE	CHARACTER	D/R	P/UP	M/UP/HAIR	ON SET
BARRY BOSTWICK	BRAD	5	7.30	8.15	9.00
SUSAN SARANDON	JANET	3	6.30	7.30	9.00
RICHARD O'BRIEN	RIFF RAFF	4	6.30	7.30	9.00
PATRICIA QUINN	MAGENTA	6	6.15	7.30	9.00
NELL CAMPBELL	COLUMBIA	6	6.15	7.30	9.00

TRANSYLVANIANS

ARTISTE	CHARACTER		M/UP/HAIR	ON SET
ANNABEL LEVENTON	ISHAQ BUX	)		
FRAN FULLENWIDER	ANTHONY MILNER	)		
IMOGEN CLAIRE	LINDSAY INGRAM	)		
SADIE CORRE	PERRY BEDDEN	)		
GAYE BROWN	TONY THEN	)	7.30	9.00
PAM OBERMEYER	HUGH CECIL	)		
KIMI WONG	STEPHEN CALCUTT	)		
TONY COWAN		)		
PEGGY LEDGER	CHRIS (POOH) BIGGINS))			

STANDINS: for:
ARTISTE	CHARACTER			ON SET
JOHN BIRKENSHAW	Mr. Bostwick	)		
LIZ COKE	Miss Sarandon	)		
DAVE MURPHY	Mr. O'Brien	)		9.00
TUPPENCE	Miss Quinn	)		
ERIKA SIMMONDS	Miss Campbell	)		

EXTRA TALENT:
RUFUS COLLINS	DANCE CONSULTANT		7.30	9.00

REQUIREMENTS

PROPS: As per Script, Banner, practical juke box,

SOUND: Playback *TIME WARP*, Chorus and Song

M/UP/HAIR/WARDROBE: Wet Brad & Janet

DANCE ARRANGEMENTS: DAVID TOGURI and SUE CLAIRE at Studio 9 a.m.
                       GILLIAN GREGORY at Studio 9 a.m.

CATERING: For 70 Unit and 35 Artistes 10 a.m. and 3.30 p.m.
                                           Lunch 1.15p.m. - 2.15 p.m.

RUSHES: On completion of shooting

TRANSPORT: Unit cars as arranged.

DANCE REHEARSALS: PETER HINWOOD (ROCKY) to rehears with SUE CLAIRE
                       from 9 a.m.

                                          MIKE GOWANS
                                          Assistant Director

Call sheet for filming 'The Time Warp', 26 November 1975

Oakley Court in 1999, no longer a dilapidated house but now a successful hotel just across a field from Bray Studios, Windsor

Olympic Studios, where Pink Floyd, Led Zeppelin, Jimi Hendrix, The Rolling Stones, The Beatles, Oasis and the soundtrack to *Rocky Horror* were recorded, 1999

The main stage at Bray Studios, 1999. The wardrobe hut is the small building to the right

Bray Studios, 1999

Sue Blaine at the wardrobe hut at Bray Studios, where the trannies would congregate during the filming. 1974

Peter Hinwood relaxing on set

Trevor White, the voice of Rocky

Hugh Cecil on the set, about to film the
wedding scene

Pat Quinn getting her make-up done

Ishaq Bux

Peggy Ledger

Tony Milner

Henry Woolf

Kimi Wong

Gaye Brown

Pam Obermeyer

Imogen Claire

Stephen Calcutt

Perry Bedden

Rufus Collins

Annabel Leventon

Fran Fullenwider

Lindsay Ingram

Henry Woolf and Ishaq Bux on the film set. Note the Columbia costume in the background

Anthony Milner and Ishaq Bux on the set, 1974. For once, Fran Fullenwider is barely visible

Hugh Cecil, Sadie Corre and Pamela Obermeyer on the set, November 1974

Kimi Wong O'Brien on the set, 1974

Gaye Brown and Kimi Wong O'Brien horsing around, 1974

Richard Hartley, Perry Bedden and Kimi Wong O'Brien rehearsing the song 'If I Ruled The World', 1976

TZ at the Royal Court, 1976

Neil, Richard and
Linus O'Brien, 1976

Lindsay Ingram, 1999

Peter Hinwood (now in the antiques business), London, 1999

Sue Blane preparing to judge a costume contest, 1999

Stephen Calcutt, the tallest Transylvanian, 2002

Pam Obermeyer and Sal Prio at the Rocky Horror
convention, London, 1999

Perry Bedden and Stephen Calcutt reacquainted
in London, 1999

Perry Bedden, Christopher Biggins and Yasmin Pettigrew at a London Rocky Horror convention, 1999

Hugh Cecil, 1999

Sadie Corre now with her costume from the film, which she presented to the author as a gift

Kimi Wong O'Brien

Annabel Leventon and Gaye Brown, 1999

Jonathan Adams, 1999

Perry Bedden and Imogen Claire, 1999

Lady Stephens, the beautiful Patricia Quinn today

The skeleton clock in 2002, to be auctioned at Sotheby's. The description runs as follows: 'An inlaid mahogany coffin-shaped long-face clock. Behind the wheel dial is a human skull and skeleton and decorated crossbones in ivory. The clock belonged to the Countess of Rossalyn, wife of the fifth earl, who is said to have travelled everywhere with it. Rumour is that the skeleton is of the man who was her lover'

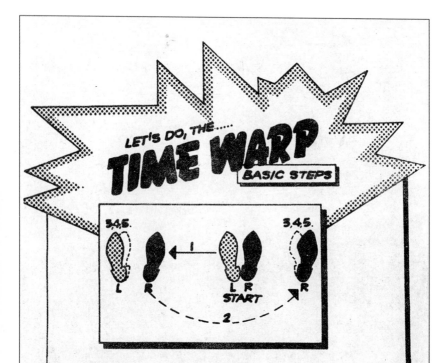

１．両手をあげながら左へ飛ぶ

２．次に右の方へ飛ぶ（タイムウォープの先祖アネッテ・ヒュニセロによるとステップは大きく）

３．両手を腰にあて、ひざをぴったりくっつけて

４．腰骨を突き出す（５回位くりかえすと狂気の道へ導きますよ）

５．腰を振る（４つのステップで狂気の道へ導びかなかったら）

６．また、タイムウォープをくり返そう

※ステップの改造やステップの回数などは気にすることはないのです。

TRANSLATED BY ″HAIR CUT″

AS FEATURED IN 'THE ROCKY HORROR SHOW'

'The Time Warp' in Japanese

'Who?' I asked.

'Me!' he said.

I said, 'I can't ask you! You've worked with John Brian, big people like that. This is not a big budget!' He said, ''Til today, I haven't worked in three months. I'd love to do it!' And of course, with people like Dick, you got the experts to make it all happen.

DE: Did you work with Jim Sharman again?

TAS: I was not asked to work on *Shock Treatment* and, yes, I think I would have liked to. I get quite upset when films are made and I'm not asked to be on them. People ask me which was the best film I ever worked on. The most enjoyable was *The Deep*. We were on the water, out in the Caribbean and the Virgin Islands. That was great. When they ask which is the most successful in the way of 'best', I always answer, first *The Rocky Horror Picture Show*, then *Aliens*, *Batman* and *Superman*. *Rocky* is always first on my CV, as art director.

DE: You still obviously work a lot.

TAS: And I also lecture and teach at Kingston University, on TV and film media. I enjoy teaching people and I enjoy seeing people learning. Like with directors, I always ask for the script. A lot of times, directors will find a location and bring me along. I'll ask for the script and they won't have it with them. They won't have figured in doors and levels, and then they'll come to realise that they have entirely the wrong location. Either the script is wrong or the location is wrong. It has to be one or the other. You have to be sorted out.

DE: So how do you budget a film as art director? That must be the main part of your initial work.

TAS: Well, you read the script. After discussions, you get to know what's in the director's mind, then you assess it. I break down scripts and then I work out the weight of every set, what is worth the money.

Budgeting a film is an art. I get asked my opinion quite a bit. I'm getting wise to that now. They'll get my information and go to someone else with my information. Sometimes they'll even use my name on the proposal. In all fairness, they usually do phone up and ask.

DE: Any favourite stories you tell your students?

TAS: Spielberg taught me to walk around a set with a baseball cap on. He sees the top of his hat as the top of the frame. If you have to move your head to see something, you have to move the camera to see it. Not a bad story, huh?

DE: Do you ever keep souvenirs of your favourite sets?

TAS: I've still got those gravestones today, if you want them.

<<<<irememberdoingthetimewarpiremememberdoingthetimewarpi>>>>

After hearing Terry talk, we felt we had to include the following story, told by Brian Thomson. It concerns the 'on-the-hoof' design-and-build techniques of film-making. It is the acme of pragmatism.

BRIAN THOMSON: During one stressful day, Jim Sharman asked me where the secret passage into the laboratory was. Either I'd forgotten or I'd never known… But there wasn't a secret passage. 'Well, how does Doctor Scott get in?' Jim asked.
    'I don't know. Just push him through the wall!' I snapped back. And that was the story behind one of the best moments in the amazing film, when Doctor Scott comes crashing through the wall.

<<<<irememberdoingthetimewarpiremememberdoingthetimewarpi>>>>

And, of course, the lurking horror only sensed yet never seen in the depths of Castle Furter was given life and form in the phenomenon known as the Transylvanians, Frank and Riff Raff's fellow travellers.

Scott's speciality subject is Transylvania. The Transylvanians were the cool people, but they were the outcasts. And yet they got to wear the clothes and dance that famous dance. It was to research the reality of the Transylvanians that spurred him on to begin these interviews. So, in no particular order, let's meet the Transylvanians.

Christopher Biggins

10 June 1998
'You make me shiver with anticipation'

Scott met with Christopher in his home in Hackney, London, which was then being refurbished. He lives with his partner, Neil. Well known in British showbiz circles and completely pleasant in every way, Christopher began his association with the *Rocky* circle when he played King Herod in *Jesus Christ, Superstar*. He was recently seen as the host of *Gay Date Mate* on Sky One in the UK, as well as in *Absolutely Fabulous – The Last Shout* and the recent video release of *Joseph And The Amazing Technicolour Dreamcoat*. Despite such talents, in *Rocky* he had no lines, and as a Transylvanian he did not sing in the film, only lip-syncing to studio recordings of 'The Time Warp', 'Hot Patootie' and 'Sword Of Damocles'. Biggins, as he is known to everyone, completely embraces his *Rocky Horror* past and showed up at Rocky Con '99 to give everyone a glimpse of just how fit he really is.

The kitchen was therefore the venue for the interview. The rest of the apartment sported many photos of Christopher, some with celebrity friends, including one with Joan Collins, with whom he has a Scrabble-playing relationship. He bubbles with infectious enthusiasm to the extent that he offers answers to questions without having to be asked. With typical panache, he was quick to offer Diet Coke and quiche as immediate refreshment. The gesture also heralded a very generous interview.

CHRISTOPHER BIGGINS: Did you know that the party for *The Rocky Horror Show*'s 25th anniversary was in the Cobden Club? It's the same club where the Ellen DeGeneres' coming-out party took place. I must go to see the show. I hear that Jason Donovan is really very good. It surprised me. He's apparently taken to it like nobody's business. I hear he's having a ball. Do you know, after the Cameron Mackintosh show last night, someone came up to me and said, 'I must tell you, you've been a hero of mine. *Rocky Horror* and *Rentaghost*.' Do you know about *Rentaghost*?' It was a wonderfully eccentric English children's show. Absolutely mad as a hatter. Directed and produced by a mad Irishman called Jeremy Swan. It was another show with a big cult following. I think it's still repeated on Sky. It's about three spooks that come back in costumes of different periods. It's just hysterical.

Scott Michaels: You're said to be a very cooperative interviewee.

CB: Am I? Such a reputation! Have you seen my bio on the *Rocky* website? It is so interesting where they get this information. It's fantastic. Quite incredible.

SM: So you'll set me right?

CB: You should certainly try and speak to Kimi Wong O'Brien. And have you spoken to Imogen Claire yet? Obviously, I'll give you Gaye Brown and Annabel Leventon's numbers. Gaye is the one with the red wig and Annabel had the blonde wig. Peggy Ledger's dead now, sadly. She was wonderful. Incredible. She was getting on when she made the film. She was quite elderly. She really entered into the spirit of it.

SM: You must have been around when it first came out?

CB: I was lucky enough to see *The Rocky Horror Show* about a week after it opened at the Theatre Upstairs, so it was really fantastic. My friend Raynor Bourton, who played Rocky, had a terrible predicament because he got glitter into his foreskin. It swelled to enormous size. He had to wear a huge bandage on it. He was in absolute agony, poor boy. A real nightmare for him. I've seen him since, so he's all right now. No lasting damage!

Chris Malcolm's career, of course, has been long taken over by his producing these new tours and things of *Rocky Horror*. You knew he had that terrible accident, don't you? He's always very pleasant. He was the original Brad, of course. I think he didn't do the movie because he probably thought it was beneath him to play a Transylvanian. I was a friend of Richard's and I knew Jim Sharman because he directed *Jesus Christ, Superstar*, for which I auditioned about ten times. I kept getting called back. In the end, Jim asked for me to be a Transylvanian.

SM: We'd heard Chris Malcolm was offered Ralph Hapshatt and just hung up the phone.

CB: Sounds likely. Not unsurprising. At least he got something out of it, in the end. Do we know how much it's taken money-wise? $250 million, I think. It has to be one of the biggest-grossing English films? Maybe because it's Fox, it doesn't count. Is it Lou Adler and Michael White that make the money? And O'Brien, of course. I wonder if Jim Sharman got a percentage? Do you know what Richard sold it for? A pittance, I imagine. I wonder if he gets anything from the film? I would have thought that, because the film made so much money, it would have been a nice gesture to share the wealth with the actors.

SM: You must have known most of these people from the London theatre scene at the time?

CB: Most, yes. Nell was from Australia, though, and I think Sharman knew her; that's why she was asked to do it. She's now in New York with her nightclub, Nell's.

SM: I think you must have a very good memory of the filming. Someone said that there was a bit of cliqueiness about...?

CB: I would have thought there was more of a problem because of the drugs. Pam Obermeyer was nice. The filming was actually great and such fun. We were stoned every day. It was extraordinary. Drugs everywhere. Everyone was so nice, like a real family. The only person who was a bit iffy was Barry. And Susan. They were a little aloof and didn't join in with everybody else. It was no surprise that she went on to be such a big star. I thought she was wonderful in *Rocky Horror*.

We did all the filming at Bray Studios. The wedding scene was at Bray. The interiors as well. We had to drive out every day. It was a real bore. I had a van at the time and I would pick up Sadie [Corre]. She had so much energy. It was like 5:30 or 6 in the morning, and I was dazed. I could hardly drive, let alone listen to conversation.

We all made £100 a week, during the filming. It was for ten weeks, I think, £1,000 total. I went out and bought a sofa-bed at the end of the run, which I needed for my flat.

I must say that the filming was all very professionally done, but there were all sorts of precarious things going on. It wasn't exactly the biggest-budget shoot I've ever come across. I don't think they would get away with doing it nowadays. They weren't as safety conscious as they could have been. We were quite high up, and it was quite a set. It was easy to have an accident. Especially with Sadie. She was about 56 at the time, and Peggy was getting on. They were treating them as spry young things, like us! [Laughs] Having said that, it was really good fun.

SM: There was a rumour that it wasn't you in the film as the Transylvanian but Meat Loaf in drag.

CB: Oh no! *Really?* How funny. Meat Loaf was absolutely adorable. I never met anyone as nice as Meat Loaf. He was really, really fun, charming, professional. I liked him enormously. I can understand why women find him attractive. He's like a big bear. There is quite a sexuality about him. I've never experienced it myself, but I can see how people could. But he doesn't turn me on. Pat Quinn told me a story about Meat Loaf getting hurt – I think it was Meat Loaf – when he crashed through the ice from the vault.

SM: It was actually Ken Shepherd, a stuntman.

CB: Oh. Well, I think he cut himself while crashing through that glass on the motorbike. We all stopped filming for the day and I think he had stitches. Are you going to talk with Tim?

SM: *I wish. Maybe the day hell freezes over...*

CB: Tim is being odd about the *Rocky Horror* thing. If it wasn't for *Rocky Horror*, he wouldn't be where he is today. He was, without a doubt, sensational. He gave the performance of a lifetime and I don't think he's ever given another performance as great as that role. He is superb and he's done really well for himself. I didn't think he was very good in *Annie*, the film, and I can't think of anything he's done since that I thought was as brilliant. It's odd to forget your roots.

SM: *Are you a fan of the movie?*

CB: Me? I could even show it to you, if you like. [He does so, on video, and comments as the action plays.]

Costumes? They were all made for us. There might have been a problem with Sadie being so small. I was in the wedding scene. I've seen the movie three or four times. There I am on the left, with the dark suit, with glasses. There's Fran, there's Gaye. There I am in the left-hand corner with Gaye, and then we run after the car. I think the others were just extras, really...

When Tim sings 'I'm Going Home', I think I'm in that, in the theatre, though I can't remember. I think I was here for this. No, I don't think any of us were. But I don't recognise anyone. I think it happened after the ten weeks. Then those were just extras probably because they [the producers] wouldn't pay us another £100...

SM: *Did you know you are the focus of a legendary flaw in the film, where Fran feeds you the same éclair twice?*

CB: No, no. *Really?* How funny. Aaah, look! Peter Hinwood... He was as...well, you know. But he was absolutely enchanting. And so beautiful. He had a beautiful body. And Jonathan Adams is absolutely off the wall. It was pretty well done, wasn't it? The pool and everything...

Of course, Susan was really ambitious. And the Americans got a much better deal than the English, you know. Susan, Barry and Meat Loaf...

And Charles Gray, I knew him. He's still around. I haven't seen him in years, and I'm sure you could talk to him. He's probably getting on a bit. [Charles Gray has since died.]

We were never asked to sing, just lip-sync. There might have been a few of the Transylvanians that did sing on the soundtrack. I am on the cover of the album. Look, it was recorded at Olympic Studios, London, 1975. Ode Records is the label. I used to have stills of myself, too, from the film, but I think I gave them away.

SM: Something tells me you went to the premiere?

CB: Indeed. The theatre was not the Odeon, Leicester Square, but the other one. You know when you come out of the Empire, it's the one on the right-hand corner. We all came out and it was like suicide time. You know the movie was a complete flop when it opened. We went to the premiere and everyone left the theatre wanting to slit their wrists. It was like coming out of a morgue. And then it suddenly took off, in such a big way. But if you'd asked me then, I never thought that, 25 years on, it would still be popular. No, not at all.

SM: Have you seen any of the revivals?

CB: I have to say that I went to see the last big revival at the Piccadilly Theatre and I hated it because the audience interrupted so much that you didn't hear any of the show. I thought it was terrible. It's fine to do it in the cinema, but in the theatre, if you paid money to see it, I would be really angry. It's a very strange thing to me, but there you go.

SM: So you wouldn't have wanted to have been in one?

CB: I was never asked! But I would have loved to have been the Narrator at one of these revivals. Very good from their point of view, I would have thought.

And tragically, David Toguri died. He was wonderful. Lovely man.

‹‹‹‹irememberdoingthetimewarpirememberdoingthetimewarpi››››

Peter Hinwood

9 December 1998
'The sword of Damocles is hanging over my head'

The part of *Rocky Horror* was played in the film by Peter Hinwood. To say that Peter in 1974 was the object of lust for men and women alike alone qualified him to play the character that could safely be said to have been the Shag Of The Century. Only by recruiting from the United States or possibly Australia could the Charles Atlas seal of approval have been given to an alternative casting, and even then, though finding 'the body' might not have been a problem, matching Hinwood's angelic features would have called for the skills of a real-life Doctor Frank N Furter.

Scott met with Peter in his shop in Chelsea, a shop which had then recently been featured in the publication *London Living*. Peter talks candidly, a stream-of-consciousness retrospective of a 25-year waking dream. These are the thoughts of a man whom the majority of London, straight or gay, men or women, would have killed to have been able to meet, let alone have a date with. Just what is it like, we all wondered then, to be that beautiful?

It was a time when at the crossroads of sexuality was emerging something called porno, not just dirty-old-man Soho sleaze pornography or the rarefied aesthetes' erotica that had to masquerade as 'art'. The cult of the body beautiful had arrived. The body beautiful and the mind dirty. *Boys In The Sand* porno stars like Casey Donovan, the precursor of the Jeff Stryker 'superpornohero', were becoming legitimate. The Andy Warhol films starring the raunchy, street-sexy Joe d'Allessandro were cultural currency. The old regime of the under-the-counter/brown-wrapper-only magazines like *Health And Efficiency* were giving way to the in-your-face blatant porno magazines. *Rocky* was as different to Charles Atlas as a bull is to a bullock, the latter anodyne and de-sexualised, the former a flagrant fantasy of sexual availability.

PETER HINWOOD: I live in Marble Arch now. I've been there about 18 years. I am a cat person. As you've gathered, I've kept a low profile ever since the movie came out. I don't even own the video. In fact, I don't own a video player and I've never been to America. I've only ever seen the film once since the premiere. One is always critical of oneself. It did not get a good reception.

The person who played Rocky when I saw it at the Chelsea Classic was a sort of acrobat and I am not. In the show, there was a guy doing somersaults. My version of Rocky was so different to that.

I was on holiday and my friends told me that I had to audition for it. I mimed to a Bryan Ferry record onstage in a cinema in King's Road, and they told me I had the job! I was never an actor. I was just someone they picked off the street. They had no idea what my abilities were when they got me to mime to a song onstage.

I wore a hoop earring in my ear at the time. In those days, people would stare at me in the streets quite often. I was used to being looked at. At the time, people would stop traffic in their cars to have a look at me, and I was sort of glamorous. Of course, I did own a red MG TC, which I bought for £150. 1948. I ended up buying American cars. Ford Mustangs.

But I remember I still thought at the time that it was odd I was picked for the movie.

SCOTT MICHAELS: *Would you call yourself a child of the swinging '60s?*

PH: I was born on 17 May 1946. When I was younger, I was constantly invited out. It was great in Chelsea in those days. I went out every night 'til four in the morning, so I had my thrills quite a lot. At the time, I was into smoking a lot of dope. It doesn't mean to say that I don't have a nice time now, leading a quieter life.

SM: So what was the life of a film actor like?

PH: I remember getting up very early in the morning and driving in with Jim Sharman. I remember sitting for hours on end with bandages all over me. It felt like I was wearing a plastic bag.

I just remember getting up at 5:30 every morning and getting home at 8:30 at night. Every night I went out to eat in a restaurant, so by the end of it I really hadn't made anything at all. I was paid £150 a week for ten weeks and nothing after that. No royalties. I think I had a bad agent. The Transylvanians got only £100 a week.

SM: Can you remember much about the events during the shoot?

PH: I remember the hairdressers always doing funny things to my hair. I went to a trichologist during the filming. They massage the head. The trouble was probably from putting a lot of bleach on it. It wasn't my natural hair colour.

They padded my swim trunks. I remember them being a peculiar cut and them having to put foam rubber down the front of them. It kept moving around and jumping up. They were leather.

I remember when I hopped to the floor off the box, my feet were very slippery from the bandages. I almost fell when I jumped. And I had bad problems with the high heels. I was told to run for my life from the dogs. I'm sure they were really hunting dogs, but they were controlled. I just did what they asked of me. I just went for it. I did the best I could. I had a feeling that they probably should have had someone else more acrobatic. It turned out that it didn't matter.

SM: All that stuff in the pool at the end must have been daunting.

PH: The pool was in the larger sound stage. It was a proper pool. Deep. But I had a stand-in. I had to go up the tower and up and down ladders.

When we had to model for the plaster casts, I remember we were almost stripped naked and workmen put plaster all over my body. It was quite an experience. They did the front and the back. I didn't shave my chest. The hair may have come out in the cast. I can't remember. I never had much chest hair.

SM: And have you any idea whose voice was supposed to be yours in 'Damocles'?

PH: No, I don't know who I mimed to in the film. I have no idea.

SM: How did you find the Americans were to you?

PH: Susan and Barry were great buddies. I suppose they were the only Americans. Apart from Meat Loaf, of course. I never realised she'd become such a sex symbol years later. Susan and Barry were doing their own number together whilst we were filming. They kept themselves pretty separate. They were the only proper actors, and they seemed above everyone else, in a way. They were Americans and trained for movie-making. I got the impression they felt we were amateurs. The film didn't make me uncomfortable. I had friends like Nell around, and everyone was nice and friendly. The gay overtones didn't bother me, maybe fractionally wondering what my family would think. I don't think the film is at all erotic. It was a laugh. I have loads of polaroids from filming. I haven't looked at them in years, but I'll drag them out for you.

SM: Did Rocky *not bring you a flood of work?*

PH: After doing the film, it was difficult to know which way to turn. People were offering me photo shoots for magazines and it felt like I was sort of taking a step backwards by doing that.

I only did a couple of other films. *Tam Lin.* Roddy MacDowell was very nice. We went up to Scotland to film. Joanna Lumley was in it. Siobhan Cusack, Stephanie Beacham. Joanna had great real spark. Ava Gardner was quite something. One or two friends of mine were entertained in her apartment. She was quite a diva. On the set, she liked good-looking men. She was like Frank N Furter. She was a great flirt.

I worked for Dino De Laurentis too, in *Odyssey*. I played Mercury. I got the part because this man called Mark Palmer, who was a famous model agent in those days, got all his friends from the Chelsea area to line up for a photograph. We all had long hair and looked freakish. Two or three of us were spotted and they asked me to have a part in this film. I was 18 or 19. We went to Rome and Yugoslavia. It was a great experience but, in retrospect, kind of frightening.

SM: How come you landed a career as an antiques dealer, then?

PH: During the filming of *Rocky*, I had a day off and was in Christies. I saw a friend who I've known for many years and was a neighbour of mine. We were both looking at the same picture, and we decided to go halves together for it. I've been buying and selling art for years. He suggested that we work together, so I stopped the other career and have been doing this ever since. But we are partners.

SM: Is it true that you showed a fan out of your shop when they asked for an autograph?

PH: I did receive one fan letter from an American and I never replied. I've always felt guilty ever since. It's the only fan letter that ever reached me. And no, I've never had to escort anyone out of my shop.

SM: I can't believe you weren't asked to be involved with Shock Treatment.

PH: Well, I wasn't. Hearing about *Rocky* again is slightly embarrassing, but I'm used to it. I never think anyone really knows my name, either. No one I work with knows about the *Rocky Horror* thing. There is one woman who has been here for years who knows. I don't get much attention. I never drop the fact that I was in the film into a conversation. I wouldn't want to disappoint people. It would depend on my mood. If

I felt bright and healthy and feeling good, I might. It *is* nice to spring it on people when they least expect it. I don't know if the girls here know about it or not. They probably will after this.

SM: Did you remain friendly with any of the cast?

PH: No. I rarely, if ever, see anyone from the film. It was such a short period in my life. Tim Curry was in the shop a few weeks ago. He just came to have a cruise around and see the place. I don't know why he came here. Maybe out of curiosity. He said he'd come back, but he never did. What happened to Nell. Is she married? I have a little flick book of Nell dancing. You flick the pages and see her dancing. There are about a hundred little photographs.

I think Rufus Collins dead. He was in the Living Theatre for years and years. I knew all these people from the Living Theatre. Derek Jarman, Andrew Logan. He was a great character. He had a friend named Leonardo Tribilio, who played Sebastiane in Derek Jarman's movie. Leo was his lover, and they were in the Living Theatre together. He lived in India for a long time.

I lead such a reclusive life now I've moved to where I am, in the middle of Marble Arch. When I was in Chelsea, Mick Jagger lived around the corner and I could just pop out and see people. In those days, everything was wild and everyone was free. AIDS didn't exist then. Promiscuity in those days was quite common. Where I am now, there is nobody I know around. I'm terribly antisocial. I quite like being on my own. I'm not in a relationship now.

SM: So what are your thoughts about the whole phenomenon now?

PH: *Rocky Horror* is extraordinary. In the beginning, it was perceived as such a disaster, and yet it's lived on for so long. I found my costume, the trunks, in the bottom of my underwear drawer a couple of years ago. I put them in one of those rock 'n' roll sales. They weren't star material, I'm afraid. Only about £400. There was a rhinestone R on them.

SM: If you came to a convention, you'd have gotten a whole lot more for them. Would you ever think of coming to one?

PH: No, I don't think I could attend a reunion. Well, maybe. It's just that I'm generally antisocial. I don't even go out with friends. I might change, you never know. I mean, look, who wants to see me 20 years later? I almost didn't call you back. I hope it wasn't a great disappointment meeting me.

SM: A few days later, I received this letter...

Dear Scott

After searching high and low for the album of polaroids, I now realise that I must have destroyed it along with the script during a massive clear-out some time ago. Your hopes are dashed. I'm very sorry and now regret mentioning it, but...I never expected you to turn up or anyone else for that matter and by now I feel quite far removed from those days when my unusual looks made me feel a bit of a freak, so Rocky was just about the last straw in that aspect and I felt even more insecure about my identity and future, so have kept quite a low profile ever since. Here are a few scraps from my modelling career. Sorry to disappoint you.

Best wishes,

Peter

PS I enquired about Rufus and understand that he died some time ago. I cannot confirm this and am racking my brains to think of someone who knows for sure the truth. When I find out, I will let you know.

SM: A few weeks later a package arrived for me and in it was Peter's copy of the original shooting script with Mick Jagger's phone number. The attached letter read:

Dear Scott

For what it's worth, here is my script as promised, for your *Rocky* memorabilia collection.

Best wishes,

Peter Hinwood

The script is a fascinating document, complete with rewrites and handwritten notes. I treasure it.

‹‹‹‹irememberdoingthetimewarpiremembedoingthetimewarpi›››

Yasmin Pettigrew

22 July 1998
'God bless Lili St Cyr'

As we have just mentioned Rocky Horror's trunks, we want to introduce an honorary Transylvanian. The lighting technicians, the stage hands and the backstage staff rarely get credit, and so we're pleased that we can bring Yasmin Pettigrew in here. She probably knew more about Rocky Horror's trunks than anyone because she held the wardrobe together for years.

If she was Jewish instead of Scottish, Yasmin Pettigrew could be called a *yenter*. She has a kind heart and a penchant for glamour. She's been in the thick of more London showbiz action than you can shake a stick at. She's also acted and lately taken herself to university, where, at just short of what the French call 'that certain age', she got herself a fine degree.

SCOTT MICHAELS: *Were you a* Hair *girl too?*

YASMIN PETTIGREW: I was indeed, but before that I worked for Lauren Bacall. I was working on *Applause*, in the West End. 1971–2. I remember telling her about the stage door man being nice to me and she said, with mock reproach, 'YAAAAASSMin… All drunks are nice when they are sober.' She asked me to do her tea leaves. I don't know where she got the idea that I could. But I did. I know she has a reputation but she never shouted at me, or raised her voice to me. Everyone else got bitched at. She gave me this lovely silver silhouette of her in *Applause*. It's gorgeous. I was with her for nine months. I have the nightdress from *Applause*. My job was to make La Bacall tea and read her mail. I would sort her letters, the ones that want a photo and the ones she will never see. They go straight to the agent, 'cause they are fucking nasty.

There was a girl who would sit in the front row of Her Majesty's Theatre every performance. Almost every time. She was in New York as well. She would do the lines before Bacall said the lines. Bacall says to the box office manager, 'Can you say to that girl that you sold those seats, because this is getting out of hand.' So they did, she came into the show, but she was further back and she saw the seats were empty. She went to the newspapers and said that Bacall was trying to get her banned from the theatre. Nasty press for Bacall. Bacall says, 'OK. Let her have the fucking seats then.'

Then, this huge bouquet of roses arrives at the theatre and the card reads, 'I hope you've learned your lesson.' Next thing we know, the girl's trying to chat up the stage door guy, trying to get backstage. Unbelievable what lengths people will go to. If you get a lot of that, there comes a point where you just need to hang onto you. I'm sure I'm right when I say that, in New York, Tim Curry actually had to move a couple of times because his address was found out and weird people were hanging around.

But, yes, I did *Hair*. That's how I got involved. I was in Norway with Straker doing *Hair* and then ended up coming to London. I helped with Rock Bottom's and Straker's costumes, too, but that was way on, when *Rocky* was at the old Essoldo, the King's Road theatre.

SM: *Sue Blane brought you in to do wardrobe, right?*

YP: I knew Sue Blane. You know she's never had that problem with credit, like Thomson. She's all her own, that one. Sue worked in Scotland, at the Glasgow Citizens with Tim Curry, and then she came down to London. The first corset came from the Citizens wardrobe, an old Victorian corset that she'd sequinned up.

When Tim Curry read the *Rocky* script for the first time at the Theatre Upstairs, he said to me, 'I've got this feeling! I think it might be another *Hair* on our hands.' He'd never said things like that unless he was sure. 'I'm really getting off on this part.'

Tim did not get the part – like *get into* the part – until he got the high heels on. He tried on those shoes, shoes that were far too small for him and this character that was a transvestite-cum-Doctor Frankenstein...well, he got his character. He says that, too, or he did say that.

I went out with Tim to get him a pair of high heels made. The ones he had were just a big pair of women's. We had no money in this show. We went to a shop in Soho and they said, 'We don't make for that kind of show.' Silly of them, really, because *Rocky* won the Musical Of The Year award that year. I used to have to go to all the sleazy sex shops to buy the suspenders and corsets, not Marks & Spencers, like nowadays. I think I was pretty famous in those bookshops in Soho. After about three years, all that outrage got to be more and more normal.

I haven't spoken to Tim in ages. I considered Tim a real buddy, though I haven't seen him in the flesh in years. We were so close at one time and I don't think you ever lose that. We never talked about work.

Tim could have easily taken advantage and gotten a lot of adulation from *Rocky*, but he was just a jobbing actor. That's the big difference. It wasn't his baby, it was Richard's and Tim was just hired. I've never liked another Frank I've seen. I've liked the actors as people right enough but never what they did with Frank. Philip Sayer was the second Frank and Peter Blake was the third.

I went to America to visit Tim after the film, before he did his rock tour. Tim came to New York from LA 'cause he's recording his album. A friend of mine told me I could have his flat while he goes on holiday. His name was Jim. So Tim came to stay, too, and it's the three of us.

Then Jim goes and it's just Tim and I. He took me everywhere on Manhattan. He'd just been in a big hit, *Amadeus*. We went to Sardi's. Everywhere. He asked me what I wanted to do. I told him I wanted to go to see *The Rocky Horror Picture Show*. I hadn't seen it yet. He has his agent arrange tickets for us, no problem. We get to the theatre and pick up our tickets. Next thing we know, the fucking manager, at the top of her voice, says, 'Excuse me, I just want to know if you are really Tim Curry!'

Well, the whole place nearly mobbed him, so we had to leave before the movie. This is just a funny story, 'cause we were really looking forward to it, and the whole cinema turned. The entire balcony was staring. He had done the initial acknowledgement by smiling and waving, but it just didn't stop. Sometimes you just cannot deal with that. Daft, but he kept apologising to me. He felt really bad. I think it must have happened to him a lot.

SM: I hope Richard likes what we're writing.

YP: Richard O'Brien is not opposed to it; he's just unsure as to how these things are done. Same with Hartley. Richard Hartley gave a lot of photos to Brian Thomson and didn't get them back. But Brian just misplaces things. You need photos, too. Ziggy Byfield. Why should I think of him? He's called Trevor now. But he went to Japan and toured in *Rocky* as Frank. You should speak to him.

SM: You had the privilege of seeing the whole phenomenon develop. It's rare that that happens, isn't it?

YP: It's quite interesting how the show has changed over the years. It's had to, to survive. The Upstairs was so small, and the stage as well. When they did the explosion bit and they did 'Science Fiction' reprise, it was happening over your head. They were actually above you, on this frame. The place was so small. That's when Julie Covington was in it.

I became involved at the Chelsea Classic. I was only a little minor helper when I started. I was always gluing sequins on shoes. Glue on those sequins, girl! It was a wonderful venue for the show. Brian got it all draped in scaffolding tarpaulins with 'Acme Scaffolding' printed all over.

Angela Bruce took over from Pat. Angela still works. She did *Hair* with us and she was a great Usherette. Angela started as Pat Quinn's understudy. Then she went in and did the Usherette by itself at one point. She came in at the Chelsea and took over for Pat because Pat was filming. Pat's schedule allowed her to do Magenta, but she could not make it in at the beginning of the show. So, to cover her ass, Angela did the Usherette. Something like that happened. Then Angela took over permanently.

And Belinda Sinclair took over from Julie Covington, because Julie just didn't want to continue with it. *Rocky* started as a three- or four-week job and I think she was signed to do something else. Julie is very funny. In theatre 20 years ago, when musicals were around, if you did them, you weren't taken seriously as an actor. Julie might very well have been that way. I would back Pat's statement about the *Evita* thing. Julie did the original *Godspell* with David Essex at the Roundhouse.

SM: Were you involved much in the film?

YP: I went up to the set at Bray a lot of times. We had nice times. I was still working on the show then. I didn't do anything official on the film. I bought some pieces here and there for Sue. Sue does such great designs.

I met Meat Loaf when he started on the film. When I met him, I met this big BIG boy, who was so nice and quiet; he didn't smoke or drink. About four years later, he tried to drag me onstage at one of his concerts at Wembley. He didn't get me, but he got O'Brien up.

SM: And you actually got to act with them all, eventually!

YP: Yes, I was in *Shock Treatment*. I had a huge bouffant, in the audience with Gaye and Annabel. Gaye was pregnant with her son Charlie when we were filming. We did that at Lee, a tiny studio in

Wembley. I was one of the first to hear 'Little Black Dress' on guitar. Richard sang it to me years before it was in *Shock Treatment*.

SM: And are you still as close as you were at the time? So many people like Tim seem to live so far away now.

YP: Brian Thomson lives in Australia. I'm still in touch with him. He just won an award on Broadway for *The King And I*. He's designed *Grease* at the moment. That's how he got back in touch with me.

Poor Richard Hartley was in the middle of that O'Brien/Thomson fight. There was a disagreement about the show. I think a lot of pettiness came about. What it comes down to is that Richard wrote the fucking show. No contest. I can imagine Richard being a bit possessive about it. It is his baby. He's never said that to me, but if you think about it, if you set down and create this phenomenon, which gives these people jobs, you would get upset if everyone else gets lauded for your creation.

We all got the impression that Richard was jealous of Tim. Richard played Frank once. He's gone on quite a few times as Frank. I think Riff is a better part, anyway. I think there's an aspect of Richard in Frank. That 'Don't Dream It, Be It' attitude, that's very Richard.

SM: You must regret all the fighting that seems to have gone on. Was it all down to mere jealousy?

YP: Obviously, there was a lot of input from others, but their egos are in the way. I don't think Richard Hartley has an ego about it. His idea is that he did the music for Richard O'Brien and it ends there. He ended up in the middle of these two guys in Australia. It was a drag. They were all mates.

This was from the production, I never heard about this from the film. The actual split happened with a disagreement about how the show was being produced and directed. In the end, Brian tried to get Richard barred from the rehearsals, or vice versa. I wasn't there, but I remember the tidal waves reached back. The shit really hit the fan in Australia.

I love Brian. He's a good friend, but whoa! He has an acid tongue and he knows it. He can be a real bitch. He says it. You cannot say someone is an angel when they are not, but he is a great designer. A great guy.

SM: And there have been a lot of deaths and entrances. I recently attended a memorial service for David Toguri with Sadie Corre.

YP: Telling me. David had cancer. They told him he was clear two years ago, and it still came back. We all were at his memorial. Richard and Sue. That was a really affectionate service. Gaye couldn't come because of her hip operations. I was sitting with Charlotte Cornwell and a couple of others who did the television version of Rock Bottom [*Rock Follies*]. There was me, O'Brien, Hartley, Sue Blane, Straker. Straker sang brilliantly. Toguri did the film of *Rocky* and he did *Hair* and *Rock Follies* and he directed *Rocky* onstage, of course. He goes way back and through all our lives. He's beloved and deeply missed. He could take a cripple and get them to look like they're dancing. He's responsible for a lot. It was he who picked Kimi for the show that Richard met Kimi in. He goes from the London Palladium right through. He did *Guys And Dolls* and then he'd do Danny La Rue. He did 'Crazy Little Thing Called Love' for Queen.

The lighting guy's name was John Morton, and he was a stormtrooper in one of the *Star Wars* movies. Now he signs autographs for conventions since the *Star Wars* people got in touch with him; he's doing futuristic designs. He's even going to write some books for them. He asked me what was going on for the 25th anniversary of the film of *Rocky*. He would love your idea. He came out of the London School of Economics. They met up with my friend Roger in strip clubs. They were doing follow spots in Soho strip clubs. Roger asked him to come and do lighting for *Rocky Horror*.

SM: I get the impression that you were all very supportive then.

YP: We all stuck together and we still keep together. We had a close personal life together. It's not just because of *Rocky*, because we were in other shows together as well. Because *Rocky* became a hit, we were all living off its glory. All of this lot were the stars, getting the treatment. But because we were already around and went to each other's houses, and had dinners and parties and Sunday lunches together, it was just the way it was. Michael White used to let us have such great parties in the theatre. We had that big catwalk for dancing. That was when Rock Bottom played. I still have my programmes from that. Brian was famous for making cakes, and we had great parties in his home. He had the Hollywood sign made up in his backyard. We would go *en masse* to parties. Andrew Logan's Miss World first started with us lot all there. I have the original pictures from that. I entered as Miss Whiplash or Miss New Bondage or something like that.

SM: So, they certainly can't take that away from you, like the song says.

YP: Darling, I kept everything. For years, I didn't have to buy trousers. I just wore the *Rocky* trousers. I have the boas from the film. At least one of them. I wear them now. Some of the costumes came from Malcolm McLaren's shop. I've got all the old programmes too. I think I still have my original *Rocky* masks and I've got some of Sue Blane's original drawings. I bought Nell's shoes at Sex – not the tap shoes, obviously, but for the film – and I still have them. They still fuckin' fit and they ain't leavin' this bitch's foot!

<<<<irememberdoingthetimewarpirememberdoingthetimewarpi>>>>

Perry Bedden

15 December 1999
'I was feeling done in, couldn't win'

Perry Bedden was not only a Transylvanian. He's played more parts in *Rocky* than a single Transylvanian could metamorphose into and spent more years involved with the beast than is good for any man.

DAVID EVANS: *So you were in the show as well?*

PERRY BEDDEN: Was I in the show! It was the main part of my life. *The Rocky Horror Show* ultimately did my head in. From 1976 'til 1977 – then I left – came back in 1980 at the Comedy and did it 'til the show ended in 1981. Then I did a German one that was supposed to tour, but the producers pulled out after three weeks; Cameron Mackintosh and some Germans were producing it, and the German producers pulled out. We were playing enormous places, thousands of seats... I played Riff Raff. Cameron brought us back, apologised, and that's when I went off to Australia with Brian. I was in Sydney and a guy named Wilton Morley [Robert's son] was about to launch *The Rocky Horror Show*. I thought, 'Oh no, please, not again.' I went to meet him and told him, 'It's very unlikely I'll do this. I'm not in Australian Equity.' I was on a working holiday visa, so I could work. I gave him a ridiculous price so he wouldn't want me, but he gave me my ridiculous price and he said he wanted me. He rigged the whole Australian Equity thing, and I played Riff. That went from 1981 and I was on a six-month contract, to do the major cities. We did six to eight weeks in Sydney and we were about 75 per cent full, so it wasn't great business. Then we went to Melbourne and it just took off. We were supposed to do six weeks and we did 16 and started losing our dates for the other cities. So we had to rearrange that, and we went to dreadful places, mining towns like Mount Isa. We were doing three shows a day. *The Australian* newspaper did a cartoon of all the miners in their fishnet tights. Nothing flew in the theatre. The stages were really basic. We just threw some boxes together and that was the stage. I just hated it.

DE: *So, unlike Frank N Furter, stardom didn't sit lightly on you?*

PB: I finished my contract and I knew it was going on. I thought, 'Should I, shouldn't I? I will.' And I did. We had amazing success. The biggest grosses of all time, at the time. We were treated like stars. A plane would fly in and would take me to a VIP room to have me interviewed. I found it very difficult. I didn't like the whole thing. What

I liked was the King's Road, where people clapped and you could go home, and I could just disappear into the night. It didn't happen like that in Australia. But I did it 'til Christmas of 1982. For about 18 months, again. When I got back here and my agent asked if I would like to go to Italy to do it, I said, 'No way!' I was absolutely cursed by the show. I should never have gone back in at the Comedy.

DE: Just to backtrack a moment, what else came after Superstar *in your career?*

PB: I was still in *Superstar* when Rocky began. The first time I auditioned for it was in 1976 for Riff Raff. I played him as a punk. I had dyed blonde hair, and my costume was full of pins. I remember the front-of-house photograph – I got a T-shirt from Sex – all over the front of it was this print and across it in painted strokes was the word *sperm*. They refused to put that picture up in the front. I was so angry with them all. Really pissed off with them.

In between, I did *Hair* in 1975. I think it was the first revamp of it, directed by Rufus Collins. Then I did *West Side Story* and odd bits of television. I didn't really want to do *Rocky*, from the word go.

DE: So, what did you think about Rocky? *I felt sort of validated by it.*

PB: When I first saw *Rocky*, it was the most wonderful thing I'd seen. Same way I felt when I saw *Hair*. I'd never seen anything like it, in a theatrical sense. It didn't validate me like you say it did you. It was just a piece of theatre that went beyond anything I'd seen before. It just hit the G-spot and it was something I wanted to see again. I suppose I was aware that I was watching a piece of magic. It was something that never happened before, never heard music like that before. At that time there were a lot of rock operas going around, and this was rock 'n' roll with a twist – and what a wonderful twist to have. *Hair* was the same sort of feeling. For me, *Hair* was much more liberating and validating.

DE: Any really special moments?

PB: The thing that always got me was when 'Over At The Frankenstein Place' started, which is fairly early on in the piece. I realised that this was going to be a great evening. Before that, really, but that was sort of like putting the icing on the cake. People weren't trained singers. It was one of the first musicals where you didn't have to sing. Chris Malcolm and Pat Quinn were not professional singers. Ritzy could sing. Julie could sing and Tim could sing, but you didn't have to be able to sing.

DE: *It was certainly unpretentious.*

PB: Yes. Going back to the rock opera thing – everyone tried it, and it was going on and on, then *Rocky* came along and you realised that it wasn't trying to be anything. It was just a bit of fun, as far as I could see. Fun with good songs and a great experience. We knew the budget was small, but it worked.

DE: *Why the endurance?*

PB: Because it's got a transvestite and it's got sex in it. Plus it's got good songs and a story. I don't think it was shocking. I wasn't shocked at all at the time. I took my mother and father along and they weren't shocked. My baby brother wasn't shocked.

DE: *You have a very unshockable family.*

PB: I worked for Andy Warhol in *Pork* at the Roundhouse and we would talk about vibrators and shitting on people's faces. That was shocking. Not a guy in drag. *Pork* only ran for about a month.

DE: *A bit too real, perhaps?*

PB: *Rocky* was magical. The latest productions don't have it, since it went into a proscenium. That's when it lost it. At the Comedy, we never had anything shouted at us. The show worked because it happened all around you. It had to be. It was very claustrophobic, especially going into the auditorium, with the ghouls. The ghouls were there in the auditorium, and you weren't supposed to see them move. They would just be there, and suddenly you would see their eyes move, and people would point and say, 'It moved!' Just as the curtain went up, the person they'd been looking at for half an hour – freaking out – you would just go for them. Some people would scream and some people would flee the theatre and never come back. By that time, we didn't show people to their seats. It lost all that. It used to make me so angry, because it worked so well. They had an usherette in nylon jacket, black trousers and a torch in their hand. That was it. They just clock someone, look at them all night and, when you heard the band tuning up, you just go for them. That's what the phantoms were. It used to terrify me when I went. They were horrible masks, really vile. Maybe only one or two ghouls would show people to their seats, but you had three or four placed around strategically.

DE: *It was really clever and original, don't you think?*

PB: I was a great friend of Lionel Bart's, and at his funeral Cameron Mackintosh said, 'You realise we are not going to have anything like that any more. Today, musicals come to me packaged. They're all done – the music, the lighting, the lyrics, the set and the choreography. You don't start at the beginning and work out. It's already done for us, and you have to work in.' It's very true. As with Richard O'Brien...they both worked with other people. You can't do that today. You can't work with the director and the designer, costumes and lighting.

DE: *Partly because it's become producers' theatre, not directors'?*

PB: That's a judgement over time, really. Over time, things change. It's not a fault of current production – I think it's the only way big producers like Cameron can work. As far as *Rocky* was concerned, Michael White didn't make it happen. He handed them half the money. There will be nothing of that sort of substance again. *Miss Saigon* –

however wonderful it was to see – was an old story. Mind you, when *Rocky* came along, there were still big musicals. Big original ones.

DE: *But* Rocky *was a play with music, not a musical. More like a Sam Shepard thing.*

PB: No. I would call *Rocky* a musical. It was a piece that Jim found, got a bunch of people together to put it on and it was a big success, not knowing, obviously, what success they had. Just a load of kids having fun.

DE: *And that's more the point to what Cameron Mackintosh was saying, surely – that 25 years ago, one did things in the theatre because you had faith in the doing.*

PB: [Cameron Mackintosh] couldn't survive on that, but he still does things like that. He lets things happen. He may not make money at it, but he does experiment.

DE: *But that's a totally different point of view to what the Royal Court was about. There was a man there called George Devine, who founded it. He had a motto: 'Here we give you the right to fail.' That's not experimenting; that's just doing it because you believe in it. Nicholas Wright believed in Jim Sharman, liked him and Brian a lot, had seen Richard performing, and was also convinced by the demo tape that the two Richards made together. That was what* The Rocky Horror Show *was initially all about. That's not experimenting; that's faith.*

PB: I think you have to experiment 'til you get to that position where you have the faith. I think everyone had faith in themselves anyway.

DE: *Remember the* Rocky *slogan in NYC, 'Give our regards to Broadway, and tell them we're on our way!', in Times Square?*

PB: I remember walking in there and thinking, 'Ooh. Big mistake.

Why did it get like this?' It wasn't there, was it? Something that shouldn't have succeeded. It was in a cabaret setting at the Belasco. People were having drinks while the dialogue was going on. It was dreadful to watch.

DE: *Thank God for that man in New York who shouted at the screen for the first time. He put the relationship to the show back with the audience.*

PB: God, yes. It's just for me the relationship started in 1973 – though I didn't start performing until 1976 – ending in 1983. That's ten years of my life, stuck with this thing around my neck. It just drove me insane in the end. I just hated it and despised it. It all got silly in the end. Once, we were about to go on tour – I don't remember when, it was in Europe. We started rehearsals and David Toguri was directing, [Peter] Straker was going to play Frank and I was going to be Riff Raff. Yet again. We had about a week of rehearsals and the whole thing fell apart. I'd had enough.

DE: *And now? So many years on?*

PB: I've embraced it from a distance. I really enjoyed the Recat Time Warp Convention. Very much so. I felt very proud for the fans. I did chat with Biggins and Stephen [Calcutt]. I thought the fans were all wonderfully behaved. I was expecting hystericals and some were. The effort they made – I really got off on that convention. I loved it. I did an interview about the meaning of *Shock Treatment* and I got completely lost on that one.

DE: *We know that the lips were an afterthought – as an opening to the movie. When did Richard sing the backing track to 'Science Fiction'? Or had Pat sung it previously?*

PB: It was always going to be Richard singing. It was just the visual part that changed.

I was always aware that Richard was singing it. I heard Pat onstage at the convention talking about it.

DE: *It's only by talking to as many people as possible that you get to the bottom of stuff.*

PB: Surely you could get Brian when he comes to do *The King And I*?

DE/SM [groans]: *We wish. To be honest, we've written to Brian, and got no reply. And we've tried via various friends and stuff. As of today, it seems he doesn't want to know.*

PB: Oh. Sorry about that. I can't help you there, but I can sympathise. I try to think how his mind is working. I've written to him, too. I got an address from Sue Blane. We were together for ten years. Even just to say, 'I don't want to see you.' It would be better than nothing. Having the nothing leaves me in limbo of wondering if he got it, if he lives there. I'm sure he has got it. It's very hurtful. It's not something you can actually forget. I think he's gone the way Tim has gone. He's cut away that piece of his life and anyone associated with it. I don't understand it. If I could, I'd feel better. I think that's part of it. I was part of that *Rocky Horror* bit and he just wants to forget. From knowing Brian, I can well see him doing that.

DE: *There seems an untoward amount of bad blood generated between the main players in this phenomenon.*

PB: I was there in Australia when Brian barred Richard from the theatre.

DE: *I understand that when the money Richard O'Brien had been diverting to Brian – even though he had no need to do so – stopped, there was even more ill feeling?*

PB: I can kind of understand that, as part of the creative team that got the show on the road. Because Brian and Richard had this fall-out in

Australia...and I can understand Richard saying that Brian is not going to design the next production of *Rocky*. But the next production did come along and Richard said that, the part of the team, which was Blane and Hartley, too... He suddenly changed the format. As I remember, at the time I was working – decorating for Hartley, actually – and it was just as the revival was coming on, and rehearsals were starting, and Richard said that Brian had been in touch with him and wanted to know if there was anything in the design that was taken from the original.

DE: *Anything you remember especially about the filming?*

PB: Not huge amounts, but I'm finding out! I always thought that the vocalist for Hinwood's 'Sword Of Damocles' was the man in The Easybeats, the 'Friday On My Mind' band.

DE: *Did you sing?*

PB: As a Transylvanian, we just worked with a playback. We worked with David Toguri, of course, and Gillian Gregory, who was his assistant. But we were there more or less all the time. The Transylvanians were basically in the wardrobe hut, playing charades – teams being hosted by Gaye Brown and Christopher Biggins.

DE: *Nothing too glamorous, then?*

PB: Except April Ashley came on the set. That was a fabulous time. I came onto the set and everyone was whispering. Tim, I think, went over to her. She was sort of over there, but she was April Ashley. I remember Britt being around, too, but more after the fact.

DE: *Just give me a little titbit. I know you're holding out on us!*

PB: There is one little story I could tell you. When they were filming with the tank – when Rocky was being created – you see Tim having a strange expression. Brian and Jim had an argument, and they got to this scene. Jim wanted to know what the colours of the rainbow were. He didn't have a clue. Brian was there, and Jim asked him. They were actually filming. Brian went, 'Yellow! Indigo! Blue!' Brian was yelling these things, and Tim was going for the wrong knobs. You actually see him doing that. You see Tim going for one and stopping and going for another one.

DE: *That accounts for a lot of that performance, then. Anything else?*

PB: Well, you were just talking about the RKO logo thing – interesting that Fox wouldn't let them use their logo, yet it was a Fox production. The Coca-Cola objection, too. From the first stage production. Coke wouldn't allow their logo in the movie, either.

And the movie was all going to be in black and white until Frank shows up, when only his lips would be red. Then he was to turn, and it all goes to colour. That would have been wonderful. Well, as far as I'm concerned the film never worked, anyway, so I don't think it would have made any difference. The reason they didn't do it was because it was too expensive. They would have had to do it in colour and then take it back to black and white.

DE: *And now you're out of the business altogether, is that true?*

PB: Doing what I do now is the only time I've ever taken control of my life. Now I look after a man who's had a stroke. I'm a carer. I got into that doing volunteer work for AIDS. I wanted to get into that field, but the pay is so bad. I got this job privately. There are certain aspects of the business I miss, because I was into it since I was 12 and did *The Sound Of Music*.

I was in an Internet chatroom one day, and I realised that another person in the room was a fan of the show, by their screen name. I went to them and didn't tell them who I was, but told them I was in the movie. They came back with, 'Oh yeah, sure. What were you?' I told them I was a Transylvanian. He was asking a few questions that only someone in the film would know the answers to. I sent him back an answer and he never came back to me again! I've been into the Australian *Rocky* website. I don't think they believed who I was.

<<<<irememberdoingthetimewarpirememberdoingthetimewarpi>>>>

Peter Robb-King

17 November 1999
'He had a pick-up truck and the devil's eyes'

DAVID EVANS: Why do face painting and a certain sexual allure go together? They just do. Remember going to fancy dress parties where make-up was a very carefully worked out part of the fancy? For men and women alike? Men and make-up go together like repression and liberation, like the forbidden and the irresistible. Scott and I talked to a man who was responsible for the perfection which is the iconic image of the red, red lips of Lady Stephens!

Peter lives with his wife, Sue, also in the make-up trade, in a large Edwardian house on the outskirts of Maidenhead. As we drove out to lunch, he took Scott and me via Bray Studios and laughed at the irony that, of all the movies he's worked on, he has only ever worked at Bray Studios once! On *Rocky*. He kindly gave up his time between flying visits to work in America, his latest film being a David Mamet script being shot in Boston.

DE: Had you seen the show before you started working on the movie?

PETER ROBB-KING: I'm not sure if I saw the show before we did the production. I think I have subsequently seen it. Terry [Ackland-Snow]'s situation was different than mine. The art department probably had many weeks to design and build the sets. Our department was definitely a late arrival. If we were lucky, we had two weeks.

However, our whole approach embraced the perception that it was based on a stage show, but in fact the detail on the make-up was much more extraordinary. If you look at any stills from the stage show, they are not even close to the end result on the film. From memory, there were 52 elements to Tim's make-up alone, which means that there are 52 different parts to the whole. They were meticulously demanded. It needed to be that fine. There was a particular desire on Jim [Sharman]'s part. That's what he wanted.

DE: The original stage concept was certainly very raw.

PRK: We could have gone with the stage make-up, but it would have been much more slapstick and much more crude. You wouldn't have got the end result as we now know it on the film. But you would still have got the effect of that show. Looking at the photographs of the new stage production, again it isn't nearly as detailed as it was in the film.

Even if we had had some information given to us regarding a particular look, without checking, I don't know who originated those ideas. I don't know how much Jim's input was on the stage production. There were four make-up artists. There was myself, Jane Royal, Ernie Gasser and Graham Freeborn. Graham died at 42 of cancer. I don't want to say [Ernie] died, but he was pretty old then.

DE: It's amazing how long Rocky's *life has been.*

PRK: On every film I've worked on subsequently, it's become a discussion point. There we were in America in 1999 and they are still seeing this show. I was there two weeks ago on Hallowe'en. It still runs all the time. It's strange that the whole image thing has become an issue.

In a way, the whole thing was supposed to be tacky. It's a tacky story, yet the detail in it is very extreme. It was measured. The eyebrows were measured to make sure. It was like a painting. Considering the time period and what was available on the street, it's a miracle that the film got made. There was a lot going on socially, when the film was made. To get anybody to show up early in the morning to sit through that, and then perform. It wasn't a quick make-up. I think it took us an hour and a half to do Tim.

DE: *Have you run into him since?*

PRK: Tim played Darkness in *Legend*. He is an extraordinary actor, in that he would put himself in a role that another actor wouldn't be capable of doing, because of his desire to cooperate with the team. On *Rocky*, it was very interesting, because the whole layout where we prepped them was also fascinating. It was a completely different scenario to any other film that's probably been made. There is more make-up on Tim than there would be on a man playing a woman, but the interesting thing is that Tim was not playing a woman. Even with that amount of make-up, I never saw it as an over-made-up look. He looked correct for the character. He looked amazing. [His] opening scene, when he came down on the lift, it was an extraordinary thing to film. There was an electric atmosphere on the set. Although it is a musical, it was a show as well.

DE: *So at last you had something to go by?*

PRK: There must have been some drawings or photographs. It wasn't just invented out of thin air. I don't know what Pierre [La Roche]'s involvement was before I was there. It's not unheard of when a company brings in an outside individual. He clearly knew someone in the production. He probably in real life had a look himself. They wanted to have his input on the image of the film. He did no actual work on the production. It's possible he did drawings. He definitely had an input. Was he given a job to design? Was it that he wasn't allowed to work because of visas? I do know that he wasn't around during the movie. I think the actors would probably have known him. I definitely met him. He did exist. He may have had some sort of product availability – pencils. The make-up we used was a different range than was usually available.

I actually did Tim behind closed doors, only because of the layout of the studio. We had a separate room, and the hairdressing room was alongside it, which was not intercommunicating. You came out of one door into the other. There was a long three-person room where the rest of the artists were made up. So in a sense they were communing with each other during the whole of that period of preparation, whereas Tim was isolated.

The producer actually delivered a sound system to be put in the make-up area so that we could play records while we were working. That was unheard of in those days. My assistant, who was in his late 50s, used to kick it whenever he came in the door. He couldn't stand it. The younger members of the team thought it was fantastic. The music was in a corridor which ran along the corridor right outside the room.

DE: Music while you work, huh?

PRK: There was a huge concentration requirement. He needed to concentrate to enable me to work and vice versa. It wasn't a job we could rush. We weren't only doing make-up but tattoos as well. They went on every day. Well before anything was available for that process. They weren't stuck on.

It was always under pressure of time. No matter how long it took, you still had to do it as fast as you possibly could. There was always a dilemma that people needed to be on the set. I was doing Pat as well. Jane Royal did Nell and maybe the Narrator. Graham Freeborn did Meat Loaf.

SCOTT MICHAELS: And what about the Transylvanians, my special interest?

PRK: The Transylvanians? The Trannies were all talented in their own right. Far from just extras. Some of them were quite elderly. I don't think any of them were first-timers. They weren't cast that way. Either their talent or work. The choreography – I distinctly remember David Toguri doing the step routines with them. 'The Time Warp' was absolutely fascinating. The version with Charles Gray was just hysterical. It was so out of character. The dialogue in the script is hysterical, but all to be said without being tongue in cheek. Totally seriously.

We had a team for the Transylvanians' make-up. They didn't work that often, so we had to bring help in. But we set the look for them.

I have to mention Nell's make-up. If you look at it, either by choice or design, she shaved her eyebrows off. She accentuated a look. You couldn't do this play looking straight or normal. They chose to make themselves look right for the part. When we did the movie, it was totally refined. It was very, very detailed, much more so than almost anything else, except for *Last Of The Mohicans*, where we were on the same level of research and skill. It was so precise. Same premise as *Rocky*, except 20 years later.

Nell and Peter Hinwood were both King's Road people. I didn't do Peter. He was a very nice person. He was an actor who, at the time, clearly had problems with the filming. It wasn't an area he was knowledgeable about. It was tough for him. A cold stage and a cold situation. It's tough if you're not sure what you are meant to be doing as an actor. If you're not trained, it's even harder. You are surrounded by people and in underpants. He was a very nice person but clearly not a film person. You don't see it in the movie, but you certainly saw it on the set. I think, of them all, in a way he was the star of the film, because it was his body that everyone liked. Everyone.

DE: And who was in the hair department?

PRK: The hairdresser was Ramon Gow, a complete... Let's just say a well-known personality. He was a good friend of mine. Very extroverted. We knew we were getting great stuff. What we didn't realise is how much of that great stuff was never going to be in the movie. That was the irony of this film. We never put onscreen what we filmed, because a lot of it was cut, and a lot of it was put together. The editing was – without pointing fingers – interesting, to put it mildly. You could say now that the editing was brilliant, because it's become this mega-hit. At the time, you weren't aware of that success, and you could say that it's a strangely-put-together film, which is one of the quirks that the public picked up on. I've never spoken to Jim subsequently, whether that was deliberate or pure finance at the time.

DE: We've been told that there were a lot of drugs doing the rounds.

PRK: There are two problems with our department. It's a double-sided coin. We do make-up and hair. When anyone discusses the hair side of the coin, they usually just say make-up. This is partly because it was the case historically, and because on television it is both. As far as your question, I know for a fact that the hairdressing department was pretty lively on that film. Pretty busy as far as the mother's little helpers were concerned. They lived the lifestyle that I didn't live at the time. It's a miracle that everyone showed up at work every day.

Ramon and his assistant were both pretty notorious. They were old enough in themselves to be able to deal with that and show up. Ramon did it for years. In a sense, he was completely isolated. He would have got away with anything he did. Even if he didn't show up, he would have got away with it because his persona was such... He would have been able to invent an answer that satisfied everybody. I, of course, didn't have that background. Ramon and I got on very well and worked together a few times. So yes, there was evidence of that sort of thing [drugs] going on, but it never affected the film.

SM: Tell us about the lips!

PRK: Pat's lips were done several weeks after the event. It was scheduled for one day, one small unit. This was pre any available technology. My problem was covering the skin around her lips and quite a large section of her face to stop it from photographing. Black make-up does photograph as black make-up on white skin. You can see all the pores. We extended the range of make-up to various inks to colour it more strongly, but you could still see the texture of the skin. The way we solved it was using polarising lenses, which they operated so that, at the point where the polarisation was perfect, they actually blacked out the skin tone to a level where they thought they could get away with it. I think we added printing ink, but if you use anything on the skin that doesn't come off, you won't be re-employed. It's quite difficult to black things out.

They told me the day before that Pat had a cold sore across both the lip area and upper lip. These are actually the lips that you see on the movie. I managed to disguise it. The irony is, in my head I remember thinking on the day, 'This is probably the worst day that we could have chosen to do this scene.' We had no other choice. To make her head stationary in the frame, we had to lock her head in a brace, to stop her from vibrating. There was a great degree of skill in making those lips look good. The lips are the shot. The shot is the lips. She was great to work with, but it was a pretty odd experience. Again, the film had not been finished, so we had no idea what we were adding this to. In hindsight it's fantastic, but at the time it was a day's work to deal with this problem, completely out of context. I don't recall a stills shoot for the lips. If there was one, I didn't do it, and it's possible that Pat didn't do it. Peter Suschitzky probably shot it. The lips may have been an afterthought. It would be interesting to see if the opening title shot says, 'Lips filling frame – singing.'

SM: I just checked the script that Peter Hinwood gave me. Here's how it was supposed to open:

1   *The first image is a set of red velvet cinema curtains; soft drum roll.*

2   *They split optically to reveal the distribution company logo. Fanfare.*

3   *A small white screen – academy size – appears in the middle of the wide-screen format.*
    On the sides of the image are stationary sprocket holes of celluloid. Science Fiction Double Feature* musical introduction. Film head runs down numbers 10–1 Start. Very scratched. During the song we see snatches of the films mentioned in song. They look old and scratched, and they are intercut with flashes of white screen, burnt celluloid, etc.

4   *The day the earth stood still – the end sequence of the robot carrying the hero, 'Michael Rennie…'*

Flash Gordon – Buster Crabbe in Action

'And Flash Gordon…'

Claude Rains in bandages and dark glasses

'Claude Rains was the invisible…'

Etc.

DE: *And the floorshow make-up?*

PRK: I don't remember there being any discussion about this. There is an area of decision-making – I don't dictate too many areas of work. I probably would have given them that advice. I am not fanatical about writing it down. It probably was a design that we created.

DE: *But the sequences in the pool? They must have been difficult.*

PRK: Wet make-up, yes. That was one of the biggest problems with the film. Tim came out of the swimming pool and looked, to put it mildly, stunning. The water enhances the make-up and sets it even more. He came out of the pool for the first few takes and he looked perfect. It was the absolute opposite of what we required. You could not get this stuff to run. We had to break it down with oils. The only thing that does damage make-up is friction. We had to fake it for the camera. We accentuated it deliberately. In the pool, things have gone wrong for Frank and he is deteriorating. His life is changing, and it was a point required to be made in terms of film.

The audience doesn't see things unless they're pointed out to them. We did a movie once where there was a yellow plastic duck in every scene. This was a serious movie – a major big budget movie. It [the duck] was never seen. On the wing of an airplane. The art department did it deliberately. The company didn't know it was done. I suppose, if you did freeze-frame it, you would see it. It took weeks before they even let the crew know. They were just having a laugh.

DE: *And when* Rocky Horror *came out?*

PRK: I didn't go to the premiere. We aren't important enough to be asked. We would only be invited if we had a particular 'in' with someone. The rare occasion we have been invited, because they want publicists, the production designer or the costume designer might get to go. I think we saw it at the crew screening.

DE: *Do you still rate your work on* The Rocky Horror Picture Show?

PRK: I think *Rocky* must be in the first six of my films that I've chiefed. The first one I ever chiefed was in 1971 or 1972. I'd been training for four or five films. Started in 1968. I came to do hairdressing in college. The college authorities were quite surprised. They then decided to do beauty training. It required a special agreement for a man to be allowed. I preferred beauty and make-up to hair. Then I applied what I'd learned and what I'd developed for myself to television. I knew nothing about it, and I qualified for two jobs. Every company turned me down because I was a man. There was no sex discrimination machinery to put it right, back then.

The BBC told me, 'We can't employ you, but why don't you try films?' I tried it and they turned me down, but they put my name on file. In that year that I was finishing my training, they set up a programme to train people. I was chosen and worked on the studio payroll. I got into Elstree Studios, on *The Avengers*. They took four people in. The one other make-up artist was on probation for three months, so she dropped out. The two hairdressers are still close friends of mine. They were both connected to the industry.

Subsequent to that, they ran out of money, so I was the only person that did...and still am. That's how I got in.

We now have two children in their early 20s. They were fanatical about *Rocky*, not because I worked on it, but because they saw it prior to knowing that. They played that tape so many times, they almost wiped it clean. They were fascinated by the whole background story. This film is that phenomenal that all those different age groups find it fascinating. We knew at the time that the music was very good.

DE: And it still follows you, haunts you?

PRK: People that I work alongside now, 25 years later, who don't really know me except from what I'm doing with them now, if they happen to find out through another source that I did *Rocky*, they aren't only fascinated by it but are amazed that [I] created that look. That is *The Rocky Horror Picture Show*. That's what it's all about. That story applies equally now as it did 25 years ago. I spoke to John Comfort about *Shock Treatment* while he was in pre-production for it. He had gotten a different crew. I'm not going to say it was a bad film, but you cannot recreate that original idea. It's a totally different film. In some ways, it is nice to do a sequel, especially if you've done the original, because you have a particular interest in continuing the story.

I've been to screenings of *Rocky*, in the last ten years, where I've been in the audience, with all the interplay with the screen. People sitting there have no idea that I worked on it and, by looking at me, would probably not put that link together. I don't know what they think the people that worked on it were like, but I sure as hell think they don't think they looked like me. The nearest I got to a *Rocky* 'do' was in America. They'd shut off an entire street. I couldn't get through and so I never got to the theatre in the end.

<<<<irememberdoingthetimewarpirememberdoingthetimewarpi>>>>

Gaye Brown and Annabel Leventon

25 June 1998
'By the light of the night'

And yet another pair of Transylvanians...

Scott met Gaye Brown at the Labatt's Theatre in Hammersmith, and together they drove to Annabel's home, about an hour away, in Berkshire. They had lunch, after which Scott stayed and talked for about four hours. Annabel has a beautiful home and still acts, although her interest seems to lie more in directing drama. Gaye teaches acting and still works professionally, despite having thrice undergone major hip surgery for a painful arthritis condition. Both now have children. Gaye's son is 17, named Charlie, and Annabel's son is 14, called Harry.

SCOTT MICHAELS: *So, tell me all about the Planet Transylvania.*

GAYE BROWN: Sadie Corre was all right. She just drove you mad in the mornings! I haven't heard from Henry Woolf in ages. Imogen Claire still looks remarkable. She stayed punk. She was punk before the movie, and she is still punk. Imogen would be good for you to talk to, because she also worked on *Shock Treatment*.

Peggy Ledger died. Now she was a very interesting woman. She was the only one clothed in *The Dirtiest Show In Town*. She wore a tutu all the way through. She was a fascinating old bird. Such a lady.

Tony Milner is interesting; I don't know what's happened to him. Perry Bedden was the assistant, I seem to remember.

Tony Then was a model. The Chinese man in the white wig. Not really an actor. So charming.

Hugh Cecil had alopecia. He would drive me in. The bald one.

Kimi is lovely. Kimi Wong O'Brien. You must get a hold of her.

ANNABEL LEVENTON: I spoke to Kimi a few times on the phone about five years ago. She was trying to organise a 25th anniversary concert version of *Hair* with the original cast. She wanted to be involved. She was on the case, ringing up about what she had and who she could get. The whole thing collapsed in a heap and we never met up. She might consider a get-together at Joe Allen's or something. She is keen to keep in touch with people. The divorce was very acrimonious. We could probably muster a meeting with her and a few of us. Maybe Pat Quinn could have us all over?

Fran Fullenwider was very famous at the time. She had the hots for Richard. She used to tell Gaye all about her dreams of Richard O'Brien.

SM: *Were you asked to be in* Shock Treatment?

GB: We were both in *Shock Treatment*. We were housewives in the studio audience, when Barry Humphries was on. We sang the Denton song, with Judith someone, an American woman. We had a few lines and we sang.

We had Steve Debrow and Robert Longden who were behind us. He was playing Chris Biggins' part, because Chris was supposed to do *Shock Treatment* and didn't. Off the wall, onstage. He's very eccentric. Anyway, *Shock Treatment* just bombed.

AL: Gaye gets a lot of attention from *A Clockwork Orange*, though. [Gaye played the opera singer in the milk bar.] I directed Jonathan Adams in a revue in Oxford. It is true, I did get him to do it, and I cast it all, but then I backed out of it. The producer didn't want me to direct. I've directed him since as well. Comedy things at Battersea. Give him my love when you see him.

GB: How is Pat? And have you spoken to Tim at all? He comes to London once a year. Straker would know. They are in touch still. *Rocky* has done a lot of damage to people. When it became a cult, it became too powerful for the individuals involved. They get caught, literally, in a time warp. People got trapped. Nell, Pat, Richard… They are all great, but they have since had limited success. *Rocky* fitted Tim absolutely, and he can't find anything else now. He looks like an underpowered version of that, and I saw him in a musketeer thing and it looked like he was doing a very tacky parody of Alan Rickman in *Robin Hood Prince Of Thieves*.

Because when he played Frank he was butch as well, it created an amazing impression, but where does he go from there? How do you give it what it deserves *and* move on? If you don't stay on that gravy train when it's rolling for you, you are a fool. If you stay on it until it runs its course, you may find that that's it. That's *The Rocky Horror Show* and that's where you belong. That's generally what happens. You need to go do Shakespeare in the park or something. He did a play here called *City Sugar*. He was brilliant, after *Rocky*.

AL: Watching Tim filming and watching him conserve his energy and then perform, we were amazed. He was completely focused. This is a wonderful lesson for any actor. This is how a movie star should behave. He took the work very seriously and gave it 110 per cent, every time. No shot was any less than the other. The physical and emotional energy. Watching him do that, and then seeing Nell, who is crazy and great – ten takes and she bursts into tears. Tim was very clever because he realised he was the pinnacle.

SM: *And yet he's distanced himself.*

GB: We can see Tim's reluctance. He cannot be a role model or an agony aunt. Or being looked up to like that. It must be very difficult. He wasn't one to let go and giggle a lot. Very held back. He was uncomfortable with a lot of things. He bonded with me and Annabel in *Hair*. He kept saying, 'Well, you understand because we've both been to university,' and I thought, 'That really doesn't aid to understand what's going on here at all.' He held onto things a lot.

AL: No one ever knew him intimately at all. I loved the fact that he was so supportive of Rock Bottom, this all-girl band we had with Diane Langton. Tim was absolutely wonderful. We were very intrinsically linked to *Rocky Horror* because we did our first concert at the theatre where it was on. It was more of the same in a funny way. Tim sat down in our music room once, around that time, and played a couple of songs he had written. That's I think the only time I've seen Tim relaxed with himself. He was wonderful when he was with Straker. They were a wonderful unholy duo. When he is relaxed, he is wonderful.

Tim gave me a necklace for good luck. We were doing *Hair* in 1968, 1969, and he went off to Paris when the show opened there. This teeny little black girl named Florence gave it to him for good luck when he left.

GB: When I and Annabel went to Paris to do the show there, Tim took my flat in Paddington. The necklace had been given to him and he gave it to Annabel. Then he was desperate for it back. When Tim went off to America after *Rocky*, he asked for it back for luck!

AL: When *Rocky* went to Los Angeles and New York, they gave it a bigger band, prettied it up. Americanised it. Therefore they lost it. They turned it into something it wasn't. It started tatty and rough and imaginative. Never a grand show. The American thing dressed it up. They lost their nerve. It should have never been taken to America. They could have kept it exactly the way it was intended on Broadway and it would have taken New York by storm.

AL: I can tell you that Mike Gowans, the first assistant, is in Hong Kong.

GB: Annabel has a video from 1989 when Philip Sayer died. He took over from Tim in the play for a year. Everyone who had anything to do with the play or the movie turned up. Some people still had their costumes. Yasmin, Pat Quinn, Richard and Jonathan and everyone who ever did it did the Time Warp again. People who hadn't done it in years did it and it brought the house down.

AL: I don't know if Pierre La Roche is still alive, but he's the one that created this wonderful make-up of Pat's and everyone's, including us.

SM: *Were you in other scenes in the movie as well?*

AL: We were both in the wedding scene.

GB: We kept saying to Rufus, 'Run over the child!' Fact is Rufus couldn't drive. It was some kind of miracle that he didn't run over the child.

AL: Because he was wasted and, second, because he couldn't drive!

GB: There was lots of dope around. That was good. Annabel doesn't remember. We were so bored, we would have done anything. We had an awful lot of hanging around to do, and we weren't treated very well. We would be stuck up on the ramp in Frank's lab, while they walked around with cups of coffee. We weren't allowed down. We would get quite annoyed. We would start saying, 'Tea...tea...' and then they would say, 'Stop whingeing. Just stay up there. It's too difficult to get you all down.'

SM: *Why is it that Peggy Ledger was the only Transylvanian to have lines?*

GB: Peggy was the only one that had lines? Did she really? [In fact Rufus Collins also had a line.] Well, we'll soon have those out. Don't worry, she doesn't get paid any more. Don't worry, Peggy was quite old. She was in her 70s when we did *Rocky*.

AL: Jonathan Adams is very eccentric but a very solid person. Not likely to go off on a tangent. He is charming and delightful. Tony Milner was a very good mimic and he had Mike Gowans' voice down to a T. He would announce, 'Tea!' and we would all rush off. Then they couldn't get us back, because there were too many of us! They didn't operate by union rule. It was pretty vague. It was good fun, but also very irritating because you didn't get your tea breaks. Gaye brought her own knife and fork, because she knew they recycled the cutlery, so she brought her own napkin and a silver knife, fork and spoon. She wanted to make sure she didn't get contaminated.

GB: Meat and veg tastes better from silver.

AL: Sometimes, when we were waiting on the side of the set because we couldn't leave the vicinity, we would sit around for hours. The mob – that's what we called Michael White and his guys – all wore shades, even in this darkened studio, and long leather coats, like Nazis. Quite extraordinary. They would walk through and not speak to us.

GB: Now, we were all personalities and acts in our own right. We didn't feel like extras, nor were we picked to behave like extras. In the end, we just started playing these stupid games. In would walk the heavies. I don't know what happened, it was never discussed. Whatever we were doing, be it screaming with laughter or just chatting, we would just stand up in silence. Nobody would look at anyone else, and they would walk through, and then we would sit down and carry on.

AL: We were helpless with laughter. They were completely undermined. Michael couldn't figure out why we were doing it. We behaved completely like children. They treated us like children and we behaved like children.

GB: And we got huge crushes on people. I was completely besotted with Graham Clifford, the editor. Shrewd judge, wasn't I? He went on to become a hugely successful director. He did *Frances* and *Twin Peaks*. I was mad about him.

AL: I was totally enamoured with Suschitzky. He was Cronenberg's cameraman on *M Butterfly*. The best people to have crushes on are the cameramen. And the editor.

GB: Have you spoken to Peter Hinwood? Peter is wonderful. He was the top male model for *Vogue*. Don't know who dubbed the voice.

AL: You get unbelievable street cred if you drop in that you've been in *Rocky Horror*. I was away with my son and I saw *Rocky* was showing. It was about two years ago, when he was about 12. The children insisted on sitting in the front. I had no idea how crude it was. They were paying me so much attention. 'I saw you in the wedding! That was you!' Their attitude was completely transformed. When they discovered I was in *Rocky Horror*, they couldn't get over it. It's still very important.

GB: It's very strange to see people dressed like Annabel and me at the film. I remember I was in Dallas seeing the film, and watching these kids perform. My friend whispered to me, 'Go on and tell them that it's you,' but I didn't.

AL: I would like to see it. I've never seen it in those conditions.

GB: I saw the live show recently at Wimbledon. Now the audience come dressed like Transylvanians. They put in all their stuff. The fans make the show go on for hours. It's a bit boring, actually. It's a real drag. I think if the audience rules a live show, you've lost the show. It's a party for them, instead of it being a theatre show. Not everybody is a fan. Some people have just come to see the show. Maybe now that's just part of the show.

AL: Gaye was the bride's mother in the wedding. I was the Jackie Kennedy clone. Little pillbox hat.

GB: Annabel was with Biggins. She was wearing turquoise. I got completely hysterical during Rocky and Frank's wedding. There's this man, dressed up as a woman, marrying a man. There's me, a woman dressed up like a man, being paid money to do this nonsense. I got completely hysterical and couldn't stop laughing. Extraordinary situation.

AL: We were not in the ending scene when Frank sings 'I'm Going Home'. Those were extras. They did extra endings and, once we'd all gone, they couldn't finish the movie. The last 20 minutes is all trying to find an ending. They only booked us for eight weeks.

GB: We shot for eight weeks at Bray. We worked six- and sometimes seven-day weeks. The house is now a hotel. A very posh hotel. Then it was owned by this woman who lived in France who just never came back.

AL: Doing the motorbikes at night in the rain at the house was fun. We had to have brandy. That was nice, I do remember that! It was us two and Kimi, I think. We rode on the backs. That was a bonus. Being up all night is always fun, anyway. We went pillion. They dressed the drivers in *Rocky* costumes. We didn't actually drive them. We were the only three at the castle on film. We rehearsed in the drawing room at the house.

GB: The accident with Meat Loaf? I remember he had to drive up the ramp and across and down again. It caused quite a lot of trouble. It was bloody hard to do. He wasn't much of a motorbike rider, really. I don't think it was a serious accident.

AL: I remember them trying to film the motorbike going past us.

GB: I don't remember what I did during that. Probably as little as possible, I imagine. I remember Jim Sharman saying to me that the idea of being in a film is to be seen. 'Why don't you stand near the camera? Don't avoid it.'

AL: The dance scene was the most fun. That was wonderful fun. David Toguri rehearsing us every day, that was our warm-up, really. We had to be on the set at 7am and do an hour of warm-up.

GB: Annabel got eye trouble at the time. Problems with contact lenses. It was OK, because we were wearing dark glasses, but every time we had a break, Annabel had to go and sit in a dark corner. I'd known Richard from way back and Annabel knew him from *Hair*.

AL: I was very close friends with Tim Curry for quite a long time. One of the reasons they asked us to do *Rocky* was because of Rock Bottom. Michael White had lent us the *Rocky Horror* theatre in Chelsea to do our first show. He lent us a Sunday night, the one night in the week when *Rocky* wasn't on there. But we were all part of that whole theatre and music scene.

GB: The *Jesus Christ, Superstar* people are the same bunch. Most of the same people did *Hair*. The guy that was the choreographer on *Superstar* was the assistant director on *Hair*. Jim Sharman directed *Hair* in Australia and he came here to direct *Superstar* and *Hair*.

AL: I think Jim knew Nell beforehand. Nell was the first punk. She invented punk. I remember her with her two-tone hair, cut across here. I've never seen that before. She brought it with her. In fact, I think it was pre-punk. This and David Bowie. David probably started it. It was all the King's Road thing. Doing *Rocky* was like a favour and for fun, for our friends. I would never put it down as one of my most notable performances, but it was great fun to be involved with; I would have hated not being in it.

GB: You want to be in films that are created by your friends. You are supportive of them and you want it to work. At the time, it was just an ordinary film. It didn't get big 'til much later.

SM: *Is that how all the Transylvanians felt?*

AL: We were all so different. Pam Obermeyer was a sharp, clever girl, and wouldn't take so much shit.

GB: Henry Woolf, he was a short Napoleon-looking man. Used to mock a lot. He'd start yawning and say, 'That's really really interesting.' He adored Annabel. His head came up to my boobs.

AL: Henry was the one who got Harold Pinter writing. Pinter wrote

The Birthday Party, The Homecoming, The Caretaker. He used pauses in his work. He wrote 'pauses'. Henry got him to write his first play, when he was at Bristol. Pinter was a discontented actor. Henry told him to stop talking and write it down and promised him he would get it produced. He got it to BBC radio. It was *The Room*. We loved him. You make such intimate friends on these things. Very intense.

GB: Ishaq Bux was not what you would call one of the crowd. He did his best, but he stuck out like a sore thumb with us.

AL: Doing this film was not just a job, because we were surrounded by mates. It was something we really enjoyed because we were supporting friends.

GB: It was like being in a play.

AL: It was special because I'd never been an extra before, and it was like being part of a company. It was quite a closed company.

GB: We were invited to the cast and crew screening, but not the premiere.

AL: On the credits, both of my names are spelled wrong. I couldn't believe it. It was the first time I'd seen my name on film credits and both were spelled wrong. So rude.

GB: We have no memory of being invited to the premiere. Biggins went because he goes to those things.

SM: *So tell me about Rock Bottom.*

AL: I'm most proud of Rock Bottom, even though it fizzled out. It was a great idea, sort of like The Spice Girls, but all grown-up. It snowballed so fast that we lost control over it and it got sort of hijacked by a television company and made into a programme called *Rock Follies*.

We were supposed to do *Rock Follies*. It was written for us and about us. The three of us. They denied any part we had in it, except that we were actresses who had auditioned to be in it. That's the story they put out. That was the basis of the court case. One of us was not available at the exact time they wanted to go into production. They could have easily put it back a month and sorted it out. They wanted all the honour and glory. They also wanted complete control. We carried on after that. We did several more concerts that year. You couldn't really carry on after that, though. They took our looks, our names. Rula Lenska played Gaye.

GB: Even Annabel's mother was a character. They took the idea of the group and put in on television. We lost our recording contract and our credibility. We looked like copies of *Rock Follies*. And we were the originals.

AL: I sued the TV company, the writer and the producer. If you take your work to a producer, it's confidential. It took us eight years to get into court, for 16 weeks in the High Court, and we won, hands down. The television people took our names, our heights, everything. We lost our group. We all sued, but I was the major one that sued.

But that's how I got my house in Primrose Hill and Gaye got her house, with the settlement. Now, if the show goes out anywhere, it has to say, 'Based on an idea by Gaye Brown, Annabel Leventon and Diane Langton.' So taking that through as far as it could go, I'm bloody proud of what I did. I have lots of court stories. And of course, we had legal aid. We had to contribute what we could, but we could not have brought the case without it.

GB: They should do the court case for television. It was hilarious, and extraordinary. Howard Schuman, the guy who was the writer for *Rock Follies*, denied he was a good friend; he actually denied knowing us and that we were really close friends. They accused Annabel of being a paranoid schizophrenic...

AL: ...and that I deluded myself into imagining that I had invented this group. And so powerful were my delusions that I persuaded my mates of the same thing. I did a week in the witness box. The judge was brilliant.

GB: The group was a bloody good idea and wonderful fun, probably the most exciting thing I've ever been part of. And then also winning the court case. Having a judge saying he believed me as an out-of-work actress over the head of drama at Thames Television, Verity Lambert. We won half a million in compensation.

AL: Tim and I played the leads in his first ten-penny play. I think Tim put me up for that part, because he already had it. He was certainly there when the name Rock Bottom was born. He remembered that very well. In a way, we were all part of the same crowd. Nearly all our friends were offered parts to be in it turned [them] down because they didn't want to be disloyal to us. Tim did neither of those things.

GB: Rock Bottom were three actresses that were fed up with working in things that didn't suit us. We were bored. We thought we needed to do something ourselves. All the girl groups until then didn't have individual personalities. We were completely uncontrollable. We were singing and comedy and ourselves. We were a combination of the female Marx Brothers and the female Rolling Stones. We had all the passion in the singing, but when we started singing, one of our very first songs that no one had heard before, they were screaming with laughter before we even started. By the end of the first verse, they were all on their feet cheering. It was one of those wonderful fusions. We thought it was hysterical.

AL: Gaye and I wrote a song first; Diane [Langton] wasn't around at the beginning. We thought it was hysterical. It was 1950s cliché. We jammed together, and we wept with laughter when we sang it. We thought it was the stupidest thing we've ever heard. Diane got really cross and said, 'NO! It shouldn't be like that. You don't understand, that's exactly what I felt when I was 15. We've got to sing it serious.' So we then found a fusion of us taking the piss and also meaning it. It was a really special combination.

GB: The fact is that we were all over the hill. 1973 is when we formed the band. I was 32, Annabel was 30 and Di was 39. We thought we got something from each other. We could do the harmonies when we needed to. We all had such different voices.

AL: When Gaye sang a verse, she had a dark, smoky, blues-jazz voice, Diane has incredibly strong wonderful Broadway voice and I am melodic. A strong central voice. Everything that was different worked. Gaye was six feet tall, with scarlet and pink hair, I was extremely blonde. Diane had black hair and tits that stuck out...

GB: We wore ridiculous platform heels. It was the most bizarre combination, visually, that anyone could imagine. But all of us were not only strong, sexy and proud of it, but also adored each other. When any one of us did anything any good, the others just shrieked with laughter. There were so many constraints on women in those days, and we just kind of said, 'Up yours. We're going to do what we want to do!' It was groundbreaking. Our audience was almost completely gay, because they were also breaking ground at the same time. We were all coming up at the same time, to be recognised.

AL: One night, we were singing [backing vocals] with Peter Straker and singing 'Proud Mary'. He had to change his trousers, over some Mickey Mouse shoes, and we were singing the 'Rolling...rolling...' part. He had a problem changing, and we were doing this for 20 minutes.

SM: *He changed for 20 minutes?!*
AL: The accidents always worked well with us. When he finally got back onstage 20 minutes later, Diane shouted at him, 'WHERE THE

FUCK HAVE YOU BEEN?!' It brought the house down. We behaved like ourselves onstage. In a funny way, that's what The Spice Girls did, too. They were packaged and put together. They took a lot on board, consciously or unconsciously, of what we were doing over 20 years ago.

SM: It's like in Rocky *or not in* Rocky, *everyone was part of the same group.*

GB: That was our connection, really. We all knew a lot of people from *Rocky Horror*. And of course we'd all been to see it. That theatre was the theatre to go to in the West End, in Chelsea, the King's Road. It's astonishing. They were turning people away. Two shows on a Saturday night and there were queues around the block. Rock Bottom started the Sunday-night concerts at the *Rocky* theatre. After that, they had them all the time. In fact, all over London, after that. We were the first people to do that. It was a wonderful time, you know, being in London, then.

<<<<irememberdoingthetimewarpirememberdoingthetimewarpi>>>>

Fran Fullenwider

'But that's just one small fraction of the main attraction'

Scott spoke with Jill Searle at the Ugly Agency, which specialises in 'different-looking' people. Jill looked after Fran for years.

Easily the largest of the Transylvanians, Fran Fullenwider was born a daughter of an affluent American diplomat in Texas, 'where everything is bigger and better' (hear that, Meat?). Fran came to London in the 1950s, studied ballet and attended RADA. Jill Searle remembers that, sometime in 1972, Fran came to Ugly with hopes of getting a secretarial position, but at that time the office was quite small – there 'just wasn't enough room for Fran in the office'. But Jill suggested that she get work in front of the camera. It was a good suggestion. Fran became the first large model to promote lacy lingerie, while in 1972 she was named Miss Roaster Wrap and came in second in Andrew Logan's Alternative Miss World Pageant.

Fran went off to Italy, where in film work she was best known for a string of romantic comedies in Italy for her good friend Federico Fellini, her last role being that of Glenn Close and Jeremy Irons' mother in *House Of The Spirits*. Her alternative celebrity was enhanced by innumerable appearances as a pin-up girl appearing on postcards and calendars.

Fran was well liked on the set of *The Rocky Horror Picture Show*. She passed away, aged 51, after suffering from a heart attack on 16 November 1997. She always swore that her surname was real.

‹‹‹‹‹irememberdoingthetimewarpirememberdoingthetimewarpi›››››

Patricia Quinn

Pat Quinn was asked to recreate her Magenta for the movie, with one big difference...

SCOTT MICHAELS: *Now tell me about the genesis of your being in the movie.*

PAT QUINN: Jim Sharman, John Goldstone, Brian Thomson and I went to lunch. They wanted me to play Magenta in the film version of the play. I asked about the Usherette and they told me they weren't using an usherette. By the way, a lot of people don't know what an usherette is and the ice-cream girl in cinemas went out of fashion. Now you have kiosks. In fact, I really once was an usherette in real life! I was at the Notting Hill Gate Classic. I used to go down the front and watch all the movies, and when the time came for the interval, I would go and get my ice cream tray and sell ice cream.

So, I had the practice and knew how to carry the tray. I asked about the song 'Science Fiction' and Jim said he had another idea and just wanted me for Magenta. I said, 'Well if I can't sing the song, Magenta only has four lines, so I don't want to do it.' The Usherette is my showcase. I was so arrogant at that age that I just didn't snap up the role right away.

Michael said, 'Listen, we'll go along to John's house, and I want to show you the set.'

I couldn't imagine what it was going to be like, coming from a small stage show and to open it into a movie. It's another world. Of course, Magenta is there all the time! Onstage, I was so bored with the four lines.

So then he showed me the sets. The pink laboratory, this is the tank that Rocky's born in...

I thought, 'Oh God, this is great! This is fantastic! I'm doing it! I don't care who's singing "Science Fiction"!' because I suddenly saw it all! It was stunning. And the costumes were great!

Well, I have to say it was the result of just great imagination from Brian Thomson and Jim Sharman. I think that's why Thomson is a bit upset now. A team made this film.

I think I got £300 a week for the film. I remember they said there were only two cars that would be going to Bray. The Yanks had one and Mr Curry had the other, because of his make-up and how long it took. They told Little Nell and me to catch a bus from Marble Arch.

So, Nell and I had a meeting and Nell said, 'No car, no picture.' Dear Richard was so upset that he said, at his own expense, he would hire a mini-van for us. But we said we wanted a chauffeur and a limo. In the end, we got a car. Oakley Court was just next door to Bray. It was so dilapidated. It was freezing cold and rain came in. We had to catch it in buckets.

SM: This is great. Tell me more movie stuff.

PQ: In the film, they wouldn't let Jonathan Adams play the Narrator. In the play, Eddie and Doctor Scott were played by the same actor. They wouldn't let me play the Usherette and Magenta. This was probably because they couldn't afford another actor. It's not that they wouldn't let me be the Usherette – they used my lips for the song – it's that they didn't let me sing the song. They couldn't figure out how to use an usherette on the screen. I really don't think the Usherette would work on the screen. They had to come up with a different idea and decided on my lips. Jonathan chose Doctor Scott, and Charles Gray had been cast as the Narrator.

I remember when we filmed the wedding scene and you could hear Richard's voice singing 'Science Fiction' right across that field. It seems like we were always freezing in a field.

When we got there for the wedding shoot, we were curious to see what Jim Sharman had conjured up. The whole idea of the American Gothic theme – that church, etc – it was a surprise! We thought, 'What's this all about, and why are we the Gothics?'

Richard and I had a funny relationship, I'm not quite sure why. It wasn't easy at that time. I think it's something to do with fancying each other, but we were both married. Maybe a sexual tension, I don't really know. He wasn't that nice to me. When he sang that song to me when I left the show, 'The Day Magenta Went Away', I guess those were his true feelings. Maybe I was difficult. In work, I am very serious.

'The Time Warp' and 'Sweet Transvestite' were switched around in order for the movie because of the Transylvanians arriving.

'Once In A While' was dropped because of length. Barry Bostwick was sick because it was dropped. After all, that was Brad's song and we did it on the stage all that time. But that's the name of the game. *Voof!* On the cutting-room floor.

SM: But you were pleased with the filming?

PQ: Absolutely. Peter Suschitzky was our lighting cameraman, son of the famous Wolf Suschitzky. We weren't allowed to see the rushes, so Richard, Little Nell and I would sneak in and see them. I loved it. Richard called Peter [Suschitzky] the Prince of Darkness, not because of the material but because of the lack of light in the film. Probably because it was never daylight in the film. It all took place in one night. Lots of people visited the set – Britt Ekland, but she was with Lou Adler after all.

Amanda Lear, Salvador Dali's muse, visited the set. He used to paint her quite a lot. Amanda *was* King's Road.

When Magenta came in with the gong and says, 'Dinner is prepared,' through a hole in the wall. I loved it. The gong was like that movie logo, and I could hardly hold it because it was so heavy. It was a brilliant idea, and I used a Katherine Hepburn voice. Oh God, we had such fun. Only because we did the play, and we knew it inside and out. That was the thrill. We were a family. It was a joyous thing to do. It was Jim Sharman's first film, so there were a lot of continuity flaws. I don't know why he wouldn't let us see the rushes, because I like seeing them. I can see where I can improve myself. It's very teaching.

SM: *Any hiccups?*

PQ: We had no idea that the Meat Loaf corpse was under the table during the dinner scene. I just laughed and couldn't stop, and Richard hits me and tells me to shut up! Nobody told me. We were going around serving the Meat Loaf, flinging it around, and Frank using the carver! I remember there was a big red table cloth and it had to be done in one shot, because everything was going off the table, and the continuity people would have had a nightmare!

Poor Tim had to get it right in one shot. He gets up and pulls off the cloth, and there's The Loaf! I was shocked, because I didn't even know we were supposed to be eating him. Then Nell ran out and cried. The actual meat was a big leg of pork. Tim had one of those electric carvers that were quite new at the time. Pat Quinn was not in on the joke and I wonder now if the rest of them knew it was coming, or if they purposely didn't tell us. The other thing I thought was quite clever was that Rocky didn't know how to use the cutlery, because he was just born and Nell gives him a nudge to get it right.

SM: *Fabulous set for that scene.*

PQ: Brian Thomson was the set designer and he was a genius. Like that dining scene. Brian thought, 'These people are from Transylvania, and this is how you dine.' I never thought about things like that. We had piss pots from the hospital and jars. He has that famous painting on the wall of that woman pinching her nipple. Or maybe that's in *Shock Treatment*. Also, wasn't it brilliant that he had the RKO tower in at the end of it? I have drawings of all of these.

SM: *What were the Americans like on the set?*

PQ: Susan Sarandon used to sit and do needlepoint during the filming. She was doing 'Home Sweet Home' on a pillow. I thought, 'Good Lord, how quaint!' I think it ended up as a prop on the set! I was talking to Barry one time, and he says to me, 'You thought I was Brad, didn't you?' I said, 'Yeah.'

And Richard O'Brien really wanted to be Frank N Furter, you realise, not Riff Raff.

SM: *Did you think at all how the play was pushing the sexual boundaries?*

PQ: I was very shocked by the bed with Frank and Rocky in it, because in the play they don't go to bed; it was all implied. I didn't realise it was so gay of a movie, and thought it was a bit crude. In the play, we never got the sexual thing. We never saw them go to bed. I thought the bits with the silhouettes and Frank having sex was completely tasteful, because it was clever. The only thing that bothered me was the bed. The fact that he was giving Brad a blow-job didn't bother me, but implying that he and Rocky had sex in that bed did.

To me, on Transylvania, they wouldn't have had sex.

Then of course Richard and I chased Rocky. That's when we did the thing with the mop, which was all new. Richard bites my neck then. There is some photograph somewhere with my neck and a huge love bite. I also made sure that my face was facing the camera!

I wonder whatever happened to Peter Hinwood? Probably in Pimlico. Peter Hinwood used to drive up and down King's Road in a red sports car looking divine. His voice was dubbed for the song in the film. He was a muscleman. He never spoke in real life. I don't know who did his voice.

SM: *Shall we cut to the lips?*

PQ: All right, I remember Tim, Richard and I were in a car, going to the studio and Tim asked Richard, 'So who is singing "Science Fiction"?'

And Richard replied, 'Me.'

I said, 'You rotter!' Richard took away my song!

It was the last day of the shoot when Jim Sharman came to me with an idea for the 'Science Fiction' sequence. His inspiration came from the poster by Man Ray called *Lips Over Hollywood*. It's a mouth with red lipstick, in a blue sky, above the Hollywood sign.

Jim said he wanted to have a mouth singing the song and he wanted my mouth. I said, 'My mouth, his voice? How much?'

I was so angry. I was actually paid nothing, or next to it. My agents really screwed up on that deal. They really wanted me for that scene and look how famous those lips are now.

They were in the process of editing *Rocky* when I arrived at Elstree Studios to film the lips scene. They blacked my face up completely and applied the lipstick. They put a piece of felt over the camera lens and cut a hole in it so the camera could film through it and not pick up any other of my facial features. It was all very primitive.

It was very difficult to keep my head completely still, so they made a clamp with those flaps that are on theatrical lights. They put my head in it so I couldn't move at all. I was in that contraption for two days. I had to post-sync it to Richard's voice, with Jim Sharman directing the entire time. He told me precisely when to lick my lips and when to smile and all that.

It was so sad, because Elstree Studios was finished. No movies were being made. I was the only person sitting out in the sun with my face covered in black make-up, with this little crew, filming the lips…

<<<<irememberdoingthetimewarpirememberdoingthetimewarpi>>>>

Richard Hartley

'I'm your new commander, you are now my prisoner'

The movie was, above all, a musical, somewhat old-fashioned in format, in an era when very few films approaching the style of the classic Hollywood musicals were even contemplated because of the cost. It goes without saying that the soundtrack of the movie is therefore as important as the film footage itself. It was created by Richard Hartley from the ashes of the first incarnation. It wasn't all plain sailing.

DAVID EVANS: *So how did you feel about the film when that came along?*

RICHARD HARTLEY: In Los Angeles, the play's producer was Lou Adler and he wanted to take care of it, so he got David Foster to do it at the Roxy. The musical director was Perry Como's MD. I was crestfallen when I wasn't asked, but I had gone on after *Rocky* to do two films. Then the film of *Rocky* came around.

Jim phoned me up and told me there would be a film.

'Do you think Phil Spector would be a good guy to do this?'

'Sure,' I said and hung up on him.

It was Lou Adler who was instrumental in getting me involved, after things didn't go well for it musically at the Roxy. In terms of it being a rock 'n' roll show, Foster and the other guy turned it into a very slick... Well, let's just say it didn't work. It never worked in America, even with people like Meat Loaf in it at the Roxy.

So with the film, Jim then said, 'Who should we get in the band?'

I said, 'This is kind of English and I think we shouldn't be going to America for musicians. If you want to do that, fine, but I think we should have the guy that played the guitar in the original show.'

Count [Ian 'Count' Blair] always wanted to be a Rolling Stone. His was a rough kind of sound, which is perfect for *Rocky*. And he knew about old-fashioned rock 'n' roll, which is where Richard's ideas came from, as well as my arrangements.

All the arrangements are steals from all my favourite records from when I was a kid. Both Richard and I share the same rock 'n' roll heritage. The score is peppered with quotes from him and me, even some of the tunes. Try 'Don't Dream It' and 'Over The Rainbow'. Listen to the cow bell in 'Sweet Transvestite'; it's very 'Honky-Tonk Women'. If you listen to the beginning of 'Sword Of Damocles', if you slow it down, you might find another song there, a Brian Hyland song called 'I Only Met You Just A Couple Of Days Ago'; and when Brad and Janet sing 'Dammit, Janet', that comes straight from a Bobby Vee record. He always had cascading strings.

But as far as our basic band was concerned, I said, 'We should get the same sax player, same guitar player as we had onstage. I'll play on some of it as well, and then perhaps we should get the two guys from Procol Harum.' I knew that the drummer was a great R&B drummer. The gothic feel gathered momentum with our discussions of where the film would go with the D of P [director of photography, Peter Suschitzky]. Peter was known in the trade as the Prince of Darkness; both he and his father did very dark work.

We rehearsed initially with the band for a couple of days in railway arches near Waterloo. Then we got into the studio. One of the reasons that nothing came about for what seemed like ages was because everyone was so stoned. With the arrival of the Procol guys, this had become real rock 'n' roll. When the roadies came in around midday or one o'clock to start work, the first thing they did was to roll a joint. I think the second thing we ever did was 'Sweet Transvestite' and we couldn't get it to work. It just wouldn't hang together. We changed the arrangement for the film, we added bits and breaks for the brass, and the way that he started was different. It didn't work.

Then we tried it a bit slower and it kind of clicked. We found a tempo where everything fitted together. Finally, they sent Timmy down so that he could sing it through and he did. It worked. Then we slowed down other songs and they sounded better, too.

DE: *These songs need to be performed, don't they?*

RH: Yes. Because the songs are so simple, they have to be sung by somebody. Just putting down the track wasn't enough. Like with 'I'm Going Home'. I've played it a million times. We started recording it one evening and it didn't work, and so I thought, 'I'm the wrong man. Rabbit, you play it.'

Then Timmy showed up and it was done. Done in an hour.

Sometimes we would just interchange people and it would work. By then, Tim had had a few offers for this, that and the other and was looking towards his future in the music business. That fired him up, too.

DE: So how long did it take?

RH: All the backing tracks were done in four days. Then there was the 'Science Fiction' saga. Originally, in the show, Pat had sung it, but Jim started saying, 'Oh, who should we get?'

I said, 'We should get Richard to sing it.' I remembered back at Richard's flat that day when he sang it first to us, really slowly. I said, 'Richard should sing it. It's his song. It's the whole story; the whole show is in that song.' That's when the Procol Harum drummer came into his own, because he was brilliant at that. He played on Dusty [Springfield]'s 'I Only Want To Be With You'.

DE: Which studio did you use?

RH: We did it in Olympic, the studio built by The Rolling Stones. It's owned by Virgin now. I've used that studio ever since. The Who, Zeppelin, The Eagles… Olympic was the biggest rock 'n' roll studio in the world. It's all revamped now. We did the backing tracks and the vocals all before we started shooting, apart from Rocky's.

SM: So, finally I get to ask it, the $64,000 question. Who dubbed for Peter Hinwood?

RH: Well, we did that with a couple of people. Originally we used this guy who was one of Straker's backing singers. That was the one that Peter Hinwood originally mimed to. Then it was decided to change the voice, so we got in this Australian guy, Trevor White, and it got more complicated. Meat Loaf was one of the six session singers. He would always come down, because he had nothing to do and he wanted to sing back-up. You can hear him on a lot of them. He sings in the chorus of 'Hot Patootie'.

DE: More secrets, please, more!

RH: Jim Sharman wanted 'The Time Warp' to sound like 'The Wizard Of Oz'. We recorded 'The Time Warp' straight and we slowed the tape down and then they sang up a bit. The five singers were Liza Strike, Helen Chappelle, Clair Torrey, Brian Engel and Barry St John, all of them fantastic. Liza and Helen were always in huge demand. They sang on everything in those days. Led Zeppelin, Elton, Cat Stevens tracks... So, there is normal singing and speeded-up voices an octave higher fed in, so it has that funny sound to it. By doing it like that, it sounded like there were ultimately 18 singers, technically. 'The Time Warp' on the record is probably the best transition from the stage show. Basically, it's a Chuck Berry song. It has that 'Chuck Berry meets The Rolling Stones' thing. That really came off well, I think. We added all sorts of other things – the brass arrangements, then the strings.

SM: I always thought the Transylvanians were like the Munchkins in The Wizard Of Oz. *There is a kind of* Wizard *thing here, isn't there?*

RH: You're right.

‹‹‹‹iremberdoingthetimewarpirememberdoingthetimewarpi›››››

Trevor White

For so long unrecognised and therefore unacknowledged, Trevor White – the owner of the singing voice of Peter Hinwood's Rocky Horror – now lives in Australia.

A former guitar player with Sparks, Trevor was previously also a member of The A-Jays and, later, Jook, along with Ian Hampton, Chris Townson and Ian Kimmet. He once sold his electric guitar to Marc Bolan, then a member of John's Children. It was Marc's first. After Sparks, Trevor released one solo single, 'Crazy Kids', with Martin Gordon on bass.

Trevor now works as a record company associate. He is much in demand as a session singer and can often be seen on Australian television backing international stars on Channel 9's *The Midday Show*.

The other singers often worked as a team and were greatly in demand at the time, contributing to albums such as Pink Floyd's *Dark Side Of The Moon* and Elton John's *Madman Across The Water*. They have collectively and separately worked with such bands as Led Zeppelin, Deep Purple and Procol Harum.

SCOTT MICHAELS: Literally hours before this book is being published, I tried one more time to locate the singer, Trevor White. I sent a blind e-mail off to a website that mentioned Trevor and included my telephone number. By a bizarre twist of fate, I currently work as a bartender at the Royal Court Theatre, and when Trevor phoned me I was in the basement of the Royal Court, changing a keg of beer. Just an odd juxtaposition, I thought. Trevor lives in Sydney with his wife Chemene, and their son Ryan. Trevor has another son, Simon, who is also a musician. He agreed to let me have a short interview with him the next day, regarding his involvement with the film.

SM: Tell me a bit about your musical background.

TREVOR WHITE: I'm originally from Essex. My first professional gig was as pianist/vocalist with a band called Sounds Incorporated. I think they were one of the first groups managed by Brian Epstein that didn't come from Liverpool. As well as being a great band in their own right, during the '60s Sounds backed such artists as Sam Cooke, Little Richard, Jerry Lee Lewis and Gene Vincent whenever they would come to England. In 1964, they were the opening act for The Beatles on their world tour, which included Australia.
SM: So you knew Brian Epstein?

TW: I joined *Sounds* in the late '60s, a while after Brian had died, although we were still with NEMS Enterprises, along with artists such as Cilla Black. The band had a couple of very big hit records in

Australia, due to The Beatles' tour. Subsequently, we came here to Australia many times on extended tours. At the end of 1971, while in Australia, the band broke up. Some of the guys returned to the UK, and others, myself included, remained here to do our own thing.

SM: Were you involved with Jesus Christ, Superstar *in Australia?*

TW: I saw Jim Sharman on television talking about doing *Superstar* in Sydney and how they were going to have auditions. As it turned out, out of 800 or so people, I got the role of Jesus. Jim Sharman directed it here and Brian Thomson designed it. Because Robert Stigwood held the rights to *Superstar*, he decided to open it in London the following year, so he brought on Jim and Brian again to do the show in London.

SM: How did your involvement in Rocky *begin?*

TW: In 1974, when my contract with *Superstar* was up, I returned to England for a break. While I was there, I met up with a friend I'd known in Australia who was working for a theatrical agency in London. Discussing work prospects, he told me that Jim Sharman was in town, doing a movie version of *Rocky Horror*. As it happened, he was looking for someone to be the 'voice' of *Rocky*. Apparently, several people had auditioned, but nothing had been settled. My friend suggested me to Jim, and they arranged for me to meet with the film's musical director, Richard Hartley. Hartley played a bit on the piano, I sang for him, and Hartley said, 'Terrific. You've got the part!'

SM: So what did you have to do?

TW: Some time later I went off to Elstree Studios for the vocal session. They just set up a microphone, and I sang along to the music track as I watched a black and white loop of the various scenes played out before me.

SM: So you had to sing to a man that was miming to someone else?

TW: Right. It was a little tricky. For example, on 'Sword Of Damocles', for technical reasons here and there, the visual was a little out of sync with the music. It was so tempting to go with the music coming through my headphones, but it was more important to be right in sync with Rocky's performance on screen. Jim told me that the deal was that I wouldn't get a credit. I can understand why not, because you couldn't have something like Barbra Streisand in the part of so and so, sung by so and so. But had I been thinking at the time, I would have said, 'Fine, but put in "Additional vocals by…"' But that didn't happen.

SM: I can understand that, but they did release a soundtrack…

TW: And I was very curious. So I checked it out, and I wasn't on it! But years later, a 25th anniversary CD was released, featuring previously unreleased material from the movie. I bought it and, sure enough, it's my voice. I thought, 'Well, nobody asked me…' and that's the way it stands. I haven't been in touch with them, and they haven't been in touch with me.

SM: Anything else?

TW: When Rocky was carrying Frank up the RKO tower, I was asked to record the breathing, panting and the Tarzan yells. That was just thrown in for fun, but I don't know if they used it or not.

SM: Interesting. It must have been exciting for you though.

TW: I've done so many recordings for commercials and shows and albums. *Rocky* really was just another session – except that the mechanics were different. I've never had to go to a studio and lay down a track to a black and white loop before. Who could have imagined that the whole thing would become so huge?

SM: So you knew Jim and Brian. What about Nell?

TW: I'm one of the few that didn't know Nell. Everyone that I worked with in *Superstar* knew Nell really well. I did actually get to meet Tim Curry over coffee with Brian at the Chateau Marmont in LA. I think I was touring with The Kinks at that time. It was pre release of the film but after I laid down the tracks.

SM: The Kinks?

TW: Yeah, a friend of mine was in the band and said to Ray Davies that he had a friend (me) that he used to be in a band with, and since you are looking for someone for an American tour... I auditioned for Ray and toured with them. That was a great experience.

SM: Tell me about the Olympics.

TW: In Australia, I'm involved in a lot of different projects. My partner, John Gillard, and I write songs for television, sports, and all sorts of things. We knew the Olympics were coming up in September 2000, and we had previously written lots of sporting anthems for television, including the music for the World Cup Soccer, Commonwealth Games, etc., etc. So, we thought we were qualified to write for the Olympics. We knew Ric Birch, the director of ceremonies, and asked if we could submit a song for the opening ceremony. 'Sure,' he said. 'Submit away!' We worked long and hard and came up with something we thought was right. I think they had something like 4,500 entries, and they chose three. Ours was one of them.

SM: What an accomplishment! Which one was it?

TW: We wrote 'Heroes Live Forever'. It's on the official opening ceremony CD, and it went double platinum here in Australia. Vanessa Amorosi, who is a sensational singer, sang it.

SM: Well, thank you, Trevor. Thanks for helping me complete this part of the puzzle and give you a bit of recognition for your part in all of this.

‹‹‹‹irememberdoingthetimewarpirememberdoingthetimewarpi›››››

Susan Sarandon

'You were caught with a flat, well, how about that!'

And the lovely Susan, then so much in love. Young and fresh and especially fragrant from having featured in a huge campaign for a feminine soap product called Dermasage, as well as an unmissable commercial extolling the virtues of Magic Lady panties in 1973, Susan Sarandon arrived in Britain. Although she only knew it as a gut instinct, she had landed on The Edge.

The following quotes are taken from interviews Susan has given:

'I look at it and I think, "Wow, we must have had such a good time." But I remember it was hellish. Bray Studios was hardly heated. It was an hour's journey each way. Everything was very slow. No one had done films before but me. And I had pneumonia...'

'I'm very proud of it. I think the spirit of the film is just a marvel. "Don't Dream It, Be It" is something I'd love to stamp on my kids' foreheads. Drag is something that everybody should have in their culture. And in their closet...'

31 AUGUST 2000
Scott had sent a copy of the unedited manuscript of *Rocky Horror: From Concept To Cult* to Susan's agents and had been told that Susan would grant him an interview. Scott phoned Susan's office as previously arranged and a man named Brian Pines put him through to Susan on her cellphone, in her car, in New York City.

SCOTT MICHAELS: *Had you seen the show in Los Angeles before the film offer came?*

SUSAN SARANDON: Yes, that's how the movie offer came around. I was already friends with Tim and a couple of others – Jamie Donnelly [who played Magenta in LA]. I had met Tim there and seen the stage production and was just blown away by his performance. So we became friends, and one day when I went by to see him, the day they were auditioning people for the film, just to say, 'Hi.' It had never occurred to anyone. I mean, I wasn't submitted for it. They had a break and I went in and said, 'Hi,' and they said, 'Oh my God, what a great idea. Would you be interested in being in the movie?' I read it. Nobody had ever found a way of making Janet funny. There were a lot of people that could sing it better, but no one could make her funny. I just did a parody of every *ingenué* I had ever played, so it ended up being funny. I thought, 'Well, if I can get there, I just have to get over my phobia of singing.'

SM: I read, in the early 1980s, that you did Rocky *because you were scared to death of singing.*

SS: So my story checks out.

SM: Did you see a production in London while you were here?

SS: No. I've never been in London long enough to see anything. Is it open there now?

SM: Yes. It's really never stopped. Did you and Barry feel any alienation being the Americans on the set?

SS: Barry was incredibly experienced in the theatre. He had done *Grease*... I felt like the odd one out because everyone else had been in the show... And Meat Loaf, who was also American, he had a music background. So for me, it wasn't the Americans and the Brits. One of the sets didn't have a roof, and another one was very cold. I remember finally I got the nerve to start asking for something to keep us warm and at that point I remember somebody in production whispered under their breath, 'American stars...' But really, I didn't feel divided that way at all.

SM: Do you have fond memories of working with Jim Sharman?

SS: Yeah. They had very little money to work with, only $1 million. It was a long ride to the studio each day and long hours. My remembrance of it was that everybody was pretty busy, trying to get through it. He really didn't talk to me about my character. I had a pretty enjoyable time, except for the fact that, physically, we were falling apart. He seemed to have some idea of what he wanted, but really you are fighting with budget and time and always need more than you have. The others had their characters down pat. I know that the opening of the film was supposed to be in black and white, until you see Tim's lips in the lift, in red, and they couldn't do it. That was just too bad.

SM: Did you feel like Rocky is more substantial that just an hour and a half's 'family' entertainment?

SS: Clearly, there is something that is really speaking to kids at a certain point of whatever transition they are in. It creates an atmosphere...a safe one...a supportive one for kids. Lonely kids. For kids that are trying to find their place outside of the cheerleader group. There has got to be something about that which speaks to them and gives them acceptance for whatever gender-bending or questioning that you have, and acceptance for who you are. I think it is a very political film. Every film is political, and so is entertainment. I think it is very entertaining, and I'm very proud to have been in it. The energy of it still stands up. Certainly, it wouldn't be around this long if it wasn't clever and [didn't have] something unique.

SM: In my research, I've found quotes that you don't really understand the fascination with Rocky Horror.

SS: Nobody has ever tried to figure out what it is that everybody is fascinated with. Nobody has ever offered an explanation about why kids get together, for decades, to see this play. I went to see it with my daughter and a few other people… Natalie Portman. We snuck in. In LA, the stage show, the audience was pretty much in hysteria. You couldn't understand what anyone was saying. It was obscenity. Chaos. So it had lost what it had before, what made it clever, but people were still going. There were kids doing the stage thing; their parents had done the stage thing. [Laughs] I don't know… I have my own theories, but I don't know if anyone has done a real study about it in a serious way. So what happened to Pat?

SM: She is still acting, and she is still pretty visible in London. Do you understand why the film wasn't a success when it opened?

SS: Sure. I mean, how could it have been a success? Nobody had ever made a movie like that before. They didn't know how to market it.

SM: Do you think it lost a lot in the translation from stage to film?

SS: No. Live theatre is always much more spectacular. The fact that some people fall flat on their face and survive…it's all in the moment and very unique and special. You can never get that experience on film. I think the spirit of it is there. Because it was low budget, it was still pretty grungy and simple. If Steven Spielberg had done it, or someone that has more cinematic experience, [they] could have done something basically more interesting, but in a way it was presented very close to how it was onstage.

SM: You can choose whether or not to answer this, but were you and Barry 'involved' during the filming?

SS [laughing]: I'm certainly not going to answer that.

SM: Now, a couple of anally retentive questions about the film. Pat mentioned that you were doing needlepoint on the set. A pillow that said 'Home Sweet Home'. Can you verify?

SS: Oh really? [Laughs] No, I don't remember.

SM: *When they made the plaster casts of you, did they use your body or just your face?*

SS: They used our bodies. There weren't any extra bodies around. They used us. It was this old stuff that was hot and not very dermatologically safe, I might add. It was hard. I don't think anyone had body doubles.

SM: *Are you doing this 25th anniversary in Vegas?*

SS: I can't, because I'm committed to the opening of the *Rug Rats* movie in Vegas the next weekend and I can't go twice. At the moment, we haven't worked it out.

SM: *Any other comments?*

SS: People were just fighting for their lives in terms of getting there and getting made up. Tim was there hours and hours in a row. We didn't just hang out. I don't remember cross-stitching. I certainly embroidered all the time. It was very therapeutic, I can remember that. Something that said 'Home Sweet Home'? That doesn't sound like me.

‹‹‹‹irememberdoingthetimewarpiremememberdoingthetimewarpi›››

Barry Bostwick

19 December 2001
'Oh, Brad...It wasn't all bad, was it?'

In the war, the Second World variety, a goodly percentage of British manhood who were not overseas thought of the visiting Americans as 'over-sexed, over-paid and over here'. There was an element of that feeling on the set of *The Rocky Horror Picture Show* surrounding the presence of Barry Bostwick, Susan Sarandon and Meat Loaf. The three

Americans were cast in the film at the 'suggestion' of Twentieth Century Fox.

Having almost given up being able to make contact with him, finally Barry was generous to share his lunchbreak with me, via telephone from his dressing room on the set of *Spin City*. After a brief conversation about that show, his former co-star Michael J Fox and his work for Parkinson's syndrome, we began our conversation about how the *Rocky Horror* experience was for Mr Bostwick.

BARRY BOSTWICK: Peter Hinwood was always very, very sweet. Because he didn't actually sing, I think he probably felt a little out of the loop.

SCOTT MICHAELS: *Had you seen the play before the offer of the film came about?*

BB: Oh, sure. I had friends who were in the stage production at the Roxy in LA, so I'd seen it a number of times. I wasn't a groupie or anything, but I liked it a lot. I was really impressed with the sort of grunge theatre. I remember Kim Milford, who I'd known from New York. When Kim came around at the beginning of the show, while the cast was circulating through the audience, he came and started sucking my toes. I thought to myself, 'Well, this could be an interesting evening.'

My training was at the NYU School of the Arts, and a lot of our training was in street theatre and guerrilla theatre, and *Rocky* sort of went along with what I had been taught. Because I really loved musicals – prior to *Rocky* I did *Grease* on Broadway – it was something that was just cool and different enough. I was never interested in doing musicals like *Oklahoma!* and those old chestnuts. I wanted to do things that were strange and groundbreaking. So I was attracted to *Rocky* not only because of its form as a piece of theatre; I was attracted to the people who were putting it together. I liked their credentials. They were the *crème de la crème* of British fringe theatre. Richard, Jim and Brian had a sort of kitschy approach, visually, and story sensibility. I just wanted to work with cool people. They were cutting edge at the time.

SM: Would you use the word dangerous?

BB: No, I wouldn't. Because I came from an off-off Broadway point of view, I was living on the Bowery, in a loft, right around the corner from Café La Mama, so *Rocky* wasn't that strange to me. I might have been playing a character who was very strange to me; I was not at all like that person in reality, so playing Brad in *Rocky* didn't shock me, Barry.

SM: How do you think Tim Curry was with it?

BB: I thought Tim gave his all, but he just wanted to get it down and over with, once and for all. I think he'd just...done it, and he wanted to get past it. From what I can gather, he was indeed just over it, but when the movie came along, he saw the potential for documenting the performance. So many musicals that we did back in the 1960s and 1970s would run for a short time and you would never get a cast album out of them. So what would happen is you would work on something for months and months and then walk away with nothing to show for it, other than a memory.

I think, if I was Tim, I would have done it just because I wanted to see my performance on film. I would want to see it, purge myself and put it on film so I could look back on it as a sort of historical document. I think he didn't want to dwell on it but just to get it over with and have fun with it and be done with it and finish it off. In fact, by the time the movie was made, they were *all* pretty damn tired of it. They just wanted to get over it and move on with their lives, so many of them had been doing it for years.

SM: It has been said in the past that both you and Susan auditioned for the film together. How did that come about?

BB: My manager at the time, Bob Lamond, was best of friends with the casting director. I think they sort of manipulated a kind of duet audition, thinking we were perhaps the best couple playing these two parts, so by putting us together in one audition, we were basically doing the final callback. We had that feeling that they were bringing their first choices together. Susan had had some movie experience and I had a lot of musical experience.

SM: I realise this is personal, but were you and Susan a couple at the time?

BB: Not at the time, no.

SM: When you came to Britain, did you get the sense at all of being separate, by being 'the Americans' on the set?

BB: I think so, only because the others had been doing it for so long as a team; there weren't too many new people involved, other than us. We were the newcomers. Even Meat Loaf knew everyone already. It was a cold winter and everybody just wanted to get it done. I don't mean to harp on about the 'Let's just get this over with' attitude. There was excitement about doing it, but it was a very hard shoot. It was done with so little money. There was nothing luxurious about how we were treated or the manner in which it was shot. It was shot on an unheated stage, no toilets on the stage. The mansion was leaking and there were holes in the roof... We were standing in front of these huge propane heaters, like jets blowing hot air into a room from which it was all leaking out of cracks. We were standing around wet all of the time. It just wasn't... It was a hard shoot. A *hard* shoot.

I don't think we were intentionally isolated from the English group. It's just that it was happening so quickly, it just took a while for us to get friendly. It was a long drive to work every day. We were living in London and had to drive to Windsor. We were constantly whisked back and forth. It was just slightly uncomfortable, which gave an edge to the piece, I'm sure. I loved just standing off to the side and watching them putting the set together, or watching other people's performances. I was as much an audience member as a participant in the whole shoot. I loved everybody I worked with and I loved the whole experience.

It was also my first time in England, so I was discovering Britain at the same time I was discovering these people, so in a way there was a parallel between my character coming into a foreign environment like Frank's castle and me, Barry, coming into London. It was daunting and exciting and anxious-making.

SM: How did you find working with Jim Sharman?

BB: He was a quiet director. He didn't talk a lot. He was very specific about what he wanted. He didn't become your best friend. I actually became better friends with his assistant, who I sadly lost track of. But Jim was a very sweet quiet guy with a vision. Like I said, he didn't go out of his way to become my best friend. He had enough on his plate. I think he trusted that we were bringing to it American energy and enthusiasm and innocence. The only direction I would get from him was to calm things down a bit. One of his real achievements was to create a consistent acting style. I would suspect that was very difficult with so many different kinds of actors. There is a slight over-the-top acting that was required, yet it had to be very grounded in reality and very real. Sort of 15 per cent hyperness that had to be added on top of every character's reality.

SM: Sort of comic-book-like?

BB: Yes, but without being so buffoonish that you didn't believe the characters' predicament. That was difficult. We had to play everything we were involved with as the characters totally straight, just heighten the jeopardy…let the cartoonishness come out in the colours in the camera angles and the edits. If we had been acting up a storm, doing non-believable performances, I don't think it would have worked. I think that's what his talent was, keeping us down to a real honest performance level with that slight hyper energy… It's not just believing in a moment, it's *really* believing a moment.

SM: Like Richard O'Brien's original obsession with B-movies?

BB: Exaggerated but not beyond reality. That was the hard part. The minute I started doing something that was just too stagey and over the top, Jim would pull me back and correct me. I'm sure there were many takes when I was a just too hyper and self-aware of the style, or what I had imagined the style to be.

SM: *Were you surprised when the film wasn't successful when it was initially released?*

BB: I paid no attention to it. I didn't even know it was released. I was probably involved with something else that was taking my attention. I couldn't tell you where it opened, when it opened. I don't remember reading a review... It's funny but, by the time we had finished making it, I was done with it. The journey was the important thing. The destination was meaningless.

SM: *Do you understand now why it wasn't successful when it was released?*

BB: Sure I do. There are 1,000 reasons it became what it became. I don't think I have new insight into that. I have no real point of view, other than everything I've said in the past and everything others have said. I think I was taken aback that it became so popular in areas other than urban areas. That's what was surprising to me, that it was successful in Des Moines, Kansas City and La Jolla, places where maybe there wasn't a big homosexual community or that sort of subculture to support it, yet it still blossomed amongst the normal – quote/unquote – kids of suburbia. It showed the depths to which we didn't understand the kids of suburbia. Their hidden or submerged dreams and needs weren't being addressed, even through their schools, their communities and parents. When *Rocky* finally became the coming-of-age show to see, I understood that, because their parents were probably the people that originally turned it into something. It's multi-generational.

SM: *Now you have children, don't you?*

BB: A five- and a six-year-old.

SM: *You wouldn't feel uncomfortable sharing the film with them when the time came, would you?*

BB: No, I don't think so. No. I would wait until they were teenagers, until they would understand not only some of the scenes, but [also] that it's just a big send-up. Certainly, by that time, I'll have to explain to them the cultish aspect of it. 'Why this worked at this point is because the audience did this...' It really became an audience show rather than a movie. I know people who have seen it on DVD who weren't hip to the environment of what it grew to, in the theatre, because of the people doing it in front of the screen, and they would wonder what was so good about it.

SM: *The way it was originally intended?*

BB: We were just making a musical, like *The Sound Of Music*. In fact, I like it better now without the audience. Because, as a piece of film history, it's structured so well, and visually so exciting. And musically it's for all ages, because the music is from all ages. I don't think it will ever really date itself because it is of no date. It's a science-fiction movie.

SM: *There is nothing in it to specifically say that it was made for 1975; it all carries very well in that way.*

BB: It's a fantasy. I think the only thing that will date it will be some of its special effects.

SM: *That will be the 2025 edition, when they re-release it with all of that [BB laughs]. Kimi Wong O'Brien was telling me a story about an accident you had on the set, regarding the lift not operating correctly, and you could have been hurt pretty badly. Do you have a recollection of that?*

BB: I think it fell. I seem to recall that it was a moment where we were either getting on or off of it. I do remember it being a potentially dangerous situation. There was a fire at one point, I know that. In the drying booth. When we were doing the water scenes, we would warm up in this plywood booth, which was heated. One day, it caught on fire and everyone was concerned that it wouldn't spread to the rest of the set. They did manage to stop it, but the fear was the possibility of us being in there at the time.

SM: *In fairness, it does sound like an absolutely miserable shoot.*

BB [laughing]: It was just freezing. Cold. Every time we would have to trudge across the field to that house... As exciting as it was to be in the environment, we were definitely making a low-budget film. It was one step above a Corman movie. I'm sure everyone else said the same thing. We were there from September 'til Christmas Eve, I think.

Susan and I came in early, because we had to pre-record the score. I remember we did it rather quickly. I loved Richard Hartley. He was a really nice guy and made us very comfortable. He was enthusiastic about our performances. He knew what he was doing, so there wasn't a lot of bullshit. When it came time to doing it, we just did it. That was nice.

A lot of times when you are working on a low-budget film, you are dealing with a lot of people who are just learning their craft. One great thing about this film, you got a sense that you were working with people pretty much at the top of their game, so there wasn't a lot of wasted time or energy. We didn't have to do things 20 times because they didn't have a clear vision. The arrangements were done, we came in and learned it and did it. It was the same visually with the filming itself. There wasn't a lot of the movie that we shot that isn't in the film, except for my song.

SM: *That was going to be my next question. Any comments about them cutting out the song 'Once In A While'?*

BB: I was disappointed when I found out they cut it, but I also understood it. It was the wrong song in the wrong place in the show in the beginning. It wasn't a time when you wanted to sit back and hear a ballad. You wanted to just move forward in the film. Onstage, it worked because it was a moment of the calm before the storm. In the film, it just didn't work. Have you seen a version with that song in its place within the film?

SM: No, which is odd, considering it has been released with the 'Superheroes' ending...

BB: I think, if you could imagine that song being at the end of the actual sex scene between Brad and Frank, you would see the juxtaposition between the funny scenes between me and him and her and him. If the action had stopped for me to sing a song about it from my character's standpoint, you wouldn't have given a shit. 'We don't care what Brad thinks now. Let's just go and look at the crazy people.' From a purely filmic standpoint, it was a wise thing to cut. I'm glad to finally see it, because I think it was well shot and I thought I did a good job. I was glad to see they didn't cut it because my performance sucked.

SM: I read that your underpants in the film were your choice...

BB: I don't know. I think it's something I could have done. Those are the kinds of decisions that are made at the time, and only in retrospect – because *Rocky* has become what it has become – does it make any difference. Any movie you make, you make 100 decisions a day based on whim and instinct. None of it has any meaning, other than to entertain. People like to read things into it.

SM: You know what fans are like...sort of like Trekkies; it all becomes an obsession. I did catch your speech in Los Angeles at the 20th anniversary of Rocky, at the Pantages.

BB: I remember that. I put glasses on and did the speech like I was Brad now and said something like, 'You guys are just wasting your fucking lives... Get on with it.'

SM: *And do people shout your nickname at you?*

BB: What, 'Asshole'?

SM: *Yes.*

BB: Oh, sure! A good bulk of my fanmail is from *Rocky*. I try to honour it as much as I can, but it's hard to keep up with that group. It's an ever-widening society. I haven't been to another convention after that 20th at the Pantages. That's the last time I had anything to do with it.

SM: *I'm answering my own question, but I'd like a comment from you. It's no secret that the actors weren't paid very much…*

BB: You always know what the next thing on my mind is. It's amazing. You're a good interviewer because you go to the next thing I was thinking, and I didn't know if I should talk about it. I don't want to sound like there are sour grapes, but they were incredibly ungenerous with the profits from the film to those of us who didn't have a piece of it. When it came out on video, they didn't have to give us anything because there were no union rules in place. When *Rocky* was released on video, we went to them and said, 'Hey guys, we've been here for you for the last 10 or 15 years,' or whatever it was. 'We've helped you out, done press, done documentaries… Give us a taste!' They said no, and I think it was from that moment on that everybody just said, 'Well, I'm moving on.' It's not that we don't love it, or aren't proud to be part of it, but why spend the energy putting another $5 million in their pockets?

SM: *That has to be difficult for you, which is why I'm even more grateful that you've taken the time to speak with me. It's like you're trapped in a – for want of a better term – time warp with this thing that won't go away, and there isn't any payback. Did you get anything from the DVD release?*

BB [laughing]: I think we get a little piece of the Australian soundtrack. For a while, occasionally, I would get a cheque – $1,000 here, $800 there. At the time, I said it was cigarette money. We did get something from the original soundtrack, but not from the others. I don't think we got anything from the audience-participation album, even though we were in the background throughout. I think it was at the 20th anniversary, Lou Adler came up and gave us a jacket with 'Rocky Horror Anniversary' on it. That was what he wanted to give me, a jacket! It was at that point I thought, 'I *have* a jacket. I don't need a jacket.' It's too bad, because I really like these people. I've never had any problems with them, other than their lack of generosity when it came to sharing the joys of what it reaped.

SM: *It is a cash cow, with dolls and everything. Though I don't think they made a doll of you.*

BB: I haven't seen it. Or, if they did, I'm not getting any piece of it, and I probably should. I mean, look at all the trading cards and things like that. We don't get anything out of that, and now, under normal circumstances, if it was a big feature, there would have been some merchandising deal. We've got nothing. But again, this has nothing to do with the fans, nothing to do with my love of the movie. It just has to do with the reality of showbusiness. The older you get, the more cynical you get about the business of showbusiness.

SM: *I'm really pleased that you're doing so well. And I hope I'm not overstepping myself when I say I hope things are well for you health-wise now.*

BB: I had prostate cancer, and everything seems to be OK with that now. Make sure, when you get a little older, to get your PSA test. It's just a blood test, but if you catch it young enough, it can save your life. It did mine. I was just lucky enough to catch it in the PSA test and pursue it. I work for a couple of foundations working to find a cure for prostate cancer. It's something that can be found out early enough and solved. So far, you just have to keep on top of it, getting the test done every few months.

<<<<irememberdoingthetimewarpirememberdoingthetimewarpi>>>>

Meat Loaf

25 October 1999
'Hot Patootie, bless my soul, I really love that rock 'n' roll'

Meat Loaf could only be American. Had he been English and insisted on such a nickname, he would have been called Mince.

Repeated calls requesting an interview to the press representative handling Meat Loaf's tour of this country promoting his 'autobiography' proved fruitless. As a result, the following is the authors' précis of a three-part special broadcast in Britain on Saturday 23 October 1999.

The programme was specifically about the Meat Loaf album *Bat Out Of Hell*, and yet there was no mention of *The Rocky Horror Show* throughout the transmission, even though the pedigree, inception, gestation and birth of Meat Loaf's juggernaut beast betrays many parallels with the progress of both the beast and the beastmasters of *The Rocky Horror Show*.

Much mention was made of Meat Loaf's Broadway and theatre work, such as appearances in a rock version of *Hamlet* and *More Than You Deserve*, Jim Steinman's three-hour musical, produced by Joseph Papp, in which Meat served with Kim Milford, who was later to play *Rocky* in Los Angeles.

All who appeared in the documentary confirmed that Meat Loaf was about showtime. He came from the theatre and was refined and made practicable by rock 'n' roll.

His manager (and also Jim Steinman's, *Bat*'s composer and songwriter) is David Sonnenberg, who seems to have been with the duo pretty much throughout their early careers and was assiduous in hawking the original tapes around to the record companies for years with no success.

Oh, that the *Rocky* wannabes had such a man on hand. The very act of hawking, of having hawked, inherently means that, when success starts to bite, the record industry all jump on the bandwagon not to admit to having turned down the product because they didn't believe in it but to say, 'Yeah! What a great record! I always said it would be a hit.'

Such a groundswell goes on to form a tidal wave of positivism that sweeps through all the organs of the industry – the hard media, radio, television, other companies...

Jim Steinman wrote the original songs in 1974/75, exactly when *The Rocky Horror Show* was being performed in Los Angeles. He admits that all the songs are story songs – like those in country and even grand opera – for this genre allows greatest 'theatricality'. Steinman, as Richard O'Brien, is a self-confessed 'gothic' freak.

The project to turn the collection of essentially disparate songs into a mainstream rock/music-biz record was turned down many, many times until it was recognised and taken up by legendary guitarist Todd Rundgren, who somehow saw the potential in Steinman's inherently, irrevocably theatrical, theatre-based songs. He points out that all the participants had a sense of humour, as did many of the songs, either lyrically or thematically. Without the sense of humour, the songs would have stood even less of a chance.

The people who turned down the Steinman/Meat Loaf collaborative project were not at all dumb. The record business and the theatre were entirely at opposite ends of a continuum. Crossover projects were generally seen as non-viable.

Don't forget, most music-biz people had never even been to the theatre and didn't understand when artists' ambitions veered in any other than a chart direction (*viz* Cat Stevens' *Revolussia* project and the Brian Protheroe/Martin Duncan *Lotte's Elektrik Opera* collaboration). Actors were perceived as different beings from rock 'n' roll stars and, indeed, rock 'n' roll stars (preferably performer/ writers, but by no means exclusively so) are far more centred on themselves/their project. They are not like actors, who are by nature and who by profession set themselves up for hire to interpret – and possibly contribute to – and build upon creativity that is not particularly their own.

Having agreed to take on the project, Rundgren proceeded to

simplify Steinman's theatrical, 'musical' versions of rock songs and translate them into recordable, 'proper' rock 'n' roll songs.

It seemed pretty much acknowledged – especially by Max Weinberg, the drummer – that Meat Loaf was essentially an actor 'playing' the part of a rock 'n' roll singer. Indeed, Meat Loaf himself agrees that he 'plays the part' of each of the 'lead' characters in the songs he sings. Real rock 'n' roll stars are always themselves – at least, they always inhabit the same created persona, even though they might change or adapt – by 'look' or hairstyle or costume or attitude – that persona for each record release.

Rundgren himself financed the *Bat Out Of Hell* project on his Bearsville Label and it took a year to complete. Warner Brothers, the parent company of Bearsville, rejected the product, which both Rundgren and Sonnenberg, the manager, continued to push for over a year. Then Steve Popovic, originally an A&R man, signed it to Cleveland Records.

The record found little or no initial success in the USA and, because it was so underwhelmingly received at first, it was vastly under-promoted. But it was a hit both in UK and in Australia, where it knocked The Bee Gees from the No.1 position.

However, in America, on home turf, the unsung Meat Loaf machine kept touring. Prophets are famously ignored in their own countries. Persistently, it gigged and gigged, often returning to the same town several times to consolidate the fanbase. Todd affirms that any acts that persistently and assiduously keep pounding the tarmac, not for a year or so but for many years, will build up some kind of an audience. Touring to Meat and co was essential, and Meat always gave 150 per cent of himself in the performances.

By direct contrast, Tim Curry never had a 'proper' manager and never a real office situation in the USA. He wasn't that fascinated or taken over by the substance of rock 'n' roll, only by the idea of the celebrity and the image. He therefore only ever toured when it seemed that there was a chance to capitalise. The music biz isn't that easily duped. It needs to see some sort of blood on the stage before it believes. It's a real Doubting Thomas.

Let Max Weinberg have (almost) the last word: 'Like some of the greatest Broadway musicals, some records, like *Bat Out Of Hell*, will be listened to forever.'

But, let's face it, guys, Meat Loaf was damned lucky. Not especially attractive, not especially talented, vocally, he did, however, play the part of the rock 'n' roll performer to the hilt and invested his recorded material with that same contagious energy. Thus, ultimately, he was allowed to convince. His audiences were more than willing to suspend their disbelief. Despite always performing and eventually returning to dramatic roles in movies, the success was never repeated. Meat was already too big. There was nothing left to grow.

Meat Loaf was an out-and-out professional. As witnessed by his participation in recording the soundtrack album, he obviously recognised that one day he might have to promote his song as a commercial single release. After all, those were the days before Jim Steinman and before *Bat Out Of Hell* was even a shadow on the night sky.

<<<<irememberdoingthetimewarpirememberdoingthetimewarpi>>>>

Sadie Corre

Monday 9 March 1998
'Prepare the transit beam'

Another Transylvanian is about to appear.

Easily the most identifiable Transylvanian in *The Rocky Horror Picture Show*, Sadie's credits have been plentiful, from her early work with Noël Coward, Marlene Dietrich and Hughie Green to projects that included a stint in Lord Snowdon's documentary *Born To Be Small*. Her film performances include appearances in *Chitty Chitty Bang Bang*, as the Slavemaster in *Dark Crystal*, *Legend*, as an Ewok in *Return Of The Jedi*, *Who Framed Roger Rabbit*, and in *Return To Oz* as a Munchkin. *The Rocky Horror Picture Show* is not her only claim to cult films. Sadie played the title role of a ventriloquist's doll in the British horror film *The Dummy*, the forerunner to *Magic*. Sadie had to provide her own costume for *The Rocky Horror Picture Show*, because of her size, and, like many 'little people', sometimes Sadie is cast in projects as a male. Sadie had a play based on her, written by Stewart Permutt, a four-parter called *Singular Women*. Sadie's part was a little woman in a pantomime.

At the time of our meeting, Sadie was in her 80s and an active member of the Grand Order of Lady Ratlings, a society devoted to British women in showbusiness. She told me she never did circuses because she is scared of clowns and the smell makes her sick. Sadie, by the way, is four feet three inches high.

SCOTT MICHAELS: *Do you still act?*

SADIE CORRE: Before I had my hip done, I did two commercials, and one of them was running up and down stairs. I don't know how I did it. It was agony. I went into hospital in September and they said, 'Sorry, Sadie, can't do you. Don't have a hip to fit you.' I had to leave and go back in November.

SM: *Where were you born?*

SC: I'm from Sussex. I was five when I said to my mother that I wanted to be on the stage. We used to go to the pub, and in the billiard room they had a stage. Me and my friends used to get on the stage and entertain everyone. I was down in Brighton with my aunt and I was dancing away in the garden when this woman who was renting an upstairs flat got me to dance for her.

SM: *So it wasn't a case of 'Don't put your daughter on the stage, Mrs Worthington'?*

SC: I had my first public appearance at the age of seven, on Hollis Pier in Brighton. A hat came over my eyes and I fell flat. That's when I thought I should be a comic. I wore a pink jacket with little white fluffy buttons.

SM: *Did you train professionally?*

SC: I went to [Italia] Conti's, which was *the* school in those days. I went there when I was around 11. I was in a play by Noël Coward. We had a scene called 'Seaside Scene', and everybody... Well, it got too much. Noël would sit upstairs in the circle, and in the end he said, 'I'm sorry, but its getting too much. Everybody's got to stop this ad-libbing, except Sadie of course. She can do the little bit she's put in.' He was very nice. He was marvellous to us kids. We would wait to go on, and drink 'champagne', which of course was ginger ale. We all used to dive down and get the ginger ale off the table and Noël would check our glasses.

Professionally, my first job was in *Madame Butterfly* as Trouble. All my friends say that I've been trouble ever since.

SM: I have to ask about *Chitty Chitty Bang Bang*.

SC: *Chitty Chitty* is 30 this year. I think there's going to be a convention in New York. We did it at Pinewood. I remember the snow was tremendous, and it was freezing cold. We didn't have proper dressing rooms. One woman would keep opening a window, and I would keep shutting it. Eventually, when I joined the Lady Ratlings I ran into her again.

There was a long table that everyone was sitting around in the film. The kids would sneak under the table with these rubber truncheons, hitting everyone's knees. I said to one of them, 'If you hit me, you'll get kicked right where you don't want to. Never touch me.' I was on top of the table, and I had to jump off it. I had a long gown on and [had to] jump to a chair and onto the ground. I didn't enjoy it like I did *Rocky Horror*.

SM: *What's this with the Lady Ratlings?*

SC: Phil Collins' sister Carol is our Queen Ratling this year. Phil was an extra in it. Phil's mother's friend runs a child actors' agency. His mum is about 85 and hasn't got a line on her face. I hate her! Someone from their school was in *Oliver!*. Dick Van Dyke had his children there. The Child-Catcher was marvellous. It frightened us a bit. We were Vulgarians in *Chitty* and in *Rocky* we were Transylvanians. Trannies, they called us. I am the most popular one!

SM: All over the known world!

SC: My first flight was to Jersey, but the second one was to Australia, in 1968. I did *Snow White And The Seven Dwarves* for six months. I was Sneezy. I don't like gags about people stuttering, but the whole PC thing is just out of hand. Dwarfs get more work, particularly male dwarfs. My problem is pituitary. That's in the neck. I was born normal at about seven and a half pounds. At 18 months, I stopped growing. I used to suck raw steak, because they thought it might help me grow. They sent me to the country, thinking that might help. That's how ignorant they were.

SM: I can't imagine what it must have been like for you.

SC: I've done everything in the business bar a circus. I started legit. When I left Conti's, I went with Hughie Green. I started smoking when I was 21. Of course, I get remarks all the time. I only smoke when I have a drink. I can't enjoy a drink without a cigarette.

SM: How did you get into the Rocky *film?*

SC: An agent that I didn't know called me out of the blue and asked if I would like to go and interview for a film. I figured, 'Why not?' So I went to the theatre where *The Rocky Horror Show* was on. I saw Michael White and was there for about five minutes. He asked me if I could dance. I said, 'Of course I can dance. I've been dancing all my life.' They asked me if I would see the show. I thoroughly enjoyed it. It took me a long time to get my money for it, but eventually I did. My friend Sheila recommended me.

SM: Tell me about working on the film.

SC: When we started rehearsals for 'The Time Warp', I said it was easy.

David said, 'I haven't finished yet, Sadie. You wait'. That was David Toguri. He died of cancer. He was a lovely man. We rehearsed at Bray Studios. Terrible place to get to. Christopher Biggins used to pick me up, and Pamela and Peggy. One day there was a strike on the underground. It was a nightmare of buses and trains. I was so late. We came every day. Chris picked us up because it was such a peculiar journey. The first day, I got off the train and met up with a lovely coloured lady [Pam Obermeyer]. She was doing *Rocky Horror* too. We went the wrong way together going through fields and mud. Finally, a minicab came, honking like mad. We got in, and it was a *Rocky Horror* cab.

Some of the people in the wedding are Transylvanians, too. I was just there for 'The Time Warp' and the Meat Loaf bit. He had to go up the balcony on his motorcycle. We were to jump off, onto mattresses. By the mattress was the iron tank, and when we did it a woman Transylvanian jumped off too soon. We did rehearse it, but she got it wrong. I missed the tank by that much. It was Fran Fullenwider. I was shaken and I was furious with her. No one would speak to me for a couple of days. She just didn't time it properly. I was dancing with Chrissie Biggie. I kept in touch with Pam Obermeyer, for a while.

SM: I've heard conditions for the Trannies weren't great. Conditions for everyone in fact.

SC: There were no dressing rooms at Bray. We were all changing in the wardrobe department. I said to Pam, 'Bugger this.' I went upstairs and found a drawing room. I found a man in charge and asked if we could use it. No problem. Peggy was a bit snooty and that put my back up. She didn't want anything to do with us, and when she found out we had a dressing room she said, 'Oh, this is where you are.'

I said, 'Yes, Pam and I, but no one else!'

SM: What about costumes?

SC: When we started *Rocky*, we just turned up. No one said anything about the plot. I had to come up with my own clothes, because no one had anything that would fit me. They provided the bow tie and the shirt. I had the jacket and trousers. We sang along to a tape. One of the Transylvanians used to do an act with two others. I think it was Annabel. We all wore dark glasses, which was good. I could see, with all the lights. I've still got my shooting schedule. It's at home somewhere and I've got one picture with the bald guy. We filmed for about two weeks. Some of the others were guests in the wedding scene. I don't think Pam was, but Peggy was. We didn't know the first thing about the wedding scene until we saw the finished film. I saw it in America on television.

SM: Any favourite moments?

SC: A lot of it was ad-libbed. When Tim Curry came up to me in 'I Can Make You A Man' and did the shimmy thing, it was ad-libbed. And I was with Chris Biggins on the balcony during the filming. There was a giant statue of David in front of him. We were dancing to 'Whatever Happened To Saturday Night?' and Chrissie was throwing me over his shoulder and all around. I said to him that they won't ever even see us. He said, 'Wide angles, darling. Wide angles.' We pitched in and bought Chrissie Biggie a shaving bag for picking us up every day. We were all at lunch and gave it to him. He was thrilled to bits. I got it at Fortnum & Mason, so it must have been nice. He appreciated the fact that we thought enough to buy him something. He used to live above the Phoenix Theatre in Charing Cross Road. He had a one-room flat there. We've kept in touch.

SM: And since Rocky? *It's a long time.*

SC: I worked with Tim Curry twice after *Rocky Horror*. He's a lovely man. One was a BBC2 thing that David Toguri did the choreography for. I was in *Legend*, too. Tim played the Devil in that. Oh, that poor man with that make-up again. The man I worked with in *Willow*, who was a midget, started an agency for little people and called it

Willow. He's the one that got me two of the commercials I've been in. And I did *Dark Crystal* with Jim Henson. That was hard work.

Jimmy was a slave driver. We did the walking. We had to wear these heavy costumes and I couldn't see a thing. In the end, my knees collapsed from the weight. One day, we had a break and Jimmy came up to us telling us all about the story. When he finished, he asked if we had any questions. I said, 'Yes,' and he said, 'Yes, Sadie?' I said, 'When can we have a tea break, please? I'm dying for a cup of coffee.'

I was also the arms of the Caterpillar in *Alice In Wonderland*. I had all green make-up on my arms and I put them through a cloth. I was a cat at the Palladium with Norman Wisdom. He used to do the most atrocious things to me. I was walking downstage and he put his foot out and tripped me. I landed on my shoulder. It was agony. In between shows, I went to the Middlesex Hospital. They told me I couldn't work now. I went back and told Norman that I couldn't go on. Norman started begging me to come back. He didn't want the understudy going on. So I said I would, only if we cut all those scenes!

SM: And Sadie personally?

SC: I don't have any kids. I've got four nephews, a sister, a brother that was killed in the war. I had a sister that died when she was 36 of Hodgkin's disease. A niece in Australia. When Kenny Baker was young (long before his career as R2D2 began), he fell in love with me. 'No, Kenny, I like you very much.' He married Eileen, and they had two boys. Eileen died. I wrote him a sympathy note, but never heard. His partner Jack Purvis died as well. They were a musical double act. Jack was tinkering under a car and it rolled over him. He was paralysed.

We were both in *Born To Be Small* by Lord Snowdon. I got very friendly with Tony [Snowdon]. We went boozing together. When I was a Munchkin in *Return To Oz* in 1985, Lord Snowdon was taking photos there. I didn't want to go up to him, but he saw me and yelled, 'SADIE!' He gave me a big hug. He was lovely. And we were in the Womble movie, *Wombling Free*, in 1978. I was Madame Cholet, Jack was Uncle Bulgaria.

SM: And what do you think of the whole Rocky *thing now?*

SC: It's amazing that *Rocky* is so popular. In Australia, it's really big. I got a lot of get-well wishes when I had my hip replaced. My niece, Diana, sent me a ton of get-well messages from *Rocky* fans on the Internet...

‹‹‹‹irememberdoingthetimewarpirememberdoingthetimewarpi›››»

Richard Pointing

23 March 1999
'Don't get hot and flustered'

Time to pay a bit of respect to another techno-whizz, this time a costumier who physically brought his design and manufacturing skills to dress the cast. Richard Pointing and his team were hands-on. This all leads, of course, to what exactly it was that went into Rocky Horror's shorts, other than Peter Hinwood's bits.

Scott met Richard at the costumiers Angels & Bermans.

SCOTT MICHAELS: How do costume people like you get involved?

RICHARD POINTING: I don't recall how I got involved. I was always with Immy [Imogen Claire]. I worked with Peter Suschitzky on *The Man In The Iron Mask*. He worked with Ken and Shirley Russell a lot. They did a whole series of cult movies, including *Tommy* and *Lisztomania*, with Roger Daltrey. I remember going to a viewing with Sara Kestleman and Imogen, as usual. After it was over, there was complete silence. Then there was one voice saying, 'What the *fuck* was that?!'

SM: John Comfort was production manager on Tommy *and* Rocky *as well. Horses for courses...*

RP: So there. Maybe his production office called me. I was young and enthusiastic. I lived in Duncan Terrace, in Islington, at that time, in a basement flat. For *Rocky*, we turned the first floor of the house into a sort of workroom. A lot of the costumes were made, and certainly fitted, there.

All of the Transylvanians came to Duncan Terrace to be fitted. We made stretch pants for each of them. A friend of mine, Marie, who died a few years back, made them for me. I remember Fran Fullenwider arriving at Duncan Terrace for her fitting. They would come down to the basement, and I remember the light disappearing as she came down the stairs in a tent dress. I think she brought a little white poodle with her. She used to drive around town in a Mini. Oh, she was wonderful. Marie had to get two tape measures to do Fran.

I remember some of the Transylvanians costumes being picked up at two in the morning for filming a few hours later. I know that Gill [Dodds] and I volunteered to work all night the evening before, because Sue Blane seemed unhappy with some of the things. It was something like a 36-hour stint. And we were all union at the time. Gillian Dodds was my assistant. The last two days of filming, there were a lot of parties going on, because it was near Christmas time. I had to come home this particular night and Gill wanted to stay on to party. She got a lift from someone else, who unfortunately crashed the car. She went through the windscreen and lost an eye. She is Marcus Dodds' daughter. He was a great conductor who did a lot of film scores.

SM: *Something tells me you had a good time on this movie.*

RP: The film had such a wonderful atmosphere from beginning to end. You just felt like you couldn't wait to go to work. It was a party every day. I remember drugging up one evening. We were knocking back a bit of booze at the time. Well, not me so much, 'cause I was driving. Sometimes I would stay with Jon Berkinshaw, who was known as 'Mother', who lived in the cottage next door to Bray

Studios in the cow shed of what is now Oakley Court. Jon stood in for Barry Bostwick but eventually came to the wardrobe side and for years worked with me as an assistant. He died last year.

The rain sequence was done early on, and I made plastic underwear for Barry and Susan. Barry said he couldn't believe how well he was looked after. I loved Barry and Susan. Barry was absolutely lovely. Never any problems. The costumes were forever damp. Not wet. But they used to call me the dorm mistress.

SM: Any bits of costume trickery?

RP: When Rocky had to get the bandaging off rather quickly, Jim said that it had to happen in less than a minute. I suddenly got this idea of a string, with the bandaging wound backwards and forwards around it, so when the string was cut and pulled out, the bandaging would just fall to the ground. For me, they didn't use the best take. I remember slightly cringing seeing Pat tugging it quite a lot to get the string out. On a different take, it was perfect, but it wasn't good for the camera.

SM: Is there anything you'd care to share about Peter Hinwood's costume?

RP: The gold shorts were gold kid leather. I have to say that I made them myself... Hope that's not showing off too much. Peter did the padding himself, I think. I remember Jim coming to me and saying, 'What's he got in the front?' I think it was a sock. We did some sort of mock padding for Barry's Y-fronts. Sue Blane wanted it to look like those trunk mannequins you would see in shop windows. No distinction, but a definite bulge.

SM: You might be pleased to hear Peter sold the famous trunks and got 400 quid!

RP: Cheeky thing.

<<<<irememberdoingthetimewarpiremem berdoingthetimewarpi>>>>

Lindsay Ingram

17 July 1998
'He thought you were the candyman, didn't you sweetie?'

Attention! Attention! Trannie on the starboard side!

When we met, Lindsay had just turned 50 and, as Mrs Meller, become a grandmother. She has a daughter in San Francisco with her boyfriend, a son with a little daughter and another son whose birthday was the day Scott met her at her home in Poole, Dorset. Lindsay is obviously incredibly close to her children. Although she expresses some regrets about not having the ambition for acting, she loves her life. She gave Scott a four-leaf clover, something he could think about on the four-hour train ride back to London…

SCOTT MICHAELS: *What was your life before* Rocky?

LINDSAY INGRAM: I was in Sir Laurence Olivier's Theatre Company, but they don't care about that! The last year of the Old Vic, before it moved to the new National Theatre on the South Bank, I worked with Anthony Hopkins, Diana Rigg and Maureen Lipman. There was a gang of us and we were real mates. Maureen and I shared a dressing room. I worked with Lesley Joseph.

SM: *You must have seen the stage production of* Rocky *first?*

LI: I saw the play the first week it opened at the Royal Court Upstairs. When we saw it at the Royal Court, we had no idea it would blow up into what it became.

SM: *How did you come to be in the movie?*

LI: I was auditioning for a Sam Shepard play at the Royal Court, *Tooth Of Crime.* Sam is the best American playwright since Tennessee

Williams, a fantastic writer and musician. He wrote *A Lie Of The Mind*. Absolutely inspires the imagination. He wrote the screenplay for *Paris, Texas*. Definitely [America's] greatest playwright. Anyway, the auditions were down to two of us. Diane Langton and myself. Sam and Richard Hartley were doing the auditions. They said I couldn't sing well enough, but the acting was OK. They hired Diane. Then they asked me to be involved in *Rocky*. Nell came to see a play I was doing, playing Patti Smith. That's one of the first times I met her. Nell was called 'Sunny'. She'd just come from Australia. She hadn't been here for very long. She was very nice and sparkly. Nell never put on any airs. She was gorgeously natural and straightforward with people.

Anyway, out of that audition came the Sam play and the *Rocky Horror* film.

SM: Filming must have been quite an experience.

LI: Tony Milner, Henry Woolf and I used to do the journey to Bray together. We formed a sort of brotherhood, or a unit. We went in a VW camper van. Henry was very interesting. He thought about things. The backstage atmosphere can be very cliqueish. When you are with a group for a short time, you are drawn to certain ones. I was very drawn to Henry that way. Also, getting the lift in helped as well. Other people can be quite scary, and you aren't drawn to them the same way.

Rocky was such good fun, but at the time it was just a job. I do remember it with fondness. We made £100 a week and there was lots of pot on the set. The Transylvanians were the outcasts. In fact, they were the unacceptables!

SM: What other scenes were you in?

LI: The wedding was freezing. I thought I'd die. We were in these summer outfits. Mine was blue, with a white hat and sunglasses. It was so cold. It was so particularly cold. I was close to tears in that summer dress. I'll never forget how cold that was. Everything freezes up. Then there was the scene in the lab. Meat Loaf's stuntman crashed. Another stuntman ran to help him and broke his leg *en route*. One running to help the other. They were both carried out in the end.

I've still got my red shirt from the film, but we couldn't keep our costumes. I've got one of the original badges, but that's it, as far as memorabilia goes. You don't suss that it's going to be a cult thing. I think the Time Warp was the real beginning of line dancing!

SM: *And the rest of the cast?*

LI: I can remember some funny nights in Pat Quinn's flat with her first husband, Don Hawkins. Mick McKenzie, a film-maker, is a mutual friend of ours. He wrote the Pankhurst play. Pat's a lovely woman.

Barry and Susan were really on another level. They just walked in and did their job. You know, when I think of *Rocky*, I think of Philip Sayer, because we were very close. He took over from Tim at the King's Road for about two years [and, like Tim, developed a terrible back problem because of the shoes]. Philip was only 42 when he died and the most stunning, talented man. He was a great friend and a lovely man. There was also a very nice guy who was one of the producers, John Goldstone. He went on and did Michael Palin movies.

SM: *What came after* Rocky *for you?*

LI: I was in the audience in *Shock Treatment*. Annabel and Gaye were immediately behind me. I had very short hair. We were there for a week's filming. I remember being on the way to the filming, hearing that John Lennon had been shot dead. It was really early in the morning and I was in Holland Park, passing the tube station. I think it was 9 December. I never even saw the film. I wrote to Richard once to ask if we could do the play and he wrote me back saying that [Samuel] French's own the rights, that he didn't have anything to do with it. French's bought him out. He may get residuals, but he does not own it.

SM: *What keeps Lindsay occupied these days?*

LI: I don't like acting too much any more. I wouldn't mind the odd telly job, but directing is much more exciting. I could never sell myself. I could never get into that. I didn't want to, really.

I am a drama lecturer now. I teach acting/theatre studies. It's a further-education college, but we are just now getting into higher education. We are going to start doing a university-type course. Because there is so little going on here in Dorset – it's a cultural wasteland – our college is actually a professional venue, so we get all sorts of professional national touring companies coming in. Our students can then crew for them and do workshops. From that point of view, because we are the only ones, we are quite lucky. If you are living in London, you wouldn't be working with these really good groups.

My students come in and they know how to do the Time Warp! It's so wonderful. I don't ever talk about it, but it gets around, and they think, 'She was there, then.' I've seen the film a few times. I have the video, and my kids used to play it all the time. Those lips were a really wonderful opening to that film!

With my students, it's amazing street cred. My students can't believe I was in it. That's been for me, a lecturer, the greatest part of it. It's allowed me an acceptability. They can relate to it…

<<<<irememberdoingthetimewarpirememberdoingthetimewarpi>>>>

Stephen Calcutt
27 July 1998

Now for the tallest of the Transylvanians. Scott met Stephen at the Peasant, in Farringdon Road, just south of the Angel. Stephen had been at an audition and joined Scott afterwards, wearing a smart suit.

SCOTT MICHAELS: *So that's what working actors wear to get work. Nice suit.*

STEPHEN CALCUTT: I've been acting for 28 years. Anyone who earns a living by doing nothing but acting in this business is a success. Even if

I am never a film star, I've been around the world and played every part you can possibly imagine, everything from Adolf Hitler in a Black Sabbath video to a frog in the Walt Disney film *Return To Oz*. I've had a marvellous time in the process.

SM: So what got you the part in Rocky?

SC: I got into it quite by accident. It was tough at first, but then I suddenly got the phone call asking me to audition for the film version of *The Rocky Horror Show*. I'd heard of it, but I didn't know anything about it, really. I went to the King's Road for the audition and I got the part. My brother and I went to see the show. I think we were very lucky, because we got two cancellations and it was full.

It was absolutely amazing. Being so innocent, being brought up in a church school, I thought, 'Oh, my God! Now I'm working on this film!' I thought they are going to put me in corsets and tights. What were my parents going to think? I was really excited and so glad I was going to be wearing stretch leather.

What you have to remember is that I was probably one of the youngest people working on the film. I was 22. I was in awe of all these people, because they all seemed so experienced and had done so much. I couldn't believe I was working with them. I was so sweet and innocent, and they thought it was so funny. I had only been working part-time as an actor before. I think the first ever job I got was working with Fran Fullenwider. We were friends for years, then I heard she had given up showbusiness and gone back to America.

SM: It must have all been very strange and exciting.

SC: On the way to Bray Studios, off the main road, there was a field on the left-hand side of the lane, and that's where the mock-up church was, for the wedding. I was in the wedding scene. Frank Lester, with the glasses, is dead and gone now. Leukaemia. I thought Koo Stark was absolutely lovely. You can see me running after the car. I wore a wig in the film, because they were filming the wedding first. We all had to have short 1950s hair. Immediately afterwards, we went to the castle and got our wigs.

If you were to ask me how many were in the cast, I would recollect about ten of us, but in actuality I think there were 17 Transylvanians. We rehearsed in Oakley Court and filmed there. I think we filmed 'The Time Warp' there. The house at the time was deserted but the books were still on the shelves, the billiard cues still on the table. But everything was rotten and decaying. It was freezing cold and damp. Of course, now it's a five-star hotel.

I remember the portakabins and also the fact that they only had a small gas heater. They tried to wash the clothes but they couldn't get them dry, so we had to put on cold, wet clothes. My bow tie was like a humbug. I can't remember what colour it was. I think it was a cream colour with black stripes. We had this black stretch leather, but unfortunately it only stretched one way. Sideways. Every time you tried to sit down, it wouldn't stretch with you. We only did one master shot of 'The Time Warp'. They did the close-up editing later. It was one enormously long take. We wanted to do it more, but they wouldn't do it. They were happy with the one master take.

We were doing a dance rehearsal and David Toguri stopped everyone and called Pam and myself up for a demonstration. He said, 'Everyone watch these two. This is how it should be done.' We were made an example of. It was amazing. Pam Obermeyer was my dance partner, other than Sadie in 'The Time Warp'. I did 'Hot Patootie' with Pam.

SM: Have you any particular memories of your fellow players?

SC: Some of the people in the film I've only ever seen in the film. Showbiz in London is very incestuous. Some were probably friends with Richard O'Brien. Rufus was a dancer and I've never seen him since. The only one who appears on television regularly is me.

Imogen Claire was very kind to me years later. She got me a job on *Flash Gordon* but I never saw her after that. David Toguri and Richard O'Brien were in it, too. I played one of the Aserians and Richard was one of the Tree People.

Tim Curry was around the West End a lot. Always so nice. Some years later, he did a series about the life of Shakespeare. He was William. I only had a day's work as an Elizabethan, in this mock-up of the Globe. There were hundreds of people on the set. Tim saw me and shouted, 'Hello, Stephen!' He called me over. He brought the entire production to a halt while he stood and talked to me. Everyone wondered who I was. I'd like to think he's the same now.

In my opinion, Pat Quinn is one of the best actresses in the country. A couple of years ago, when things were at their worst with the recession, I got a walk-on job in *An Inspector Calls* at the Garrick Theatre. That little job just turned things around for me. I was told that the cast changed every six months and Pat was supposed to be in the next cast. However, they refused to even give her an audition for the part. If you are not one of the 'right people', worked at the Royal Shakespeare, you just didn't get the part. They were not even interested in Pat. I think that's so terrible.

Tony Cowen is a Jewish actor who used to be with Ugly [the agency], like Fran Fullenwider.

Ishaq Bux was a very nice man, once you got through the reserve. He was in a lucky position, because there were very few people like him in London at the time. He had the market cornered for all those Middle Eastern types. If you made the effort, he really was very nice.

SM: *Were you aware of all the illegal substances abroad in Transylvania?*

SC: As I've said, I really was very young and innocent at the time, [but] I knew there were drugs around. I remember one time someone offering me a cigarette, but I wouldn't take it. It was going on all the time. In the period we were working on that film, it was a continual party. Whether we were working or sitting around on the set, it was one massive party all of the time

SM: *Which must have taken away the pain of some of the painful bits.*

SC: Everybody got hurt on that set. We were dicing with death. They wanted us to be there when Eddie was riding the cycle around the ramp, hurtling at us. If you notice, we are all jumping out of the way. I jumped over to the ladder and slid down it. It really was dangerous. It required split-second timing. Everyone connected to it got injured. Meat Loaf got injured, his stuntman, his stand-in.

We were off for the week when they needed people for the motorbike scene, when the bikes approach Frank's castle. By the time I got back to them after they'd called, it was too late. I always was very upset, because I wanted to be in that scene.

SM: How did you get on with Barry and Susan? Was it stars versus Transylvanians?

SC: Barry was so intensely ambitious, as I've discovered American actors usually are. He just never has gone as far as Susan. When we were filming, Barry had never worn glasses before. He came to me and asked about wearing glasses and how to live with glasses. All through the film, you can see him doing little things with his glasses that I told him about.

Any time the film comes up in conversation, there's a little anecdote that I always tell. This is true and funny, but it's also very tragic as well. One day, Barry and Susan were watching me during one of the dance rehearsals. They came up to me after the rehearsal and Susan said, 'Stephen, we were just watching you rehearse, and we just thought we had to say to you that we think you are really marvellous, and in a year or two, you're going to make it big, and be a star…' Then I always pause and think, 'Whatever happened to Susan Sarandon?' She came back to America and became a star. I wrote to her a number of times through her agent, and whether she got them or not, I don't know. I never ever received a reply. I always thought that you hear wonderful stories in Hollywood about people like Kirk Douglas and Lauren Bacall, who went to drama school together. They agreed that, if they ever made it, they would remember the other and help them out. Lauren, of course, became a star at 19 and remembered Kirk and helped him out. I thought, if Susan really believed that I had all that talent, I just hope that in a year from now, she'll be in America and read this book and perhaps my message to her: 'I'm still the same person, and I've still got the talent and the ability! It's not too late, Susan! Give me a ring!'

SM: But one day the Rocky *party was over, right?*

SC: When we finished filming, they told us all very strictly to hand in our costumes. But a number of them did keep things. I didn't.

We all got invited to the premiere, at a cinema in the Haymarket somewhere. I came out disappointed. I thought the stage show was so great. Tremendous pace and energy. What I didn't realise was that they were clever enough not to emulate the stage show. It's much slower and really good. Although the lips look good in the film, onstage it was supposed to be an English cinema usherette, but you don't have them in America, do you? To everyone in England, when they saw the stage show, it was a great joke. It was an incredible joke. It was a 1950s usherette, great big busty blonde in a white outfit, a beauty spot, thick make-up and lipstick. She would have suicide blonde hair, a tray full of ice creams and drinks.

SM: Would you say you need as much luck as talent to succeed as an actor?

SC: It's always been tough for me to be an actor. I was told that I would never make a living as an actor because I was too tall, because I'm six foot seven and a half. I had to fight for years against tremendous prejudice to be an actor. I overcame it all, and I've had a good career. Every year I was getting better work and making more money. Suddenly, we had the worst recession, and we had our lives and careers ruined.

In the middle of it, when I thought things couldn't possibly get any worse, I went out on a beautiful summer day on my bicycle and was knocked down from behind by a drunk driver. I had a depressed skull fracture, multiple broken bones and damage to my neck and spine. I landed head first, and I wasn't wearing a helmet, I got compression of the spine, so I lost an inch and a half in height. The odd thing is, now that I've lost that inch and a half, I'm just on the edge of what people consider to be acceptable for an actor. It took a long time to fight my way back to health, and I eventually got back to work. The last two years have been very good; 1996 was the best year I've had as an actor.

When people ask me about my career, I always say to them, jokingly, that I am basing my career on Orson Welles. I started right at the top and I am gradually making my way down to the bottom. It is odd, if you think about it, and probably for the others that were in the film as well, that none of us knew at the time that we were making a film that was going to be the most successful and popular film we would ever work on in our lives!

SM: But you went on and kept acting, at least.

SC: I went on to work on the *Star Wars* films, but not in the same capacity as we did on *Rocky Horror*. My father went off not long after *Rocky* and left me with my mother and a young sister to support. I had a number of years when I could not choose what work I did. I auditioned for a part in the Space Cantina in the first film, but they used animatronics instead. They then asked me if I would stand in for Chewbacca and double for Darth Vader. I worked all through the film.

The Two Ronnies did a spoof of *Star Wars* and I did Darth Vader then. In 1996 I auditioned for a television commercial for Tunes throat sweets. They did an exact recreation of the council chamber scene. I played Darth Vader on that. I made more money on that one day for the commercial than I did for all three of the *Star Wars* films. They had a woman from Lucasfilms to oversee it and all the costumes and props had to be authentic. They followed the same camera moves. They would not allow the commercial to be made unless it was absolutely true to the original, except for the punchline.

And I was in *High Spirits* where Peter O'Toole inherits an ancient castle in Ireland. I was a ghost of the master of the house who was killed in a riding accident. All my face is smashed in and I have a horseshoe sticking out of my face. And I've been in tons of videos, too.

Black Sabbath, 'Trashed' and 'Zero The Hero'. Debbie Harry, 'Rush Rush'. The Eurythmics' video disc. T'pau, 'Secret Garden'. Depeche Mode, 'Walking In My Shoes'.

SM: Do you go to the Rocky *conventions and stuff? Reunions?*

SC: I know they had a big party for the anniversary in London. I don't know if they asked any of the others, but they certainly didn't invite me. I was very upset about it. I thought they had hundreds of people there, and there were only about 20 in the whole film, and they didn't ask us. Seems odd. You know, O'Brien has taken legal action in the past against people putting together sub-standard shows.

I've got a real copy of the film, which I bought before the film was released on video, and I have my original *Rocky Horror* T-shirt that we were given at the time and a whole box of eight-by-tens that I bought from Mick Rock.

I was approached to be in *Shock Treatment*, but my agent never even told me about it. She turned the job down, because evidently they only wanted to book us as extras and she had a part for me on the BBC for a Charles Dickens serial. She knew it was much more money on that and I would get overseas repeats. She never even bothered to tell me about it. I only found out much later. I was absolutely furious and she could not understand that it was something I would have done for nothing just to be in it and to meet all of the people again. It didn't have the original Brad and Janet, though.

One of the other Transylvanians, Tony Milner, said to me, 'Life is just a big shit pie, and every day we eat another slice.' At the time, I thought it was the most awful thing I've ever heard in my life! I thought that couldn't possibly be true! Now, of course, I'm 46 years old and I've been through this terrible business and the recession, and I think, 'He knew what he was talking about!' Tony and I used to end up auditioning for the same films and commercials and things. I just don't know what he's doing.

SM: But it's not all just shit pie, surely?

SC: Last year I went off to stay with friends of mine in California for Christmas. One day they took me out into the mountains, in the middle of nowhere. We pulled into a lay-by to look at the view at the top of this beautiful mountain. There was one other car there, and we got talking to this American guy. It turned out he was a gold prospector. I thought it was fantastic. Somebody spending their life looking for gold. He got a case out and showed us all his gold nuggets and precious stones that he had found all over America. Just casually he asked me what I did. I told him, 'I'm an actor.' He asked what I've been in. I told him, 'My work is mainly in England, but the one thing I've been in that most people know of in America is *The Rocky Horror Picture Show*.' The moment I said that, it was like an explosion. He went absolutely bonkers! 'Oh, my God! You were in *Rocky Horror*! I have to have an autograph! I have to have a photograph! Wait 'til I tell my wife! She's nuts about the film!' I could not believe that you couldn't even go to a mountaintop in the middle of a vast wilderness without the first person you bumped into being a *Rocky Horror* fan! Some 25 years later! Of course, the film was made in 1974 and a few years later they established the residuals in contracts, so we make nothing on it... Even with the make-up and hair in the film, and I was only 22, but look at me now. I don't look too different...

(A few days later, after Scott had sent Stephen a Rocky convention T-shirt, he received a letter from Stephen. We are reproducing the relevant part because Stephen articulates a feeling that was expressed many times by those we interviewed.)

'Thank you very much for the T-shirt. I was both delighted and appalled. Pleased to be given a lovely present, but I really would like to know what merchandise they are using my image on and how they can get away with it without paying a single penny to us. Is this something recent or have they been selling these items for the past 25 years? I was not happy with the convention, really. I found it all very strange. Most of the people there were not even born when the film was made and I felt that they had no interest in me as a person at all, just that I had worked on the film...'

(Stephen is still active in the film industry, most directly standing in for characters in Harry Potter and James Bond films.)

<<<<irememberdoingthetimewarpirememberdoingthetimewarpi>>>>

Henry Woolf

7 July 1998

Scott telephoned Henry Woolf at six in the evening at his home in Saskatchewan, Canada.

SCOTT MICHAELS: Would you talk to me a little about your background with Rocky *and being a Transylvanian?*

HENRY WOOLF: My wife, Susan Williamson, was at the Royal Court in *The Sea*, Edward Bond's play. I think it was 1973 or 1974. *Rocky Horror* had just opened, in the little Theatre Upstairs. They had no proper dressing rooms, so she happened to go upstairs for something and there was Raynor Bourton standing in a little bowl, putting gold paint [glitter] on himself. She asked what he was doing and he said that they'd just opened in a little fill-in called *The Rocky Horror Show*. He said they thought it might run a week. It went on a wee bit longer than that. It ran for years.

SM: But you didn't have to audition or anything?

HW: They just offered the part to me. We were all acting away. We worked a great deal in London. In fact, we lived around the corner. They asked actors who were known. As it had been put on in the Royal Court, and I've worked at the Royal Court for years, they knew me. I'd had quite substantial parts at the Court, and when I saw I would be playing almost nothing in the movie, my tiny ego was a bit pricked.

I was punished for my elitism because I left the shoot after two or three weeks to do a play in Edinburgh, *The Iceman Cometh*, in which I sat for 5 hours and 40 minutes onstage. So that was my punishment for leaving *Rocky Horror*, but I survived it. Nevertheless, I think it's a terrific movie. It's a very, very good movie. I thought Tim Curry, Pat Quinn and Susan Sarandon were all marvellous in it.

SM: Do you have personal memories of the other members of the cast?

HW: Pat Quinn is an old friend. I've been in several plays with Pat, and I like her enormously. If you see her again, give her my best. I often think of her. Tell her Henry sends his very best love and to Quinn as well. Pat's a great girl. A very good actress. Very good. You might tell her, if you speak to her, we were in Canada and we watched *The Box Of Delights* with her late husband.

Peggy Ledger was quite full of beans.

And Fran Fullenwider, of course; I liked her very much. I'm very sorry to hear that she's dead. I gave her one of my pet kittens on the condition that she not feed it to her huge pet python.

You know, I think I was in it because I was part of that particular theatre scene of the early 1970s. Of course, Tim Curry had been working at the Court. When he played Frank, he had already been working downstairs at the Court.

Annabel Leventon is a very good actress. I'm not saying the others weren't. They were more on the music scene. Annabel is a very distinguished actress.

Funny thing that my bios only include movies. It doesn't say that I directed Harold Pinter's first play, for example. I did get him to start writing. He's a loyal friend. He's just given me the North American premiere of his latest play, *Ashes To Ashes*. Over and above New York. They open in January, we open in August. Good pal. He's a good egg. I'm so glad he's done brilliantly. He is one of the very few people to realise that conversation is not used to communicate but to avoid communication. David Mamet has copied this. It's usually used to defend oneself or attack another. It's a territorial exercise. He's the very first person to ever actually put that into dialogue. Mamet does it later, but he's always been a fanatical follower of Pinter. If you see Annabel, please give her our love.

SM: Any particular incidents you may remember?

HW: The last day I was on *Rocky*, Meat Loaf came round this kind of circular ramp on his Harley. He toppled off and the bike came off the ramp about 12 or 15 feet up. A very large extra stepped forward and caught the bike and Meat Loaf, who otherwise would have been seriously hurt. The extra snapped his ankle. This man saved the day. If Meat Loaf had been badly hurt, that would have been the end of that. For at least a long time. I can imagine that tiny Sadie could have been crushed quite easily. The day before I left for Canada, I worked with this same guy, who was working on a movie with The Sex Pistols. I asked him if they were grateful to him for saving the day?

Not at all, he said.

Did they give you an extra few pounds? No.

Did anyone visit you in the hospital? No.

He got no thanks, just a broken ankle. It was a sad story.

He saved Meat Loaf's stand-in from really serious injury. I just wish this chap got a bit of recognition. Even thanks or flowers.

I was the photographer in the wedding scene. I had the first line in the movie. It was shot as if it was a lovely summer or spring day. It was a freezing November day. We all used to gather in my camper and drink brandy to keep warm. I used to have a Volkswagen camper and we used to just huddle in there, with a stove on, and drink brandy. It was on the set, outside a sound stage, at Bray. Later on at Bray, it was in a house. We rehearsed 'The Time Warp' at the old house.

SM: So no real horror stories?

HW: I didn't mind the shoot. Quite honestly, the shoot was fine. I was treated quite beautifully. I just didn't want to play one-line photographers. Do give my best to Richard. And to Kimi, if you see her.

Hugh Cecil

14 July 1998
Next alien please...

Hugh Cecil's career in showbusiness began with his first magic set, purchased by his mother, when he was 11, and it hasn't stopped yet. Though many think he shaves his head, Hugh has alopecia, an affliction that caused him to lose his hair permanently one summer. He also really does wear a monocle. Scott arrived at Hugh's very eccentric house, which looked like one that kids would call haunted. He also has two significant garages and looks to be something of a gardener. He and Scott sat in an East Indian-styled room and Scott formed the impression that Hugh likes to travel a lot. Hugh is now in his 80s and still performs magic. He is also a Punch and Judy artiste.

HUGH CECIL: Hugh isn't my given name. It's Cecil. And neither is Cecil my surname. I'm really Cecil Ware. My son Neville Ware was a radio star. He doesn't like to be seen. He teaches drama at Soberton.

SCOTT MICHAELS: *So tell me about the casting for* Rocky.

HC: I did not shave my head. It just happened. I was in a holiday camp for the summer season. The first time I arrived at the camp I got alopecia. My look has made me a lot of money. That was around 1950. Until fairly recently, I painted eyebrows on, and I would show up for a job and they would just have me take them off, so I stopped doing it.

I got involved with *Rocky Horror* after a call from Ugly [the agency]. We were to meet in the King's Road, outside the theatre, the cinema where the stage show was. We were auditioning for it, although we were really chosen already. Jim chose them from photographs. They didn't commit themselves immediately, in case they made a mistake. We were all booked, in actual fact. For six weeks.

SM: *Were you told you had to dance?*

HC: Well, I did it, but I couldn't dance. I got the sack from *Scrooge!*. I lasted two and half days and got the sack. I can't dance. Easy as that. It wasn't long after *Scrooge!* that I did *Rocky Horror* with David Toguri. He said, 'Don't worry about it. If you're a half a beat off, it doesn't matter. You are still in character.' I felt a lot better because of that. Peggy Ledger was my Time Warp partner. She was fine. We didn't sing, but we sang along, sort of voice-over.

SM: *Were you in other scenes, too?*

HC: I was in the wedding scene. I have a photo of me by the church on the set. I had a wig on that they made specially for me. It was a wonderful wig. A hairdresser saw it and said it was a £250 wig. It was really, really marvellous. I have a monocle. I have brought it along in the past to shoots, but I don't really recall. I probably did. I have the film on tape.

SM: *Do you have particular memories of the time at Bray Studios? Or the people?*

HC: Gaye Brown used to pick me up to go to the studio, when we were filming. Chris Biggins I know. *Rocky* was probably beneath his dignity. I do remember that we played Scrabble in our off time.

SM: *And the recreational substances?*

HC: The drugs didn't come my way.

SM: *And what do you do now?*

HC: I do mostly television now. I meet up with Stephen Calcutt quite frequently. Oh, and modelling work, of course.
I've done a few pop videos. They all become famous after I've been

with them. I was in a Spice Girls video. I got kissed by them, by Baby Spice. I was in a Boyzone video, too, and a Samantha Fox one. I've sold cigars. Lots of ads. I was in *The Last Days Of Pompeii* and in a Hammer Film, *Frankenstein And The Monster From Hell.* Not at Oakley Court, though! I've been in *Dad's Army* for nine years. I was the only one who stayed the whole run, beginning to end.

SM: Are those garages full of cars?

HC: I'm a big American car fan. I like AMC cars the best. I have a Rambler. My first American car was a Hudson. I have an AMC Matador that was used in *The Man With The Golden Gun.* I happened to know the man who bought it from the studio. I have a Studebaker, too.

‹‹‹‹iremembertdoingthetimewarpiremberdoingthetimewarpi›››

Pam Obermeyer
24 November 1998

Sadie called Scott with an old number for Pam, and when Scott called it was the home of an old boyfriend, who nevertheless called Pam to tell her to call Scott. Thus are connections made. Pam was the only person Scott interviewed who brought her own tape recorder to the interview. When asked at the convention what she had been doing since *Rocky*, Pam replied enigmatically, 'Therapy.'

PAM OBERMEYER: I was not in the wedding scene. My Afro was my real hair. I still have it underneath these braids. David Toguri – I worked with him in *Hair.* I went back to Nottingham after *Hair*, to recuperate from *Hair* in a lot of ways, and was in a group called Truth. I didn't hear about David's death 'til I was leafing through an old Equity magazine. He was an excellent director. He was human. A very approachable, friendly, nice person.

Jim Sharman was a wonderful, lovely guy. I worked on *Superstar* and *Hair* with him. Thank you, Jim, if you ever read this! I was quite shy then and I had these tinted glasses, because I was a bit paranoid. He let me keep my glasses on through the show. That was the sweetest thing for him to do. Very sweet of him. He knew I needed them.

SCOTT MICHAELS: *What was the work like?*

PO: We rehearsed in the old house. It was wonderful. While we were working, it was great, but when we weren't, I didn't feel very comfortable. On my face, they waxed out my natural brow line and they put gold glitter on my face. I loved my glasses. I wore a paper pirate hat with a skull and crossbones on it. I think I sort of looked like the lion in *The Wiz*. While working, I was like a fish in water. But I was socially awkward. I didn't have a huge part; I was just a Transylvanian in a couple of scenes. There were a lot of parties, but I wasn't invited because I wasn't part of the 'in' crowd.

SM: *Several people have said how cliquey the set was.*

PO: I would say that I felt on the periphery of the cast. There were people that were in a gang that naturally gravitated toward each other. I felt like an observer. It's just how it was. It wasn't necessarily a bad experience; it just makes it what it was. I did feel, in Sadie, that she was a mate. We supported each other. She was a bit of an outsider, too. There was the sparkly crowd. Gaye and Biggins – they were 'the crowd'. I believe that Stephen, Sadie and myself were the outsiders, not part of the sparkly crowd.

I was in the car going into the studios in the mornings with Biggins and Annabel. I would sit very quietly and listen to them. I liked Sadie because she has a big laugh too! Perhaps when I talk to Sadie more, it will bring up more stories. There was the American contingent as well.

SM: *And what about the Americans? Were they 'the stars'?*

PO: Susan Sarandon was extremely serious about her work. I respected that. I was walking past her and made a comment and she was totally concentrating on what she was doing. Barry Bostwick still gets cast in those roles, sort of the affable good-looking suave American. Meat Loaf just scared me.

SM: So what are your remembrances of things past, the other actors?

PO: Tim was just so out and out... I remember him getting trapped in the elevator. Richard O'Brien, the way he looks, the way he is – that's him, and he's carried that through right to the present day. Obviously, he's traded on himself. That was the real him then, as it is now. Kimi Wong O'Brien. I often think of her. I remember her and Richard when we were in *Superstar* and them coming towards me with Linus in a pram. They had him dressed in little multi-coloured mittens and a little hat.

Nell – I loved her tap-dancing routine and that squeaky voice. And Peter Hinwood...well, he was a god. He had the tan and the body. Beautiful. I just loved looking at him. But I heard a few cast members saying he was too perfect.

The stuntman incident was very scary. It happened on the other side of the ramp. I heard the kerfuffle but didn't see it happen.

Perry was in *Superstar* with me, of course. Biggins I really remember being very expansive, very ebullient, very up front. He wasn't intimidated by anyone. Anyone he wanted to speak to he would speak to. No qualms about it. He said, 'Life is too short. You want to speak to them, go and speak to them.' I've always remembered that. Imogen's claim to fame was 'Maltesers melt in your mouth, not in your hand'; she played that as a Spanish dancer.

I remember Fran getting her make-up done. I was quite fascinated with Fran.

Peggy, bless her. She told me, in her very posh voice, 'You're far too nice to be in this business.' I did feel an odd vibe from Peggy. That's how it is. You get thrown together.

SM: But you didn't keep up with them all?

PO: I was not asked to be in *Shock Treatment*. I'm strictly a Transylvanian. It was great when they turned up the music and we were dancing. It was just wonderful.

I haven't really mixed with a showbiz crowd of people, which has been to my advantage for a number of years. That's it, really. My name is Bethany Brown now. I'm involved in the business at a level I like. I do my job and go home. I'm really interested in writing. I've done lyrics, poetry, skits. What I tried to develop was that I could be immersed in what I do and financially supported by it. It's happening more so now. I worked with my husband for many years, singing, songwriting, and doing studio work.

SM: Do you have any souvenirs?

PO: Just memories. I don't have any of the costume. It wasn't ours to keep. I have seen the movie several times but I don't have it on tape. I don't think I saw the film in its entirety for many years, but when I did, it was great! I remember my bits. And Sadie. It all slid into place. It was a tiny experience, but it meant quite a lot to me. I still have my call-sheets.

‹‹‹‹irememberdoingthetimewarpirememberdoingthetimewarpi››››

Peggy Ledger

Peggy, sadly, is no longer with us. She was born in Dublin, petite, just about five feet tall, and had been in the business since she was a young woman, although she left to marry actor Hugh Whitmore Ledger and have children. Her husband was a founding member of Equity, the actors' trade union. She also dabbled in the antiques business and taught ballet.

When Peggy did *The Dirtiest Show In Town*, as the only fully clad performer, thus capturing all the notices, she got her own Equity card. She did the show from May 1971 to March 1973 and was the only cast member never to miss a show. She was 74 when she appeared in

The Rocky Horror Picture Show and was the one of the few Transylvanians given lines. In 1974, Peggy appeared in the BBC serial *Ann Of Avonlea* and, also for the BBC, she appeared in the dramatisation of *Cheri*, by Colette.

She appeared in *Space 1999* and worked for Yorkshire Television from July 1977 to March 1978 in the series *You're Only Young Twice*, about a ladies' retirement home.

Sadly, she was not asked to appear in *Shock Treatment*. Peggy died on 4 July 1981. Her fellow Transylvanian and co-star Christopher Biggins gave the address at her memorial service.

<<<<irememberdoingthetimewarpirememberdoingthetimewarpi>>>>

Tony Cowen

How many Trannies were there? Seventeen? Here's another.

Scott rang Tony, attempting to get an interview. Tony had a very brusque demeanour…

SCOTT MICHAELS: *Tony Cowen?*

TONY COWEN: Yes.

SM: *My name is Scott Michaels.*

TC: So, you're the one that's been trying to get hold of me. Who are you?

SM: *I'm researching the Transylvanians in* The Rocky Horror Picture Show, *hopefully for a book.*

TC: Well, I don't live in London, so next time I get in town I'll call you.

SM: *It is really important that I get to speak with you.*

TC: In America, they started this cult society about the film and they used our pictures quite a bit. None of us were very pleased about it. We didn't get paid hardly anything to be in it and they promised us more. It took quite a bit of cheek to do it. None of us were very happy about it.

SM: Oh...

‹‹‹‹iremberdoingthetimewarpiremberdoingthetimewarpi›››

Imogen Claire and Perry Bedden
16 July 1998

The ever-resourceful Scott had almost run out of Transylvanians available and willing to be interviewed. Then he collared Imogen Claire.

Imogen was in *The Lair Of The White Worm* and played the mother, who was cut in half. She was in *Little Shop Of Horrors* in the downtown scene and loved working with Frank Oz.

She worked with David Toguri many times, but the first time was in *Rocky*. She used her Transylvanian costume in the film *Absolute Beginners*. She was supposed to play Pola Negri in the Ken Russell version of *Valentino*, but Negri's family and the estate objected and sued to stop her portrayal. Imogen is married to John Rothenberg, an Australian with whom she has been for 20 years, having met at the National Theatre.

Scott met Imogen and Perry Bedden at the same time. He said he felt completely at ease as they interviewed each other!

IMOGEN CLAIRE: When they were doing *Rocky* at the Royal Court, the management rang my agent saying they wanted to see me to possibly play someone called Magenta in this new show Upstairs at the Royal Court. I asked when it was scheduled, as I was in a show in the West End and wondered if I could get out of it. My agent told me I probably couldn't get out of it, so I rang Equity and asked them. No. It wasn't even worth my going to the interview, because there was no way I could get out of my contract. So I didn't do it. I told Jim and he was sad. Jim Sharman was just the sweetest man. When they were doing the film, he asked me if I would be in it, because he really wanted to work with me.

When I couldn't do the show, my agent said, 'Oh, don't worry. It's only three weeks upstairs at the Royal Court. Sounds ghastly. It will never go anywhere.' But something inside of me thought differently. I thought the world was ready for this. You must remember that the Royal Court Theatre at that time was the centre for new writing. John Osborne and Joe Orton had begun there. It was the centre of 'art', if you like. If people came to London, they came to the Royal Court to see what was on. They knew what they were going to see would be interesting. That's why all those celebrities went to see *Rocky*. They may have gone because of the reputation, which didn't take long to start. There was a huge fuss about it. It was scheduled for three weeks, extended to five, until they got the Chelsea Classic.

PERRY BEDDEN: I remember when Jonathan King came along and wanted to do the cast album. That was out by the time it got to the Chelsea Classic. It was almost done overnight. I think it's the best album ever. They get residuals from that album still.

SCOTT MICHAELS: So Jim would have specifically asked for you for the movie?

IC: Celestia Fox called my agent because they wanted this motley crew. There was a lot of people who knew Jim from *Jesus Christ, Superstar* and a lot of people like me, who Jim wanted to work with, and then they needed the oddballs like Stephen Calcutt and Sadie and Biggins, who was fat.

PB: Even though we knew Jim, we still had to meet with him, for an interview by Celestia Fox.

IC: I went to see Celestia, to the King's Road at the Chelsea Classic, where it was playing. I left my crutches outside, because I had a broken foot. I walked in, and there was Jim and Celestia and Richard. We chatted. I stood up and walked out. When I told Jim later that I could hardly walk, he said, 'I wish I'd known. I'd have had you on crutches in the film!'

SM: It seems that filming was not uneventful?

IC: Remember when the stuntman was on the bike? He was extraordinary. The shot is cut just as the bike turns. He realised the bike was going to crash and we were all jumping out of the way. He passed out. He came round to turn the ignition off or we'd have all gone up in flames.

PB: I just remember that bike being very, very big and the ramp was not very wide.

IC: Tony Milner was such a good actor, wasn't he?

PB: They found a little man that took over from Henry Woolf, because the shooting went on for longer than they thought. His name was Tony Cowen. We didn't like him too much, I seem to remember.

IC: But who cared? You just had another smoke and off you went.

PB: We used to play charades in wardrobe. Gaye Brown used to organise it, remember? 'You do this, you do that!'

IC: There was a lovely man, Richard Pointing, who was the wardrobe man on the film. I've worked with him loads of times, because he always worked with Ken Russell. I used to travel to the studio with him. I'd just finished doing the film *Tommy* and Richard was the wardrobe man on that as well. I was Jack Nicholson's nurse.

SM: What came after Rocky?

IC: I gave up acting in 1978 because I lost my nerve. I started doing choreography. I wouldn't go onstage or television. The thought of performing... I completely lost my nerve. Debbie McWilliam was casting *Shock Treatment* and she rang me up and said Jim wanted me for a 'whatever happened to *Rocky*?' film. I said I couldn't possibly work. She said, 'Oh, I'm sorry,' and then Jim came on the phone. 'Listen, it's a personality part, five days over three weeks. That's all you have to do. Please come.'

So I went to the studios and had my fitting. Sue Blane and I shrieked. I got my costume together with Sue, because the budget was tight. Jim came to me and said, 'Oh, I assume you are doing it, then. Thank God for that'. I did my five days, the first week of the shoot. I was there on the daily rate. Debbie came to me at the end of the week and said, 'Imogen, this is the moment when you say to me, "Please, Debbie, will you double my money?"' I just said she was being silly, but she did it for me! So, for the next two weeks, I got paid on the daily rate, double what the original deal was. I made a lot of money.

I remember Michael White's girlfriend at the time, Lindall Hobbs, making the video of the making of *Shock Treatment*. She was there with cameras up our bums the entire time. I remember one day, you [Perry], me and Rufus sitting there, and there was Lindall, filming. They were lining up a shot [for] some television documentary, so we had three cameras on us for three different purposes.

SM: Has the cult caught up with you yet? Do you have fans?

IC: When I played New York a couple of years ago, because I had *Rocky* on my CV, the fans were waiting outside the stage door. The fans track you down. We were playing the Brooklyn Academy of Music – the Royal Court of New York, if you like – and leaving the stage door there were always at least a half dozen of them. And then, when I played Plymouth a few years ago – same tour, *Salomé* with Stephen Berkoff – I had white face and black lips, sort of the same make-up.

Across from the stage door was a cinema that showed *Rocky*. We would leave while the fans were queuing up and they would mock me. It haunts you in a way. I quite like it because it's not a problem for me. For the likes of us, the Transylvanians, we did the film and we did *Shock Treatment* and it doesn't affect our lives hardly at all. I think the leads – Pat, Richard, Nell and Tim – it completely changed their lives.

SM: *Film-making in the mid 1970s seems to have been a very small world.*

IC: All the crew on *Rocky* had worked on *Tommy*. It was the same group of people I'd been working with all summer. The crew would play the *Tommy* soundtrack and we would have to stop and think, 'What movie are we on?' It was so bizarre. There were a lot of us that were in Ken Russell's repertory company. When they did the premiere of *The Devils*, I went with Ken and his wife, Murray Melvin, Brian Murphy. We were filming *Tommy*. We got dressed at the studio and went to the premiere. Then Ken said he had to go to the television studios for an interview. By that time, he had been drinking for so long; he's watched the film. He did wallop Alexander. We were filming the next day, so we couldn't go out to play. I turned on the television and saw Ken hit him. I was hysterical.

SM: *I bet they wish that movie had survived, as well as* Rocky.

IC: The fact that the *Rocky* film is timeless, that's largely to do with Brian, Sue and the script, the fact is that people are still wearing those clothes. Sue bought my frock in Berwick Street market.

PB: It was Brian's idea to use the lips from the Man Ray painting. I remember Jim was stuck for credits. Another scene where Brian didn't get credit. There was a lot of in-fighting.

IC: *Rocky* is one of the biggest films ever, because of the number of times it's been shown. Up there with *Gone With The Wind*.

SM: *And you had no objections to the Americans being imported into such a very British cast?*

IC: Susan and Barry were so lovely. Barry was such a laugh. Susan and Barry were only stand-offish at one time. The dressing rooms were terrible. Appalling. The wardrobe where they had to get dressed was across this cold area to this hut that was the wardrobe. Because it was the first day of filming, everyone was there. A huge scene. They had flown in from LA and hadn't been treated like gods by people. They were then thrown into this very cold day and they walked from wardrobe all the way across the field where we were filming and I think they were very pissed off. But that was the very first day. After that, they were gorgeous. Especially Barry. Years later, when I did *I'll Take Manhattan*, he came to my Winnebago, rushed in, and we squealed with laughter. We sat and had coffee and shrieked about *Rocky*! I didn't think he'd remember me, so I didn't bother to seek him out.

I think, because it was Fox's money, they chose Susan and Barry because they were up-and-coming stars. I think Fox said, 'Fine, we'll give you money, but you use these two Americans.' I think it was a stroke of genius. Different cultures are just that. They were perfect. It was made up of totally unknown people, including the director. Susan did a Billy Wilder movie immediately after *Rocky*. I used to hear a lot of her, because she's a great friend of Rupert Everett and Rupert is a good friend of mine.

PB: I always thought it was Jim's idea, for authenticity.

SM: *Any thoughts about Tim Curry?*

PB: Tim had a major problem with *Rocky*. He wanted to cut away from it totally and do the big singing thing. I just think he just wanted to get away from anyone questioning his sexuality. I remember Brian got a call from Tim about an invite to a *Rocky* convention. I remember him screaming, 'I don't want anything to do with *Rocky Horror*!' He went hysterical and he never turned up.

IC: Tim's career is quite solid now. He's ruthlessly ambitious. I think him showing up for the 15th was probably because it was Fox-backed and it suited him. *Rocky* did affect their lives and Tim was right to be careful. That could have been his only job. He had to prove himself. A lot of people can do one thing and nothing else. When you think of Terence Stamp in *Priscilla Queen Of The Desert*, he was an established actor when he did it. Tim wasn't. He needed to establish himself as an actor.

SM: *Have you kept much of the film memorabilia?*

IC: I bought a whole load of stills and gave them away. But I still have my tailcoat, waistcoat and shirts. When I did *Absolute Beginners*, which Sue designed and in which I played a lesbian, as usual, she said, 'I don't know what we're going to put you in.' I told her I still had my things from *Rocky*. She said, 'We'll get you a nice pair of trousers and high heels, and that would do, wouldn't it?' I've still got them in a suitcase under my bed!

<<<<irememberdoingthetimewarpirememberdoingthetimewarpi>>>>

Anthony Then

And yet another lost Transylvanian…

In the not-so-PC days, Anthony was affectionately known as 'Chinky'. He wanted to become a proper ballet dancer, but because of his height (five foot six inches) he fell well short of the mark. He started a career in choreology, the system of notating dance steps, and taught in the London Institute of Choreology. For extra money, he took up jobs in commercials and films. Aside from *The Rocky Horror Picture Show*, Tony also appeared in a four-hour epic, *Doctor Frankenstein*, and a 'gong-fu' movie, *Blade Of Vengeance*. Tony once said of his experiences, 'I've never felt compromised. Not at all. I saw it as an extension of my experience in the theatre.'

After working as a choreographer in California and Las Vegas,

Germany and Italy, Anthony returned to his native country of Singapore, where he co-founded the Singapore Dance Theatre. He passed away at the Communicable Diseases Centre in Singapore on 16 December 1995.

‹‹‹‹irememberdoingthetimewarpiremerberdoingthetimewarpi››››

It would indeed be churlish not to mention here those erstwhile and totally anonymous persons on film sets called stand-ins. We know they're paid to be patient and, unlike understudies in the theatre, they know they will never appear as the characters for whom they are 'standing in'. So, for that reason alone, other than Jon Berkinshaw, whom Richard Pointing has already mentioned, let's gave a name-check to those we know of.

Liz Coke was Susan Sarandon, Gerry Paris was Tim Curry, both Richard Smith and Dave Murphy were Richard O'Brien, Tuppence and Melita Smith were Patricia Quinn, Erica Simmons did for Nell Campbell, AN Other and Alan Harris alternated for Peter Hinwood and Eric Kent inhabited Meat Loaf's ultimate space.

Thanks, guys.

‹‹‹‹irememberdoingthetimewarpiremerberdoingthetimewarpi››››

Ishaq Bux

Ishaq Bux was unfortunately not well enough to met Scott. He comes from a long line of entertainers in his native India. A well-known face on British television, he has also appeared in the films *A Passage To India* and *Raiders Of The Lost Ark*.

Ishaq has said that his chief memory of the *Rocky* shoot is being led by David Toguri through numerous dance rehearsals. 'We had to do quite a lot of rehearsal. They wanted to be very sure before they did the real thing.'

Scott received the following letter from Ishaq's daughter on 4 August 1998.

Dear Mr Michaels

My father, Mr Ishaq Bux, has just received two letters from you via the Oriental Casting Agency regarding *The Rocky Horror Picture Show*. In your letters, you expressed an interest in meeting my father for an interview. Sadly, however, this will not be possible as speaking is very painful for my father due to his heart condition and shortness of breath. He is also paralysed and wheelchair-dependent.

I hope you understand that, in these circumstances, it would be very difficult to grant your request.

I know from past conversation with my father that he enjoyed his time in *The Rocky Horror Picture Show* and had only good things to say about its cast and crew.

My father and I wish you all the best in your work.

Regards
Miss R Bux

Subsequently, Isahq Bux passed away shortly after this letter was received. Rest in peace, Ishaq.

‹‹‹‹irememberdoingthetimewarpiremembderdoingthetimewarpi››››

7 'Say Goodbye To All This And Hello To...Oblivion!'
From Mary Shelley To Richard O'Brien

This chapter must be the ultimate of all the 'whatever happened to...?' features that most initial failures never have written about them. Oblivion is usually a one-way street. Resuscitation is not a widely practised art in movieland.

SCOTT MICHAELS: *Rocky Horror* changed my life. There. I said it. Now, it may sound like a cliché to use that description when referring to a movie, but wait... I can explain. I can positively trace my existence as it is today to this film. If I hadn't met those few particular people at the old Punch and Judy Theater in Detroit...well, I can't imagine where I would be now.

I grew up in Detroit, in a very blue-collar neighbourhood. It never is cool to be different, but it was especially uncool in Detroit. Around 1978, well after *The Rocky Horror Picture Show* 'cult' began elsewhere in the country, it finally hit my town. I never heard a word about this piece of celluloid until one evening it was used as a human-interest story on the local news station. I saw. I wanted. That was for me.

The report showed scenes of mayhem in the movie house, with hundreds of people throwing food, dancing and singing in the aisles – it was something I wanted to belong to. *The Rocky Horror Picture Show* was rated R in the States, which meant that you had to be 17 or with a parent to see it. At that time I was only 16 and barely had my driving licence, so I practically (what I am saying is, *I did*) beg my 26-year-old brother to take me to the local cinema to see this film for the first time. I didn't really get it at first, but I did get the amazing feeling of camaraderie involved with this. I didn't even know what I was doing, but dammit if I didn't bring hotdogs and toast.

For the next year or so, I felt like my life had really begun. I became obsessed with it. I had to see it. Had to. When Dori Hartley mentioned in an interview that seeing *Rocky Horror* was 'like a fix', I knew what she meant. I bummed rides, walked miles in the dark, hid in hedges from the police (I was breaking curfew laws) and endured as much agonising criticism as humanly possible, but I had to see those characters. *Rocky* was my rebellious phase. It simply wasn't cool to paper your school locker with pictures of a man in fishnets. I did. And it made me a better person.

No one ever got it. Neighbours around the theatre tried to get it shut down, because of the disruption late at night. The arguments I would have with my parents about going, the hassles from classmates about liking that 'fag' movie.

I begged the theatre managers to give me a job at the movie house where it played. My wonderful position was frisking people for bottles of booze and monitoring the audience. If anyone had lighters, there I was. I had to bust smokers, confiscate meatloaves…but afterwards, the real fun would begin. A team of four of us got to clean the mess. It took us all about six hours to do the job. I still remember the smell of stale beer and rice. It takes me right back.

I moved away from Detroit to Chicago for ten years, then to LA, where I weirdly lived just down the road from Tim Curry. Funny, that. As much as I would love to speak to him now, I never had the nerve to approach him then, when I saw him on his daily walks through Griffith Park. Wherever I lived, I always managed to squeak in a showing of *Rocky*, though not as often as before. When the 20th anniversary of *Rocky* was being celebrated at the Pantages Theater in Hollywood, I was there to see Pat Quinn, Richard O'Brien, Barry Bostwick and Sal Piro in person. It was a moment I treasure.

Cut to 1998. I moved to London, England, the birthplace of it all. I went to the opening night of a play called *Always*. I thought I recognised one of the people in attendance as Pat Quinn. I was too frightened to go up to her. I loved her. No, you don't understand, I adored her. A while later, my partner was hosting a talk show that was looking for a guest and he very kindly asked my input. Without hesitation, I suggested Pat Quinn. Much to my surprise, he got her. And I met her.

We got on really well. I started telling her about myself and my current writing project and Pat suggested we get together and write her book. Pat and I had many meetings in her home. She was very generous and forthcoming with information. I put together a proposal for a book based on Pat and her life but couldn't find an interested publisher. It sat there.

Now, the basis of my being in London is my relationship with my partner. The laws were only starting to change here in the UK, and the authorities were only beginning to acknowledge same-sex partners. The very first step in my application for residence was handing in my passport and being forbidden to leave or work. This period lasted a year and a half. I therefore decided to go on a Trannie hunt. I wanted to meet all of *Rocky*'s Transylvanians. I always thought of them as the Munchkins of Transylvania. They were the freaks I adored. I spent so many evenings with them in my youth, I felt I owed it to them now. I wanted to know their names. I wanted to find out all about them. It became a real labour of love, but once I found my first one, Sadie Corre, all the pieces started to fall into place. Phone numbers were becoming available and a lot of the Transylvanians were really helpful finding others.

I have to thank many people for helping me obtain interviews for this book: Graham Norton, Sadie Corre, Christopher Biggins, John McKay, Kimi Wong O'Brien, Perry Bedden, Peter Straker, Yasmin Pettigrew, Sue Blane... You guys are my heroes. That's right, my heroes. It is an honour to know you. I also want to thank my old friends Marianne Babich, Michelle Martin, Cheryl Zahler, Jennifer Gerious, Marlene LaHaise and many others that I spent my weekends with. They made my youth a more bearable place to be.

Theatrically, *The Rocky Horror Show* was a supremely conventional piece, as far as form went, and in any fair comparison with traditional morality plays, it was a classic. As well as being about stardom, the play's also about dictators (good and evil), sin and repentance.

Rocky's roots go deep and draw fully from a centuries-old well-spring. Tap the show's frivolous casing and its bell will sound not cracked but as sound and true as that of Big Ben itself. It's one of the reasons for its timeless success.

The film ensured a sort of immortality for Richard O'Brien's concept. However, the substance of the play had already been diluted in the making of the film. Brad's song was dropped and 'Superheroes' omitted, on which grounds no one is sure, except any Hollywood-approval quotient has always been a compromise between the libertine and the latter-day saint, between the free thinker and the fundamentalist. Every age has had its libertines. Don Juan, Sir Francis Dashwood, the Bloomsburies…there's no need to go on, but the tradition of tinkering with human beings by the divine or the occult is centuries old. Greek gods often arrived on Earth to cause havoc. Shakespeare has Oberon and Titania creating mayhem in *A Midsummer Night's Dream* for no other reason than it pleased them to do so and the sight of human beings in dilemma is amusing. As far as I know, no one as yet has proved a direct lineage to a Shakespeare play, but as I am no classical scholar, just keep on holding your breath… Humans behaving badly through no fault of their own, only to awake to rediscover the moral truth and to correct their errant ways, has been the stuff of theatrical success down the ages. There but for the grace of God go we all…

Oddly, even die-hard fans sidestep the sex issue. In his book *The Rocky Horror Picture Show Book*, Bill Henken places huge emphasis on the 'family fun' nature of the Rocky experience and at times appears to be apologising that there could be any sexual content or implication inherent in *The Rocky Horror Show*. He seems to side with the non-holistic view of sexual behaviour, that it somehow exists apart from the sexuality of the whole person and is a separable phenomenon. Like what you do isn't who you are. Like it's OK to dress up in corsets, ripped fishnets and fuck-me pumps, but it's only my feminine/masculine side coming out and 'I'm not in the least gay, really.'

It seems a little odd that the cult status now ascribed to *The Rocky*

Horror Picture Show and its devoted acolytes was first established in America, the land where the theatrical reality of the original show was renounced. Perversely, it was the cinematic unreality that was ultimately embraced. It's not unlike the growth of a major religion which only ever becomes big after the reality that spawned it is long past. The stories and hearsay and legend added onto the initial core create a phenomenon that ends up way out of sync with the original. And a thought: is a cult a cult because it is cultivated or because it is an abbreviation of the umbrella culture beneath which it shelters?

There must be comparatively few people *vis-à-vis* the massed devotees of the movie who even remember the original.

DAVID EVANS: I watched the film again in September 1999 for the first time in years. Terry Ackland Snow had said that watching the film was even better for the passing of time. As I watched, I pondered how much has changed for the better in our lives since we stepped through *Rocky*'s particular time warp and how much has remained unchanged, given that most of us have since stepped back. And even more questions, like 'Just who de-Medusa'd Doctor Scott?' 'Just how did Peter Hinwood kick off both his shoes in one take in one shot?' 'Just how did they all manage to have their shoes on when they get out of the pool?' 'Just how was the lightning superimposed?'

It was brave and original at the time to suggest that men take fantasy to bed and women take reality. Columbia is not interested in the fantasy of Eddie or in Eddie's fantasies; she wants the real thing. She wants Eddie. I pondered the blurring of parameters time has effected in what men are and what women are. Words like *gay* and *lesbian* now have a reality. They are words that can now be applied to real people and not merely to media or medical phenomena. Loves that dared not speak their name can now be shouted from the rooftops and even embraced in Cabinet. So why is it that the majority of human beings are still excluded by dint of species from the joys of Planet Transylvania? Sooner or later, ultimate freedom and absolute pleasure are too much to cope with on a permanent basis. It's almost like not being able to cope with heaven.

'How sentimental!' do you cry? Maybe. Because, of course, like Riff Raff, we all have to keep control. But when Tim Curry's lipstick comes off at the end, that is the precise moment when the film, like Doctor Frank himself, collapses.

It is ironic that, although in places like South Africa both play and film were banned for years and willing and eager audiences were legally proscribed from seeing it, in other places audiences had no interest in going to see the piece in the first place. Until, one night, one metropolitan midnight... But that would spoil Sal Piro's story.

<<<<irememberdoingthetimewarpirememberdoingthetimewarpi>>>>

Sal Piro

5 November 1999
'Sane inside insanity'

DAVID EVANS: We met Sal in the Crypt Café of the Parish Church of St Martin-in-the-Fields on Trafalgar Square. Spooky, huh? And it was no accident! Scott had made the appointment a couple of days previously and today, Friday, was its rescheduled time. Sal had been due someplace else. Sal had actually been confined to bed with a horrid cold. But, ultimately, there was Sal. In the flesh. The man who made the myth made man. Sal is the man who said, 'Rocky Horror is a style. It preaches freedom as a way of life.'

In order to have *The Rocky Horror Show* reap the success it deserved, Richard O'Brien needed his Sal Piro. Sal looked to me as though he could build or tear down pretty much anything, although it emerges more and more that accidentalism is the real key to success. Star-bangs and celestial event management can never be planned for but can, to compensate, be thoroughly over-analysed in hindsight. It is certainly the tale of *The Rocky Horror Show*.

Sal Piro has become one of the major authorities on the *Rocky Horror* phenomenon. I would hazard that he knows more about its post-movie incarnation than Richard, Chris Malcolm or any of the producers, franchisees or licensees. Sal, like Saul of Tarsus on the road to Damascus, is a man o'erta'en by the sheer force of the event he had not planned for, only Sal is a truly willing victim of this accidentalism.

Sal was 26 when he first went to see *The Rocky Horror Picture Show* and it is to the movie that he has his allegiance. He is a child of three American movie-going generations and was himself a movie buff throughout high school and college. Obviously, he has since seen stage productions of *Rocky Horror*, but viscerally it is the movie that hits the spot for him.

Sal is, of course, American. Across the pond, and for all practical purposes, the show/the play for years meant zilch. Prior to 1976, when his life was literally consummated and then shaped by the experience of seeing *The Rocky Horror Picture Show*, Sal Piro had been a nice Catholic American boy. He had been through high school, where he had always been an achiever. He is a natural president. Whatever club he joined, he always ended up taking charge of it.

He grew up a confirmed extrovert and, after graduating from high school, where he enjoyed participating in drama activities, he became a seminarian. All things would have pointed to him being a natural candidate for the priesthood. Had he followed that path, I have no doubt that Sal would have accelerated way past bishop and would have ultimately made cardinal.

However, after three years at Seton Hall University, in New Jersey, he began to teach high school and ended up heading classes in religious education. That is, until...until nuns were brought in to replace him and, at 26 years of age, a secular life beckoned. Was it the revving of motorbikes in the night? Was it the sounds of hovering alien spacecraft? Or was the lure of a life apart in Thespis's theatre, as powerful a magnet as the theatre of the church?

Whatever. Sal decided to cross the river and move into Manhattan, where, heeding the call of the Great White Way, he planned to pursue a career in drama. So, naturally, he first had to become a waiter, although it wasn't long before he landed a part in an off-off Broadway show that ran for some three months and for which he garnered some pretty decent reviews.

During late 1975 and into 1976, the management of the Waverly

Theater on Sixth Avenue in Greenwich Village had begun to run midnight performances of grungy B-movies, cheap to rent from the studios and calculated to lure the pink dollars out of the pockets of the nocturnal weekend denizens of Greenwich Village, Soho and Chelsea. Screenings of movies like *Pink Flamingoes* and *Night Of The Living Dead* featured prominently. Like the London punks who embraced the first London stage production, the gay audiences have always been eager to find somewhere else to discover and populate for themselves. They soon gravitated to yet another cruisy cinema in the post-Stonewall New York of clones, plaid workshirts, drag queens and disco. Trends in taste and fashion always seem to find a cradle in the bosom of the gay population and as we all know, the hand that rocks the cradle... The Caterpillar boot and shoe company should be so grateful.

Tim Deegan, the Fox executive so powerfully endorsed by Michael White as being the only one at Fox who championed the picture, persuaded Bill Quigley of the Walter Reade Group to persuade the Waverly management to take the otherwise-dead-in-the-water *Rocky Horror Picture Show* to replace *Night Of The Living Dead* for midnight screenings, the first of which was scheduled for April 1976.

Other than in Los Angeles, where the film had been playing at one screen or another since it opened in September 1975, the film was going nowhere. Tim Deegan must have been either desperate or inspired, like Saul on the road to... He apparently not only didn't like the movie; he purported not even to understand where it was coming from. But he knew enough to know that it was certainly a film that a predominantly gay audience would have been likely to appreciate, as well as other creatures of the night, unknown in the respectable suburbs occupied by up-and-coming Fox executives... I'm amazed his other name wasn't Brad Majors.

What happened next is not even a long story to cut short. The midnight performances took off. Whatever the audience were doing in the dark, they weren't yet interacting with the screen, but the audiences were there, the box office sold tickets and *The Rocky Horror Picture Show* was soon secure in its midnight slot. Deegan capitalised on this success and began to persuade other cinema owners in hand-picked locations to run the movie. The theatre on campus in Austin, Texas – which Michael White insisted was first to start midnight screenings – was in fact three weeks behind the first screening at the Waverly, although, within a year, the movie was playing at over 100 screens nationwide. After two years, the number of regularly active *Rocky* screens rose to 200.

When Sal and his friend Marc Shaiman first went to see the movie in December 1976, the audiences were merely polite. It took a year to 18 months before the participative phenomenon was fully fledged, as long a time as it had taken from the birth of the show until the completion of the movie. Together, Sal and Marc saw the movie between 30 and 40 times. Then Marc went off to LA to become the masterly composer of film music he now is, leaving Sal to go it alone.

And Sal kept right on going. He remembers clearly the occasion, and credits Louis Farese with first yelling a line back to the screen. Louis was blessed with a funny, distinctive voice, and thus, when Janet first shelters beneath the newspaper, from the darkness was heard, 'Buy an umbrella, ya cheap bitch!'

Laughing Out Loud. The whole Waverly audience fell about. LOL.

Two weeks later, another line, in retort to the Narrator's suggestion of 'the strange journey'.

'So, how strange was it?'

More LOL.

The ensuing weeks saw the ritualisation of more audience comeback reactive dialogue and the first props appeared – the newspapers, the rice, the lighters and candles accompanying 'There's A Light' and Sal's big ring, which he waved on the cue, 'Nicer than Betty Munro had.'

The next most significant member in the incipient cult-ivation was Dori Hartley ('not her real surname but one she chose 'cause she liked the English sound of it and it was sorta Richard's name [Richard Hartley, the musical arranger]').

Dori first threw off her cape at the front of the gallery in her Frank N-lookalike costume and was soon identified with Sal as a core member of the growing, loyal audience that, unbidden, reinvented the theatricality of the *Rocky Horror* experience. By doing so, they breathed new life into a supine, bowed and bloodied failure.

'We're making a show with someplace to go and it's good for relieving our...tension!'

Although Sal never dressed up himself as any of the characters, he became 'president' as the result of...yes! Of an accident! Thankfully, the accident never happened, but on one of the successive occasions when the lighters – which were being brought along as props – were scheduled to be lit against all fire regulations, the Waverly management approached Sal as a readily identifiable *bona fide* audience member to act as liaison officer.

Sal agreed to make the announcement before the performance that the movie would be shut down if the lighters were lit. No lighters were lit that night and Sal made the announcements at subsequent performances and so Sal became The Leader. To quote the lyrics of another great glittering leader who was later to go on to play Frank N Furter in New Zealand, 'I'm the leader, I'm the leader, I'm the leader of the gang, I am!' Thanks, Gary.

Sal Piro became the star of the cult. His immortality was ensured when *The Rocky Horror Picture Show* featured so prominently in the movie *Fame*. Sal, like the master of ceremonies on a Victorian music-hall stage in the Palace of Varieties, became the acknowledged MC, the most famous cabaret MC, apart from Joel Grey...

In 1977, Sal and Dori and about eight or ten others who did dress up decided to form a fanclub because they wanted to have a convention. A meeting was held – it all sounds so democratic and proper and not the slightest bit dictatorial.

Nominations were taken; Dori didn't want to stand, and so Sal was elected unopposed as president. Yes! 'Recognition at last,' as Tim Curry once famously wrote. Although Sal admits to identifying with the Magenta character but emphasises that he never wanted to be her, he also admits to liking the character of the good doctor Frank N Furter. Gay and liberated and 'The Leader'. So, life imitates art imitates life...

The fledgling fanclub had no money and so soliciting members and charging them fees seemed a good way of raising some initial working capital to launch the campaign for their convention. America is a land of conventions. Everyone has them. No fetish, cause or subculture is unworthy of a good weekend's knees-up. Even gerontophiles have conventions, cheerfully chasing each other up and down the corridors of a hotel in a city near you, four times a year.

The *Rocky Horror* self-confessed business virgins and entrepreneurial *ingenués* must have been somewhat taken aback when, after a few short weeks of their activities, the fanclub had a member in Australia and, very quickly, a membership of between 5,000 and 10,000. *The Transylvanian* was the title of the fanclub's newsletter and it spread a fast word.

(A word about fanclubs. As word-spin machines and PR tools in the music business, about which I can talk with some authority, fanclubs are essential. Once these begin to build, managements would be well advised to recognise them and legitimise them immediately. The fanclubs act as one of the main media organs available to the bands or artists in question. I remember both Elton John's fanclub and the Queen fanclub being integrated into the very structure of the management company surrounding the artists and, indeed, being housed in the very same building. The people at Fox were not slow in identifying the importance of Sal and his team. Information is most advantageously disseminated in a controlled way and renegade rival outfits putting out information at odds with the management line are counter-productive and a waste of corporate energy. Ask the Stasi, the CIA, the KGB and the FBI. And MI5.)

One setback occurred at the beginning of 1978, when the institution *The Rocky Horror Picture Show* had become was evicted from the Waverly. There occurred what was tantamount to a riot outside the theatre. Some young guns up from Little Italy – probably homophobes and certainly killjoys – who had been taking exception for months to those oddly dressed in the line outside the Waverly finally snapped. No more would there be the spectacle of audience participants doing the Time Warp in the middle of Sixth Avenue.

The freaks and the weirdos were set upon and…horrors! Just like at Stonewall, the freaks and the weirdos fought back.

Moral: Not everyone in a corset's a fairy.

The *Rocky* juggernaut moved to the Eighth Street Theater, whose management knew a good thing when they saw one coming, and the movie also started playing at another Manhattan venue, the New Yorker. The fanclub grew, as did the peripheral careers of those in the movie.

The box-office receipts that had begun to flow throughout 1977 must have once again excited Lou Adler's appetite. The Tim Curry-making-proper-albums project was resuscitated. Tim's ambitions were taken off the iced back burner and Lou set him to work.

Also reactivated by the events and newly rekindled interest in *The Rocky Horror Picture Show* was the project created by Jim Steinman and Meat Loaf entitled *Bat Out Of Hell*, which was suddenly signed up. Whilst in London working on the *Rocky* movie, Meat Loaf had recorded at least five tracks with Richard Hartley, singing songs with lyrics by Brian Thomson, one of which was entitled 'Clap Your Hands'. Like Little Nell's efforts to break into the record business with stuff like 'Do The Swim' and the blighted efforts of Kimi and Ritzy, Meat Loaf in 1974 and 1975 had met with little success.

In 1977, with the burgeoning success of *The Rocky Horror Picture Show* under his generous belt, although Meat Loaf had toured and gigged much more often than Curry, both set to their new windows of opportunity with a will. Both Tim and Meat Loaf played small venues nationwide, such as New York's legendary Bottom Line. Whether they played other venues in towns where *The Rocky Horror Picture Show* was becoming established is only a matter of record…

Blatantly leaning on the growing success of the movie, Tim Curry performed at least one of the theatres showing *The Rocky Horror Picture Show*. Public awareness was considered sufficiently ready to at last launch Tim's bid for pop stardom. Lou Adler was destined to invest a great deal of money…

The movie's success also spawned a couple of theatrical tours of the play, although neither were successful and both closed before the end of their scheduled runs. Scott remembers seeing one in Detroit in 1979, a date that was sponsored by Schlitz, the brewers. There were to be only a few other Equity-cast productions of the play in the United States, where the format had never worked. The habit of audience participation is now acknowledged to have spread to any theatrical presentation as well. Although actors might not like it, audiences now love it.

And who to cast? American theatre-goers like seeing stars at work and playing in *Rocky* live was a difficult area for any actor to undertake. Paul Jabara, who had taken over from Tim Curry at the Roxy in Los Angeles, was an established Broadway and London theatrical star. There were plenty of actors who could have done it and even more drag queens around who would have fought and scratched to do it, but no one with that...that...mmmmm... No stars. Tom Hulce could have done it. Robert Downey, perhaps. But precious few others could have ensured that there were sufficient St Louis or Ogunquit or Santa Fe patrons to buy the seats.

Sal's own involvement with the vital phenomenon was growing. He had had the benefit of the ear of Lou Adler, who had always consulted him, and when the production of *Shock Treatment* was being filmed in London, Sal was flown over to appear in the movie, as well as act as Lou's unofficial ambassador.

Sal had met Jim Sharman only once before, at the Eighth Street Theater, when the director had arrived with a group of friends and proceeded to give a private lecture to his party, rather ignoring the spectacle of the audience's participation. Sal feels that, with *Shock Treatment*, Jim also didn't want to use it as a tool to further promote *The Rocky Horror Picture Show*. I intuit that Sal's was not an entirely happy experience on *Shock Treatment*, and in the event Sal's appearance was just in the background. Even though Sal had acting credentials, apparently Jim Sharman insisted on Equity-only significant casting.

But Sal's die had become well and truly cast and, two years later, in 1983, he was brought into the audience-participation album and, by 1985 and the movie's tenth anniversary celebrations, was well and truly centre stage.

However, Sal was one of the few originators of the fanclub still in position. Though he is anxious to emphasise the essential role Dori played in the cult-ivation, and though he remains very close to her, Dori Hartley had stopped performing as Frank by 1980. She retired quite early from the fanclub, even though she was back for a while in 1985. Whilst the movie was still playing away at the Eighth Street Theater, the tenth-anniversary celebration was held in the 3,000-seat Beacon Theater and was MC'd by Sal. By now, Lou Adler introduced Sal to Fox, who put him on a salary and assumed financial responsibility for the fanclub, which Sal successfully advised him to make free to the members.

The phenomenon had spread. Even in Japan, *The Rocky Horror Picture Show* found its following. Sal was amazed to witness the lines being shouted back at the screen in both English and Japanese. Sal points out that all audiences respond to the maverick nature of all the characters and each individual has their own reasons for identifying with their favourite. Though Sal admits that there is certainly a rite-of-passage element for those who first go to see the film, and that many go to see the movie because of the character Tim Curry invests in Frank, for Sal the continuing joy is the music, the story and the characters themselves. His over-riding motivation for staying with the piece for so long is the audience. It is, he concedes, essentially a theatrical thing.

The audience certainly seems more a congregation, the interactive dialogue a form of the responses elicited of worshippers. A branch of the Church of not the Poisoned but the Liberated Mind?

As to the future, *Rocky* now boasts a stalwart presence on the Internet (Sal estimates a fanclub base of some 50,000 souls) and the albums are consistently being repackaged and reissued. There is even now a karaoke version, for obvious reasons... Both gay and straight bars all over the world regularly have *Rocky Horror* nights and the loudly played 'Time Warp' still resounds from private parties, sending *Rocky* echoing throughout suburbia all over the world. The position of the show in the mythology of our time is, as one politician so disastrously predicted, unassailable!

Cover versions of the songs have never been exactly thick on the ground. Sal remembers Brian May's rendition of 'Hot Patootie' and Belinda Sinclair fashioned a disco version of 'Touch Me', also covered by Peter Straker in London in 1975 for the Pye label. (The B-side of the Sinclair version has a group of people gathered around Richard O'Brien's piano singing 'Over At The Frankenstein Place'.)

Sal calculates that he has seen the movie some 1,500 times and was even in the *Guinness Book Of Records* for this achievement until it was considered that his being on the *Rocky Horror* payroll disqualified him. Even with the passing of the 25th anniversary of the first showing of the movie, Sal has no doubts as to the ongoing nature of the phenomenon. It is now at least second generation. A third is surely not far behind. The day cannot be far away when news of the celebrity of their planet will reach those Trannies who managed to escape from the castle and return to Transylvania.

As an end-piece, I was rather chuffed, as a rank outsider, to be able to explain the significance of a little bit of Rocky mythology to Sal, the acknowledged insider. It concerned the 4711 applied 'tattoo' that Tim Curry sports. That 4711 was a rather inexpensive yet superbly respectable cologne used sparingly and yet with a certain contented thrill by middle-aged, middle-class matrons the length and breadth of the British Isles was not in Sal's canon of experience. It is now.

<<<<<irememberdoingthetimewarpirememberdoingthetimewarpi>>>>>

8 'How Sentimental'
The Sincerest Form Of Flattery?

It's said that only when you own a Volkswagen do you begin to notice all the other Volkswagens on the road. Intense research on this project reveals uncanny resemblances in other films to *The Rocky Horror Picture Show*. Coincidence? (Charles Gray should have read that paragraph aloud.)

For example, in *Little Shop Of Horrors*, complete with Imogen Claire, resident Transylvanian, it's interesting that the graphic font used for the word 'Horrors' in the interval links pre and post the commercial break were very similar in style as the lettering for *The Rocky Horror Picture Show*...

Was this deliberate or just an accident?

If it was an 'accident', it was entirely opportunistically capitalised upon. The songs have a definite O'Brien feel, racy-pacy theatrical rock 'n' roll. Ummm...

From the movie's credits, it seems that the play was first performed (at least, the songs were first copyrighted) in 1982 and the movie was made in 1986 by the Geffen Company and distributed via Warner Brothers. David Geffen has a wide grasp of all showbusiness. He started his career in the mailroom at one of the giant New York theatrical agencies, like CMA before it became MCA, and was entirely *au fait* with the Boulevard of Broken Dreams, entirely hip, one could say, to the Broadway trip.

The movie was shot was entirely at Pinewood Studios, England, although much of the score and the songs were recorded at the Record Plant in LA. It was cast in England by Celestia Fox, who would have been Celestia Something-else had it not been for *Rocky*. Her surname came from her husband, Robert, having been on the staff at the Royal Court and then being persuaded by Michael White to greater things...

Death Becomes Her is another movie born from a traceable pedigree of inspiration that is uncannily reminiscent of *The Rocky Horror Picture Show*. Made in 1992, it starred Bruce Willis, Meryl Streep and Goldie Hawn. Some of the scenes are almost a straight crib of whole sections of *Rocky*.

When Miss Streep drives up to the house of the mysterious Liesl, having been recommended by Ian Ogilvie's uncontrollably winking weird Beverly Hills hairdresser, the crashing thunder and the flashes of lightning illuminate the Gothic sculptures surmounting the pinnacles of a house that looks uncannily like Oakley Court...

When the door is opened – not, admittedly, by Riff Raff but by body-pumped, big-haired perfect male specimens of contemporary Rocky Horrors – I also thought of Peter Hinwood.

The initial shot of the arrival of Liesl's elevator, full of mystery and promise and threat, is more than reminiscent. The maker of the film would not have been ignorant of loading it in favour of a *Rocky Horror* type of audience. The arrival of Liesl to the celebrity party is exactly like Frank's initial appearance in the descent in the *Rocky* elevator!

When the arcane, occult Liesl is discovered in the chair with her back to us, if that's not the good doctor Frank N Furter reincarnated in female form, let's drink a bottle of life juice...

The morgue in the hospital, where Miss Streep is discovered in the body-bag, is awfully like Frank's Lab.

At the party with all the undead celebs – how like Rocky Horror's birthday party! – the Transylvanian atmosphere and ambience is reekingly obvious...

The Michelangelo glass ceiling. OK, in *The Rocky Horror Picture Show* it was on the bottom of the pool, but this one was the ceiling over the pool where God in Liesl form gives eternal life to all her undead clients...

Many of the characters are like *Rocky Horror* counterparts: Bruce

Willis's plain, stolid and decidedly unsexy Doctor Ernest Menville, with all his moral dilemmas, is uncannily like Doctor Scott!

Even some of the lines are redolent. Liesl says, 'I can give you the secret of life.' In *Rocky*, Frank, I believe, mentions having 'discovered the secret of life itself'.

I surmise that the whole thing is more than just a coincidence. However, the most blatant rip-off must be the occasion when, on BBC's *Top Of The Pops*, Britain's longest-running television music show, I watched in disbelief on 12 October 2001 as a song called 'Two People' by someone billed as Jean-Jacques Smoothie was played and acted out by two white-garbed dancers, accompanied by a man in dark clothes playing a multitude of electronic synthesisers in front of a multi-screen presentation of a pair of red lips on a black background miming to the lyrics. It was such a bad rip-off, too, as it appeared that the lips only had teeth in the upper jaw. Kinda sad...

<<<<irememberdoingthetimewarpirememberdoingthetimewarpi>>>>

9 'And Our World Will Do
The Time Warp Again'
Life After Rocky

Patricia Quinn

DAVID EVANS: Other than Richard O'Brien, the only member of the
original cast to have stuck with the phenomenon in any sort of hands-
on fashion is Patricia Quinn. As much as the actor and performer in
her derives some pleasure from public appearances at the conventions
and other fan assemblies, this pleasure must often be alloyed by a sense
of burdensome obligation and of being haunted by a past that will
never go away, however inconvenient. Scott, I know, would like it
known how grateful he and thousands and thousands of *Rocky* fans
are all over the world for her continuing forbearance. I would like to
add personal thanks to Pat for her honesty and co-operation.

SCOTT MICHAELS: *What did the future hold after* Rocky?

PAT QUINN: When I finished the film, I was on a high because I was
becoming very successful. I was asked to read a part for a show called
Murderer with Robert Stephens. I got the script, written by Tony
Schaffer, who had written *Sleuth*, and thought that it wasn't very good.

I went out to dinner that night and had too much wine and was
very hung over the next morning and was going to skip the audition
altogether. I was so arrogant and stupid! I did a few things like that.
There was a play of Dennis Potter's I wouldn't do because I had to
show my bosoms, or whatever. At the time, I had an American au pair

we called Scoop, who would sit and smoke in the kitchen while I was doing the dishes. She was quite clever. She would take my baby Quinn to arcades and things that a regular au pair wouldn't do. So she was sitting there reading the script and laughing. I asked her why, and she said it was good. She was pointing out the good parts, and I thought, 'Oh, Christ! I'd better get to the audition.'

So I threw on my full-length racoon coat and made it in time. They auditioned every girl in London and no one was good enough for them. There was Robert Stephens, continually looking over his little professor glasses. I began reading, and the first line was 'I'm feeling a teensy bit chilly', and she was a kind of debutante. Robert was to play the murderer who is having an affair with her.

They stopped me and said, 'Thank you!' Which is typically the end of an audition. I just wasn't any good. Michael White was the producer of this show as well and he was there. Michael told Robert that he thought I was good and Robert couldn't figure out why Michael was pushing me on him. Michael asked him if he saw *The Rocky Horror Show*. He replied, 'Yes,' and Michael said that I played the Usherette and he thought I was going to go far. Robert said, 'I saw it. Give her the job.' Tony Schaffer observed, less nicely, 'Huh! Someone comes in, obviously on Novocain, and gets the job!'

I began rehearsals for that and Robert became a bit enchanted with me. So I had a husband and child, but Robert started to seduce me. First we started going to the curry houses, then he began taking me to places like the Ritz. I would tell my husband that I was going to a play with Robert Stephens! We went to see Glenda Jackson in a play and Robert walked out in the first three minutes! Then we had dinner with a guy who was in it and Robert started giving him notes. We hadn't seen the play at all! Robert couldn't bear the theatre unless he was on the stage. He preferred the cocktails at the Savoy.

SM: *Were you around for the New York production at the Belasco Theater?*

PQ: Not really. Richard thought the reason *Rocky* failed onstage in

New York is because New York resented the fact that it came from LA. They took out all of the seats of the theatre and made it into a night club. The other side of the coin, the show lost a lot of its naïveté. It lost its gritty appeal. The great thing in it was that we all had relationships, but these people improvised and made it glitzy – the Usherette coming on and chewing gum, drinking soda and being common and punching home the song, when it was intended to be this angelic person, Miss Strawberry Time.

When Tim went to New York with *Rocky* for the Belasco opening, after it bombed they dropped him like a hot potato, because it was such a failure. He did *Pirates Of Penzance* on the stage, and I thought it was brilliant. I remember Tim was once singing at the Bottom Line in Greenwich Village, while he was in town for a convention. He was doing two shows, and Meat Loaf was there, too. Tim was singing and I stayed for the first show, and he asked me to stay for the second show. I said I would, but then I realised I just couldn't sit through another one. I went home.

I found out later that he dedicated a song to me during that show. They told him, 'But she left!' The next day, I rang his hotel and tried to apologise. I asked for Tim Curry, but they had no one registered there by that name. I then asked for Albert Hall – that's the name he used – and they put me right through. He answered and I said, 'Hello, Albert Hall. This is Primrose Hill!'

I did go to a leather bar in New York with Robin Littner, a fan. She was a gorgeous Magenta. She had lovely hair and lips. She became a friend of mine. We ended up on holidays in Greece and just great friends.

We were in this bar, watching *Rocky* on screen. They all had their caps. They set me up on the bar during the movie, like a queen of the night. They didn't talk back to *Rocky* like the audience-participation thing; this was really crude. I was shocked. When they ask Frank what his favourite drink is, and his next line is 'cum', I think that's clever. This was just gross. I didn't like it. Maybe that's why Tim doesn't like it.

My friend Lillian was just at Tim's house in LA and told me he's now doing a weekly series about the Addams Family. He was doing a show with Annie Potts, a sitcom, but it was pulled. Rightfully so, from what I understand. I was told that, during one of the Oscar ceremonies, Tim was singing to movie clips and his image of Frank came up on the screen. He just looked back and rolled his eyes. I don't understand his animosity, because Frank is the best thing he did. It's shocking to me, because it changed his whole life.

SM: And you went back to it all when? 1994?

PQ: In 1994, *The Rocky Horror Show* was in production once again, this time at the Piccadilly Theatre, for the 20th anniversary of the stage show. Starred Jonathon Morris as Frank. Windsor Davies was the Narrator. It was supposed to be a brand-new concept, by Chris Malcolm. Chris was the original Brad at the Theatre Upstairs. They produce *Rocky Horror* in the UK and Europe, Hong Kong, while Chris directs them. That's his job. Chris Malcolm had a terrible motorbike accident a while back and almost lost a leg, so now he uses a walking stick. Nowadays he's well known for playing Saffy's father in the television show *Absolutely Fabulous*. Since he couldn't work so much as an actor any more, he went into production. Richard O'Brien didn't especially want that tour to go out, but Chris was insistent that it would make money. They put a Cadillac in it, a spaceship and a Magenta who moonwalked wearing a Madonna/Gaultier bustier. They threw a lot of money at it, but it was dreadful.

One gimmick they used was bringing in different people as guest stars to be the Usherette and sing 'Science Fiction'. They had Chrissie Hynde once.

So, Chris called me just before the show closed and asked me to come in and sing 'Science Fiction' for the closing night of the show. I hadn't sung that song since the original production in King's Road and the idea sounded like fun.

Chris Malcolm wanted me to use a blonde wig for the Usherette. When we did it upstairs, there was no money for wigs, so I did it as me. I left the stage and changed into Magenta's frock and went back out.

They had to make me the wig because, since the film, my hair colour has changed. So to make me look like I did in the film, they made me a fantastic wig, much better than my own real hair. It was gorgeous. Almost too gorgeous. It must've cost a fortune. The Usherette certainly couldn't come out with that one. She's much more glammy.

As I said, I hadn't sung 'Science Fiction' since the original production in King's Road. I've been to a few of the *Rocky Horror* conventions, but I always sang 'The Time Warp' and Richard always sang 'Science Fiction'. I agreed to do it. For a fee, of course!

I thought, 'Oh my goodness, how amazing to do her again.' My Usherette hadn't been touched since King's Road. So I'd said, 'Yes!', and the regular actress who played the Usherette had to abandon her costume. I went in like a diva. It was like Maria Callas showing up just to sing her opera.

We did some publicity for the papers and went to lunch. I told Richard that I didn't have any shoes. I needed my white stilettos for the Usherette. He took me shopping. We got the tackiest, highest shoes. I went into my dressing room. It was weird to walk into someone else's show. There was a bouquet from Robert. There, hanging up, was the Usherette costume. It was so bizarre. I started to get dressed and got my ice-cream tray, looked in the mirror and thought, 'My God, there she is.'

I had forgotten how great it was to sing *that* song. The atmosphere was great. They were warming up on the stage and I strolled in. I met the band. Some of them were there from the original production. They were the same musicians from 20 years before! When we began rehearsing, the MD asked me if I needed the words! I said no. Maybe Chrissie Hynde did, but I don't. I had forgotten how great it was to sing that song. The atmosphere was great.

So the house was full and the atmosphere was terrific. It was so nostalgic. There were a lot of friends in the audience that night. The band began playing that familiar music so many years later. I walked out onstage and the place went into uproar. I hadn't experienced this sort of adulation in ages. I began to sing my song the way it was written, directed in the manner of Jim Sharman, not Chris Malcolm. It felt extraordinary. The cast in the production were getting a cult following as well. I guess a lot of the people had never seen a live-onstage production of it.

The whole feel of it brought back the magic. I came off and they went berserk. Chris was gushing on and on and Richard went to the floor and kissed my stilettos.

At a later production, Richard O'Brien and I went to the opening-night party and the actor/comic Mel Smith said to him, 'You can't hear any of the lines or the songs because the audience were shouting so much at the actors.'

I told him that I understood it perfectly! I said I didn't have a problem with it, but then again, I did it! And Mel said, 'But you actually *did* it!'

I was so flattered that he even knew who I was!

They had a spaceship, a rocket. I don't know how long it ran. Anthony Head, the guy in that famous coffee commercial, played Frank. He was quite sexy. They were trying to reinvent it.

SM: *And then they asked you to tour with the show?*

PQ: That's why, because of that night. When they asked me if I was interested in touring in the 21st anniversary tour, I thought, 'I will.' I realised the high of it. If I hadn't done that night, I wouldn't have taken on the tour. Robert was very encouraging, as well.

I was on the 21st anniversary tour of *Rocky Horror*, and shortly before I began that tour Robert had had to have a kidney and liver transplant and was convalescing in Denville Hall, the actors' nursing home.

I was in Sheffield, and Natalie Branch – I called her Wigs because she did my wigs and make-up on the show – finally dropped me home at four in the morning. There was post, including one undistinctive letter. It looked like a tax letter. I opened it and it was asking Robert if he would accept a knighthood. You aren't allowed to tell before it's announced or you won't get it. I was jumping up and down and I couldn't tell Robert because it was too late, and the only one I could tell at four o'clock in the morning was Natalie Wigs, who just dropped me off. So I rang up Natalie and was screaming at her, 'Natalie, Robert's going to be a knight!'

Robert wept when I told him. That's when I decided we needed to get married.

SM: You were obviously very happy with Robert.

PQ: The reason he and I worked is because I supported everything he did. I really looked after him. That's why I fell behind. But I really enjoyed it. I didn't miss the theatre, because I was living it through him. He travelled a lot, so I was on the sets of his movies.

Robert also needed me. A very needy person. He couldn't be on his own. So, when he went on movie shoots, it was horribly lonely for him. That's why I would go with him. Robert loved to work hard and to play hard as well, so we had great holidays. The focus of my own career was gone. I had lunch the other day with a friend who said to me that, if I had continued, I would be the Maggie Smith of today.

Robert had tons of ideas in the last year of his life. He was going to do *Death Of A Salesman* and he wanted to do something with me. In fact, that was the first time since *Murderer* he suggested we do something together. I never liked him for that, because nepotism does work. He did try his best to get me into the Royal Shakespeare Company while we were living together in Stratford. I was basically his housekeeper. It was awful for me, though. I could have, and would have, played anything. It was horrible for me to see actors going to work every day and I was just sitting there. The person I liked acting with best was Robert, because he was the best actor. He and I had done *The Box Of Delights* together and it was written by the poet laureate John Masefield.

SM: And so onwards and upwards now?

PQ: My thing today is to get back out there. I think a lot of people were very jealous of me. Before I met Robert Stephens, I was in awe of him. I was a girl fresh off the boat from Belfast and I used to go with my pennies and go to 'the Gods', the cheap seats, and I would watch Robert Stephens, Laurence Olivier and Maggie Smith's company. There they were, the great couple. I had no idea that my life would take that kind of curve.

I am still on good terms with my ex-husband, Don. For years, I had two husbands over for Christmas lunch! It's stopped now, mostly because Quinn is out of school and, of course, one husband is dead. Don was always here. He really liked Robert, and Robert really tolerated Don being here, so I was very lucky.

SM: *Was the whole cult thing and the conventions a surprise?*

PQ: When we had our London *Rocky* convention, people came from all over the world, setting up stalls selling drawings of me and just selling their own stuff. I took my son, Quinn, who was mingling about. He came running back to me and said that they were selling Robert's photograph out there. It was a shot of him and Tim Curry in *The Shout*. Robert said that was the closest he will get to becoming a cult star.

SM: *But you have your own fans.*

PQ: I do. It's amazing to me. I get lots of letters from fans. They are so nice, but I just never get around to responding to them. Not only from America, but from England as well. I get them all the time, and I'm just awful. I never respond. Robin was a gorgeous Magenta. She was a fan and has become a friend of mine. She's Dori [Hartley]'s friend in New York.

I've never been able to understand why all of the Magentas I've seen at later productions of the show were so very plump. And why do they all identify with me? The reply from everyone was that they couldn't afford Columbia's sequins! They could afford the maid's frock. And all the Columbias are minute, too.

SM: *And so* Rocky *has taken you all over the world?*

PQ: Fox put a lot of money into the 15th anniversary, mainly to sell the video, and for the 20th anniversary we were in LA. We gave 'The Time Warp' to Planet Hollywood in Beverly Hills. Lou Adler was there with Paige Hannah, Daryl's sister. So we went into Schwarzenegger's private room. There's a pool table, a cinema and special walls to take cigar smoke out of the room. Daryl Hannah came to a convention once with Lou in New York and Quinn was thrilled because she had just done *Splash!* and all of his friends wanted Quinn to get a photo with her. She showed up with Lou and came as Riff Raff, with a hump! So Quinn didn't want a photo of that!

We went to the Roxy, and it was before that night at the convention. Richard and I went onstage to say hello. Later that night, Sal introduced me and said, 'Patricia has just married an English lord and she's now Lady Stephens.'

I said, 'No, he's not a lord; he's a knight of the realm.'

So Lou owns the Rainbow Room next door. It was amazing for me to go to the Roxy because they were showing me Meat Loaf's dressing room and Tim's. I'd never seen it! So we went to the Rainbow. Lou is very protective of his stars and Richard was sitting in a booth. They asked me if I'd like to come into the kitchen. I said, 'I'm not going in the kitchen. Can't we stay here?'

But I guess that is the place to eat there. I don't think Lou is used to being disagreed with, so I said, 'No thank you, and I'd like a margarita.' They brought out one plate of calamari and four forks. I thought, 'How crude. So this is dinner and I'm sitting in my £600 frock!'

Lou asked if we wanted to come to his place. Richard wanted to see the Viper Room and its infamous back room, so Richard said, 'We'll just walk down the road.' I said that I wasn't going to walk anywhere. Lou said he would give us a lift. Lou took us to the hotel and off to the Viper Room. It was so disappointing. We couldn't find the Viper Room...

I saw Michael White recently and told him the story of our trip to LA. He repeated a quote from Lou Adler to me that goes, 'Patricia Quinn is Lady Stephens until ten o'clock, but after that she's Pat Quinn.' I thought that was terribly funny.

I recently went back to Belfast for a Hallowe'en party, by invitation of my nephew Jonathon Quinn, who is drummer with a band. He asked if I would do 'The Time Warp', because the party had a *Rocky Horror* theme. It got in all the papers and I did lots of radio promos. We did terrific interviews. At the venue, we did 'The Time Warp' with a rock 'n' roll band. The whole club were doing it.

SM: *And, in a nutshell, can you tell me why? Can you explain why?*

PQ: Can I explain the success of *Rocky*?

SM: *Yes.*

PQ: Sex, drugs and rock 'n' roll. That would seem to be it. The actors didn't get much money. There were no video contracts then, so we don't get a penny for them. I think everyone was very naïve. The great thing was that Twentieth Century Fox had the brilliant idea of putting it on late at night. That was the turning point.

I never really thought about what would happen to the film. It's funny. I thought it was amazing we ever got to make it. And I still get a royalty cheque for the original cast album. One came from Jonathan King just the other day.

I was invited to Prince Charles' 50th birthday party, thrown by Camilla Parker-Bowles. The Prince and I were chatting, and someone else entered the conversation. 'You know Pat?' the Prince said. 'She's the star of *The Rocky Horror Show*.' I was speechless!

‹‹‹‹irememberdoingthetimewarpiremerberdoingthetimewarpi››››

Chris Malcolm

Tuesday 2 May 2000
'It's gonna be all right, Janet'

DAVID EVANS: Although Doctor Frank N Furter's creation might have perished, Richard O'Brien's creation is still more than alive and well. Apart from being able to go and partake of *Rocky Horror*'s 'horsepitality' at bars and clubs throughout the world, stage productions and theatrical tours of *The Rocky Horror Show* are now popular from Cape Town to Cleethorpes. *Rocky Horror* in theatrical incarnation is currently handled by the Canadian actor Chris Malcolm who created the role of Brad in the original production.

The casting these days must often be thought bizarre by the purists and those involved in the early productions, but in the new tradition of 'all good family fun' the audiences still flock to see Ken Morley (he who played Reg Holdsworth in *Coronation Street*), who toured in the show for at least 18 months. Nicholas Parsons played the Narrator for years, confirming that the show has now transmuted into the genre of modern pantomime, a form that has brought a renaissance to the touring theatre by equipping the casts with famous television 'names'. It's almost like a Lloyds underwriting exercise, where the equally infamous 'names' insure the insured. The audiences come to see the performers, not necessarily what is being performed.

Chris Malcolm, Scots but brought up in Canada, created the part of Brad Majors in the original production of *The Rocky Horror Show* in London in 1972 – yet another wild colonial to add to the growing cast list. (The count now stands at one Canadian, three Australians, one New Zealander and an Irishwoman.)

However, Chris Malcolm's significance in the *Rocky* phenomenon is twofold because he now – with Richard O'Brien and Howard Panter, collectively known as the Rocky Horror Company Ltd – administers the international rights to theatrical productions of the show. The company grants licences for productions as far afield as Australia and South Africa. As the Rocky Horror Company, London, Chris and Howard also act as producers, controlling the various productions of the show both on tour and in regional incarnations throughout the UK.

Scott and I met Chris for lunch at Sheekey's Restaurant in St Martin's Passage, next to the Albery Theatre.

DE: *The last time we met was in 1978 at one of Freddie Mercury's bashes. Are you still down in Bath?*

CHRIS MALCOLM: Yes. I come up to London a lot, though.

DE: And this accident you had. Are you, as they say, lucky to be here?

CM: Absolutely. It was 13 years ago. Motorbike accident. The last operation to set it right was only two years ago. Basically, I have no knee. My whole leg is always straight, so I have to always sit on the outside of the theatre row or like this, with my leg up on a chair in restaurants. And business or first class in aeroplanes…

DE: So do you still act? Can you?

CM: I still have an agent, although she only really does it for loyalty. I'd do a role if it was suitable, but there's not a lot of that kind of part…

DE: You were in Unseen Hand *too, weren't you?*

CM: Yes. That's where we all met. In fact, I was in about five productions at the Court between 1972 and 1975. Are you seeing Brian Thomson?

SM: On Friday, actually.

CM: He was so inventive. *Unseen Hand* all took place by a roadside in the USA. Brian found an old American car, cut it into three to get it to the Theatre Upstairs and reassembled it. Amazing ingenuity.

DE: So how much of Rocky *had you heard about beforehand?*

CM: In the dressing room in *Unseen Hand*, I'd heard a couple of the songs – 'Sweet Transvestite' and 'Damocles', I think. Richard played them on guitar. But I still had to audition for *Rocky*. It was in some little hall around the corner from the Royal Court. I thought I was going to play the lead, this Brad Majors part. It wasn't 'til after the first read-through I realised it wasn't the lead at all. At that time, no one knew where the thing was going. There was a script but it was being rewritten almost every day. Even Tim didn't really know where it was going.

SM: So when did it all come clear?

CM: Not 'til the first rehearsal we had in the Earl's Court rehearsal room when the band came along. When we heard the music, electrified and through amplifiers, with Count's guitar and Richard Hartley on electric keyboards rather than tinkling at a rehearsal piano, then we got it. We'd been three weeks not getting it, even after Jim taking us to the Notting Hill Classic to see *Beyond The Valley Of The Dolls*. Pat Quinn said she got it, but… Anyway, that night, we all went to this piano bar on Knightsbridge Green, where Dudley Moore used to play, and celebrated.

DE: It was such a tiny space at the Theatre Upstairs. What was it like, playing there?

CM: Very crowded, you're right. For us to get from one side of the stage to the other, we had to crawl through the legs of the band, who were all squashed in behind the stage to one side. And you know we had just the one microphone, which swung about and which we all had to learn to play with like it had a mind of its own. It wasn't 'til we transferred to the Chelsea Classic that we knew that the show was going to be really big.

DE: So you had no doubts about staying with it?

CM: I was offered *Design For Living* with Vanessa Redgrave at the end of the second week we were at the Court, but it wasn't a big part and so I decided to stay with *Rocky*. And, of course, when we did those midnight shows at the Chelsea Classic just so that the other West End actors and theatre people could come and see us, then we knew we were really on our way.

DE: *A lot of the cast's agents still weren't sure. Raynor's advised him not to even try to stay and Julie Covington obviously wasn't so sure.*

CM: Julie was already committed, I think, to the job at the Globe, although I wouldn't be surprised if she chose to leave. I don't think they ever forgave her, either.

DE: *Of all that cast, she was the most likely to have had a successful career in the music business. Was she suspicious of records and music? A lot were.*

CM: She was generally very suspicious of everything. Probably rightly. But we were very lucky to get Belinda Sinclair to replace her.

DE: *Did you feel brave, when you were doing* Rocky? *Like you were in something at the cutting edge?*

CM: Certainly. It was in the best tradition of the Royal Court, too – being daring, pushing parameters.

SCOTT MICHAELS: *And you came out of the show to go back to the Court, didn't you? To work with the 'team' again?*

CM: In *Tooth Of Crime*, yes. In fact, the film was casting at the same time that *Tooth Of Crime* was playing. I knew all about it and I was wondering, because nothing was being said by Jim at all. And then I get this phone call, blah blah blah, and would I accept the part of Ralph Hapschatt in the wedding scene? I replaced the receiver. I didn't hang up; I just gently put down the phone, and I've never spoken to Jim since.

DE: *Certainly not the most diplomatic of ways to handle an actor's sensitivity, to say nothing of a friend's. Did that end your association with the show, too?*

CM: No. I went to Japan with it, with Raynor and Ziggy and Belinda Sinclair in 1975. And, of course, I moved into Richard and Kimi's flat at Oakington Road when they moved to Clapham. I stayed there for the next ten years. Bought the downstairs flat, too. But no, after the Japanese experience, I had nothing to do with the show between 1976 and 1988.

SM: *Which is when you bought the rights?*

CM: Actually, not 'til June 1989, but it was in 1988 when I suggested that [Rocky] was due for a revival in the West End in 1989. I thought it would do well and Michael Linnit was approached as a possible producer. That fell through, though.

DE: *Just take us through what happened prior to that time. Who had the rights?*

CM: Ros Chatto was Richard's agent and her office looked after the professional productions and tours for Richard. Samuel French looked after the amateur rights. After the initial run of the London production closed at the Comedy in 1980, Michael White, of course, still had the option to produce first-class productions and to be involved in the residual rights. He let that lapse in 1984.

SM: *He* what?

CM: Yes. He's said it himself, the biggest mistake of his life. But he did. So it was Ros and Richard who licensed the show from then on, a period that covered the legendary production and tour starting at the Theatre Royal, Hanley, in 1986 and 1987, which involved people like Bobby Crush. This was a really successful tour, directed by Paul Bernard. It played in Europe, too. It went as far as Italy before coming back to the UK.

DE: *Which brings us back to you.*

CM: I was co-producing Alan Bennet's *Single Spies* at the time with Howard Panter. I approached Richard about the rights and it turned out he wanted to be involved with whatever the future was, so we started our companies. It was then that Richard stopped giving Brian and Jim the share of one of his percentage points in the show. He'd done it for 15 or so years. More. He hadn't had to do it, but after 15 years he just thought that was sufficient. Even Michael isn't involved with anything of *Rocky* now. Even the film rights he abrogated to Lou Adler, and a Dutch company looks after the movie stuff, a guy called Paul Verbrought. So, we're doing well too from the American theatrical rights. Summer stock productions. Places like Bucks County Playhouse. There's been almost a 180 productions since then. We've also released the amateur production rights, too, for the USA. Did that in January this year.

SM: *That will be fascinating, to see how they're taken up.*

DE: *Something I woke up last night wondering about was what happened to the Royal Court's interest in all this? They were co-producers, after all. Initially.*

CM: They benefited, along with Michael, from the beginning.

DE: *Until his option lapsed?*

CM: Yes. And I have to say that I was rather shocked to see in the recent book about the history of the Royal Court that *Rocky* is hardly more than a footnote. I think *Rocky* deserved more. It was as Avant Garde a production as any of the Osbornes or the Bonds. And just one thing about Michael – I have to emphasise that his investment of £1,000, that was a helluva punt back then. Even if you think about inflation and, what would it be now? Ten grand? I ask myself, 'Would I invest ten grand now in something that I wasn't sure about?' That initial money was Michael's own money. Did you see those publicity pictures for the 1992 tour, by the way? We did those on the steps of the Royal Court with the blue plaque. There should be a real one.

DE: *I hope not yet. You have to be 25 years dead, I think.*

CM: Oh. OK.

SM: *Do you still see Lou Adler?*

CM: Sure. Lou and I are always sparring and I see him whenever I go to LA. Twentieth Century Fox have now given him a sort of power of attorney, sort of *carte blanche* with everything to do with the movie. Lou works closely with Tom Sherack, who is head of marketing at Fox. Sal Piro is paid by Fox, I think. There's going to be a sort of karaoke thing at the Hard Rock Café to celebrate the 25th anniversary of the movie.

SM: *Sounds glamorous. And any other plans from your side?*

CM: We hope to have a production in Russia very soon. One in Oslo, too, and in Israel.

DE: *In the true spirit of Dana International?*

CM: Shalom! I hope you're going to talk to Tim. You know, he was beautiful. He was beautiful as Frank.

DE: *I don't think that's going to be possible.*

CM: I can see why he's bitter. I still see him. I've stayed with him in LA. He gave so much to that part and to the show for what was more than three years. He's haunted by it. Fans camp out almost in front of his house. It'll never go away. I think he does get something from the movie, but I don't know. Brian Thomson is very bitter. But you're seeing him, aren't you?

‹‹‹‹irememberdoingthetimewarpiremememberdoingthetimewarpi››››

'It Was A Night Out They Were Going To Remember For A Very Long Time'
Epilogue

On Tuesday 6 June 2000, *The Rocky Horror Show* was onstage at the Congress Theatre, Eastbourne. It's a quiet town, Eastbourne. Lots of family holidaymakers, a high proportion of old people. The Congress Theatre seats 1,800 people. Stefanie Powers (she of *Hart To Hart*) had been at the neighbouring Devonshire Park Theatre the week before and even she hadn't filled its 800 seats.

So, being generous, there must have been 300 people in the Congress audience that night. Eight of those were costumed, dressed to kill (two of these were dressed to kill in wheelchairs, which would have comforted the real-life Doctor Scott, I suppose), which leaves 292, none of whom could even be remotely considered 'rich weirdos'.

As the show got started, six waved appropriate lighters, three had the requisite newspapers and for a moment it seemed as though there would be a more-or-less unaided performance by the company onstage.

However, by the end of the performance, every one of the 300 – wheelchairs included – were up in their seats doing a passable version of the Time Warp. Everyone – pensioners and lookalikes alike – was shouting, 'Asshole!' at every mention Ken Morley's Narrator made of Brad Majors and everyone shouted 'Slut!' at every mention of Janet. The participative element generated by the movie has, like a successful transplant, thoroughly taken.

This version, directed by Chris Malcolm, is out on tour. It is out and loud on tour. The sax player nowadays leaves the band and performs a virtuoso solo, which starts the second act. There are now four Transylvanian singers/dancers/ghouls. Frank now sinks away in a mock faint with the line 'Oooh, I've come over a little queer!', an aside that is greeted by the most hysterical laughter of the night. As he wanders in his Joan Crawford make-up across the stage like a knock-kneed pigeon-toed giraffe, so unsure is he of his balance in the high-heeled shoes, Frank spits rather nastily when apprehended by Riff and Magenta, 'Oh, shit!'

These are not lines Richard O'Brien ever wrote originally and none that Jim Sharman would have ever directed, and Frank N Furter is a million miles away from Tim Curry's dazzling, hypnotising, masterful creation. Tonight's Frank is an imposter.

The actor Ken Morley, once a star of the globally popular soap opera *Coronation Street*, gabbled his lines as the Narrator unintelligibly as he camply grimaced and inexplicably pouted at the audience.

Without the benefit of the explanation of the plot, what did the audience virgins think was going on?

The volume of the amplified sound was so loud and its clarity so badly distorted that Richard O'Brien's brilliant lyrics were inaudible.

Without the lyrics, the plot and most of the characters' motivation is rendered incomprehensible.

Like an out-take from a Saturday-night *Stars In Their Eyes*, the two musical invasions of an excerpt from Lulu's 'Shout' and a quick rendition of 'I'm So Excited' were so obtrusive that something about sore thumbs comes to mind. Why were these extra songs there at all? What's wrong with the original music?

There is a celebrated observation once made about sex – the anticipation of it, the act of it, the performance of it, the production of it: 'It's very easy to do but it's very difficult to do well.'

The risk of disappointing is that run by everything and everyone with an eclipsing reputation: when the first time has been the best time, anything that follows is usually a pale imitation.

But the Eastbourne audience loved *Rocky*. They had a good time and merely smiling made their faces positively ache with pleasure.

<<<<<irememberdoingthetimewarpirememberdoingthetimewarpi>>>>

Raynor Bourton

We want to give the last word to a story Raynor Bourton told us. We thought it was sweet.

SM: *Of course, at the time, no one ever dreamed that one day there might be a sequel.*

RB: No. I once asked Richard O'Brien whatever would have happened to Brad and Janet. Richard said, 'I think they'll probably go back with Doctor Scott, have a nice little lunch. Brad will put his hand in his pocket and bring something out. "What's that?" they'll ask. And, of course, it's a suspender...'

THE END

Ha! Ha ha ha! Ha ha ha ha ha ha...!!!

Appendix: The Major Players

Abe Jacobs ....Sound engineer at the Roxy, LA
Alan Blaikly ....British composer/songwriter
Alan Harris ....Stand-in on movie
Alan Ladd Jr.....................................Twentieth Century Fox executive
Alan Rickman ....British actor
Allan Jones ....British artist and sculptor
Amanda Lear ....1970s disco diva, muse of Dali
Andrew Cruickshank..Scots actor
                                           founder of Edinburgh Fringe Festival
Andrew Lloyd Webber ....Composer, theatrical producer
Andrew Logan ....British artist, sculptor, designer
Andy (from Sarm) ....British recording studio engineer
Andy Warhol ....American artist
Angela Bruce ....British actress
Angharad Rees ....British actress
Anita Dobson ....British actress
Annabel Leventon ....Transylvanian, British actress and director
Annette Funicello ....American singer/celebrity
Anny Humphries ....British hair artist/colourist
Anthony Bowles ....Musical director
Anthony Head ....British actor, once played Frank onstage
Antonia Fraser, Lady..British writer
Antony Hopkins..British actor
April Ashley ....British beauty, a transsexual
Arthur Kelley ....Songwriter

Ava Gardener...American screen star

Barrie Denham ....British actor
Barry Bostwick............................American actor, played Brad in movie
Barry Humphries.................Australian actor and female impersonator
Barry Krost ....British talent agent/artist manager/producer
Barry St John ....Backing singer on movie soundtrack
Belinda Sinclair ....British actress, replaced Julie Covington as Janet
Ben Fencham ....Set painter
Bernie Taupin ....British lyric writer of Elton John songs
Bianca Jagger ....First wife of Mick Jagger
Bill Henken ....American writer
Bill Immerman ....Twentieth Century Fox executive
Bill Quigley ....Executive of movie theatre chain
Bill Whittaker ....American writer
Billy Idol ....British singer
Billy Wilder ....American movie writer and director
BJ Wilson ....Musician
Björk ....Icelandic singer/writer
Bob Chetwyn ....Theatre and television director
Bob Ezrin ....Canadian record producer
Bob Spencer ....Movie technician
Bob Swash...London theatrical producer in
Robert Stigwood organisation
Bobby le Brun...Australian actor/performer
Brett Forest ....British actor
Brian Engel ....Backing singer on movie soundtrack album
Brian Protheroe ....British singer/songwriter and actor
Brian Thomson ....Australian artist, designer of the show
Britney Spears ....American singer
Britt Ekland ....Swedish actress, former partner of Lou Adler
Brooke Adams ....American actress
Bruce Robinson ....British actor and scriptwriter
Bruce Silke ....American, assistant to Barry Krost
Bryan Ferry ....British singer, in Roxy Music

Bryan Forbes ....British actor, writer and film director
Bryan Hyland ....American singer
Burt Bacharach..........................American composer and accompanist
Buster Crabbe ....Iconic American film star

Cameron Mackintosh ....British theatrical producer
Camilla Parker-Bowles ....British socialite and courtesan
Candy Darling ....American actress
Carole King ....American composer, singer/songwriter
Casey Donovan ....American actor
Cat Stevens ....British singer/songwriter
Celestia Sporburg (Fox) ....Theatre and film casting director
Charles Gray ....British actor, played the Narrator in the movie
Charles Laurence ....British playwright
Charlie Brown ....Son of Transylvanian Gaye Brown
Charlotte Cornwell ....British actress
Cher ....American actress, singer, writer and producer
Cherry Vanilla ....American actress
Chris Blackwell ....Founder of Island Records
Chris Malcolm ....Scots/Canadian actor, created role of Brad
Chrissie Hynde ....Pretenders' lead singer, once played Magenta
Chrissie Shrimpton ....British model
Christopher Biggins ....British actor and Transylvanian
Christopher Gibbs ....British antique dealer and connoisseur
Clair Torrey...............................Backing singer on movie soundtrack
Clive Hirschorn ....British theatre pundit
Clodagh Wallace ....British theatre and music agent/manager
Colin Chilvers ....Movie technician
Colin Higgins .....Australian/American creator of *Harold And Maude*
Colin McNeil ....Colleague of Sue Blane, costume designer
Coral Browne ....Actress wife of Vincent Price
Cynthia Lennon ....First wife of John Lennon

Damien ....British actor and performer
Dana Gillespie ....Actress and singer, well known in 1960s and 1970s

Dana International ....Israeli transsexual winner of
1998 Eurovision Song Contest
Dandy Livingston ....Singer
Danny La Rue ....British actor, female impersonator, showman
Daryl Hannah ....American actress
Dave Murphy ....Stand-in on movie
David Belasco ....American theatrical producer, early 20th century
David Betteridge ....British record company executive
David Bowie ....British singer, actor, writer
David Dale ....British actor, female impersonator
David de Yong ....British theatrical agent
David Essex ....British singer/songwriter, actor
David Evans ....British writer
David Foster ....American musical director and arranger
David Hockney ....British painter and designer
David Mamet ....American writer and director
David Meyer ....British actor
David Minns ....British music executive, art expert
David Sonnenberg ....American manager of Meat Loaf
David Toguri ....Canadian choreographer of the movie
Debbie McWilliam ....Casting director on *Shock Treatment*
Derek Dunbar ....British model, singer and King's Road authority
Derek Jarman ....British painter, designer, film-maker
Diana Quick ....British actress
Diana Rigg ....British actress
Diane Langton ....British actress and singer
Dick Frift ....Movie set builder
Dick Rowe..Executive at Decca Records
Don Arden ....British manager of rock bands
Don Fraser ....British composer and musical director
Don Hawkins ....British actor, first husband to Patricia Quinn
Donovan Leitch ....British singer/songwriter
Dori Hartley ....American female male impersonator,
original movie fan and *Rocky* devotee
Duggie Fields...London-based artist

Ed Murray (Beldowski) ....Antique dealer, friend to Tim Curry
Edward Bond ....British playwright
Elliot Gould ....American actor
Elton John ....British singer/songwriter
Eric Kent ....Stand-in on movie
Eric Roberts ....American, manager of Neil Young
Erica Simmons ....Stand-in on movie

Fran Fullenwider ....American actress and model
Franco Zeffirelli ....Italian film director
Françoise Hardy ....French singer/songwriter
Frank McKigh ....British theatrical company executive
Freddie Mercury ....British singer/songwriter

Gary Glitter ....British singer, once played Frank
Gary Hamilton ....British actor and singer
Gary Numan ....British singer/songwriter
Gay Beresford ....British model and 'walker'
Gaye Brown ....British actress and Transylvanian
George Devine ....Founder, guiding light of the Royal Court Theatre
George Harrison ....British singer/songwriter, film producer
Gerald Thomas ....British film producer, director
Gerry Paris ....Understudy/stand-in on movie
Gillian Diamond ....Casting director, Royal Court Theatre
Gillian Dodds ....Costumier on movie
Gillian Gregory ....Assistant to David Toguri, movie choreograper
Glen Conway ....Actor, friend of Kimi Wong O'Brien
Glenda Jackson ....British actress
Gloria Dawn ....Australian actress
Gloria Hunniford ....British television presenter
Graham Clifford ....Film editor on the movie
Graham Freeborn ....Make-up artist on movie

Harold Pinter ....British playwright
Harriet Cruickshank ......Casting director at the Royal Court Theatre

Harry Miller ....Australian theatrical producer
Harvey Fierstein ....American actor, female impersonator
Helen Chapelle ....Backing singer on movie soundtrack
Helen Lennox ....Make-up artist on movie
Helen Montague ....General manager, Royal Court Theatre
Henry Woolf ....British actor and Transylvanian
Hercules Bellville ....Theatrical producer, friend of Michael White
Holly Woodlawn ....American actress
Howard Panter ....British theatrical producer of *Rocky*
Howard Schuman ....American script writer and playwright
Hugh Cecil ....British actor, model and Transylvanian
Hughie Green ....British television presenter

Ian 'Count' Blair ....British guitarist in original show,
                                                    cast album and on movie soundtrack
Ian (Tarantulas) ....Unknown commissioner of early O'Brien songs
Ian Whittaker ....Property buyer/set dresser
Iggy Pop ....American singer/songwriter
Imogen Claire ....British actress and Transylvanian
Ishaq Bux ....Indian actor and Transylvanian
Ivor Novello ....British composer

Jack Nicholson ....American actor
Jack Purvis ....British actor; friend and colleague of Sadie Corre
Jackie Curtis ....American actress in Warhol Factory projects
James Dean ....American actor
James Werner ....British theatrical producer
Jamie Donnelly ....American actress in *Rocky* at the Roxy in LA
Jane Moss (O'Brien) ....Married to Richard O'Brien
Jane Mulvagh ....British biographer of Vivienne Westwood
Jane Royal ....Make-up artist on movie
Jane Stonehouse ....Friend of Richard O'Brien
Jason Donovan ....Australian actor, singer; has played Frank
Jean Genet ....French writer
Jean Shrimpton ....British model

Jean-Paul Gaultier ....French designer and television presenter
Jeanie Macdonald (Also known as McArthur)..............British actress
Jeff Stryker ....American actor and entrepreneur
Jennifer Lopez ....American singer/songwriter
Jeremy Conway ....British theatrical agent
Jeremy Swan ....Irish television director
Jeremy Thomas ....British film producer
Jerry Jenks (Jenkins?) ....Lighting expert on original *Rocky*
Jerry Moss ....American executive, co-founder A&M records
Jill Bennett ....British actress
Jill Searle ....Proprietor of the Ugly Agency
Jill Sinclair ....Sister to John Sinclair, executive of Druidcrest
                                        Publishing; now married to Trevor Horne
Jim Beach ....British showbiz lawyer, manager of Queen
Jim Henson ....Puppeteer and producer
Jim Sharman ....Director of original Rocky and movie
Jim Steinman ....American songwriter for Meat Loaf
Jim Sweeney ....British actor/singer
Jim Whittaker ....American writer
Joan Collins ....British actress
Joanna Lumley ....British actress
Joe d'Allessandro ....American actor
Joe Orton ....British playwright
Joe Rotherd (?)...................................American film producer
Joel Grey ....American actor
John Clark ....British movie art director
John Comfort ....British film production manager on the movie
John Dewe-Matthews ....British photographer and painter
John Dexter ....British theatre director
John Goldstone ....British film executive, co-producer of movie
John Lennon ....British singer/songwriter
John Morton ....British actor
John Osborne ....British playwright
John Peel ....British DJ and music pundit
John Reid ....British manager, Elton John/Queen; producer

John Sinclair ....Publisher of *Rocky* music
Johnny Vaughan ....British television presenter
Jon Berkinshaw ....Stand-in on movie
Jonathan Adams ....British actor, played Narrator/
Doctor Scott in original *Rocky*
Jonathan Bergman ....Early audience to *Rocky* songs
Jonathan King ....British record producer of original cast album
Jonathan Kramer.........................Actor; considered for original Frank
Jonathan Morris ....British actor, once played Frank
Jordan ....Late-1970s' British fashion icon and punk celebrity
Joseph Papp ....American theatrical producer
Judy Garland ....American screen star
Julie Covington............................British actress, created role of Janet

Kate Garrett ....Friend of Richard O'Brien
Keith Moon ....British drummer
Keith Washington ....British actor, singer
Ken and Shirley Russell ....British film director, writer, designer
Ken Campbell ....British theatrical producer
Ken Howard ....British composer, songwriter
Ken Morley ....British actor
Ken Shepherd ....British stunt rider, double for Meat Loaf
Kenny Baker ....British actor; was R2D2 in all *Star Wars* movies
Kim Milford ....American actor, singer; played Rocky in LA
Kimi Wong O'Brien ....British actress, singer
married to Richard O'Brien
Koo Stark ....British actress and socialite
Kris Kristofferson ....American actor, singer

Lauren Bacall ....American screen star
Lenny Kravitz ....American singer, writer, performer
Leonardo Tribilio ....Actor, friend of Derek Jarman and Andrew Logan
Lesley Joseph ....British actress
Lester Bangs..............................American journalist and music pundit
Liberace ....American musician and performer

Linda Goldstone (Seifert)...........................Married to John Goldstone, movie co-producer

Lindall Hobbs ....Australian journalist, friend of Michael White

Lindsay Ingram ....British actress and Transylvanian

Lindsay Kemp ....British actor, director, producer and mime

Lindy St Clair...British style celebrity

Linus O'Brien ....Son of Richard O'Brien and Kimi Wong O'Brien

Lionel Bart ....British composer and songwriter

Liz Coke ....Stand-in on movie

Liza Strike ....Backing singer on movie soundtrack

Lou Adler ......American record producer and producer of *Rocky* movie

Lou Reed ....American singer/songwriter

Louis Farese ....American movie-goer, *Rocky* fan

Madonna ....American singer/songwriter, screen actress

Maggie Smith ....British actress

Malcolm McLaren ....British music and style pundit, entrepreneur, artists' manager

Man Ray .....,..Artist and painter

Marc Bolan (Feld) ....British rock musician, singer/songwriter

Marc Shaiman ....American movie-goer, early *Rocky* fan

Margaret Trudeau ....Once first lady of Canada

Marianne Faithfull ....British singer, actress and songwriter

Mark Palmer ....British proprietor of model agency

Marshall McLuhan ....American writer and pundit

Martin Duncan ....British composer and songwriter

Martin Sharpe ....Painter

Martin Sherman ....Playwright

Mary Austin ....British, friend of Freddie Mercury

Maureen Lipman ....British actress

Max Weinberg ....American musician

Meat Loaf ....American singer/songwriter and actor

Mel Gibson ....Australian actor

Melita Smith ....Stand-in on movie

Michael English ....British designer and artist

Michael Linnit ....British theatrical agent

Michael White ....British theatrical producer of original show
and co-producer of movie

Mick Jagger ....British singer/songwriter and actor

Mike Gowans ....Assistant film director on *Rocky*

Mike Gwilym ....British actor

Mike Pratt ....British actor

Mitch McKenzie ....British film-maker

Mrs Shufflewick ....British actor, female impersonator

Murray Head...British singer/songwriter, actor

Natalie Branch ....Theatrical hair artist

Neil Young ....American singer/songwriter

Nell Campbell ....Australian actor and personality,
created role of Columbia

Nicholas Parsons ....British actor

Nicholas Wright ....Administrator, Theatre Upstairs, Royal Court

Noël Coward ....British playwright, songwriter, actor, performer

Paddy O'Hagen ....British actor, created role of Eddie

Paige Hannah ....Sister of Darryl, friend of Lou Adler

Pam Obermeyer ....British actress and Transylvanian

Patricia Quinn ....British actress, created roles of
Miss Strawberry Time (Trixie) and Magenta

Patrick White ....Australian playwright

Paul Bernard ....British director/producer *Rocky* theatre tours

Paul Burnett ....British publishing executive

Paul Cox (Tarpaulins) ....Supplier of tarpaulin props to original show

Paul Dainty ....British promoter and producer in Australia

Paul Jabara ....American actor, singer and performer

Paul McCartney ....British singer/songwriter and producer

Paul Nicholas ....British singer/songwriter, actor and producer

Paul Verbrought ....Dutch entrepreneur, licensee of video rights

Peggy Ledger ....British actress and Transylvanian

Perry Bedden ....British actor, Transylvanian, played Riff Raff

Perry Como ....American singer and performer
Pete Townshend British musician, songwriter, publisher and producer
Peter Beale ....Once head of Fox in Britain
Peter Blake ....Third incarnation of Frank
Peter Hall ....British theatre director and producer
Peter Hinwood ....British actor, model, played Rocky Horror
in the movie; now an antique dealer
Peter Plouviez ....Once general secretary of Equity in Britain
Peter Robb-King ....British chief make-up artist on the movie
Peter Rogers ....British film producer
Peter Schaffer..British playwright
Peter Sellers ....British actor
Peter Straker ....British singer, actor
Peter Suschitzky ....Director of photography on the movie
Peter Thompson ....British press officer for original show
Peter Wood ....British theatre and opera director
Petula Clark ....British singer and actress
Phil Collins ....British musician, drummer, singer, actor
Phil Kenny ....British musician on cast album
Phil Spector ....American record producer/company executive
Philip Prowse...........................British theatre director, writer, designer
Philip Sayer ....Second incarnation of Frank
Pierre La Roche ....Consultant/adviser on make-up for the movie
Prince Charles ....Coming king
Princess Margaret ....British royal and socialite

Quentin Crisp.................British gay icon, poet, writer and performer

Rabbit ....Musician
Ralph Richardson ....British actor
Ramon Gow ....British chief hair artist on the movie
Raynor Bourton ...British actor and writer, created the part of Rocky
Rex Cramphorn ....Australian theatre designer
Richard Chamberlain ....American actor
Richard Hartley ....British musician and arranger of the original songs

Richard Hell ....American musician
Richard O'Brien ....British/New Zealand creator of *Rocky*
and the part of Riff Raff
Richard Pointing ....British costumier with Sue Blane on the movie
Richard Wherrett ....Australian theatrical promoter and producer
Rob Walker ....British playwright and songwriter
Robbie Williams....................................British singer/songwriter, actor
Robert Downey Jr ....American actor
Robert Fox ....British theatrical producer
Robert Kidd ....British theatre director
Robert Longden ....British theatre director, writer and actor
Robert Stephens ....British actor
Robert Stigwood ....Australian/British artists' manager
and theatre and film producer
Robert Thomas ....Welsh antique dealer
Robin Littner ....American fan and *Rocky* devotee
Rod Stewart ....British musician and singer
Roger Daltrey ....British musician, singer, actor and producer
Ron Moody ....British actor
Ros Chatto ....British theatrical agent
Rudolf Nureyev ....Russian ballet dancer
Rufus Collins ....British choreographer and Transylvanian
Rula Lenska ....British actress and singer
Rupert Everett ....British actor and writer

Sadie Corre ....British actress and Transylvanian
Sal Piro ....American movie-goer, original *Rocky* fan
and now in charge of fanclub operations
Sally ....Nanny to Linus O'Brien
Salvador Dali ....Catalan artist, designer and thinker
Sam Shepard ....American playwright and actor
Sara Kestelman ....British actress
Sarah Harrison ....British style guru and PR consultant
Scott Messenger ....British actor
Scott Michaels ....American writer, researcher and *Rocky* devotee

Simon Barker ....Malcolm McLaren's assistant; style pundit
Siobhan Cusack ....Irish actress
Siouxsie ....British singer, musician
Snowdon (Lord)..British photographer
Stephanie and David ....British *Rocky* devotees
Stephanie Beecham ....British actress
Stephen Calcutt ....British actor and Transylvanian
Stephen Spielberg ....American film director and producer
Steve Debrow...Actor in *Shock Treatment*
Steven Berkoff ....British actor
Stewart MacPherson ....New Zealand theatrical producer
Sting ....British singer/songwriter and actor
Sue Blane ....British costume designer of *Rocky* in all its guises
Susan Sarandon ....American screen actress, played Janet
Susan Williamson ....British actress
Suzanne Bertish ....British actress
Sydney Terry ....British entrepreneur, manager and producer

Tennessee Williams ....American playwright
Terence Donovan ....Australian actor
Terry Ackland Snow ....British art director of the movie
Tiggy Legge-Bourke ....British royal employee and socialite
Tim Curry ....British actor, created the role of Frank
Tim Deegan ....American film executive at Twentieth Century Fox
Tim McInerney ....British actor, once played Frank
Todd Rundgren ....American musician, producer of Meat Loaf
Tom Hulce ....American actor
Tom O'Horgan ....American writer of *Hair*
Tom Sherack ....American film executive at Fox
Tom Verlaine ....American musician
Toni Tennille ....Singer, writer
Tony Cowen ....British actor
Tony Richardson ....British theatre and film director and producer
Tony Then ....Singaporean actor and Transylvanian
Trevor Horne ....British record producer and musician

Trevor Nunn ....British theatre director and producer
Trevor White ....Australian singer
Tuppence (Smith) ....Stand-in on movie
Twinkle ....British singer/songwriter

Vanessa Redgrave ....British actress
Verity Lambert ....British television and film executive
Victor Spinetti ....British actor and director
Vincent Price ....British screen star
Vivienne Westwood ....British style guru and couturier

Wally Veevers ....Film technician
Walter Burley Griffin ....Australian
Warren Clarke ....British actor
Willie Nelson ....American singer/songwriter
Wilton Morley.......................................Australian theatrical producer

Yasmin Pettigrew ....British actress and costumier
Yoko Ono ....Japanese artist, second wife of John Lennon

Ziggy Byfield..British actor and singer

Selected Bibliography

Harding, James: *The Rocky Horror Show Book 1973–1987* (Sidgwick & Jackson, 1987)

Henken, Bill: *The Rocky Horror Show Picture Show Book* (Hawthorn Books Inc, 1979)

Piro, Sal: *Creatures of the Night* (Stabur, 1990)

Piro, Sal: *Creatures of the Night II* (Stabur, 1995)

Thomson Brian (book design): *The Rocky Horror Show Book* (Star Fleet Productions, 1979)

Whittaker, James: *Cosmic Light* (Acme Books, Altoona, PA, USA, 1998)

Index